MATTHEW ARNOLD AND FRANCE

MATTHEW ARNOLD, *ca.* 1860

MATTHEW ARNOLD AND FRANCE

The Poet

by

IRIS ESTHER SELLS, M.A.

NEW AND ENLARGED EDITION

'Vous avez traversé notre littérature…par une ligne intérieure, profonde, qui fait les initiés et que vous ne perdrez jamais.'

Sainte-Beuve to Matthew Arnold.
25 January, 1863

1970

OCTAGON BOOKS

New York

To

MY FATHER AND MOTHER

First published 1935
Copyright © 1970 by Iris E. Sells

Reprinted 1970
by permission of the Cambridge University Press

OCTAGON BOOKS
A Division of Farrar, Straus & Giroux, Inc.
19 Union Square West
New York, N. Y. 10003

Library of Congress Catalog Card Number: 65-15236

Printed in U.S.A. by
NOBLE OFFSET PRINTERS, INC.
NEW YORK 3, N. Y.

CONTENTS

and the 'Ranz des Vaches', Titlis, *Rome-Sickness*, Aosta and the
Great St Bernard, the lake of Geneva and Vevey, *Obermann Once
More*. *Chateaubriand et son groupe littéraire*: a translation of
Stanzas in memory of the author of 'Obermann'. A letter to
Mademoiselle de Senancour, 1868.

Conclusion   *page* 252

The assimilation of Arnold's genius to Obermann's. Arnold and
Obermann as interpreters of the Alps. Pantheism. Arnold's
poetic period dominated by the influence of Senancour. Other
French writers. The evolution from romantic poet to critic;
Sainte-Beuve.

LIST OF ILLUSTRATIONS

PREFACE TO OCTAGON EDITION

The years that have intervened since this study was first published have naturally brought many additions to our knowledge of Matthew Arnold the poet; and, in particular, of his poetic affinities with the literature of France. It has become possible, now, to state authoritatively, in certain instances, what could only be formerly guessed at. Where not of my own discovering, these authorities are acknowledged in the addenda Notes at the end of this volume.

But this increase of information, fascinating as it is, has not had the effect of much modifying Arnold's poetic stature—unless an enhancing effect. No essential re-assessment appears to have resulted from the diligence of many research scholars; and the main trend of my study and most of the details have not been invalidated or much affected.

The most serious rectification is imposed as the result of the publication of a work that has been barely noticed by Arnoldian scholars. This is the edition of M. André Monglond's definitive volumes on Senancour. Having access only to some early essays of M. Monglond in 1935, the full significance of *Oberman* as an autobiography I did not then grasp; nor does this significance seem yet to have dawned on more recent writers on Arnold, who still refer to his pre-occupation with "the listless Senancour"; "the indolent dreamer of Jaman", in a "premature senile decay"; and so on. But it is now clear that Senancour is far from being accurately described in these terms; that he was in-

deed a very different person from what the general view of
him has supposed. And the effect of this difference has
been to establish a much more striking analogy with Arnold
than one had already perceived. It now appears that Senancour was inspired to write *Oberman*, not as the outpouring
of an ineffectual dreamer, possessed of a grievous and
repining temperament; that the melancholy of Oberman
was not due to an inactive brooding, but to a series of
misfortunes of a most positive kind, including exile, loss
of fortune and other vicissitudes resulting from the Revolution of 1789, and finally, to a tragic experience of love.
Although not known to or fully understood by Arnold, the
character of Oberman is revealed in M. Monglond's study
in a light which renders more intelligible the affinities
which Arnold felt for him.

Finally, in the realm of biographical criticism, I have
incorporated in the Notes added to this volume much
material which is entirely new; this mainly relates to
Arnold's early life and particularly to the period between
1846 and 1851. No study has yet appeared of the diaries
available for these years, nor has any careful analysis been
made of their entries. There have been references of an
incomplete kind made to them by editors and critics, from
Alan Harris's short account of the early diaries to K. Allott's
rather sparing use of them. But these have been largely
inadequate to convey a picture of the events of the years
in question; they have not always had the kindly insight
which reveals and illumines and invests the bare records
with an eager significance. In my reconstruction, for instance, of Arnold's wedding-journey, I have sought to interpret his early interests and doings in such a light, and to

show them as deeply concerned in the moulding of his outlook, and character, and poetic achievement.

I am grateful to the Cambridge University Press (and Octagon Books) for enabling me to reprint this study of Arnold's poetry, and for their consideration in allowing me to incorporate the new material which has been made available to me through the courtesy of the Trustees of the Rare Books Library at Yale, and especially of Miss Marjorie Wynne. I should like also to acknowledge the personal kindness of Professor Arnold Whitridge; and to express my thanks to Mrs. Mary Parkin Moore for some useful suggestions and a pleasant exchange of views on Arnoldiana; and to Madame Marie Cordroc'h, curator of manuscripts at the Bibliothèque Nationale, for her kind assistance in consulting the journals and correspondence of George Sand. Professor Lytton Sells has helped me in more ways than I can enumerate here.

It is a source of gratification that the text of my book can receive a new lease of life, without serious amendment, and that it can again bear witness to my continued desire to honour in Matthew Arnold one of our very great poets. My estimate was formed before the discoveries of the many scholars now engaged in their task of "exegetical scrutiny"; and it has not, I think, been much improved by them; nor changed by them; nor rendered less acceptable, I hope, to the poet's admirers.

Amherst, Mass., Durham, England.
1967–1968

ERRATA AND ADDITIONS

p. 7, line 13. Read "1846" for "1845", and see addenda, Note A.

p. 23, line 23. Read "projicient" for "proficient".

p. 31, note 2. Add at the end of this note: "See also addenda, Note O".

p. 34, line 21. Insert "note 4" after "Madame d'Agoult" and at the foot of the page the following note: "It is apparently only a coincidence that Matthew Arnold should later enter into correspondence with the liberal French Protestant 'pasteur' whom Daniel d'Agoult had desired to conduct her funeral service, on March 5th, 1876. Arnold actually wrote to M. Fontanès shortly after this event, on March 25th."

p. 37, note 2. Read "A. Harris" for "H. Harris".

p. 38, lines 11–12. Omit: "probably the only work besides *Obermann* that Matthew Arnold read"; and substitute: "probably the work, after *Obermann*, which most influenced Matthew Arnold".

p. 40, line 5. Read "several" for "many".

p. 40, line 15. Omit "(Saint Saphorin)".

p. 40, line 18. Omit "only".

p. 59, line 17. Read "Stagirius" for "Stagyrius".

p. 65, note 2. Add to this note, after "Introduction, p. 36": "The reference to Fausta indicates that at least part of the poem was written about the time of the marriage of Arnold's sister in August 1850 to William Forster; one would imagine at least when the marriage was

firmly projected. In view of the one or two other possibilities that did not materialise, it might otherwise
have been tempting Providence."

p. 89, note 2. Add, after "*A Wish*": "In a remark to Clough,
he speaks facetiously of their meeting in Heaven, but
possibly without recognizing or preserving their indi-
viduality".

p. 93, lines 9 and 10. Read "Obermann could have stayed"
for "Senancour must have stayed".

p. 108, note 1. Read, in place of present note: "J. Bonnerot
thinks the friends referred to might be Clough, Walrond and Wyndham Slade (in 'La Jeunesse de Matthew Arnold': *Revue Anglo-Américaine,* août 1930,
p. 525). But Arnold was writing on September 29th,
1848, to Clough about his visits to Thun, and appears
to be quite alone on this tour. He makes no mention
of their common friends Walrond or Slade; and he
concludes his letter, 'Farewell . . . to meet I hope at
Oxford.' Letters written by his mother and sister
on September 25th of this year also speak of him as
wandering alone in Switzerland (*The New Zealand
letters of Thomas Arnold the Younger*). The following
year he may not have been unaccompanied."

p. 112, note 1. After "*The Letters of Arnold to Clough,*
p. 91"; instead of "For the projected itinerary south
in 1849 see *On the Rhine*, which appeared first in
1852," read: "but for the above conjectured itinerary
see p. 124, note 1."

p. 124, note 1. Omit from: "Moreover", line 16, to "1851",
line 21, and substitute: "The evidence of *On the
Rhine* would suggest that Arnold returned to Switzerland by the same route as he left it in 1848. But as

he is known to have come from Austria that year, perhaps 'On the Rhine' refers to 1850, when, as appears to be the case, he returned to Switzerland after meeting Miss Wightman—perhaps to say 'goodbye' to Marguerite."

p. 126, note 2. Add to this note, after "Rhine": But see p. 124, note 1.

p. 131, line 9. Read "1851" for "1850".

p. 197, note 2. Add, after "writings": "Ménard had been a pupil of E. Burnouf at the Ecole Normale".

p. 221, line 28. Insert after "Three Sonnets on Rachel": "(see addenda, Note A)".

p. 239, note 1. Add after "Works, vol. xiii, p. 75": "(But see addenda, Note A)".

p. 240, line 21. Read "later" for "second".

p. 268, line 24. Read "Philobiblon" for "Philobiblion".

AN UNPUBLISHED LETTER OF SWINBURNE
TO MATTHEW ARNOLD

HOLMWOOD

HENLEY ON THAMES

Oct. 9th.

Dear Mr Arnold,

Your letter has just reached me, & it gives me real &
great pleasure to know that you have derived any satisfaction from my article: & especially that my choice of extracts
accords with your own judgment, as I always have great
regard to a man's own preferences in the matter of his
work, & quite disbelieve the current saying that one cannot
judge or pronounce when one has done best. It is a very
small instalment of debt that can be paid by such expression of praise or thanks as a review admits of. The passage
in 'Empedocles' cited always seemed to me to have in it
the kernel of the poem as to thought, & the stanza cited
from 'Thyrsis' is one above all which still gives me, when-
ever read or thought over, the sense of tears for beauty's sake
-pleasure's only which Chateaubriand speaks of in a passage you have translated. Whatever does that for anyone
not of a melting mood approves itself enough without
further test, but it is none the less pleasant to have one's
sense of right confirmed by authority. I have often wondered, in reading criticisms anything but malevolent, at
the choice of excerpts.

In reply to your question, I must confess to you that the
French critic quoted by me resides in a department of

France abutting on the province of Germany where MM. Teufelsdrockh[1] and Sauerteig[2] are Professors. I so often want French words for my meaning & find them easier & fuller of expression that I indulge the preference, as I write prose (I know) quicker & (I think) better in French than in English; with verse it is the other way usually. There was another long passage on speculative English poetry, pitting for example your 'Empedocles' as a spiritual study against Tennyson's 'In Memoriam' on this hand & Browning's 'Death in the Desert', 'Easter Day' &c. on the other, which I had to sacrifice to the laws of space, with regret; for writing as from a French standpoint I had been able to put things more clearly; & without this the notice of the 'Empedocles' as it stands is more inadequate than it was & looks to me all lopsided. But as it is, the article outruns the limits & it was by the editor's goodwill that it was squeezed in; as I told him, the critic of Buloz is better off for space in the *R.d. deux Mondes.* I want to see in some French review a competent introduction of your poetry to French readers, as those who would read it at all would I am convinced appreciate it better in the main than the mass of English readers. The Academy, meantime, was irresistibly provocative of attack to me in passing after its ultra-Philistine election and doctrine of this year, choosing

---

[1] Teufelsdrockh (Devils-dirt). Professor Diogenes Teufelsdrockh of Weissnichtwo (I know not where), the invented author of *Sartor Resartus.*

[2] Sauerteig (Sourdough). The fictitious philosopher-friend of Carlyle, on whom he fathered some of the overflow of his voluminous observations on life; including the exposition of his famous "Pig-Philosophy", (Schwein'sche Weltansicht), in *Latter-Day Pamphlets* (no. VIII, "On Jesuitism", August 1, 1850).

These allusions would be perfectly understood by Arnold; who used the same device when he makes Arminius his mouthpiece in *Friendship's Garland.*

before Théophile Gautier, 'le poëte impeccable', some M. Chose or other—bourgeois politicians & babes-[?]-of-letters-not men. Here I am convinced they would elect Mr John (or say [?] Jacob) Bright & Mr Coventry Patmore rather than you, were you a candidate.

Believe me, Ever sincerely yours,

A. C. Swinburne

[The signature here is almost illegible]

I am indebted to Professor Arnold Whitridge, the owner, for permission to publish this letter.

It appears to be the answer to a missing letter of Matthew Arnold's, of early October 1867, his first to Swinburne.

Matthew Arnold had evidently written to thank Swinburne for his eulogistic *Essay* on *New Poems* (published in the early autumn of this year). The *Essay*, a study of some length, had appeared in the October number of the *Fortnightly Review*. In it Swinburne had fabricated a "quotation", three pages long, purporting to be praise from a French critic of Matthew Arnold. Arnold, in thanking Swinburne for the review, had certainly voiced some humorous suspicion of this French authority, and perhaps had actually taxed Swinburne with having invented the quotation. Swinburne's reference to Professors Teufelsdrockh and Sauerteig was his way of admitting the fabrication.

To this letter of Swinburne's, dated October 9 (the year is omitted), Arnold replied the next day, on October 10. That this is his second letter is clear from a remark of Swinburne to Rossetti on October 11 mentioning that he has had "two very pleasant letters" from Matthew Arnold

since the *Essay*'s appearance. The tenour of Arnold's letter
also makes it clear that he is writing for the second time.
(See *The Swinburne Letters*. Edited by Cecil Y. Lang.
Yale University Press, New Haven, 1959–62, 6 vols.
Vol. I, pp. 269–70. Arnold's letter was first published
in the *T.L.S.*, on August 12, 1920).

Swinburne had been very anxious to write the *Essay*,
having expressly asked for a copy of *New Poems* when it
was first advertised, in July 1867; he had, with some satisfaction, drawn Lord Houghton's attention to its forthcoming appearance in the *Fortnightly*. He had earlier spoken
of his wish to write on the one hand on the subject of
Arnold and contemporary French literature, and on the
other of Baudelaire and contemporary English literature—
a juxtaposition which would have scarcely been to Arnold's
taste.

Arnold appears to have been less eager to follow up the
acquaintance, fearing to be identified with Swinburne's
circle, although he was flattered enough to allow Swinburne
to persuade him to reprint in *MacMillan's Magazine* in
1876 his early poem, "The New Sirens", and to re-instate
it in the two-volume edition of *Poems* in 1877.

After Arnold's letter of October 10, with its characteristic
remarks about Sainte-Beuve and Lacaussade, and a reference to the French critics mentioned by Swinburne
(Montégut and Etienne), there is a break in the correspondence which was only resumed in May 1868, when Arnold
wrote a letter to accompany the second edition of his *New
Poems*. This volume contained an added note on "Obermann Once More" to which Arnold refers Swinburne. He
also speaks of the death of his youngest son, Basil, which
had occurred earlier that year. Swinburne delayed until

July 3 to answer this letter; and then makes only a perfunctory reference to Arnold's bereavement. Some rather coarse remarks follow, which Arnold could not have relished.

The correspondence seems to have lapsed after this; there was a meeting at Balliol in 1876, but the only other extant letters are apparently limited to notes accompanying a courtesy exchange of publications. These appear to cover a short period only, from 1879 to 1882; but the two poets remained on amicable terms; until the publication, after Arnold's death, of the Russell correspondence, which included a reference to his first meeting with Swinburne. The occasion had been a dinner arranged by Monckton Milnes on June 14, 1863; about which Matthew Arnold wrote somewhat facetiously to his mother, as if to deprecate his presence among the rather weird set which Milnes had collected. In this (purely private) letter, he had described Swinburne, who had also been present, as "a sort of pseudo-Shelley". The injudicious publication of this passage in Swinburne's life-time had turned the latter's admiration into an almost frantic hatred.

In fact, after the pleasant exchange of letters following his *Essay*, Swinburne had eagerly sought, and accepted with *empressement*, an invitation to meet Arnold at a dinner-party expressly arranged by the Lockers (Lady Charlotte Locker was a sister of Lady Augusta Stanley, the wife of Arnold's friend Dean Stanley) on November 16, 1867; no doubt his remembered jubilation on this occasion, and his wounded amour-propre, in 1895, had combined to produce a severe shock. Probably the record of Arnold's impression on this first very occasional meeting, before Swinburne had established himself, and before the later cordial exchanges, would not have had so drastic an effect on anyone less un-balanced than Swinburne. He never forgave the unfortu-nate indiscretion; but perhaps Arnold's judgment was, in this instance, sounder than either realised.

INTRODUCTION

It is not pretended, in this study, to minimise the extent of other influences than French on Matthew Arnold's thought and art. His classical training, most important of these, played its assured rôle in Arnold's life; supplying ballast and balance to his intellectual formation, the good taste and judgment which nearly always mark his serious pronouncements, and, lastly, the rich humanity and sense of beauty that are the gifts of the ancient world to the new.

Of his debt to Wordsworth, in whose shadow he grew, to Byron, to Gray,[1] to all his English predecessors, we cannot say much here. Nor of his German interests—literary, social and theological—is it here in our province to speak; unless perhaps to wonder how much in fact Arnold was owing here, to a literature and a society whose language he never possessed with the sureness and intimacy of the French. An early interest in Carlyle, later disavowed, seems to have made him first acquainted with Goethe, for whom he formed an enthusiasm which grew to veneration with the years, but which never had on him the definite influence of a leading ideal. He read and translated Schiller; Heine he first derided and came to appreciate only in later life. It was probably the German habit of loose unrhymed lines that influenced him in his first poetic experiments,[2] but here the example of the classics may also have had its rôle to play. And, finally, the German religious criticism which he absorbed came to him chiefly through the medium

1 Who so far resembled Arnold that a contemporary poet and critic was recently able, with a certain plausibility, to refer to 'some-one' as applying to Arnold the words that Arnold himself had used in speaking of Gray (though then quoting from Gray's friend, James Brown): 'he never spoke out'. But Arnold spoke out clearly enough to those who would hear.
2 See G. Saintsbury, *A History of English Prosody*, vol. III, pp. 21, 249, etc.

of the French who, as we shall see, gave the whole subject a turn and a beauty and a conviction which the ponderous Dutch and German volumes had been powerless to impart.

Under these many directing currents the classical tradition held firm. But on the whole it operated rather as an influence in the background of Arnold's life, giving its general tone to his taste and intellectual habits, than as contributing materially to his stock of ideas. These latter are, as it were, the 'couches successives' superimposed on the classical substratum by the constant, free flow of more modern influences. And among these it is our endeavour to show that the greater number sprang from the culture which, of all others, lies closest to its classical ancestry—French.

Studied from this point of view, a surprising consistency will be revealed in Arnold's literary progress. Every step in our examination will seem by a natural transition to pass to the next: and this smoothness and general coherence will find its natural explanation in the fact that the events of Arnold's moral and literary evolution were actually so knit together; that in this progress of his there is nothing eccentric or jarring; that every stage is explained by its predecessor, and is linked on to the next just as naturally; and that discordant elements, if any appear, are to be accounted for rather by our lack of knowledge or understanding, than as due to any frivolous or erratic or inexplicable impulse in Arnold.[1]

Thus that Arnold should have his early taste for France, and early knowledge of French, might seem at first a little curious, until, turning back to his schooldays, we find that it is precisely

---

[1] Such as A. P. Kelso seems to ascribe to him (in *Matthew Arnold on Continental Life and Literature*, 1914, p. 12) when, following Saintsbury, he says: 'Matthew Arnold so far fell from his ideal of guiding English literature into the main channel of continental thought, that he lapsed into that distinctively English trait of following side-issues and fighting for lost causes'.

Rugby, alone of all English public schools of the day, which was giving instruction in French.

So the apparent arbitrariness of his preference for 'nobodies' like the de Guérins, for the genius of a George Sand rather than of a Balzac,[1] the seemingly divergent nature of his interests, in subjects so disparate at first sight as the works of Foscolo, Joubert and Amiel; or those of Senancour, Quinet, Sainte-Beuve, La Villemarqué and Renan, will be seen to have their origin in the days of his first revelation of French literature, from the oracular lips of George Sand.

Arnold indeed was no mere 'picoreur', snatching literary themes and suggestions as he found them, from a facile interest in their subjects. A deep sense of affinity with his sources impelled him from the outset; he read where his sympathies lay, and not lightly, or at hazard. The subjects he thus came to treat fall naturally into associated groups: from the early sensibility of George Sand, the author of *Lélia*—termed the *sister* of Obermann—he went direct to Obermann himself; and in his subsequent life he remained always susceptible to influences which emanated from this source of inspiration. Quinet, who had shared his own enthusiasm; Sainte-Beuve, among the first of Obermann's declared adherents, and who, in his character of 'Joseph Delorme' and later spiritual evolution, makes so strange a parallel with Arnold—even to his possession of those qualities of perfection in a second-rate *genre* to which Arnold also came to aspire; Maurice de Guérin, whose best formal works, the *Centaure* and the *Bacchante*, read like lyrical dramatisations of *Obermann*; Amiel, a genius of the same type on a different

---

1 See the short article on 'George Sand' in *Works*, vol. IV, p. 248; where, in addition to asserting George Sand's superiority over Balzac, Arnold goes so far as to rank her beside Goethe and Wordsworth. This estimate was no doubt strengthened by Sainte-Beuve's verdict: 'Mme Sand, est-il besoin de le rappeler? est un plus grand...écrivain que M. de Balzac' (*Causeries du Lundi*, vol. II, p. 461). See p. 11, note 1, below.

plane; the earlier moralist Joubert with his delicate religious affinities—to these, and to all who had comprehended Obermann, his sympathies naturally leapt. In others too, whom Obermann had comprehended, like Spinoza and Marcus Aurelius, he took an inevitable interest. If his affection for some of these writers seems due to a perverse fondness for upholding the weaker cause, for reinstating the incomplete genius, it is because it was in the ranks of such writers that Arnold saw the very qualities of greatness by which his own spirit survives—the common endowment which unites them all within the same great 'family of minds'; but which he had first seen pre-eminently exemplified in one, the author of *Obermann*.

By Obermann, and in some degree perhaps also by his love for a 'daughter of France', was Arnold's first interest in France confirmed.

With some of the above writers we shall meet in studying Arnold as poet: the others it is proposed to treat in a later work on Arnold as critic.

In conclusion, I desire to express my sense of obligation to the late Professor Sir Archibald Strong, who aided me in my first essay on the subject of Arnold. I wish also to thank very sincerely all who have assisted in the production of this work: in particular, my father, Mr F. T. Robertson, for many years Associate-Editor of the *Adelaide Advertiser*, by whom my interest in Matthew Arnold was first awakened; and my husband, Professor A. Lytton Sells, without whose collaboration this book could hardly have been completed—to my husband indeed I am indebted for help and guidance in more ways than can be enumerated here; Mrs Vere O'Brien, to whom I owe the very great privilege of reproducing an early poem by Matthew Arnold never before published; Bishop Welldon, formerly

Dean of Durham, and Mrs G. M. Trevelyan, whose kindness procured me the means of collecting some interesting information; Miss Dorothy Ward for courteously entrusting to me some original documents in her possession; Professor O. H. Prior, for his continued interest in my work; Miss Muriel Dodds for her help in connection with the early poem mentioned above; Mr Herbert Bell, and the Secretary and Members of the Dove Cottage Committee, for kindly permitting the reproduction of the frontispiece portrait of Matthew Arnold; Monsieur Paul Hazard, for his interest and encouragement; Mademoiselle C.-E. Engel, for kindly consulting documents on my behalf in the *Bibliothèque Nationale*, for much helpful information, and finally for procuring the medallion portrait of Senancour in the *Cabinet des Estampes*; Monsieur Marcel Bouteron, Librarian of the *Bibliothèque de l'Institut*, for courteously furnishing the portrait of George Sand; Dr C. Huber, Archivist of the Stadt Thun, for many delightful conversations on old Thun, and for kind permission to reproduce the Panorama of Thun in the Stadt Library; Herr Gustav Keller, Curator of the Historisches Museum, Schloss Thun, for the right to include the picture of the Bellevue Hotel; Herr C. Kurz, Staatsarchivar of Berne, and Monsieur André Bovet, Librarian at Neuchâtel, for some useful suggestions; Herr Walter Braendlin (Thun) for his courtesy in facilitating my enquiries; the officials of the Rathaus, Thun, for kind permission to consult the town archives; and finally, Herren A. Gurtner (Thun), E. Gyger (Adelboden) and Brügger (Meiringen), for permission to reproduce the photographs of Thun, Leukerbad and the Dent de Jaman.

I. E. S.

Thun—Durham
1933

CHAPTER I

DR ARNOLD AND HIS SON

Matthew Arnold's boyhood seems not to have shown him as distinguished by any marked taste for foreign languages. At Winchester he suffered some unpopularity for having, in the presence of the headmaster, referred to the work as 'light and easy'.[1] But his studies at Winchester did not include much beyond the Greek and Latin languages and a little divinity. He attracted notice by his poetic recitations, and later at Rugby by his poetic reading and original composition.[2] Some explanation, however, beyond these facts is required of how he came to possess his perfect command of the French language which he wrote in later years with so pure a style as not to dissatisfy even such a master as Sainte-Beuve.

Dr Arnold, as is well known, favoured the study of modern languages, and it is probable that it was from the father that the son acquired his taste, together with others that included a strong fondness for foreign travel. How strong was this latter preference we know from the account of the many journeys which Dr Arnold happily recorded in his Journals. Between 1815 and 1842 he had crossed the Channel no less than twelve times, mostly spending his time in France, Switzerland and Italy, and ranging between places as distant as Naples, Meran, Lucerne, the Puy-de-Dôme and the Pyrenees. In 1842, the year of his death, he was actually meditating another journey

[1] Thomas Arnold, *Passages in a Wandering Life*, London, 1900, p. 14.
[2] An early poem, written at the age of thirteen—actually in the summer preceding his entrance at Winchester—I am permitted to reproduce here for the first time (see Appendix A, p. 257). The circumstances of its composition are interesting, but more interesting is its importance in showing Arnold's poetic bent to have developed even earlier than is often supposed.

to the south of France and Carthagena with a view to his history of the Punic Wars.[1]

This love of foreign travel in an age not specially so addicted must be regarded as one of the many 'excellencies' which Matthew Arnold praised in his father,[2] and which he himself was to inherit, adding to it the poetic vision his father never possessed—a view which must be maintained in spite of the evidence of Dr Arnold's school-fellows at Winchester, who had nicknamed him 'Poet Arnold'; and in spite of the more convincing consideration that the Journals plentifully afford, of a certain delicate touch in his prose style, and an eloquence of description in which at least the germ of poetry seems budding.

But more generally informative than picturesque, Dr Arnold's Journals are chiefly remarkable for the comments and views which strangely foreshadow many of the opinions his son was to recast a quarter of a century later. Referring to Guizot's 'placing France at the head of European civilisation', Dr Arnold continues, 'he means because it is superior to Germany in social civilisation, and to England in producing more advanced and enlarged individual minds. Many Englishmen will sneer at this notion, but I think it is to a certain degree well founded, and that our intellectual eminence in modern times by no means keeps pace with our advances in all the comforts and effectiveness of society. And I have no doubt that our miserable system of education has a great deal to do with it. . . monkeyish imitation will do no good; what is wanted is a deep knowledge and sympathy with the European character

---

1 A. P. Stanley, *The Life and Correspondence of Thomas Arnold, D.D.*, London, 1858, vol. II, p. 276.
2 Matthew Arnold's actual words were, 'Ah, my poor Father! he had many excellencies but he was not a poet'. (Arnold Whitridge, *Dr Arnold of Rugby*, London, 1928, p. 15.)

and institutions, and then there would be a hope that we might each impart to the other that in which we are superior'.[1]

It is not to be wondered at, that with the circulation of such opinions through his childish environment the young Matthew Arnold should not escape their influence, and that he should begin to look, like his father, wistfully beyond the Channel for the realisation of all that could not be satisfied by life in England.

Dr Arnold seems to have struggled against this too passionate preference of his for the Continent as being a real moral weakness in himself. Some of the remarks he addressed to his wife show a pathetic desire to be just to England and not to minimise the advantages of cloudy climates and laborious days in their effect on character.

On August 3, 1829, he writes from Como:

I fancy how delightful it would be to bring one's family and live here; but then, happily, I think and feel how little such voluptuous enjoyment would repay for abandoning the line of usefulness and activity which I have in England, and how the feeling myself helpless and useless, living merely to look about me, and training up my children in the same way, would soon make all this beauty pall, and appear even wearisome.[2]

And again, with unconscious pathos, he continues ten years later to remark, from above St Cergues where he can see the morning sun on Mont Blanc:

This glorious scene...is overpowering like all other intense beauty, if you dwell upon it; but I contrast it immediately with our Rugby horizon, and our life of duty there, and our cloudy sky of England—clouded socially, alas! far more darkly than physically. But beautiful as this is, and peaceful, may I never

1 A. P. Stanley, *op. cit.* Journal, August 1830, vol. II, pp. 335–6.
2 *Ibid.* p. 323.

breathe a wish to retire hither,[1] even with you and our darlings, if it were possible; but may I be strengthened to labour, and to do and to suffer in our own beloved country and Church. . . .[2]

In 1840 he says:

I cannot deny that the meadows here [Lucerne] are as green as ours, the valleys richer, the woods thicker, the cliffs grander, the mountains. . .higher. And if Switzerland were my home and country the English lakes and mountains would never tempt me to see them, destitute as they are of all historical interest. . . .But all country that is actually beautiful, is capable of affording to those who live in it the highest pleasure of scenery, which no country, however beautiful, can do to those who merely travel in it, and thus. . .I must still maintain that to me Fairfield is a hundred times more beautiful than the Righi, and Windermere than the lake of the Four Cantons. . . .[3]

This firmly expressed conviction did not prevent Dr Arnold returning year after year to the Continent, and thoroughly enjoying his visits. Matthew Arnold has an amusing story of his father at this time whom he represents as reading Plato with his sixth form classes out of an illicitly introduced, half-bound, continental edition of Tauchnitz in several volumes.[4]

At Rugby Dr Arnold had been the first to realise the importance of putting the study of French and German on a regular footing. Until 1828 French had been taught by a visiting teacher, of no status and without authority except during his limited hours of class: even this represented an advance over the other public schools, as Eton and Harrow, where neither the modern languages nor mathematics had as yet entered into the school curriculum.[5] But after Dr Arnold's appointment the

---

1 A wish which Matthew Arnold, however, with a smaller consciousness of the desirability of character-building in England, was not deterred from forming some fifteen years later. (See *Letters*, vol. I, *Works*, vol. XIII, p. 35.)
2 A. P. Stanley, *op. cit.* vol. II, p. 346.   3 *Ibid.* p. 378.
4 See *Letters*, vol. I, *Works*, vol. XIII, p. 270.
5 A. Whitridge, *op. cit.* p. 121.

teaching of French at Rugby was entrusted to one of the regular masters, and the same policy was later adopted for German. By this innovation Arnold's successors were enabled to put French on exactly the same footing as classics and employ special masters for the purpose who were no longer, like the visiting teachers of 1828, without degree or social standing. Dr Arnold did, in effect, by his reform anticipate the whole system of modern language teaching now general in our schools.

In some respects he may be said to have gone even further. A reference to the programme of studies drawn up by Dr Arnold in 1834 shows the astonishing inclusion of Guizot's *Histoire de la Révolution d'Angleterre* and Mignet's *Histoire de la Révolution française* for the French division of the sixth form, although these works had only recently appeared.[1] It is interesting to note, moreover, that in the course of lectures he planned to give at Oxford in his capacity of Professor of History in 1841 his intention was 'to do for English history what Guizot in his Lectures on the civilisation of France had begun for French history',[2] and although this purpose was prevented by his sudden death in 1842, it is more than important as showing his keen interest in French culture. We gather how wide and impartial was this interest from a chance reference to the 'pococurante temper' in the Journal of July, 1829,[3] from which it appears that he had read *Candide*, or at least knew the passage in which the Venetian nobleman figures.[4]

It is noteworthy that Dr Arnold's great admiration for France and French culture and institutions was maintained in marked

1 *Ibid.* p. 113.
2 A. P. Stanley, *op. cit.* vol. II, p. 253.
3 *Ibid.* p. 323.
4 To this knowledge of French he added a less intimate but by no means superficial acquaintance with the German language, which he spoke sufficiently well to delight a Prussian soldier whom he met at Pont-de-l'Arche by addressing him in his native tongue (A. Whitridge, *op. cit.* p. 31).

opposition to the taste of the day. The fear of revolutionary
infection and the general disfavour into which France had
fallen with the English Tories were not shared by Dr Arnold.
His interest in the Napoleonic wars had been early stimulated
by his childhood residence on the Isle of Wight, and was
increased by the fact of his elder brother Matthew's having
served as army chaplain with the forces in Sicily and Genoa.[1]
The events of 1830, which were viewed with apprehension by
his friends, were approved by Dr Arnold, whose real lack of
sympathy with the revolution of 1789 did not prevent his
looking with satisfaction upon the overthrow of Charles X and
his too reactionary policy. His radical tendencies, however,
limited themselves to bringing back from one of his voyages
a tricolour cockade for himself and a tricolour work-bag for his
wife. But he persevered in what for the time was a very un-
English attitude, even to the point of uttering a severe warning
against the policy Lord Palmerston was pursuing towards the
French in 1840,[2] while he constantly defended the desirability
of friendly relations between the two countries.[3]

That in effect his ideas only reached, through his untimely
death, the small circle of his friends and pupils may not be
gainsaid. But strong and fruitful was their influence on more
than one of these. Not only Matthew Arnold was to profit
from his liberal environment; others of the Rugbeians were
to carry away some taste for and interest in French civilisation.

Dr Arnold himself was not over-sanguine about the results
to be obtained from the dedication of one school-hour a week
to the study of French. He did express the hope, however, that
the elements so acquired might prove useful to those students

1 A. Whitridge, *op. cit.* pp. 5–6.
2 For Matthew Arnold's opinion of Palmerston, see *Letters*, vol. II, *Works*,
vol. XIV, pp. 58–9.
3 A. Whitridge, *op. cit.* p. 191.

who wished to carry their knowledge further, and that merely the ability to read the masterpieces of French literature had very great value. In the case of his sons, who added to their school training the constant influence of their father's avowed interest, this hope was fully justified. A letter of Jane Arnold, written at Christmas in 1850,[1] describes Edward, the third son, as reading *Corinne* with enjoyment; from which one gathers that proficiency in French was not limited to Matthew alone. Other Rugbeians who went from school with a taste for French included Clough who in 1845 boasted an acquaintance with the language, and to some extent with the literature, nearly as intimate as Matthew Arnold's own.

In 1845[2] Matthew Arnold's knowledge of the language was already sufficiently advanced to permit him to enjoy French tragedy on the stage, for we have his own account of the fascination exercised over him at this early age by the great Rachel in the part of Hermione at the Edinburgh Theatre, after which he 'followed her to Paris and for two months never missed one

1 To Thomas Arnold, from Fox How, dated December 30, 1850. The letter is in the possession of his grand-daughter, Miss Dorothy Ward, to whose courtesy the author owes permission to make this reference. In the same letter is an interesting picture of Arnold reading a Christmas tale of Mrs Gaskell's, which 'moves him to tears and the tears to complacent admiration of his own sensibility'.
2 It seems necessary to assume that it was in this year (see next page, note 1) that Arnold first saw Rachel, though she played in this country in 1841 and 1842 also, and again in 1846 and 1847. Arnold himself gives no hint of the date. We may note that, in 1841, on the conclusion of her London season on July 15, Rachel had proceeded immediately to Bordeaux where she remained until August 20, returning to Paris and Montmorency for purposes of rest and study only. (See Léon Séché, *Delphine Gay*, Paris, 1910, Correspondence with Rachel, pp. 240–5.) It is possible that the Arnolds, passing through Bordeaux on their way south in 1841 (see p. 9), had marked the announcement of Rachel's coming season there: a fact likely to interest them in view of the success which Rachel had just had in England, where she had even been received by the Queen at a grand banquet given in her honour at Windsor on June 10. It may have been this coincidence which first aroused Arnold's enthusiasm, and led to his subsequent visits to the Edinburgh Theatre and the Théâtre-Français. 'Hermione', always one of Rachel's finest rôles, was the part in which she had the greatest success in England in 1841.

of her representations'.[1] To enjoy classical tragedy, particularly
that of Racine, whom he was never greatly to admire, and
Andromaque, which is perhaps the most purely classic of all
Racine's plays, exacts far more than an elementary understanding of the language. To a foreigner who would eke out
his knowledge of English by some observation of pantomime
and expression, a certain amount of Shakespeare might be
intelligible on the stage; the subtleties of French character
analysis require on the other hand a very delicate appreciation
of style, since it is on the perfection of the language and not the
dramatic incident that the psychological interest of French
classical drama depends.

Arnold's feeling for Rachel, that not time nor the appearance
of Sarah Bernhardt[2] was ever to change, compares rather
strangely with the effect produced by the great actress on two
women contemporaries. To Charlotte Brontë, living at this
time her obscure and shrinking life in Brussels, Rachel was the
spectacle of a soul in ruin, tearing itself to tatters in a paroxysm
of despair.[3] The sensitive soul of Charlotte was unable to
dissociate this personal interpretation of the performance from
its artistic value: her own life had prepared her to read into the
representation its background of passionate and heavily-loaded

1 'The French play in London', in *Irish Essays, Works*, vol. XI, p. 202.
According to his diary, Arnold spent six weeks in Paris in the winter of
1846–7, taking French lessons and seeing Rachel constantly (A. Harris,
'Matthew Arnold: the Unknown Years', in the *Nineteenth Century*, April
1933, p. 505). If this visit corresponds to the period in question, one must
assume that his memory was somewhere at fault, either in stating that he first
saw Rachel at the Edinburgh Theatre, or that his visit to Paris followed on
this experience; for Rachel was not in Scotland in 1846. On the other hand,
Arnold's diary contains no mention of a visit to Scotland in August 1845, at
the time of Rachel's season there, and there *is* a record of his having seen
her, in the part of Phèdre, during a four days' sojourn in London in August
1846 (article cited, p. 504).
2 See Mrs H. Ward, *A Writer's Recollections*, London, 1918, pp. 157–8, and
the three Sonnets on Rachel.
3 Charlotte Brontë, *Villette*, chap. XXIII.

suffering. Something malevolent she saw, too, from which she recoiled, not without a secret horror lest it should stir her own trouble into some fiercer woe. In 1839, another woman of letters, whose life was also overshadowed with great sorrow, the Comtesse d'Agoult, was writing in a curiously similar vein of a performance of Rachel in *Horace*:

A factitious talent, without tenderness, grace or love; but magnificent in disdain, and scornful irony; in a word, sublimely Jewish. Hers is in truth the reverberating, harsh voice of a race persecuted and dishonoured. She cannot—she ought not—to love. Her vocation is for malediction, imprecation, bitter and hate-bearing irony. I do not know if this is the view of most people; but that is how she appears to me.[1]

In 1845 Arnold was still very young. In so far as he can have appreciated these more sinister qualities in Rachel he found them in harmony with certain agitated stirrings in his own breast. But as yet he had suffered nothing of the 'hunger and rage' which troubled Charlotte Brontë's genius; and the dramatic spectacle of passion could not call into being elements of which he had no experience. It was the artistry of the representation that impressed him, and to appreciate this there was needed a vivid sense of the beauties of classical French.

This visit to Paris to see Rachel was by no means Arnold's first trip abroad. As early as 1837 Dr Arnold with his wife and three eldest children had made a ten days' tour of northern France, visiting Rouen and Chartres, and returning to England by Versailles and Paris. In June 1841 Dr Arnold again took his two eldest sons, Matthew and Tom, for a holiday abroad before sending them up to Oxford. At the end of this month he was already speaking of the excitement prevailing in the family over the projected tour. No prolonged stay was to be made at

1 *Correspondance de Liszt et de Madame d'Agoult*, ed. Daniel Ollivier, Paris, 1933.

Paris, the travellers planning to proceed directly to the Pyrenees. On the way they stopped at Fontainebleau, spending the night together at an inn to which Matthew returned alone nearly twenty years later with all the flush of affectionate memories coming back to him of that happy boyhood time.[1] It was raining[2] and little was to be seen on this first visit; yet, in the light of his subsequent travels, this glimpse of Fontainebleau seems curiously prophetic: as though the shades left by the passing figures of certain visitors to its green haunts have already fallen across his path. The one form moves alone, a silent wanderer; the other has a companion, like herself young, poetic, ardent. Of the second of these, George Sand, we must now speak.

[1] *Letters*, vol. II, *Works*, vol. XIV, p. 3.
[2] From the point of view of the weather the journey, as Dr Arnold said sadly afterwards, was not a great success. It rained most of the time, but there was a little sunshine between St Jean de Luz and Irun. Dr Arnold was greatly impressed by the beauty of the Landes with 'their glades of heath, surrounded by wood, and the dark iron-coloured streams fringed with alders' (A. P. Stanley, *op. cit.* vol. II, p. 243). His sons' impressions are not recorded, but the 'howling fury' of the ocean at St Jean de Luz, 'the deep-wooded combes' near Fontarabia (pp. 384–5), and the 'union of mountain and sea about the mouth of the Bidassoa' must have awakened delight at least as great as their father's.

CHAPTER II

'DAYS OF LÉLIA'

On October 15, 1841, Dr Arnold wrote: 'Our eldest son is gone up to Oxford this day to commence his residence at Balliol. It is the first separation of our family . . .'. And this separation was to mean for Matthew Arnold a relinquishment of many of his old interests and an eager acceptance of the many new ones which began to confront him on his escape into the outer world. His brother Tom followed Matthew to Oxford in the following year. With their old school-fellow Clough, who, in 1839, had preceded Matthew to Oxford, and Theodore Walrond, the companion of one of Arnold's later journeys to the Continent, the two brothers formed a little company in which were discussed with enthusiasm subjects of contemporary interest and current events in the literary, social and political worlds.

It is from this Oxford period that we must date the beginning of Arnold's interest in George Sand,[1] an interest which he maintained, with a certain amount of sympathy from Clough, during the years of study and amusement at Balliol, from the time of his graduation in 1844, and his fellowship in 1845, until the final outburst of enthusiasm which led him to undertake the difficult and out-of-the-way pilgrimage to Nohant of 1846.

To have loved George Sand in youth is a sign of health and ardour. 'This name', says one who did so,[2] 'represents many a generous passion, many a confused aspiration, audacities of

[1] For the influence of George Sand in England, see M. Moraud: *Le Romantisme français en Angleterre de 1814 à 1848*, Paris, 1933, particularly pp. 396–417. Of interest is Charlotte Brontë's account of her reading of George Sand in 1850 (see Mrs Gaskell's *Life*), in the course of which, like Arnold and Sainte-Beuve, she ranks George Sand decidedly above Balzac.

[2] E. Caro.

thought, profound discouragements, and superhuman hopes, mingled with the elegant torture of doubt.' There is need in life for the ornamentation of such idealism as Madame Sand's. Since, as Anatole France says, in one of his sagest and most exquisite essays,[1] naturalists and idealists alike, we 'are the playthings of appearance, walled in as we are within ourselves as if enclosed within a rock, solitary and deceived in the midst of the world;... since every image of things that we can form corresponds, not to the things themselves, but to states of our own souls, why should we not preferably seek and enjoy appearances that inspire charm, beauty, and love? Dream for dream, why not choose the pleasanter?' It is what, he continues, the Greeks did, and this with a full consciousness of the sadness and bitterness and doubt which they felt underlay the facts of life and nature. And it is what George Sand did too. The immense efforts of George Sand were concentrated on this end—for we may to-day waive all her eloquence in favour of offending against social institutions—of making the ideally beautiful a common and true fact about life. 'Le sentiment de la vie idéale, qui n'est autre que la vie normale telle que nous sommes appelés à la connaître'—these were the words which sprang to Arnold's memory in middle age, as the most delightful recollection of the George Sand of his youth; as the 'ground-motive' of all that was most beautiful and typical of her art.

We have the first mention of his interest in a letter to Clough, probably written about 1845.[2] In this letter Arnold makes the sound observation that *Indiana*, George Sand's first independent novel, is not 'pre-eminent among the author's other novels'. In spite of this adverse verdict, however, Arnold proceeds to

1 'George Sand et l'Idéalisme dans l'art', in *Œuvres Complètes*, vol. VI, *La Vie Littéraire*, pp. 300–7. Trans. A. W. Evans.
2 *The Letters of Matthew Arnold to Arthur Hugh Clough*, ed. H. F. Lowry, Oxford, 1932, pp. 57–9.

quote from memory a long enough passage to persuade us that
he was very familiar with the text. What attracted him particularly is clear from the mention he goes on to make of the
letter which the heroine, Indiana, writes to Raymon, and which
contains an epitome of the ideas George Sand was then pressing
on the world—the invitation to social revolt, and to a kind of
romantic idealism in which the liberty of the individual is
affirmed against the restrictions imposed on it by a conventional
society and a traditional set of religious and ethical values.

George Sand had herself slipped the yoke of these in a
remarkably simple manner. Without the burning questioning
or anxious self-doubt which were to torture a later generation
of sceptics, she had jettisoned with apparent ease the whole
fabric of ethics, religion and society, as traditionally upheld
before 1830. This memorable year was in fact a year of revolution in other worlds than the political. Literature also, which
had long been brooding over its inner ferment, had opened
itself to revolt. The ideas of Saint-Simon were rife. Madame
de Staël had already, it is true, some time earlier proclaimed the
independence of women: but Corinne and Delphine had been
women of genius. George Sand was now taking up the cudgels
not merely for the woman of genius, but for the woman unhappy in marriage.[1]

The source of Arnold's attraction to these ideas seems to
have been at first a desire, natural in the young 'Liberal of the
future', to outstrip his more 'tight-laced'[2] companions, and
even perhaps to shock the more conventional of them. In the
ranks of the more advanced thinkers, an enthusiasm for George
Sand was an index of enlightenment. But this transitory impulse in Arnold must very soon have given place to a sincerer

---

[1] René Doumic, *George Sand*, Paris, 1922, p. 111.
[2] H. F. Lowry, *op. cit.* p. 59.

interest. In the letter quoted above he goes on to refer to *Jacques*, a later novel in which the theme of revolt is again developed; here, however, the 'femme mal mariée' has given place to the 'homme mal marié'. Jacques is, in fact, a kind of stoic, a sublime sufferer in the cause of a rotten society which has unjustly bound to him his young and charming wife, Fernande.

It is doubtful whether this general theme of redress for social wrongs, whatever prestige its adoption might have given him, would have much appealed to Arnold if he had not at this time been suffering from a kind of unrest predisposing him to its acceptance, if he had not been already beginning to feel those 'qualms of vague misgivings' which Clough was to record in himself a little later.[1] In his essay on George Sand[2] Arnold recalled many years afterwards this period of youthful un-folding, of early agitation—'days of Lélia' he called them; 'days of Lélia' and 'days of Valentine'; when the young man, with the stirrings in him of some as yet dimly apprehended power, for which all the placid regularity of his school and home training had not prepared him, turned with devouring eagerness to these novels of passion and revolt; 'days of Lélia' whose 'ineffaceable impression' was to linger long after their stormy inception, and mark the days to come.

'Ah, no, I was not born to be a poet, I was born to love. . . . What I wanted was to live a human life; I had a heart, it has been torn violently from my breast. All that has been left of me is a head, a head full of noise and pain. . . .'[3] The echoes of these imaginings sounded strangely through the English college atmosphere and peace of her quiet cloisters.

1 H. F. Lowry, *op. cit.* pp. 61–2.
2 *Mixed Essays, Works,* vol. x, pp. 298–327.
3 George Sand, *Lettres d'un Voyageur* (IX, au Malgache: 15 mai 1836); quoted by Matthew Arnold in the above essay.

'The world remains in all its vileness and in all its hatefulness; this is what men call, "the triumph of good sense over enthusiasm".'[1] Yes, the demands of the heart must be heeded; its free, frank expression allowed; not rendered stony cold by mute repression and servitude.

'For ten thousand years I have cried in infinite space: *Truth! Truth!* For ten thousand years infinite space keeps answering me: *Desire, Desire.*'[2]

The spell of this new world had laid its charm upon the soul of Arnold. The poetry of renewed life seemed contained in that spell, the wonder of an unknown, uncharted land. And floating about his exaltation he caught the murmur of a distant, beautiful countryside; a real world, where a stream took its quiet way between green, cressy banks, and a thousand pastoral noises were faintly heard, amid the stir of simple, happy, rural existences. Over this land hung a glow, a poetic vision transfiguring it, tenderly idealising, the maternal spirit of George Sand hovering over her beloved Berry. For it was from Berry that these soft idyllic noises rose; and made a humming tranquil background for the almost too strident note of revolt. In this way had George Sand, with skilful art, employed the memory of her childhood life at Berry, and thrown its poetic glamour over her rebellious notions.

All the beauty of her native haunts seemed to have passed into these early novels and there shed its revivifying influence. Who, said Arnold, years later, in his essay on George Sand, can forget the lanes and meadows of *Valentine*? And the page of almost Thyrsis-like beauty which follows, describing the exquisite nature-background of the novel, is practically taken from the text. The images of the 'winding and deep lanes

1 George Sand, *Jacques*, xcv, De Sylvie à Jacques.
2 *Id. Lélia*, lxvii, Délire.

running out of the high road on either side, the fresh and calm
spots they take us to'; of 'the grave and silent peasant whose
very dog will hardly deign to bark at you, the great white ox...
staring solemnly at you from the thicket'; and of that one 'lane,
where Athénaïs puts her arm out of the side window of the
rustic carriage and gathers May from the over-arching hedge,
...with its startled blackbirds and humming insects, and
limpid water, and swaying water-plants,...and yellow wag-
tails hopping half-pert, half-frightened on the sand'—of 'that
lane with its rushes, cresses, and mint below, its honeysuckle
and traveller's joy above', are George Sand's. The translation
only is Arnold's.

It was by this dream-like beauty of description that George
Sand wielded her power over Arnold. As early as 1853 [?] he
was to confess to a difficulty in re-reading *Valentine*, except, he
added, for the descriptive nature passages.[1] It was in fact the
manner of their presentation, in a setting of pastoral beauty,
which had first won his interest in George Sand's ideas. And
it was the allurement of this calm countryside, even more than
his enthusiasm for the ideas, as yet incompletely understood,
which was to set Arnold wandering south on his pilgrimage to
the Valley of the Indre.

In 1846, the date of this memorable journey, the first period
of George Sand's literary activity was almost closed. Between
the appearance of *Indiana* in 1831 and of *Le Meunier d'Angibault*
in 1845 she had incarnated her dream of a socialistic revolution
in a long succession of novels, to which her own experiences
added a practical interest. In 1833, three years after her
triumphant escape from the Baron Dudevant and her first
success in the world of literature, George Sand had met Alfred
de Musset at a dinner of the *Revue des Deux Mondes*, to which
they were both then contributors.

1 H. F. Lowry, *op. cit.* p. 139.

Musset was at this time in the van of the Romantic movement, and already the author of the most poetical play of the
age, *Les Caprices de Marianne*, that beautiful dramatisation of
himself in which he had embodied, in the sceptical Octave and
tender, elegiac Cœlio, the two warring elements in his own
nature. Their dissension was to overcome him with weariness
later. But at the moment of his meeting with George Sand he
was the most charming of poets, gay, young and mischievous.
'Monsieur mon gamin d'Alfred' George Sand called him play-
fully. We have a picture of George Sand herself at this time,[1]
in the glow of her first celebrity, and the melancholy of 'Lélia'
all dissolved away from the laughing face; not very tall, with
a charming *sveltesse*, and a skin whose golden tint was full of
the warm caress of sunlight; her hair, dark, and with a kind of
opulent glory in it; but it was her eyes that men looked at, for
their expressive beauty.

In August Musset was visiting George Sand in her apartment
on the Quai Malaquais. In the autumn of the same year the two
had taken their way to Fontainebleau, and there were spent
some of the happier days of that fragile idyll which was to end
in the shattering of Musset's life and happiness.[2]

In 1841, when Arnold visited the forest, these voices had not
yet quite stolen away from its glades. In February of that year,
Musset, traversing once more the haunted ways, was still
writing, in mournful remembrance of their love:

> These are the slopes, and these the flowery bushes,
> And these are the silvery steps on the silent sand—
> Love-sick pathways, filled with our talk—
> Where *her* arm enlaced me round.

The adventure took place just after the appearance of *Lélia*
in 1833.

1 See R. Doumic, *op. cit.* p. 130.
2 See Émile Michel, *La Forêt de Fontainebleau*, Paris, 1909, chap. III, pp. 117–19.

Indiana had already appeared in 1831, *Valentine* in 1832. Of these three, by far the most important in its reaction on Arnold's thought was *Lélia*. In *Lélia*, indeed, lies the clue to those profound and far-reaching influences which were to modify the whole of Matthew Arnold's literary career.

Lélia, in form and inspiration, is not, strictly speaking, a novel. There is no real subject. The heroine is a woman who has loved, been deceived, and renounced love, to the despair of the young Sténio, who still believes in life, and who is forced to bear the sceptic raillery of the beautiful and world-weary Lélia. The theme giving unity to what is otherwise a dreamy succession of reflections, is that of a universal desolation, an unquiet sensibility which seeks with pain a cessation of its sorrowful existence. In effect Sténio finally seeks his release by suicide, while Lélia is destroyed by the jealousy of Magnus, the priest she has also tried by her beauty and fatalistic philosophy.

An accent of deep melancholy appears in these pages. The friends of George Sand were astounded at the appearance of *Lélia*, detecting a new version of the plaint of Werther, of Obermann, and the Byronic heroes. Lélia had become, in her turn, the personification of that strange evil, the *mal du siècle*.[1]

'How often, O Lélia', says Sténio, 'have you appeared to me the symbol of that untold suffering which the spirit of enquiry has brought upon man. Do not you personify by your beauty and your sadness, your *ennui* and your scepticism, the excess of suffering which arises from the abuse of thought!' He adds, 'There is arrogance in such suffering. . . .'.[2] 'O cruel and incurable! listen to yonder bird, he sings of the sun, of spring,

1 R. Doumic, *op. cit.* p. 124.
2 *Lélia*, XXIX, *Dans le Désert*.

GEORGE SAND IN 1833

From a drawing by ALFRED DE MUSSET

of love; this little creature's song is sweeter than yours, who can sing only of grief and doubt.'[1]

Thus we see in *Lélia* the first instance Matthew Arnold had yet encountered, of a type of character which was to fascinate him henceforth; the embodiment of a malady brought upon the soul by indulgence in an excessive intellectualism, operating on a highly developed sensibility.

Lélia, which began to appear in the *Revue des Deux Mondes* in August 1833, was composed during the first stages of George Sand's friendship with Sainte-Beuve. It is in this year that the critic appears in the rôle of George Sand's literary confessor. The novelist had written to thank Sainte-Beuve for his reviews of *Indiana* and *Valentine* in the *National*, and inviting him to call on her. In March, 1833, the two were reading together the first manuscript draft of *Lélia*, and also that of *Volupté*, Sainte-Beuve's own novel which he was then composing. But our chief concern among Sainte-Beuve's occupations at this time is with his preparation of the preface, dated the 18th of May, for a second edition of *Obermann*, the little-known masterpiece of Étienne Pivert de Senancour.

Sainte-Beuve had already given a preliminary article on this work in the *Revue de Paris* in January of the previous year. Some years since, 'Joseph Delorme' had read and been deeply influenced by *Obermann*, in whom he had recognised a precursor of the romantic melancholy of Chateaubriand. It was not, however, till after the death of the latter that Sainte-Beuve was to assert definitely the priority and superiority of the genius of *Obermann* over that of *René*. But in 1833 a circle of distinguished adherents had already formed about Senancour. In this year George Sand was introduced to him by Sainte-Beuve, and in June had written her article in the *Revue des Deux Mondes*,

[1] *Id.* xxviii, *A Dieu.*

with its profound expression of reverence and admiration. *Lélia* was composed under the direct stimulus of this new interest.

In his Preface to *Obermann* (first published in part in the *National*, 1833), Sainte-Beuve, referring to the yet unpublished manuscript of *Lélia*, expressly points to this influence of *Obermann* on *Lélia*, 'nom idéal', he continues solemnly, 'qui sera bientôt un type célèbre'.[1] And when *Lélia* eventually appeared, contemporary criticism was not slow in describing the heroine as the '*fille*' or the '*sœur*' of Obermann. But more than the spiritual affinity noted in this word existed between the two works; their similarities were due to no mere accident of temperament only, but, as we have seen, to the direct influence of *Obermann* on George Sand.

At the same time the immediate stimulus had proceeded from the moral crisis through which George Sand was then passing. The introduction to *Obermann* took place at a critical moment in her life, when everything was inclining her to receive a philosophy so much in accord with her own outlook. At this moment George Sand was suffering intensely from the unhappy experiences of her marriage; in the moral crisis of these days she regarded herself as a woman who had outlived her past, and who was henceforth immune from all temptations to further deception and disillusionment. In her fancy she saw herself with heart dried up, and her faculty to love cold and withered. But such a state of mind could not represent more than a phase in the evolution of George Sand's strong and vigorous genius. At the end of 1833 she was already excusing herself to Sainte-Beuve and begging him not to be alarmed by this assumption of 'airs sataniques'.[2] The adventure with Musset in the autumn of this

1 'M. de Sénancour. *Oberman*', in *Portraits Contemporains*, Paris, ed. 1870, vol. 1, p. 178.
2 Sainte-Beuve, Correspondence with George Sand, in *Portraits Contemporains*, vol. 1, p. 510.

year completely dispelled the last of her melancholy, and proved to her, as she wrote elatedly to Sainte-Beuve, that she had still a heart to love. Indeed, in this respect, George Sand was to remain perennially young.

She was not long after this in repudiating the influence of Senancour, and by 1837 she had expressed her final attitude towards the author of *Obermann*, an attitude in which were mingled affection, respect and admiration, but from which she was careful to dissociate a too personal expression of enthusiasm. But in 1840 her sustained allegiance was shown in the Charpentier edition of *Obermann* which she brought out in that year, with an important preface.

This preface (repeated from the article of 1833), in addition to its contribution to the literary appreciation of *Obermann*, is of great interest in throwing light on George Sand's own state of mind during the composition of *Lélia*, although the latter novel is not actually mentioned. Not Sainte-Beuve himself had analysed the situation with such shrewd and delicate understanding.

'Obermann', says George Sand,[1] 'c'est la rêverie dans l'impuissance, la perpétuité du désir ébauché.' (Obermann is the dream of powerlessness, the continuance of unformulated Desire.) Three great classes of melancholy souls there are, she continues: the first, of which Faust and Werther are the types, represents the exaltation of ambition or of passion opposed in its free sway, or the struggle of man with things; such is the bird which dies suffocated in its cage. The second class contains those who suffer from the consciousness of some power or genius which they have not the will to realise; such is the eagle which, wounded in its flight, beats painfully its wings and resumes its way. René is the type of these. The last class is of

[1] Preface to *Obermann*, Paris, 1840, p. 4.

those who have the sentiment of clear and undeniable, but incomplete, faculties; such is the bird that sits on the reef, to which nature has refused wings, and which exhales its calm and melancholy plaint on the strand 'whence set out the boats and whither return the wrecks'. Of these last is Obermann.

Where then, we may ask, in these three classes of *malades*, is the place of Lélia?

Before the answer is forthcoming, we must turn back a little in time and recall the period between 1800 and 1830. These years represent the aftermath of the Revolution. During the 'grande mystification du consulat' the national spirit had found expression in the war and movement of those days: this was succeeded by its diversion and repression under the Constitutional Monarchy. The French genius began to turn to scepticism, and from scepticism to suffering; and by 1830 a whole crop of moral diseases had sprung into being.

In 1803 *Obermann* was already written. Composed in complete obliviousness to the stirring events of the period, *Obermann* is one of those extraordinary works of art that seem to bear no trace of their age; almost anachronisms, they may be said to reach out towards a future as yet untraversed and undivulged, and only come into their own when the progress of years has revealed truths of which such works are the prophets. Obscurely and painfully, in an almost complete moral isolation, Senancour had evolved the literary expression of the troubled soul of 1830, a generation before its time.

Beside the three great classes of *malades* George Sand now places a fourth to contain the representatives of her own agitated age; the class of those in whom suffering does not come through rebellion against a society which opposes its passion; nor through the possession of power without will; nor yet from the paralysing consciousness of imperfection: but those in whom

suffering is the outcome of the soul's struggle to realise its
destiny, but before whom destiny flees like a dream; those in
whom the will to act remains, but from whom the power has
ebbed; in such souls the faculties are withered; belief and love
are dead. Desire alone survives, cutting, anguished desire, the
more terrible because it is doomed. These are the souls that
have been the victim of some disease of experience, deception
or disillusionment, who have suffered the last divorce from
hope and feeling. And this class of souls approaches nearest to
Obermann, hearing his sad cry, O! if I had but lived![1] and
answering (in the words of George Sand): Obermann, be con-
soled; you would have lived in vain.

In this class we divine the place assigned to Lélia, in the
family of sick souls; it is by right of this title that Lélia dare
invoke Obermann as the witness of her unappeasable sorrow.
Mine is the history of a heart, says Lélia sadly to Pulchérie,
'égaré par une vaine richesse de facultés, flétri avant d'avoir
vécu, usé par l'espérance, et rendu impuissant par trop de
puissance peut-être'.[2] *Lélia* is, as it were, the realisation of that
of which *Obermann* is the untested but hopeless prophecy; the
fulfilment of the melancholy which in Obermann is not the
result of experience, but which is suffered by anticipation, by
virtue of some strange proficient sense. 'J'ai tout examiné, tout
connu', he says, 'si je n'ai pas tout éprouvé, j'ai du moins tout
pressenti. Vos douleurs ont flétri mon âme. . . .'[3] In Obermann
the fire of life had never mounted; his heart was already in
ashes.[4] In Lélia the fire had burnt once, and consumed her. In

1 *Obermann*, ed. G. Michaut, Paris, 1931, XII, vol. I, p. 65. All successive
references to *Obermann* are to this edition of M. Michaut's, in the 'Textes
Français Modernes'.
2 *Lélia*, XXXV.
3 *Obermann*, XLI, vol. I, p. 164.
4 'Je ne connais point la satiété', he says; 'je trouve partout le vide' (*Id.* I,
vol. I, p. 4).

both is the same aspiration to recovered life. But for both, the world and its joys remain only as 'la vaine beauté d'une rose devant l'œil qui ne s'ouvre plus'.[1] In this they are alike—in their incapacity to live. Obermann desires to live, but is imprisoned in his strange melancholy; Lélia, pursuing life, sees it elude her like a phantom. Sainte-Beuve so describes her:

L'idée réelle de Lélia...est l'impuissance d'aimer et de croire, la stérilité précoce d'un cœur qui s'est usé dans les déceptions et dans les rêves. Le front reste uni et pur, les cheveux sont noirs, abondants comme toujours; la taille élégante et haute n'a pas fléchi. Le regard se promène avec dédain ou sérénité sur le monde, l'intelligence des choses n'a jamais été si limpide; mais où est la vie, où est l'amour?[2]

Lélia comme Obermann [says a modern critic[3]] est pleine d'aspirations comprimées, d'un ardent désir de vivre qui se consume dans un découragement absolu; elle a des élans désespérés, elle voudrait retrouver la candeur des illusions, le prestige qui illuminait le monde devant ses yeux, et toute expérience tentée ne sert qu'à lui faire mesurer sa chute. Son cœur est 'moins ardent que son cerveau, ses espérances plus faibles que ses rêves'.

And so, as it is to the mountain heights that Sténio leads Lélia, to assuage her sorrow in a silence unknown to the plains, it is in Alpine solitudes that alone is revealed to Obermann the sense of the infinite within him. As Obermann in one hour of *rêverie* lives through ten years of his life, Lélia, in her retreat in the monastery of the Camaldoli, grows old in the duration of her briefest ecstasy.

Lélia and Obermann are alike the symbols of a state of society which has exhausted itself, and which consumes the remnant of its days in mortal regret for its lost vivacity. 'The hour of

---

1 *Obermann*, XXII, vol. I, p. 91.
2 Article on *Lélia* in *Portraits Contemporains*, vol. I, p. 500.
3 J. Merlant, *Sénancour*, Paris, 1907, p. 268.

agony and revolt' has passed away; the power to feel and enjoy is gone; but the mind is still clear, the soul still retains its feverish grasp on Desire.

'For ten thousand years I have cried in infinite space: *Truth! Truth!* For ten thousand years infinite space keeps answering me: *Desire, Desire.*' [1]

Matthew Arnold never forgot the striking impression these words made on him. Many years later, in 1865, travelling as Commissioner on the Continent, and approaching Naples and the site of Lélia's cell on the mountain of the Camaldoli,[2] he recalled his old interest; he engaged his driver to take him, not to Sorrento, nor to Pompeii, but to the mountain monastery. Only the reluctance of the driver and the unsafe nature of the road dissuaded him from the project. He carried away from this experience a sense of deep disappointment; as of one who has been brought by chance to an open drawer, and seen there a familiar packet tied with faded ribbons: he hesitates, the drawer is closed, and the packet shut away.

From the revolt of *Indiana*, the despair of *Valentine*, and the melancholy of *Lélia*, George Sand passed in 1834 to the stoical conclusion of *Jacques*:

Life is arid and terrible, repose is a dream, prudence is useless; mere reason alone serves simply to dry up the heart; there is but one virtue, the eternal sacrifice of oneself.[3]

This novel was written at Venice, under the influence of the

1 The death of Lélia, LXVII, *Délire*; quoted by Matthew Arnold in his essay on George Sand, *Mixed Essays, Works,* vol. x, p. 306.
2 Not the convent commemorated by Wordsworth in three sonnets, and which lies on a ridge of the Apennines some fifteen miles east of Vallombrosa; but the monastery at the famous viewpoint above the bay of Naples and smoking Vesuvius.
3 *Jacques,* XXIX, De Jacques à Sylvie; quoted by Matthew Arnold in his essay on George Sand, *Mixed Essays, Works,* vol. x, p. 307.

spirit of renunciation in which she and Musset had parted. It was at Venice, too, that were composed the *Lettres d'un Voyageur*, for the benefit of the readers of the *Revue des Deux Mondes*; these letters Arnold placed among the four most representative of her works. Several mediocre novels followed; and then *Mauprat*, her first masterpiece, in 1837. In this book George Sand created in Patience, the rustic disciple of Epictetus and Jean-Jacques Rousseau, her first successful study in peasant character.

Un hiver à Majorque, composed in 1838, contains some charming descriptions of the sojourn with Chopin on the Balearic Isles; and marks the beginning of the association between the novelist and the musician, an association which lasted until the publication of *Lucrezia Floriani* in 1847. Chopin was not unreasonably alienated by this romance, in which, as the Prince Karol, he plays so poor a part; while Lucrezia, otherwise George Sand, the beautiful actress who has renounced love and retired with her children to the deserted shore of Lake Iseo, appears as a benign, maternal figure, who admits Karol to her affection only as she might add 'one duty the more to the life of austerity to which she is dedicated'.

Les Sept Cordes de la Lyre, *Spiridion* and *Consuelo* are spiritualistic novels belonging to the time when George Sand was beginning to write more impersonally under the influence of Lamennais, and of a minor writer, Pierre Leroux, the founder of the *Globe*.[1] Her object at this period seems to have been an attempt to embody in novel-form the socialistic philosophy of

1 Pierre Leroux in 1831 had been one of the earliest and most enthusiastic of the supporters of *Obermann*. In his *Discours aux Artistes*, which appeared in the *Revue encyclopédique* of 1831, he had dared to place Obermann among the group which contains the names of Werther and Faust, René, Adolphe and Joseph Delorme; and again alludes to *Obermann* in the introduction to his translation of *Werther*, the *Considérations sur la poésie de notre époque* (see J. Levallois, *Senancour*, Paris, 1897, pp. 170–1).

Leroux; it was no doubt owing to his influence that she proceeded to give 'le peuple' the chief place in her writings. From
these novels to the purely pastoral stories of the next period
was a logical transition. *Jeanne*, the first of these, was written
in 1844, before the last of the socialistic novels had appeared.
La Mare au Diable, the first important member of the pastoral
series, followed in 1846. It was early in this year, fired by his
reading of *Jeanne*, that Matthew Arnold had got out 'Cassini's
great map at the Bodleian', and was tracing an itinerary to
Berry, locating the tiny villages and roadways which he planned
to include in his pilgrimage.

CHAPTER III

A VISIT TO NOHANT

[*Introductory note:* In this chapter I have tried to explain the origin of Matthew Arnold's interest in at least two prominent French writers, an interest which a careful study of his later writings has led me to trace back to his meeting with George Sand.]

The village of Nohant lies in the very heart of France, in a modest countryside which before 1830 no famed beauty nor historic interest had made known to the world outside. For the most part the country hereabouts is one of flat spaces and wide, calm horizons; in the distance can be seen the low hills which begin to rise towards the volcanic heights of the Puy-de-Dôme; on the east the region is separated from Lyons, the nearest large town, by the mountains of the northern Cévennes. It was in this 'pauvre coin du Berri', as she called it lovingly, that George Sand passed most of her childhood; and it became, in her tender remembrance, 'the sanctuary of her first, her long, and her continual dreams'.[1]

The château of Nohant stands in the *Vallée noire*, the melancholy and charming spot which is so delicately painted in *Valentine*; down this valley flows the Indre, not a large stream at this point, whose music for long had fallen on the ears only of the indifferent or, as George Sand called him, the unreflecting peasant, calmly ploughing his field in 'an eternal childhood'.[2]

In 1846 there was still no railway as far as Nohant. To Arnold, descending in August of this year from the post which had brought him to Paris, with all the spell upon him of that

1 Notice to *Valentine*, March 27, 1852.
2 George Sand, *La Mare au Diable*, ed. 1927, p. 21; quoted by Matthew Arnold in his essay on George Sand in *Mixed Essays*, *Works*, vol. x, p. 315.

apparition of beauty,[1] the prospect of a journey so far south must have appeared a daring and exciting enterprise.

From Paris he travelled by rail to Vierzon, where he changed into a diligence for Châteauroux; at Châteauroux he had to change again for La Châtre into a 'humbler diligence'; and from La Châtre he pushed on to Boussac by, as he says, 'the humblest diligence of all'. Just before reaching La Châtre he had passed Nohant, and its château by the roadside. The garden, dimly seen beyond its high walls, was rich in flowers; roses, clematis, geraniums and many summer blooms made of it 'un nid parfumé', to which the sweet scent of the oranges, citrons and pomegranates on the terrace contributed their peculiar freshness. Where the meandering alleys crossed, benches had been placed that invited to repose; and long shadows fell from the cedars and two tall firs that rose above the garden.[2]

Matthew Arnold gazed with shy awe at the house of the great authoress, but it was not his intention to present himself just then; the diligence carried him on, and after the change at La Châtre he found himself proceeding up the *Vallée noire* to the higher reaches of the Indre. By nightfall he had left the valley and was in a wild bare heathy country of silent 'landes'.[3]

This was the spot that George Sand had chosen for the scene of *Jeanne*, the first novel in which she had left all her socialistic and mystical preoccupations behind and given herself up to the sincerest and most original bent of her genius, the portrayal of peasant life and its simple world.

1 In 1866, Arnold speaking to his mother of his sister's plan to visit France wrote: 'Paris will not astonish her so much as if it was the Paris of twenty years ago, and she had arrived at it by post instead of rail; one comes too rapidly upon Switzerland also nowadays; but what is unchangeable in Switzerland itself remains'. *Letters*, vol. II, *Works*, vol. XIV, p. 75.
2 Aurore Sand, *Le Berry de George Sand*, Paris, 1927, pp. 163–5.
3 'George Sand', in *Mixed Essays*, *Works*, vol. X, pp. 299–300.

'Jeanne' is in fact the first peasant woman to enter French literature as a romantic heroine, and the first illustration of the doctrine that George Sand was to develop in *François le Champi*, *La Mare au Diable* and *Les Maîtres Sonneurs*: that goodness and charm are the natural qualities of the heart which lives close to nature.

The portrait of Jeanne is exquisitely drawn. We see her, one of those peasant girls 'au visage grave et pur de lignes, au regard noyé de rêve'[1] who still exist, and were almost a type a hundred years ago. But in spite of her success in drawing this character and the singular charm of the heroine, George Sand had not yet found in this novel her ideal of a harmony between her peasant actors and their environment, as she exemplified it later in *François le Champi*. The simplicity of the *cadre* is spoiled in *Jeanne* by the introduction of a party of bourgeois, among whom appears Sir Arthur, the rich Englishman who wishes to marry her. In spite of this discordance, the setting remains predominantly rural; the fresh air of wind-blown uplands breathes through the whole. As Arnold wandered from Boussac to Toulx Sainte Croix he felt its pure elemental qualities, as he had felt them in reading; and stopping at sunrise by the Pierres jomatres[2] on the platform of Toulx Sainte Croix, he gazed on the 'scrawled and almost effaced stone lions',[3] solitary reminders of the English occupation in the fourteenth century, with the

1 R. Doumic, *op. cit.* p. 297.
2 Arnold calls them *Pierres Jaunâtres*. They were druidic stones. The curé in *Jeanne* is represented as explaining to Guillaume, the young Baron de Boussac, that the word *jo-mathr* is derived from a verb meaning 'faire saigner et souffrir la victime sur la pierre expiatoire'; and here refers to the sacrificial rites for which the stones were used. Arnold evidently had not lingered over this passage; or perhaps thought 'jomatres' a Berrichon corruption of 'jaunâtres'.
3 '...les trois lions de granit, monumens de la conquête anglaise au temps de Charles VI, renversés par les paysans au temps de la Pucelle, brisés, mutilés, et devenus informes, qui gisent le nez dans la fange, au beau milieu de la place de Toull' (*Jeanne*).

mountains of Auvergne in the distance, and the calm, quiet beauty of the countryside entering into him.

Matthew Arnold never lost his youthful sense of joy in visiting haunts made dear by their literary associations; this long and ambitious journey to Boussac was only the first of many pilgrimages so undertaken. But at twenty-three his heart may have beaten with a specially romantic pleasure.

At all events, emboldened by his elation, Arnold dared to send a note to the great novelist, begging permission to call; the note could not have been written in such 'bad French' as he modestly professed later, nor so inadequately expressive of his homage; for it met with a prompt response from George Sand inviting the young man to lunch.

The eventful meeting took place just before midday. A servant in typical Berrichon dress, complete with square coiffe and crossed fichu, introduced him into the dining-room. A lustre of red and white Venetian glass, suspended above, would shed on this room the light of its fifty candles at a later hour. The room was panelled in grey; magnificent cut crystal lay exposed on the great table-cloth, which had belonged to Marshal Saxe and bore his mark, in red cotton, of two little crossed swords. From the blackened rafters above hung a number of old-fashioned burnished copper vessels.[1]

Madame Sand was surrounded by her children and friends. Among those present was Chopin; it was the year before the appearance of *Lucrezia Floriani*, and the last year of his connection with George Sand.

This one[2] meeting with the great novelist remained indelibly fixed in Arnold's memory. The conversation was

[1] Aurore Sand, *op. cit.* pp. 101–2.
[2] According to Professor Saintsbury (*Matthew Arnold*, 1899, p. 74) Arnold saw George Sand again in 1859, but see *Letters*, vol. I, *Works*, vol. XIII, pp. 137, 140, 141; and *Mixed Essays*, *Works*, vol. X, p. 302.

naturally directed to the subject of the young stranger's wanderings. Arnold was a little shy at the outset, a little tremulous at his temerity; but soon reassured by Madame Sand's gracious and easy manner. Sometimes she spoke to him directly, and sometimes she addressed her companions. Arnold listened intently; all that passed the lips of George Sand that morning had for him the authority of an oracle. Madame Sand ascertained that he was going on to Switzerland;[1] he would then probably pass through Lyons. Was he intending to follow up other literary associations in Switzerland? If he were going to the lake of Geneva and Lausanne he would not fail to visit 'Imenström', the home of Obermann.

The conversation passed naturally into a discussion of Senancour, whose death had occurred in January of that year (1846), and was still an event fresh in the minds of George Sand and her circle. It was years now since the recluse of 'Imenström' had faded into the sick and solitary hermit of the rue de la Cerisaie; and yet the death of Senancour had seemed like the snapping of some great spiritual force. No one before Senancour had rendered the soul of the Alps into literature, and interpreted the secret of their mountain solitudes; no one would do so again in the same way. George Sand refrained from showing too much enthusiasm. She had by this time outlived the phase of *Lélia*, and now viewed Senancour in a rather more sober light. She felt herself, however, grow moved before this young man's interested expression; it was a pleasure to throw open a gateway to new worlds for the young generation to pass. Moreover, from a practical point of view she could not disown her interest in *Obermann*. Since her edition of 1840, several reprints had been called for: one had appeared actually in the preceding year, and a new and corrected one was to appear in

1 *Mixed Essays, Works*, vol. x, p. 301.

1847. This sustained interest was perceptible in the peculiar inflection of her voice as she spoke of *Obermann*: in all her remarks could be felt a sort of reverent and melancholy regard which did not escape Arnold. With the name of Senancour, he heard pronounced, a little later, that of Sainte-Beuve; he learned of the sanction that great man had given the genius of Senancour; a scrap of information which he carried away to explore at leisure.

Among other *bouts de phrase* that he took away was some conversation on a work Madame Sand had been doing on a certain Maurice de Guérin, a disciple, like herself, of Senancour. Maurice de Guérin's interest in *Obermann* had not been merely a temporary phase like George Sand's, but had left an enduring influence on his work and character. Arnold enquired where this work was procurable: he learned that it had not as yet been published, except for an important fragment Madame Sand had herself brought out in the *Revue des Deux Mondes* on May 15, 1840.[1] She added that he would find it more readily available in a volume of her novels published in 1844 where she had again reproduced it.[2]

Madame Sand had returned to the subject of his prospective travels. If he were staying at Vevey he would do well to go on to Chamouni.... It was only later that Arnold learned of George Sand's own famous 'course à Chamouni' in 1836 with Liszt and Madame d'Agoult, the 'Arabella' of the *Lettres d'un Voyageur*. 'Arabella' had not in fact greatly enjoyed the

1 *George de Guérin*, vol. XXII, pp. 569–91.
2 *Œuvres Complètes*, Paris, 1843–4, vol. XIV, pp. 293–327. The contents of this volume are: *Un Hiver à Majorque* (pp. 1–197); *Pauline* (pp. 197–293); *George de Guérin* (pp. 293–327); *Mouny-Robin* (pp. 329–56). The fact that Arnold about 1847 (see the essay on Maurice de Guérin, in *Essays in Criticism, Works*, vol. III, p. 87) was haunted by a passage in the *Centaure* of Maurice de Guérin which had appeared as early as 1840 and 1844, suggests that he had not known it much before this date (1847), and supports our view that it was his visit to George Sand which revealed it to him.

irruption of 'Dr Piffoël'[1] and children on the scene, but Liszt had been enchanted. . . .

The name of Liszt had been more than once pronounced that morning. Liszt had known Madame Sand in the early days of her liaison with Musset, to whose young sister Herminie he was then giving music lessons. A few years earlier, in 1830, Liszt had shared in the wildest dreams of the young Romantic Movement and had caught its enthusiasm for the ideas of Saint-Simon. The reading of *Lélia* in 1833, and particularly that of *Leone Leoni* in the following year, had turned him immediately into a fervent partisan of George Sand, who found, as she rather plaintively said, that she had been preaching 'du Saint-Simonisme sans le savoir'.[2] Her novels had, in fact, seemed a practical illustration of Saint-Simon's ideas. It was the perusal of these two early books, passed on to her by Liszt, which had fanned the romantic flame of the young Marie d'Agoult, and which had inspired her to defy the claims of her ill-assorted marriage and escape with Liszt in 1835. The following year, at their first meeting at Chamouni, George Sand had fallen into the arms of the beautiful countess, whose intrepidity she had long admired.[3] But Madame d'Agoult had not been so eager to welcome George Sand. The friendship between Liszt and Madame Sand was not altogether to her taste. For there was certainly great sympathy between the two. One of George Sand's attractions for Liszt was her love of music, for which she had a considerable gift. And another link was their common interest in Senancour, whom George Sand had presented to Liszt in 1833, at the time her enthusiasm for *Obermann* was at its height. In 1836 Liszt, travelling through Switzerland, had

1 The name under which George Sand appeared at Madame d'Agoult's hotel at Chamouni in 1836.
2 Notice to *Valentine*, March 27, 1852.
3 See the *Lettres d'un Voyageur*, vol. x.

been inspired by the memory of *Obermann* to compose two pieces in his *Années de Pèlerinage, La Vallée d'Obermann* and *Le Mal du Pays*;[1] and had even taken the famous Third Fragment in *Obermann*, on the expression of the 'romantic' and the 'Ranz des Vaches', to serve as *épigraphe* to the latter piece.[2] The theme was the traditional love of the Swiss for this call of the herdsman on the mountain tops; which, according to Rousseau, is so strong that a Swiss in exile from his native country will burst into tears at the sound. . . .[3]

Matthew Arnold listened eagerly to the conversation around him. He looked at the assembled guests curiously, among them the young man 'with the wonderful eyes', Chopin, who was a kind of present link with all these interesting associations.[4]

---

1 A. Monglond, 'Senancour et un voyageur au Brésil, Lettres inédites à Ferdinand Denis', in the *Revue de Littérature Comparée*, janv.-mars, 1931, p. 104 and note; see also R. Bouyer, *Obermann précurseur et musicien*, 1907, p. 78.

2 J. Merlant, *Sénancour*, p. 309.

3 No doubt Arnold knew Wordsworth's allusion to this tradition in the *Descriptive Sketches taken during a Pedestrian Tour among the Alps*:

> 'Lo! where through flat Batavia's willowy groves,
> Or by the lazy Seine, the exile roves;
> O'er the curled waters Alpine measures swell,
> And search the affections to their inmost cell;
> Sweet poison spreads along the listener's veins,
> Turning past pleasures into mortal pains;
> Poison, which not a frame of steel can brave,
> Bows his young head with sorrow to the grave.'

The theme is repeated in a later Sonnet of 1820, *On Hearing the 'Ranz des Vaches' on the top of the Pass of St Gothard*.

4 Chopin had for some time played an intimate rôle in George Sand's life. She had met him first through the Countess d'Agoult, whose salon Chopin had frequented in the days before her elopement with Liszt. In 1836, when Liszt and the countess were staying at the Hôtel de France in the rue Lafitte, and sharing a salon with George Sand, Chopin had resumed his visits. It was shortly after this that a little coolness had arisen between the two *dames*, owing to the unfortunate way in which Balzac in his *Béatrix*—at first called *Les Galériens* or *Les Amours forcés*—had made capital out of material furnished him by George Sand; to whom the artless countess had been a little too confidential in relating the sufferings of Liszt and herself. George Sand had in effect been much provoked by Marie's ironical attitude towards her *engouement* for Chopin. Nor had the delicate and aristocratic Marie d'Agoult much in

Out of the floating fragments of conversation that surrounded him only one or two other names reached him. At the real life behind this friendly family circle he could not even guess. He would one day ascend the Faulhorn, following in the tracks of Liszt and Marie d'Agoult, in the first year of their romantic passion. But at present all was confused to his mind.

The impression Arnold himself made on George Sand was one of singular freshness and purity. Years afterwards, recalling his visit in conversation with Renan, she spoke of him as having seemed to her like some 'Milton jeune et voyageant',[1] a description of himself which Arnold very much enjoyed.

Towards the conclusion of his visit, tea was introduced, and, with that *boisson fade, mélancolique*, subjects of home interest—life in Oxford, English literary lions. They spoke of Byron, the most vehement and forceful of the *âmes maladives*; of Bulwer Lytton; and also of Arnold's own literary projects.

With what a sensation of pleasure did Arnold find his way at last through the garden and out of the gate, bearing a flower in his hand, the gift of the rustic *magicienne*.

At Lyons, we assume, he took care to acquire, among a parcel of other books, a copy of Madame Sand's edition of *Obermann*,[2] and her *Hiver à Majorque*, or perhaps some back numbers of the *Revue des Deux Mondes*, whose pages he turned rapidly to

common with George Sand, whose bourgeois manner and cigar-smoking habits were very irritating to her. But the Countess d'Agoult, as 'Daniel Stern', could not afford to fall out with such lions of contemporary literature as Balzac and George Sand, at a moment when she and Liszt were struggling to secure a position and some financial security for their children, of whom, however, only Cosima, born at Como in 1837, was to live for long.

1 *Letters*, vol. III, *Works*, vol. XV, p. 14.

2 This is the edition Arnold most certainly had; his preference for and quotation of passages in *Obermann*, also favourites of George Sand and referred to in her *Preface*, confirm us in thinking so.

be sure that they contained the *Centaure*. Thus equipped, he went on eastwards to Geneva,[1] and round the historic lake to Vevey and Glion.[2]

1 For this route, see his projected journey, *abandoned*, in 1859 to Nohant from Geneva and Lyons, that is, in the opposite direction (*Letters*, vol. I, *Works*, vol. XIII, p. 128).

2 The reference in *Obermann Once More*, published in 1867, points to this conclusion (see Chap. XVI, pp. 245–6).

> 'Glion?—Ah, twenty years, it cuts
> All meaning from a name!'

Arnold himself states, in the essay on George Sand, that he went on from Nohant to Switzerland. His diary for this year, however, according to Mr H. Harris (article cited, p. 504), has no entry recording such a journey; the suggestion is that his memory was at fault when making the above statement.

CHAPTER IV

THE AUTHOR OF *OBERMANN*:
ÉTIENNE PIVERT DE SENANCOUR

[*Introductory note:* I have attempted in this chapter a short analysis of Senancour's thought and art.]

Obermann, Senancour's best-known work, has often been regarded as a true chronicle of the author's life and thought, and the two names, Obermann and Senancour, used almost interchangeably. Yet Senancour himself never wished to be identified with the hero of *Obermann*. This book was a work of youth, and did not represent his mature thought. *De l'Amour*, which appeared a year later than *Obermann*, in 1805, was an attempt at a more systematic kind of writing; and in this, and in the second and third editions of the *Rêveries*, he attempted to incorporate all that he himself thought of value in *Obermann*. The *Libres Méditations* of 1819, probably the only work besides *Obermann* that Matthew Arnold read, was undoubtedly intended by its author to be the definitive expression of his philosophy of life.

This book does indeed mark a stage in the spiritual development of Senancour far beyond that attained in *Obermann*: the vague melancholy and scepticism, or at most pantheism, of the latter having become a hopeful seeking for the proof of Divinity. The two last works projected by Senancour, *De la Religion éternelle*, and the final rehandling of the *Libres Méditations*,[1] show him in his old age to be a sincere though undogmatic Christian thinker.

These contradictions in his thought, of which Senancour has

1 The first of these was never completed; the second for long was lost.

been often accused, melt away when they are envisaged as stages in his spiritual progress. His reluctance to republish *Obermann*, however, was in part due to his sense of apparent inconsistency, and in part to his feeling that it most unworthily represented his final attitude. For his great preoccupation in later life was that he should appear as a moral thinker rather than as an artist. In 1832, when Sainte-Beuve approached Senancour over the question of a second edition of *Obermann*, he had much difficulty in persuading the author to leave the text untouched. Sainte-Beuve was particularly anxious to overrule Senancour's objections, for he had long divined the real place of *Obermann* in the literary history of the century: it was his great object to establish the priority of *Obermann* over *René* as the precursor of the Romantic Movement.

We can, nevertheless, in spite of Senancour's hesitations, accept *Obermann* as a sincere record of its author's experiences at the time of composition; and though it is not possible nowadays to identify, as Arnold did [1] (following Sainte-Beuve), all the events noted in *Obermann* with Senancour's own personal history, the differences are mostly external; the reappearance of the majority of Obermann's ideas and sentiments in other works of Senancour is evidence that they represent the author's real convictions.

Certain external differences may be mentioned. The chief of these relates to the extent and duration of Obermann's wanderings, and how far these are coincident with Senancour's own experience. Most of the letters of Obermann are addressed from the Alps, in particular from Geneva, Lausanne, Saint Maurice in the Valais, Fribourg, Thun, and the imaginary 'Imenström' on the Lake of Geneva. Apart from visits to Paris,

[1] Arnold says definitely, in his review of the 1863 edition of *Obermann* (in the *Academy*, Oct. 9, 1869, p. 1): 'It is Senancour himself who speaks under Obermann's name'.

and Lyons, a comparatively brief sojourn at Fontainebleau, and a journey to Thièle near the foot of the Jura, Obermann's wanderings are in general confined to the great mountain-block of the Bernese Oberland.[1] The itinerary which the letters show him as tracing out, over a period of many years, embraces a rough circle starting from Geneva and Montreux (Glion), across by the Schwarzsee to Thun, thence over the Gemmi to the Rhône valley, and back through Saint Maurice and Bex to the Lake of Geneva; with extensions, possibly by the Aar valley, to Lucerne and as far as the Grimsel on the one hand, and from the Rhône valley to the Great St Bernard and Aosta on the other. We know that Senancour himself visited Switzerland only in his youth where, unlike Obermann, he married. After a sojourn of some years, spent chiefly at Fribourg and Saint Maurice (Saint Saphorin), he settled in Paris, where his maturity and later years were passed. Except for one brief visit in 1802–3, he never returned to Switzerland. Fontainebleau he had known only from a summer visit in childhood to Basses-Loges.[2]

In spite of these dissimilarities, *Obermann* remains an almost exact psychological autobiography; to the readers of the thirties indeed no reservations at all occurred in their interpretation; *Obermann* was regarded as a personal confession, and its author the typical romantic figure of the age.

Obermann, however, had been published in 1804, and had been meditated for some years before this date. It was in 1789 that Senancour, then nineteen years of age, had left his home in Paris to escape the solicitations of a father anxious to establish him in Saint-Sulpice; and had, with the connivance of his mother, taken refuge in Switzerland. In a little more than a year

---

1 Whence, perhaps, it is logical to assume, the title of *Obermann* springs; rather than, as MM. Levallois and Merlant believe, from his qualities as a *surhomme*.

2 J. Levallois, *Senancour*, p. 158.

SENANCOUR

From the medallion by DAVID D'ANGERS

he had married there, for motives obscurely given, but unquestionably redounding to the chivalry and generosity of his nature, a Mademoiselle de Daguet. This marriage was not a happy one. In addition, his flight had deprived Senancour of a patrimony which would have given him, if not affluence, at least freedom from the material cares that were to be his lot henceforth. Two or three visits paid to Paris during the days of the Revolution, in an attempt to secure some remnant of his fortune, met with failure. An infirmity of the arms seems to have disqualified him from the rustic modes of life which Obermann preferred, and indeed, from all but sedentary occupations. On his return to Paris at the beginning of the century, a few friends procured him work with booksellers and periodical editors. Long separated from his wife, who had died in 1806, he lived in great retirement in Paris with his daughter, a witty and intelligent woman who venerated her father as one of the rarest intellects of the day.

In 1793, while in Switzerland, Senancour had already begun to write over the signature of *Le Rêveur des Alpes*. But it was not until 1799 that his first important work appeared, *Les Rêveries sur la nature primitive de l'homme*. Soon after this, *Obermann*, begun in 1801 in Paris, and finished at Fribourg, probably in 1803, was published: it appeared, quite unnoticed, in 1804, eclipsed by the fame that had hailed, two years before, the appearance of *Le Génie du Christianisme*.

In his *Observations critiques sur l'ouvrage intitulé Génie du Christianisme*, Senancour years later (in 1816) took pains to point out his complete ignorance in 1804 of Chateaubriand's work; researches have shown, in effect, that he was unaware even of Chateaubriand's name when the *Rêveries* of 1799, which are already in the tone and style of *Obermann*, were being composed. It is difficult indeed to see how the theatrical character of René could in any sense be regarded as anticipating the melancholy of Obermann. In the one case attitudinising, in the other perfect sincerity, are the keynotes to character.[1] Nor was Senancour by nature susceptible to influences from a quarter where sentimentality served for religious conviction and the heart was pompously invoked to override rational scruples. In his article Senancour paid due tribute to the poetry of Chateaubriand's style; but in resuming the arguments employed by Chateaubriand to bolster up his conversion, Senancour could find nothing that was solid. With intense earnestness he pointed out, as he had done already in *Obermann*, the necessity of founding religious and moral precepts on principles that were not ridiculous. 'Je voudrais', he says, 'que le cœur ne fût pas le seul guide de l'homme, parce que les mouvements du cœur étant passionnés, orageux, fanatiques, il ne resterait aucun espoir de rétablir l'ordre dans les sociétés humaines.'[2]

This highly developed intellectual bias is the most striking characteristic of *Obermann*. *Obermann*, unlike *René*, can in no sense be called a novel. It is rather a philosophical journal,[3] or poem, in which are recorded the outpourings of a soul divided by conflicting principles, one rational, leading its owner on to scepticism and materialism, and the other idealistic and sentimental, craving satisfaction for its aspirations, but shrinking with painful discouragement before the arid arguments of its materialist partner. In this volume, the word God is barely mentioned, immortality is wistfully denied; even personality explored in its inwardness yields Obermann no more than a glimpse into *le néant*; and for the soul which has so comfortlessly

---

1 See Levallois, *op. cit.* p. 174, and Matthew Arnold's note to the *Stanzas in memory of the author of 'Obermann'*; also his article on *Obermann* in the *Academy*.
2 Quoted by Levallois, *op. cit.* p. 118.
3 J. Merlant, *Le Roman personnel*, Paris, 1905, p. 99.

denounced its religious longings, there remains only recourse to the pagan philosophies. By turns epicurean and stoic, Obermann seems to seek first in the cultivation of the possibilities of this life, and then in their complete renunciation, a solution of the problem which haunts him. At times his attitude approaches that of the followers of Aristippus of Cyrene, whose cult for beauty and happiness almost verges on the stoic ideal, so much of renunciation is required that the highest in them may be nurtured, and bring forth its fruit of happiness.[1] So Obermann often seems to fancy *le bonheur* as the highest end; not the happiness of himself alone but, as he pleads, of all men around him. 'Qui pourra dire si elle [la vie] serait plus heureuse, sans accord avec les choses, et passée au milieu des peuples souffrans.'[2] But in his frequent moods of discouragement, in face of the seeming vanity of life, it is upon the frank acceptance of stoicism that he falls back. This stoicism Obermann never entirely abandoned. In part derived from classical, and to a large extent also, from Eastern sources, it remained his refuge when other philosophies failed. The serenity of the 'sage' became his ideal; and his watchwords *permanence* and *ordre*. But the actual attainment of this subdued life of the spirit was not often granted him. Once in youth, on his first arrival in Switzerland, the warring elements within him were reconciled, and he felt, he tells us, at once 'ardent et paisible'.[3] And again on the mountain tops, in a solitude untroubled by the vain turmoil of men, he was to find this peace: in such solitudes Nature had seemed to rebuke the divisions of his spirit, and

[1] The pretended Manuel de Pseusophanes (see *Obermann*, vol. I, pp. 111–13), attributed to Aristippus, is an exposition of epicureanism, hardly distinguishable from a very elevated conception of stoicism, and which might have been inspired by Epictetus or Marcus Aurelius.

[2] *Obermann*, VII, Vol. I, p. 45; quoted by Arnold in his article on *Obermann* in the *Academy*.

[3] *Obermann*, II, vol. I, p. 9.

appeared to him, in her impenetrable calm, the model of and guide to a happier existence.

So Obermann was always to turn to Nature, as the exemplar of the fixity and absoluteness which he desired and vainly sought in the flux of things about him: so he tried to attune his being to the stillness of her vast ice peaks, seeing, as by reflexion, the integrity of his own soul, a thing he might also maintain and hold to in the midst of the passing of all else in life. But, like the Stoic Cleanthes, who had taken the notion from Heracleitus, he came to be aware of the stillness of Nature as a sign of a deeper order of change, of viewless cycles of being, through which the world maintained itself constant; like the crest of a wave that flows on, itself unchanged, or the tenuity of a column of water, by which its eternal spouting seems immovable. From his readings of Saint-Martin, the spiritualist philosopher, and of the *Bhagavad Gîtâ*,[1] he took the idea of world-revolutions of degeneration and regeneration, of an eternal cyclic process in which nothing might be saved except to be again destroyed. And his soul fortified itself in stoic anticipation of its seemingly useless annihilation.

In this way, groping after immunity from the torments of desire and from his intellectual agitation, Obermann yet might see, from a mere physical change of attitude, the results of his philosophic reasoning fall away, and himself the prey of tortured longings—longings, as he says, never satiated, and yet bearing in their nature the foretaste of disillusionment.

Obermann is the history of a soul which, in its quest for Truth, is continually substituting Desire as its real end.

This dualism in Obermann leads him at one moment to regret emotions he has never indulged, and the next to long fiercely for their extinction. Torn between the exigencies of his

---

[1] J. Merlant, *Sénancour*, pp. 29, 90, 103, 145, etc.

sensibility and his reason he can find no satisfaction in renouncing either. The struggle is a painful and a weary one. Possessed neither by passion fulfilled, nor by peace attained, there is within him, he cries, 'un dérangement, une sorte de délire, qui n'est pas celui des passions:. . . c'est le désordre des ennuis; c'est la discordance qu'ils ont commencée entre moi et les choses; c'est l'inquiétude que des besoins longtemps comprimés ont mise à la place des désirs'.[1] No, he continues, 'je ne veux plus de désirs, ils ne me trompent point'; and, in the next breath, 'je ne veux pas qu'ils s'éteignent'.[2]

Tossed between these moods he walks out into the open air, 'abattu, et rempli d'ennui', and passing by a wall with flowers growing thereon, the scent of a jonquil affects his senses with sudden, joyful pain. 'C'était le premier parfum de l'année: c'est la plus forte expression du désir. Je sentis tout le bonheur destiné à l'homme. Cette indicible harmonie des êtres, le fantôme du monde idéal fut tout entier dans moi.'[3]

That conviction deserted him almost as soon as it was born. The ideal could not descend so easily upon earth, and he saw it floating away from him, as unattainable as ever. 'Je ne veux point jouir; je veux espérer, je voudrais savoir! Il me faut des illusions sans bornes, qui s'éloignent pour me tromper toujours. Que m'importe,' he continues with an accent of the deepest desolation, 'que m'importe ce qui peut finir. . . je veux un bien, un rêve, une espérance enfin qui soit toujours devant moi, au-delà de moi, plus grande que mon attente elle-même, plus grande que ce qui passe. Je voudrais être tout intelligence. . . .'[4] And then, a little later, he says sadly, 'Sans les désirs, que faire de la vie?'[5]

The sacrifice to the intellect cannot be borne; longing for

1 *Obermann*, XXII, vol. I, p. 91. 2 *Ibid.*
3 *Id.* XXX, vol. I, p. 102. 4 *Id.* XVIII, vol. I, pp. 74–5.
5 *Id.* XLI, vol. I, p. 165.

happiness and beauty surges up insistently: 'Mais quelle destinée que celle où les douleurs restent, où les plaisirs ne sont
plus....Plus de charme, plus d'ivresse, jamais un moment de
pure joie...et je suis né sensible, ardent!'[1] And again: 'Le
tourment du cœur insatiable est le mouvement aveugle d'un
météore errant dans le vide où il doit se perdre....Cette nature
cherchée au dehors et impénétrable dans nous est partout
ténébreuse. Je sens est le seul mot de l'homme qui ne veut que
des vérités. Et ce qui fait la certitude de mon être en est aussi
le supplice. Je sens, j'existe pour me consumer en désirs
indomptables....'.[2]

Elsewhere he says again 'La perte vraiment irréparable est
celle des désirs'.[3]

In this state the solitude of the mountains seems to offer
consolation and direction: but their silence, untroubled and
passionless, creates a new uneasiness in him.

'Ce silence absolu serait plus sinistre encore...c'est la vaine
beauté d'une rose devant l'œil qui ne s'ouvre plus.'[4]

For even when desire is slain, unrest does not perish: still is
left the 'fierce necessity to feel', without the 'power...'.[5]

Though dreading it more than the inanition of death,
Obermann continues to struggle towards the calm and light
his soul requires: he realises that it is only attainable through
the cultivation of the inner life, by which one may come at last
to indifference to the world of external things. The permanence
of Nature has its analogue in the soul; but he who would possess

1 *Obermann*, IV, vol. I, pp. 28–9. It was this despair at the thought of ebbing
youth and sensibility that George Sand re-echoed in her cry: 'L'amour,
l'amour, le bonheur, la vie, la jeunesse!...O mon ami! passes-tu des nuits
entières à pleurer tes rêves et à te dire: je n'ai pas été heureux...Oh! non, ce
n'est pas la force qui me manque pour vivre et pour espérer; c'est la foi et la
volonté...O mon Dieu! s'il pouvait me tomber de votre sein paternel une
conviction, une volonté, un désir seulement!' (*Lettres d'un Voyageur*,
Nohant, septembre 1834; IV, à Jules Néraud.)
2 *Obermann*, LXIII, vol. II, p. 73.   3 *Id.* XLI, vol. I, p. 161.
4 *Id.* XXII, vol. I, p. 91.   5 *Tristram and Iseult*.

such tranquillity must safeguard himself against external irritations, and on the stream of life maintain his self intact. 'La vie réelle de l'homme est en lui-même.'[1] 'The aids to noble life are all within', as Arnold said after him.[2]

'Il se peut que le vrai bien de l'homme soit son indépendance morale et que ses misères ne soient que le sentiment de sa propre faiblesse dans des situations multipliées; que tout devienne songe hors de lui, et que la paix soit dans le cœur inaccessible aux illusions.'[3]

'Les sages', he says elsewhere, with a lingering uncertainty, 'vivant sans passion, vivent sans impatience...et trouvent dans leur quiétude la paix et la dignité de la vie.'[4]

More firmly, he enunciates his ideal of manhood: 'Nous n'avons peut-être reçu la vie présente que pour rencontrer, malgré nos faiblesses, des occasions d'accomplir avec énergie ce que le moment veut de nous. Ainsi, employer toutes ses forces à propos, et sans passion comme sans crainte, ce serait être pleinement homme....'.[5] 'Sommes-nous faits pour jouir ici de l'entraînement des désirs.'[6]

He implores his unnamed friend: 'Je ne cherche point à justifier ce cœur brisé qui vous est trop bien connu....Vous savez, vous seul, ses espérances éteintes, ses désirs inexplicables, ses besoins démesurés. Ne l'excusez pas, soutenez-le, relevez ses débris; rendez-lui, si vous en avez les moyens, et le feu de la vie, et le calme de la raison, tout le mouvement du génie, et toute l'impassibilité du sage'.[7]

Arrived at this equilibrium: 'Ainsi, quoi qu'il arrive... nous disposerons des choses, non pas en les changeant elles-mêmes...mais en maîtrisant les impressions qu'elle feront sur

1 *Obermann*, I, vol. I, p. 5. 2 *Worldly Place.*
3 *Obermann*, XLI, vol. I, pp. 164–5. 4 *Id.* XLIII, vol. I, p. 183.
5 *Id.* XCI, vol. II, p. 238. 6 *Id.* XC, vol. II, p. 231.
7 *Id.* LXXXIX, vol. II, p. 224.

nous...ce qui maintient davantage notre être en le circonscrivant...et nous approcherons, par ce moyen, de l'heureuse
persévérance [variante, *permanence*] du sage'.[1]

For a moment it seems that this stoical ideal has succeeded.
'J'ai connu l'enthousiasme des vertus difficiles; dans ma superbe
erreur, je pensais remplacer tous les mobiles de la vie sociale
par ce mobile aussi illusoire. Ma fermeté stoïque bravait le
malheur comme les passions.'[2]

But the attitude was short-lived. 'L'illusion a duré près d'un
mois', at the end of which Obermann had lapsed into the old
passionate regret. 'Qui suis-je donc? me disais-je. Quel triste
mélange d'affection universelle, et d'indifférence....'[3] 'Je ne
suis point l'esclave des passions...mais enfin ne faut-il pas que
la vie soit remplie par quelque chose?'[4]

> Shall I not joy youth's heats are left behind,
> And breathe more happy in an even clime?—
> Ah no, for then I shall begin to find
> A thousand virtues in this hated time!
>
> Then I shall wish its *agitations back*,
> And *all its thwarting currents of desire*....[5]

So Matthew Arnold sighed, after Obermann and George
Sand. 'Calm's not life's crown, though calm is well.'[6]

No, it is not by renunciation of desire, Obermann discovers,
that immunity from unrest is obtained. Such sacrifice only
replaces passion by a feverish, undermining discontent, which
is more distressing than pain or suffering itself. Thus Obermann
feels his youth is passing, with all its promise and hope; its
torments are indeed passing away too, but bearing with them
all aspiration to what is beyond. Nothing is left but an unhappy

---

1 *Obermann*, I, vol. I, p. 7.   2 *Id.* IV, vol. I, p. 28.
3 *Ibid.* p. 23.   4 *Id.* XLI, vol. I, pp. 155–6.
5 *Youth's Agitations*.   6 *Youth and Calm*.

disease, and a vain regret for lost capacities. This is the sad temper of Obermann.

'J'étais rempli d'ennui. J'avais besoin de larmes, mais je ne pus que gémir. Les premiers temps ne sont plus: j'ai les tourmentes de la jeunesse et n'en ai point les consolations. Mon cœur, encore fatigué du feu d'un âge inutile, est flétri et desséché comme s'il était dans l'épuisement de l'âge refroidi. Je suis éteint, sans être calmé... je n'ai ni joie, ni espérance, ni repos; il ne me reste rien, je n'ai plus de larmes.'[1]

> My melancholy...
> Ah! if it *be* pass'd, take away,
> At least, the restlessness, the pain...
> The nobleness of grief is gone—
> Ah, leave us not the fret alone![2]

What is the real cause of this *ennui* of Obermann?

According to his own reflections, it often seems the result of contact with the distress and tumult of the outer world. We have seen that it is only in isolation from his kind, 'loin des émanations sociales',[3] before the sublimer aspects of nature, that Obermann captures even the illusion of tranquillity.

The malady has, however, roots deeper than this. Above all, there is that peculiar bias in Senancour's own nature, which is the source of his power and his originality, and is hardly therefore susceptible of analysis. A more general cause is the reaction upon him of the mental outlook of the age into which he was born.

At the time Senancour was writing *Obermann*, an almost complete intellectual liberation had been effected in France; but moral and religious aspiration had been curtailed; materialism, and rationalism, had chiefly regulated the output of

1 *Obermann*, xv, vol. i, p. 72.   2 *Stanzas from the Grande Chartreuse.*
3 *Obermann*, vii, vol. i, p. 44.

the eighteenth century. For the positively inclined thinker, the infinite field presented to speculation was of interest sufficient to absorb all his spiritual needs. A nature like Senancour's, however, was confused by the violence done to man's rationality, by a system which, while offering him an unlimited scope of enquiry, maintained the finite and limited nature of man himself. Such was the dilemma into which sceptics and materialists alike had fallen. This conflict of principles appeared to Senancour in the light of a radical contradiction in man's nature. The problem of human destiny pressed heavily on him; and the antinomy could not be solved, as Pascal had been enabled to solve it in an earlier age, by a blind but trusting faith. That age of faith and unenlightenment had passed away; what should replace it? The incompatibility between infinite thought and desire, and finite life and achievement, seemed to Senancour irreducible. The check imposed on spiritual aspiration, by which the finite for ever limits a conception of the infinite which it has itself created, and the bewilderment resulting therefrom —this is the deep-seated cause of the melancholy of Obermann. It is in this sense that Obermann has been described as obsessed by the infinite, 'malade de l'infini'. The ephemeral nature of man, persuaded of his own finality, but able to formulate the conception of an eternal universe, is his reiterated theme.

Much the same idea had engrossed an earlier age. It was the same sense of powerlessness to pass beyond 'the flaming barriers of the world' that had turned the Cyrenaics to arrest and imprison what they could of the transitory present, by the cultivation of their powers of emotion and sense. Nor was it happiness that they aimed at merely, but an exquisite appreciation of life, involving, it might very well be, suffering and heroism, so long as it were noble. 'Give him emotion, though pain!'[1]

1 *Early Death and Fame.*

'L'énergie dans les peines est meilleure que l'apathie dans les voluptés.'[1] The minor details of life, too, would have their heightened significance, viewed in this way. Epicureanism, in this highest sense, is the special philosophy of ascetic and humble lives. 'Toute la grâce de la nature', Obermann says, 'est dans le mouvement d'un bras.' Every little incident would take on a special sense and beauty to eyes whose capacity for vision had been so sharpened. Such a training would be *culture* in the best sense, an effort to the perfecting of the world as we must live in it, saved by virtue of such culture from the heaviness and vulgarity of common life. But what epicureanism has to dread, is the blunting of its appetites, and the ageing of its faculties. It is thus that Obermann experiences his keenest dejection, as he fears and watches the falling away of that heightened sensibility so anxiously cultivated.[2] He too will cling even to the capacity to suffer, as security against the consciousness of such weakening. 'Il est des jours pour les douleurs', he says, in one of those dream-like moods which overtook him so often, 'nous aimons à les chercher dans nous, à suivre leurs profondeurs, et à rester

[1] *Obermann*, Manuel de Pseusophanes, vol. I, p. 112.
[2] In a note to Letter XII, Obermann discusses the disrepute into which *l'homme sensible* had fallen, and particularly *la femme sensible*; and deplores such ridicule as tending to give a higher value to the temperament which is cautious and reserved than to that which is generous and open. Perhaps the defects of sensibility have been most fairly exposed in the person of Marianne in Jane Austen's *Sense and Sensibility*. The farewell to Norland will be remembered: 'Many were the tears shed by them in their last adieus to a place so much beloved. "Dear, dear Norland!" said Marianne, as she wandered alone before the house, on the last evening of their being there; "When shall I cease to regret you! when learn to feel a home elsewhere! O happy house, could you know what I suffer in now viewing you from this spot, from whence perhaps I may view you no more! And you, ye well-known trees!—but you will continue the same. No leaf will decay because we are removed, nor any branch become motionless because we can observe you no longer! No; you will continue the same; unconscious of the pleasure or the regret you occasion, and insensible of any change in those who walk under your shade! But who will remain to enjoy you?"' (chap. v). This reflection will be a favourite with Obermann and Arnold.

surpris devant leurs proportions démesurées; nous essayons, du moins dans les misères humaines, cet infini que nous voulons donner à notre ombre avant qu'un souffle du temps l'efface.'[1]

And it is fear for the waning of these powers that flings him back again on to the acceptance of the more ascetic stoic ideal. But at this point an element distinctively modern colours his philosophy of life. For it is above all to the example of Nature that this 'pre-romantic' instinctively turns, as pointing him away from his unsatisfied hedonism, to the other ideal, of sacrifice and resignation.

This association of Nature with human sentiments is something new in literature. Through Bernardin de Saint-Pierre, whom Senancour had read and appreciated,[2] though rejecting with the severity it deserved his doctrine of final causes, Nature had already made her entry into literature; as, in a less exotic way, before him, in the serene pastoral landscapes of Rousseau. But the engagement of Nature, not merely as spectator, but as participant of man's experiences, is peculiarly a conception of the romantic imagination. Not until the second quarter of the nineteenth century was French literature to seize definitely on and make use of this conception.

But already in Senancour the place of man in Nature was one of the outstanding preoccupations. It was in fact the consideration of this issue which he himself regarded as the unifying element of his work, beyond its many seeming contradictions and varied subject-matters. In his *Note* to the *Académie des Sciences Morales* he wrote: 'Ce qui est descriptif dans [mes] divers écrits... a cela de particulier que les résultats en appartiennent à la connaissance du cœur humain et des rapports établis entre nos mouvements intérieurs et l'esprit de la nature'.[3] It is

1 *Obermann*, xv, vol. I, p. 71.
2 G. Michaut, *Senancour*, Paris, 1909, p. 113, note.
3 Quoted by J. Levallois, *op. cit.* p. 165 and p. 173.

perhaps in accord with this aim that Obermann prefers in general the evocation of Nature in her more noble and grandiose aspects, rather than in her humble, intimate moments.

The final message of Nature to man is, however, one of discouragement. Nature, working harmoniously through continuous change to eternal changelessness, seems to reproach man and his tumultuous life. 'La paisible harmonie des choses fut sévère à mon cœur agité.'[1] To Matthew Arnold the same reproof was contained in the sight of Nature's

> Sleepless ministers....
> Their glorious tasks in silence perfecting;
> Still working, blaming still our vain turmoil,
> Labourers that shall not fail, when man is gone.[2]

In this passage we read beyond the reproach something more crushing still—the assertion of the finitude of human destiny in presence of enduring Nature. 'Il y a là une permanence qui nous confond: c'est pour l'homme une effrayante éternité. Tout passe; l'homme passe, et les mondes ne passent pas! La pensée est dans un abîme entre les vicissitudes de la terre et les cieux immuables.'[3]

> We, O Nature, depart,
> Thou survivest us! this,
> This, I know, is the law.[4]

And yet Nature is beautiful. The bitterness of Obermann is mixed with a kind of wonder that man should be unhappy before such beauty.

'Les neiges fondent sur les sommets; les nuées orageuses roulent dans la vallée: malheureux que je suis! les cieux s'embrasent, la terre mûrit, le stérile hiver est resté dans moi. Douces lueurs du couchant qui s'éteint! grandes ombres des neiges durables!... et l'homme n'aurait que d'amères voluptés

---

1 *Obermann*, LXIII, vol. II, p. 72.   2 *Quiet Work*.
3 *Obermann*, XVI, vol. I, p. 73.   4 *The Youth of Man*.

quand le torrent roule au loin dans le silence universel, quand les chalets se ferment pour la paix de la nuit, quand la lune monte au-dessus du Velan!'[1]

Once or twice this bitterness was tempered with reflections more hopeful, less sad; once or twice, his soul attuned to the vast silences about him, he was vouchsafed a moment of understanding; when he thought to catch, in the murmur of the pine-needles, some 'accents of the eternal tongue'.

'Et moi aussi j'ai des momens d'oubli, de force, et de grandeur.... Je m'arrête étonné; j'écoute ce qui subsiste encore; je voudrais entendre ce qui subsistera: je cherche dans le mouvement de la forêt, dans le bruit des pins, quelques-uns des accens de la langue éternelle.'[2]

> And thou hast pleasures, too, to share
> With those who come to thee—
> Balms floating on thy mountain air,
> And healing sights to see.
>
> How often, where the slopes are green
> On Jaman, hast thou sate
> By some high chalet-door, and seen
> The summer-day grow late...
>
> Lake Leman's waters, far below!
> And watch'd the rosy light
> Fade from the distant peaks of snow;
> And on the air of night
>
> *Heard accents of the eternal tongue*
> *Through the pine branches play.*[3]

At such moments, moments which, as Arnold said,[4] were at once 'the inspiration and the enervation of his life', is the

---

1 *Obermann*, LXXV, vol. II, p. 148.
2 *Id.* XLVIII, vol. II, pp. 19–20.
3 *Stanzas in memory of the author of 'Obermann'*.
4 In his article on *Obermann* in the *Academy*, p. 3.

melancholy half-scepticism of Obermann redeemed. His last words are a desire that on his death-bed he may be placed outside on the mountain grass, and there, in the sun, under the sky, in presence of the peace of Nature, feel again some breath of the infinite illusion pass into his soul.

Amid all the doubts and vexations which haunt him, like ghosts on which he has no hold, Obermann moves, a strange and solitary figure; a mixture never more than 'physical' of ingredients which may separate out from moment to moment and give their characteristic quality to his musings. The combination is rare and unstable, of *sagesse*, sensibility and romanticism; yet such is the originality of Obermann that the confusion within him—of sceptic, epicurean and stoic, of mystic in the presence of Nature and rationalist in that of man—is never confusing; the clear line of his personality, and classic utterance, emerges still forcefully and distinctly. The extravagances of his sensibility have indeed no counterpart in his language; despair does not make him either vehement or turgid. His expression is for the most part calm and measured, his style of almost classic purity. Reading *Obermann*, Arnold might well disdain the French alexandrine and think the best vehicle for French poetry to be—its prose! The confessions of Obermann, one might say, appear as overhung by a veil, through whose thickness the superficial reader does not readily penetrate. Like the universe which Obermann himself at times fancied as wearing a cloud of illusion, his thought is also draped; the personal utterance is controlled and the inspiration seems less violent than sad or dreary. There are moments when the words move with a mysterious air, like an enchanted monody or the language of a dream, beautiful and languorous as a dream; each word then charged with its secret importance, each sentence measuring out its slow, enveloping rhythm; and all, once uttered, seeming to slide back into profundity, or lingering only as a failing sound on the ear. Such charm of form, combined with its ever-serious undertone of impressive meaning, ravishes sense and thought together, and while the one is borne away in a confusion of delicate sensation, thought itself is lost in some higher lyric beauty.

His musings under the summer foliage of the forest of Fontainebleau are a poem of this sort:

Il est...des momens où je me vois plein d'espérance et de liberté; le temps et les choses descendent devant moi avec une majestueuse harmonie, et je me sens heureux, comme si je pouvais l'être: je me suis surpris revenant à mes anciennes années; j'ai retrouvé dans la rose les beautés du plaisir et sa céleste éloquence....Mais l'instant passe; un nuage devant le soleil intercepte sa lumière féconde; les oiseaux se taisent; l'ombre en s'étendant entraîne et chasse devant elle et mon rêve et ma joie.

Alors je me mets à marcher; je vais, je me hâte pour rentrer tristement, et bientôt je retourne dans les bois, parce que le soleil peut paraître encore. Il y a dans tout cela quelque chose qui tranquillise et qui console. Ce que c'est? je ne le sais pas bien; mais quand la douleur m'endort, le temps ne s'arrête pas, et j'aime à voir mûrir le fruit qu'un vent d'automne fera tomber.[1]

When the autumn comes, the mood is graver:

L'homme connaîtrait-il aussi la longue paix de l'automne, après l'inquiétude de ses fortes années? Comme le feu, après s'être hâté de consumer, dure en s'éteignant.

Longtemps avant l'équinoxe, les feuilles tombaient en quantité, cependant la forêt conservait encore beaucoup de sa verdure et toute sa beauté. Il y a plus de quarante jours, tout paraissait devoir finir avant le temps, et voici que tout subsiste par-delà le terme prévu; recevant, aux limites de la destruction,

1 *Obermann*, XIX, vol. I, pp. 75–6.

une durée prolongée, qui, sur le penchant de sa ruine, s'arrête avec beaucoup de grâce ou de sécurité, et qui, s'affaiblissant dans une douce lenteur, semble tenir à la fois et du repos de la mort qui s'offre, et du charme de la vie perdue.[1]

The beauty of the passage attenuates the thought and degree of suffering beneath it. But in Obermann language is a vesture which covers but does not conceal the interior pain. Even here there is a gloom that is saddening; more often his calmness hides a terrible anguish.

> A fever in these pages burns
> Beneath the calm they feign;
> A wounded human spirit turns
> Here, on its bed of pain....
>
> Yet, through the hum of torrent lone,
> And brooding mountain-bee,
> There sobs I know not what ground-tone
> Of human agony.[2]

Such is the character of Obermann as Arnold must have seen it; and such were the ideas the English poet was assimilating during the period 1846–9, after his momentous visit to Nohant. Illimitable were these latter to prove to Arnold, in suggestiveness and inspiration. Before verifying their influence, it is interesting to read Matthew Arnold's own statement of the characteristics in Obermann which most impressed him. They are, in the order in which Arnold gives them,[3] his 'inwardness', 'sincerity', 'renouncement', 'poetic emotion' and, lastly, his 'exquisite feeling for Nature'. The words are significant.

1 *Id.* XXIII, vol. I, p. 92.
2 *Stanzas in memory of the author of 'Obermann'.*
3 In his article on *Obermann* in the *Academy*, p. 3.

CHAPTER V

POEMS OF 1849:
FIRST 'OBERMANN' POEMS: ORIENTALISM

The first reference made by Arnold to his actual reading of *Obermann* occurs in a letter to Clough dated November 1848.[1] But the traces of the influence of this reading on him seem to place it somewhat earlier. Arnold's own positive and generous acknowledgment has been, one suspects, too often regarded as mere poetic exaggeration—if it has been regarded at all—and good-humouredly set aside at that.

'Thou master of my wandering youth'[2]—in these serious, and by no means rhetorical, words Arnold apostrophised the author of *Obermann*.

Still more definitely, in an earlier poem, he states his obligation:

> The eternal trifler breaks your spell;
> But we—we learnt your lore too well![3]

Senancour would have desired no fuller recognition. Yet none, save Arnold himself, has ever made it.[4]

Arnold's first volume, *The Strayed Reveller and Other Poems*, appeared early in 1849. It is not possible to assign dates to the various poems in this collection, but there are signs to show that most of them were written in the period between 1846 and 1848. In early February 1849, Arnold quotes a line of *Resignation* to Clough, as though he had but just laid down the pen from

1 Lowry, *op. cit.* p. 95.
2 *Obermann Once More.*
3 *Stanzas from the Grande Chartreuse.*
4 Nor has any critic, so far as I am aware, ever made an analysis of Arnold's indebtedness.

writing; and it seems safe to conclude that the year 1848 was his most fruitful period of poetic activity.

In the summer of 1845 Arnold with his mother and sister had visited the Isle of Man; this is the scene of *To a Gipsy Child by the Seashore*, and it has been suggested [1] that Arnold must have begun the writing of it soon after this date. Certain expressions in the poem, however, seem definitely the opinions of a later date; and it is not perhaps fanciful to argue that the actual composition of the poem was at least a year or two subsequent to the incident which occasioned it.

We are not concerned here with the poems in the volume which are clearly of classical inspiration; but putting these aside, we are confronted with a group of poems distinguished by a certain unity of mood, and singularity of thought. Into this group fall some of the early *Sonnets*, *The New Sirens*, *To Fausta*, *In Utrumque Paratus*, *The World and the Quietist*, *Resignation*, *To a Gipsy Child*, and possibly *Stagyrius* (at one time called *Desire*), a kind of litany with a characteristic note. What is perhaps outstanding in these poems is the sort of moral challenge they contain and steadfast bravery of the soul in face of some disconcerting spiritual discoveries. Modifying this, and at times softening it to a very much less stalwart attitude, is an impulse to melancholy and doubt.

This uncertain note was perhaps what was mystifying and unsympathetic to Arnold's first hearers. In *The World and the Quietist*, the poet attempts a justification of his attitude: it is the familiar one of the sceptic who hesitates to give his hand or his brain to a blind activity or untested creed.

People keep talking, says Obermann, of doing with energy what ought to be done; but amidst all this parade of firmness, tell me then what it is that ought to be done. For my part I do

---

1 H. F. Lowry, *op. cit.* p. 62.

not know, and I venture to suspect that a good many others
are in the same state of ignorance.[1]

Why [says the carping Critias (Clough?) to the poet] be
    debating still?
  Why, with these mournful rhymes
  Learn'd in more languid climes, [France? Switzerland?]
  Blame our activity...?

Critias, long since, I know,... [the poet answers]
Long since the world hath set its heart to live;
  Long since, with credulous zeal
  It turns life's mighty wheel....

  Yet as the wheel flies round
  With no ungrateful sound
Do adverse voices fall on the world's ear.
  Deafen'd by his own stir....

The same idea, of discovering the light before walking
blindly on the path, Arnold was to work out more fully in his
later social writings.[2] The text of a chapter of *Culture and
Anarchy* will be a saying of Obermann: 'Il est plus difficile et
plus rare d'avoir assez de discernement pour connaître le devoir
que de trouver assez de forces pour le suivre'.[3]

The examination of some at least of the objects of human
activity is contained in *The New Sirens*. This poem is a very
beautiful and interesting exposition of the conflict between the
intellectual and sentimental elements of man's nature; this, the
familiar obsession of Obermann, is an idea which will haunt
Arnold henceforth.

For the understanding of the poem we can refer to the gloss
which Arnold himself furnished to Clough for the purpose.[4]

The problem—the choice between the emotional and the
intellectual life—is treated by Arnold in a mood which is itself

---

1 Quoted by Matthew Arnold in the article on *Obermann* in the *Academy*,
   p. 2.
2 See the Preface to *Culture and Anarchy*, *Works*, vol. vi, p. xv.
3 *Obermann*, LXXXVI, vol. ii, p. 204.   4 H. F. Lowry, *op. cit.* pp. 105–6.

predominantly intellectual and shows a cool if somewhat wistful detachment. It is significant that he gives the speaker (one
of a band of poets), half-way through the gloss, words which
are practically those Senancour quotes from Voltaire on the
same subject: 'I [says the poet], remaining in the dark and cold
under my cedar, and seeing the blaze of your revels in the
distance, do not share your illusions: and ask myself whether
this *alternation* of ennui and excitement is worth much?
Whether it is in truth a very desirable life?'

Senancour, too, had doubted it, but regarded it as his
mournful fate, 'n'est-ce pas une nécessité que ma vie soit
inquiète et malheureuse...et que, comme l'a si bien dit
Voltaire, je consume tous mes jours dans les convulsions de
l'inquiétude ou dans la léthargie de l'ennui?'[1]

The theme of the poem is transparently borrowed from
Obermann: the personal exposition, poetic development and
embroidery, are Arnold's. And yet again, the setting, with its
images of myrtles, vines, and odorous pines, of the 'orient
hill', and 'rose flush on the frore peak's awful crown', has an
Alpine touch and memory of *Obermann* too.

Arnold's commentary shows the poem to be a kind of
address from the poet to the company of 'New Sirens'.
I dreamed, he says, you were the Sirens of antiquity, those
'fierce, sensual lovers'; but I am mistaken; the attraction which
drew me to you from the uplands and 'dragon-warder'd
fountains' of knowledge was something you claimed to be more
spiritual—nor can I still resist your charm, as I remember it
'at sunrise on these lawns'.

But now I see you wandering dispiritedly in your bowers,
where storms are creeping up; are you regretful that you have
abandoned the 'purer fire' that once you sought like me, on the
frozen mountain tops; and have descended to this 'windless

1 *Obermann*, XIV, vol. I, pp. 68-9; and see *Candide*, chap. XXX.

valley'? [The Sirens resume their revels, with revived joy, while the poet continues to comment on them.] Surely this alternation of whetted and jaded appetites, 'this flux of guesses —mad delight; and frozen calms', he says, is worth very little. As the long day waxes, they will bring you only weariness. Then love will wane, and faith fail: even emotion on which you depend will dry up, and you will desire to let fall a tear, and be free. He exhorts them: Leave your roses, maidens, for the cypress and the yew.

The temptation these Sirens represent is one with which Obermann was always struggling. He had tasted, like them, the disillusionment which follows indulgence in sensibility. For, as the Sirens boldly made appeal to the authority of feeling, against that of the judgment, claiming 'Only what we feel we know'; so Obermann also, in a certain mood, had invoked sensibility as the one source of truth: 'Je sens est le seul mot de l'homme qui ne veut que des vérités'.[1]

But this glorification of the emotions was quickly followed by depression; and the same fluctuations of excitement and apathy as exhausted the Sirens, brought dejection to Obermann. He, too, became dispirited and restless, and yearned, even as they, for the refreshment of tears, to break through his stony lassitude.

'J'étais rempli d'ennui. J'avais besoin de larmes mais je ne pus que gémir. Les premiers temps ne sont plus.... Je suis éteint, sans être calmé: je n'ai ni joie, ni espérance, ni repos; il ne me reste rien, je n'ai plus de larmes.'[2]

Like the Sirens, he was to clutch feverishly at his waning capacity for emotion:

'Je commence à sentir que j'avance dans la vie. Ces impressions délicieuses, ces émotions subites qui m'agitaient

1 *Obermann*, LXIII, vol. II, p. 73.   2 *Id.* XV, vol. I, p. 72.

autrefois et m'entraînaient si loin d'un monde de tristesse, je ne les retrouve plus qu'altérées et affaiblies. Ce désir que réveillait en moi chaque sentiment de quelque beauté dans les choses naturelles, cette espérance pleine d'incertitude et de charme, ce feu céleste qui éblouit et consume un cœur jeune, cette volupté expansive dont il éclaire devant lui le fantôme immense, tout cela n'est déjà plus.' [1]

So it fared also with the Sirens; the 'sombre day' which had opened with a dawn so fair and joyful, had worn on, and left them wearied, and uneasy, finding joy no longer more than a memory and unable to 'warm the heart anew', life and beauty dulled, and love ebbed away; recalling sadly the higher, more permanent hopes they had once aspired to, and abandoned.

In the later poems Arnold was again and again to fancy himself in the plight depicted in the *New Sirens*, never able fully to give himself to their invitation, nor to reject it.

> Ah! two desires toss about
> The poet's feverish blood.
> One drives him to the world without,
> And one to solitude. [2]

To which desire will he yield? He is unable to decide. The moon, companion of his vigil in silvery nights of later life, will speak to him long afterwards, as she had spoken to Obermann, and reproach his uncertain dis-ease:

> Hast thou then still the old unquiet breast,
> Which neither deadens into rest
> Nor ever feels the fiery glow
> That whirls the spirit from itself away,
> But fluctuates to and fro,
> Never by passion quite possess'd
> And never quite benumb'd by the world's sway? [3]

1 *Id.* xxi, vol. 1, p. 80.
2 *Stanzas in memory of the author of 'Obermann'.*
3 *A Summer Night.*

Obermann, too, fluctuated between these opposed ideals. 'Je sens, j'existe pour me consumer en désirs indomptables; pour m'abreuver de la séduction d'un monde fantastique'[1]... but 'où trouverai-je un aliment pour mon cœur quand il aura perdu cette soif qui le consume?'[2]

Obermann, before Arnold, had known the charm, and experienced the withering effect, of emotion indulged: 'Indicible sensibilité, charme et tourment de nos vaines années,... passion universelle, sagesse avancée, voluptueux abandon; tout ce qu'un cœur mortel peut contenir de besoins et d'ennuis profonds, j'ai tout senti, j'ai tout éprouvé dans cette nuit mémorable. J'ai fait un pas sinistre vers l'âge d'affaiblissement; j'ai dévoré dix années de ma vie. Heureux l'homme simple dont le cœur est toujours jeune!'[3]

So Arnold, identifying himself with this unquiet spirit, adjured the calm, contemplative Scholar-Gipsy:

> But fly our paths, our feverish contact fly!
>   For strong the infection of our mental strife,
>   Which, though it gives no bliss, yet spoils for rest...
>
> And then thy glad perennial youth would fade,
> Fade, and grow old at last, and die like ours.[4]

Matthew Arnold was, like Senancour, in youth at heart a romantic, but one of classical training and tradition; and this unfused mixture was the cause of his continual agitation, the rational side of him bringing to birth aspirations to poise and spiritual self-control which his instinctive romantic longings would not allow him to accept without an aching sense of loss.

> Calm's not life's crown though calm is well,
> 'Tis all perhaps which man acquires.
> But 'tis not what our youth desires.[5]

---

1 *Obermann*, LXIII, vol. II, p. 73.   2 *Id*. XLI, vol. I, p. 159.
3 *Id*. IV, vol. I, pp. 22–3.   4 *The Scholar-Gipsy*.   5 *Youth and Calm*.

But as Senancour sought to rid himself of his unquiet longings by taking refuge in classic and eastern disciplines, so Arnold also turned, in Clough's words,[1] to the example of 'his rehabilitated Hindoo-Greek philosophy' in search of a solution.

Resignation reflects the influence of these ideas, received at the hands of Senancour, upon the English poet. The insinuating charm of Senancour's style had perhaps been first to fascinate Arnold; his imagination had thus been captured, and his emotions excited: but it cannot be forgotten that it is supremely by the character and force of his personality that Senancour was to exercise his great ascendancy over Arnold. The appeal of Senancour is a limited one: but Matthew Arnold was already by nature disposed to receive and respond to it. The rare nobility and sincerity of the elder writer could be revealed only when they were understood; in Arnold they worked to bring to expression sentiments and ideas which he had already felt, as yet voiceless, within himself. *Resignation* was 'written from the heart, from a real stoicism, that had attained no inconsiderable power of renunciation'.[2]

In this poem, indeed, Arnold expounds the stoical doctrine which he was now resolved on embracing. We can see how for Arnold, as for Senancour, the very austerity of this ethic would have its appeal; the severe discipline would be embraced eagerly as the furthest possible removed from romantic or epicurean tendencies; these, now disavowed, could only so be resolutely extinguished.

A certain quiet disdain and calm dismissal distinguish Arnold's attitude in this poem, and serve to maintain it untroubled by the fluctuations and wistful returns upon himself which he, like Senancour, will later suffer. In the year 1848

1 A. H. Clough, in the *North American Review*, July 1853, vol. LXXVII, p. 22.
2 H. F. Lowry, *op. cit.* Introduction, p. 36.

Arnold was reading with appreciation the Oriental poem, the *Bhagavad Gîtâ*,[1] directed thereto, probably, by his interest in *Obermann*. The central teaching of this Indian philosophy is the idea which occurs repeatedly in *Obermann* and is almost the key-passage of the *Libres Méditations*: 'Tout mérite est dans la soumission à l'ordre'.[2] It is the double impress of classic and oriental influences that gives its peculiar cachet to this aspect of Senancour's thought, and which similarly distinguishes Arnold's.

Wilkins' translation from the Sanskrit of the *Bhagavad Gîtâ* had enjoyed a great vogue in the eighteenth century: from England it had passed to France, retranslated by Parraud, and appearing in 1787, just two years before Senancour fled to Switzerland. There is no doubt that Senancour had read and been deeply influenced by this book.[3] To Senancour the revelation of Eastern thought, Chinese as well as Indian, had appeared with all the prestige of its venerableness and exoticism. This interest in the East was not transitory, but was maintained all through Senancour's later life. His *Résumé des traditions morales et religieuses*, in which he asserted the idea familiar to the eighteenth century, and revived by Michelet, Quinet, Renan and other students of comparative religion, that the mainspring of Christianity existed already in the ethical doctrines of antiquity, was an outcome of this interest. In 1824, a year before, he had given a *Résumé de l'histoire de la Chine* for the same series of *Résumés historiques*, to which were also contributors, among others, Ferdinand Denis and Armand Carrel. It is noteworthy

1 H. F. Lowry, *op. cit.* Introduction, pp. 69, 70, 71 and 75. Professor Lowry (p. 71, note 3) makes the suggestion that the reading of this poem 'heavily influenced Arnold's *Resignation* and other early poems'.
2 *Libres Méditations d'un Solitaire inconnu*, Paris, 1819, Soirée IV, p. 47; and see also Rêverie XLI, 'La notion de l'ordre est ce fruit de la science dont parlent les Orientaux' (*Rêveries*).
3 J. Merlant, *Sénancour*, pp. 103 and 145.

that Senancour, in correspondence with the former, would occasionally sign himself 'le cénobite de l'est';[1] or would address Denis, on the other hand, as 'Monsieur le brahme de la Seine ou de Rio Janeiro',[2] or 'M. le descendant des sages brahmes',[3] this kind of allusion being perfectly understood on both sides, and in fact marking the ground of their sympathy. The slightly odd appellation of 'brahmane alpestre'[4] which has been given Senancour, would thus seem not un-deserved.

Moreover, among the group that was associated with the short-lived *Institut historique*, of which Senancour was a member from 1834 to 1840, was Eugène Burnouf, the great orientalist, to whom much of the responsibility for the revived interest in orientalism of the mid-nineteenth century must be attributed. It seems that Arnold himself had a copy of Burnouf's *Intro-duction à l'Histoire du Buddhisme indien*, published in 1844, for a book referred to as 'my *Bouddhisme*' is mentioned by him (as being unprocurable) in a letter dated 1858.[5] The almost certain probability is that this *Bouddhisme* is Burnouf's *Buddhisme*, since Arnold, we know, was familiar with the orientalist's writings.[6] It is possible therefore that this book, too, was instrumental in turning Arnold's interest in the direction of Hindu thought.

The various themes which Arnold took over from these sources will recur with increasing explicitness in the later poems, but already in this first volume they have practically all been enunciated. The themes—predominantly those of in-

---

1 A. Monglond, 'Senancour et un Voyageur au Brésil', in the *Revue de Littérature Comparée*, janvier–mars 1931, p. 110.
2 *Ibid.* p. 106.   3 *Ibid.* p. 107.
4 J. Merlant, *Sénancour*, p. 15.
5 A. Whitridge, *Unpublished Letters of Matthew Arnold*, New York, 1923, p. 43.
6 See *Literature and Dogma, Works*, vol. VII, p. 119, etc.

difference and submission, of the peace which comes from the control of passion and imagination, of the need of preserving the inner life intact and pure from worldly touch, and the more special ideas of illusion, of Nature as an eternal process, and also as a cyclic process—all these appear in the early poems. And these ideas we have already seen in *Obermann*. The evolution in the thought of Arnold and Senancour presents indeed an almost startling parallel; not only their general conclusions being in harmony, but also their spiritual progress to these conclusions. So, with similar hesitations and backward glances, together they draw near their ideal, alike persevering to attain a common goal, of self-restraint, self-dependence and sacrifice, sought in isolation, in face of Nature's silence, impenetrability and calm.

Resignation, which is among the longer and more important of Arnold's early poems, is a fair epitome of these ideas. The first two lines, with their expression of unflinching resolve and steadfast purpose, are expressive of the bolder, more positive aspirations of the young stoic. (In a later poem, *Courage*, he will elaborate this ideal again, and even more firmly.) The serenity of mild natures, freed from the sway of passion, is next extolled. This is the *sérénité* which Senancour thirsted after: the 'sérénité' and 'paix'[1] of the *sages*, who '*vivant sans passion, vivent sans impatience*, et...trouvent dans leur quiétude la paix et la dignité de la vie'.[2] But

de grands obstacles s'opposent souvent à cette tranquille indifférence. Pour *recevoir le présent comme il s'offre*, et mépriser l'espoir ainsi que les craintes de l'avenir, il n'est qu'un moyen sûr, facile et simple, c'est d'éloigner de son idée cet avenir dont la pensée agite toujours, puisqu'elle est toujours incertaine. Pour n'avoir ni craintes ni désirs, il *faut tout abandonner à*

---

1 *Obermann*, XLVI, vol. I, p. 214.
2 *Id.* XLIII, vol. I, p. 183.

l'événement comme à une sorte de nécessité, jouir ou souffrir selon qu'il arrive, et l'heure suivante dût-elle amener la mort, n'en pas user moins paisiblement de l'instant présent. Une âme ferme, habituée à des considérations élevées peut parvenir à l'indifférence du sage.[1]

Such a spirit indeed would resemble those whom Arnold praises,

> . . . Milder natures, and more free—
> Whom an unblamed *serenity*
> *Hath freed from passions,* and the state
> Of struggle these necessitate;
> Whom schooling of the stubborn mind
> Hath made, or birth hath found, resign'd—
> *These mourn not that their goings pay*
> *Obedience to the passing day.*
> These claim not every laughing Hour
> For handmaid to their striding power;
> Each in her turn, with torch uprear'd,
> To await their march; and when appear'd,
> Through the cold gloom, with measured race,
> To usher for a destined space
> (Her own sweet errands all foregone)
> The too imperious traveller on.[2]

The conception of the poet's function is also reminiscent of Senancour's description of *l'homme supérieur.*

> The poet, to whose mighty heart
> Heaven doth a quicker pulse impart,
> *Subdues that energy to scan*
> Not his own course, but that of man.[3]

L'homme supérieur a toutes les facultés de l'homme, et il *peut éprouver toutes les affections humaines.* . . . Celui qui fait céder de grandes pensées à des idées petites ou personnelles. . . n'est pas un homme supérieur. . . . Il fait quelquefois ce que les passions humaines peuvent faire; *mais il y a dans lui une chose*

---

1 *Ibid.* pp. 183–4.   2 *Resignation.*   3 *Ibid.*

impossible; c'est qu'il le fasse par passion. Non seulement
l'homme supérieur...n'est point passionné pour les femmes
...mais je prétend qu'il n'est pas même ambitieux.[1]

> He...for no moment's space
> Envies the all-regarded place.
> Beautiful eyes meet his—and he
> Bears to admire uncravingly....
>
> Blame thou not, therefore, him who dares
> Judge vain beforehand human cares;
> Who needs not love and power, to know
> Love transient, power an unreal show.[2]

And as Arnold points to this ascetic ideal, Obermann too
describes one in whom he has known and seen exemplified the
beauty of such living:

> Cette vie passée dans l'indifférence au milieu de tous les
> agrémens de la vie, et dans l'ennui dans une santé inaltérable;
> ces chagrins sans humeur, cette tristesse sans amertume, ce
> sourire des peines cachées, cette simplicité qui abandonne tout
> ...ces regrets sans plainte, cet abandon sans effort, ce dé-
> couragement dont on dédaigne l'affliction; tant de biens
> négligés, tant de pertes oubliées, tant de facultés dont on ne
> veut plus rien faire: tout cela est plein d'harmonie, et n'appar-
> tient qu'à elle.[3]

Of such are the stoic souls whom Arnold describes in another
poem in this volume, *To a Gipsy Child*; the souls

> who weigh
> Life well, and find it wanting, nor deplore;
> But in disdainful silence turn away
> Stand mute, self-centred, stern, and dream no more.

These souls, though they have never known the 'superfluity
of joy',[4] or 'the longings vain'[5] that agitated the 'New Sirens';

1 *Obermann*, LXXXIV, vol. II, pp. 191–2. 2 *Resignation.*
3 *Obermann*, LXXXIX, vol. II, pp. 226–7.
4 *To a Gipsy Child.* 5 *Ibid.*

never suffer on the other hand the dispirited reactions that follow such indulgences; never taste the weariness, 'which is the full-fed soul's annoy' [ennui]. The Gipsy Child, in whom Arnold fancies the possession of the coveted stoic qualities, has, like Obermann, renounced life even before beginning to live, and in youth is already lined with the depression of suffering endured, as it were, in foretaste; of disillusionment known by expectation. Such was the singular experience of Obermann, which George Sand had noticed in him as the most grievous aspect of his melancholy. But Senancour while renouncing, had endured all the agonies of renunciation—'Je ne connais point la satiété: je trouve partout le vide'. The Gipsy Child has more fully resigned itself, it knows no rebellion: a 'meek anticipant' of 'sure pain', it has 'foreknown', and submitted itself to the 'vanity of hope', and desire. To the same conclusion, though his heart rebelled, his reason had driven Senancour. And so too Arnold envies the calm of his Gipsy Child; and he also accepts the vanity of life; with Obermann, dismisses the idea of 'cette éternité que l'homme croit ajouter à ses passions d'un jour'.[1]

> The World in which we live and move
> Outlasts aversion, outlasts love,
> Outlasts each effort, interest, hope,
> Remorse, grief, joy;—and were the scope
> Of these affections wider made,
> Man still would see and see dismay'd
> Beyond his passion's widest range,
> Far regions of eternal change.[2]

The thought contained in this passage, of the contrast between man's unlimited hope and finite destiny, is peculiarly the conclusion of Obermann's saddest meditations. The spectacle of the everlasting heavens was to him also an impenetrable enigma.

1 *Obermann*, LXXXIX, vol. II, p. 226.　　2 *Resignation*.

'Il y a là une permanence qui nous confond: c'est pour l'homme une effrayante éternité. Tout passe, l'homme passe, et les mondes ne passent pas! La pensée est dans un abîme entre les vicissitudes de la terre et les cieux immuables.'

But, says Arnold sadly, 'Fate's impenetrable ear'[1] remains deaf to man's prayer. 'Nature impénétrable';[2] and again, 'Nature partout accablante et partout impénétrable':[3] Obermann in these terms had already bowed to the mystery of the world.

In *A Question: To Fausta*[4] a more wistful tone prevails. The ephemeral grace of human dreams and friendships is again Arnold's theme: resisting this sad conclusion, he is yet carried away by it; the hesitant, questioning note of the poem is in contrast with the stouter affirmations of *Resignation*.

In the latter poem, Arnold seems almost to approach the 'poet's rapt security' which he desires, and seeks to draw from the presence of inanimate Nature around him; his highest hope is the moderate one, that he may some day find a place among these silent companions, and be merged and lost in their life, in the life of the world, 'of plants and stones and rain' that will survive him.

In this poem of *Resignation* Arnold seems to lend himself also to the ancillary notion of world-cycles of change behind 'the eternal mundane spectacle'; seeing, beyond the visible world,

> Beyond his [man's] passion's widest range,
> Far regions of eternal change.[5]

1 *Resignation*.
2 *Obermann*, LXXV, vol. II, p. 148.
3 *Obermann*, IV, vol. I, p. 22.
4 In the volume of 1849 this poem is simply called *To Fausta*. Presumably a pun was intended in the name Fausta—which occurs also in *Resignation* —applied to his sister, who married William Forster in 1850. A piece of humour of this sort would undoubtedly have delighted Arnold and his family; on the other hand, he would early have seen the undesirableness of giving it too much prominence and have relegated the name to a sub-title.
5 *Resignation*.

The passage is interesting as showing Arnold preoccupied with the idea of 'change' rather than of 'permanence' in Nature. The latter concept is more characteristic of him, as it is, on the whole, of Senancour also. The idea of Nature's immutability, and the contrast of her quiet labour with the tumult of life in the inhabited plains, is reiterated so constantly in *Obermann* that Sainte-Beuve proposed the word 'permanence' to represent its central thought.[1] But the notion of change, *within this fixity*, is implicit in the idea. Senancour himself has a beautiful image to explain it, of the agitated summit of the tree which yet never moves from its place.[2] 'La mobilité qui me caractérise...', he says, 'est constamment une grande inconstance.'[3]

But in Nature, he goes on to say, man can only guess at the existence of these workings: they are performed so quietly that only the flux of man's nature can supply him with the clue to them. 'Sans les souvenirs apportés des plaines [he says], l'homme ne pourrait croire qu'il soit hors de lui quelque mouvement dans la nature; le cours des astres lui serait inexplicable; et jusqu'aux variations des vapeurs tout lui semblerait subsister dans le changement même. Chaque moment présent lui paraissant continu, il aurait la certitude sans avoir jamais le sentiment de la succession des choses; et les perpétuelles mutations de l'univers seraient à sa pensée un mystère impénétrable.'[4]

In the sonnet *Quiet Work*, the very title of which, 'paisible travail', seems taken from *Obermann*, Matthew Arnold caught up this idea and worked it out fruitfully, showing Nature in her calm pursuit of order, labouring tranquilly, and noiselessly,

---

1 *Portraits Contemporains*, vol. I, p. 163.
2 *Obermann*, XC, vol. II, p. 232.
3 *Ibid.* This sentiment of the universal movement of matter came to Senancour from the Stoics through his favourite Montaigne—'Je peins le passage et non l'être'.
4 *Obermann*, VII, vol. I, p. 47.

through man's discordant life, and long after he has passed away, as 'sails that gleam a moment and are gone'.[1]

Senancour, on the mountain tops where he had attained the same vision, had also his lesson to learn from their vast silences,

> Of two duties kept at one,
> Of toil unsevered from tranquillity;

reproaching himself, ardent but sterile, 'au milieu *du paisible et éternel travail des êtres*'.[2]

Je ne saurais vous donner [he says again, with his grave intentness], je ne saurais vous donner une idée juste de ce monde nouveau, ni exprimer la permanence des monts dans une langue des plaines. Les heures m'y semblaient *à la fois et plus tranquilles et plus fécondes*, et comme si le roulement des astres eût été ralenti dans le calme universel, je trouvais dans la lenteur et l'énergie de ma pensée une succession que rien ne précipitait et qui pourtant devançait son cours habituel.

Quand je voulus estimer sa durée, je vis que le soleil ne l'avait pas suivie; et je jugeai que le sentiment de l'existence est réellement plus pesant et plus stérile dans l'agitation des terres humaines. Je vis que malgré la lenteur des mouvemens apparens, c'est dans les montagnes, sur leurs cimes paisibles, que la pensée, moins pressée, est véritablement plus active. L'homme des vallées consume, sans en jouir, sa durée inquiète et irritable; semblable à ces insectes toujours mobiles qui perdent leurs efforts en vaines oscillations, et que d'autres, aussi faibles, mais plus tranquilles, laissent derrière eux dans leur marche directe et toujours soutenue.[3]

For in the eternal cycle all that is ephemeral in us will be swallowed up: 'L'œuvre est déjà commencée, et les siècles de vie subsisteront quand nous, nos plaintes, notre espérance et nos systèmes auront à jamais passé'.[4] And again we are re-

---

1 *To a Gipsy Child.*
2 *Obermann*, XLIII, vol. I, p. 181.
3 *Id.* VII, vol. I, pp. 45–6.
4 *Id.* LXXXV, vol. II, p. 199.

minded of the same thought in *Resignation*, in a passage which we now must quote in full:

> The world in which we live and move
> Outlasts aversion, outlasts love,
> Outlasts each effort, interest, hope,
> Remorse, grief, joy;—and were the scope
> Of these affections wider made,
> Man still would see, and see dismay'd,
> Beyond his passion's widest range,
> Far regions of eternal change.
> Nay, and since death, which wipes out man,
> Finds him with many an unsolved plan,
> With much unknown, and much untried,
> Wonder not dead, and thirst not dried,
> Still gazing on the ever full
> Eternal mundane spectacle—
> The world in which we draw our breath
> In some sense, Fausta, outlasts death.

With the thought of man's limitations uppermost, Matthew Arnold has an admission, however, to make in his favour. In the sonnet *In Harmony with Nature*, after treating with some disdain the idea that man can ever emulate Nature's coolness and strength, he adds, rather sternly,

> Know, man hath all that Nature hath, but more.

In this 'more', Arnold is perhaps thinking of the power which Senancour had recognised in frail humanity, to embrace in thought more than he can attain in being. It was the poignant sense of this disparity between men as they are, and that of which they have the consciousness they *might* be, which is the characteristic lament of Obermann.

'Dieux par la pensée, insectes pour le bonheur',[1] we are indeed superior to our destinies, greater than the unconscious

---

[1] *Obermann*, XLV, vol. I, p. 202.

order around us, greater than it has any need for us to be. With our consciousness we penetrate the Universe, our thought going beyond our being, as the shadow which grows more vast than its cause, but which a second may annihilate.[1] Arnold concludes: we must either surpass Nature, or remain enslaved by her: 'Fool, if thou canst not pass her, rest her slave!' We must rule our environment, says Senancour in a passage which was perhaps in Arnold's mind—disposing of things not by changing them, but by mastering the impressions they make on us.[2] Such a solution of the tyranny of Nature, in the view of Obermann, is the greatest work of human wisdom.[3]

But that Arnold is as uncertain as Obermann of our real title to superiority is shown in his wavering, in two other sonnets of this group, between the ideas that 'the will is free',[4] and yet that we are, on the contrary, hemmed in by 'Mountains of Necessity'.[5] Our 'liberté absolue est si incertaine', says Obermann; and our 'liberté apparente si limitée'.[6]

The only certainty is the inexorable roll of Nature in her eternal cosmic order. And yet even this may be an illusion. *In Utrumque Paratus* is the dolorous cry of the dreamer who has thought to put his finger on the secret truth of the world; obeys the decree:

> —O waking on life's stream!
> By lonely pureness to the all-pure fount
>   ...the colour'd dream
> Of life remount!

then, drawing near the heart of Nature, finds himself in presence only of an illusion.

The idea of the world as an illusory appearance occurs

---

1 *Obermann*, XLVIII, vol. II, p. 19.
2 *Id.* I, vol. I, p. 7.   3 *Ibid.* p. 6.
4 *Lines Written in Emerson's Essays.*
5 *To a Republican Friend Continued.*   6 *Obermann*, I, vol. I, p. 6.

frequently in Obermann. Himself he often described as the dream of a dream, and reality as the infinite illusion, 'l'illusion infinie'.[1] As he says sadly, 'Je suis sur la terre comme une ombre qui s'y promène, qui voit et ne peut rien saisir'.[2] The world as a universal lure, in which man is flung from deception to deception, is an idea that haunts his more mystical pages.[3] This is the conception of Mâyâ in Indian doctrine, from which Senancour undoubtedly took the idea.

Another distinctively oriental thought which he took over from the same source and which certainly influenced Arnold, is that article of Hindu cosmogony which involves the idea of the world as a scene of change from degeneration to regeneration. This is a development of the idea of movement in Nature, which we have already noticed in Arnold (see pp. 72–3). It appears to have made a deep impression on him, for years later, in the *Epilogue* to *Haworth Churchyard*,[4] he refers to it in terms which are almost Senancour's own. At the end of the requiem poem of the Brontës, the poet adds, with a grim sort of consolation:

> Unquiet souls!
> —In the dark *fermentation* of earth,
> In the *never idle workshop of nature*,
> In the *eternal movement*,
> Ye shall find yourselves again!

Senancour had already observed, commenting on a more general aspect of this 'dogme oriental':

Je vous avoue que ce système de la réparation du monde ne me choque point du tout. Il n'est pas moderne, mais cela ne peut lui donner que plus d'autorité. Il est grand, il est spécieux. . . . Je croirais volontiers que cette hypothèse d'une dégradation

1 *Obermann*, Dernière Lettre, p. 246.
2 *Id*. LXXXIX, vol. II, p. 225.   3 *Id*. LXXI, vol. II, p. 137.
4 This epilogue was not printed until 1877, in the second collected edition, although *Haworth Churchyard* had appeared in 1855.

fortuite, et d'une lente régénération, d'une force qui vivifie, qui élève, qui subtilise, et d'une autre qui corrompt et qui dégrade, n'est pas le moins plausible de nos rêves sur la nature des choses.[1]

And again:

La force qui meut [le monde] paraît vague, inquiète, énervée ou balancée par une force indéfinissable: la nature paraît empêchée dans sa marche, et comme embarrassée et incertaine. Nous croirons discerner une lueur dans l'abîme si nous entrevoyons les mondes comme des *sphères d'activité*, comme des *ateliers de régénération* où la *matière travaillée* graduellement, et subtilisée par un principe de vie, doit passer de l'état passif et brut à ce point d'élaboration, de ténuité, qui la rendra enfin susceptible d'être imprégnée de feu et pénétrée de lumière.[2]

The verbal similarities between this passage and Arnold's epilogue are striking: the *ateliers de régénération* and the *matière travaillée* must certainly have furnished Arnold with the idea of the 'never idle workshops of nature'.

The use of the word 'fermentation' also suggests direct borrowing. In another passage on the same subject Obermann concludes:

Si cette fermentation silencieuse et terrible qui semble ne produire que pour immoler, ne faire que pour que l'on ait été, ne montrer les germes que pour les dissiper, ou n'accorder le sentiment de la vie que pour donner le frémissement de la mort; si cette force qui meut dans les ténèbres ['in the *dark* fermentation'] la matière éternelle, lance quelques lueurs pour essayer la lumière; si cette puissance qui combat le repos et qui promet la vie, broie et pulvérise son œuvre afin de la préparer pour un grand dessein; si ce monde où nous paraissons n'est que l'essai du monde; si ce qui est ne fait qu'annoncer ce qui doit être; cette surprise que le mal visible excite en nous ne paraît-elle pas expliquée? Le présent travaille pour l'avenir, et l'arrangement

1 *Obermann*, LXXXV, vol. II, pp. 196–7.
2 *Ibid.* pp. 197–8.

du monde est que le monde actuel soit consumé; ce grand
sacrifice était nécessaire, et n'est grand qu'à nos yeux. Nous
passons dans l'heure du désastre; mais il le fallait et l'histoire
des êtres d'aujourd'hui est dans ce seul mot, ils ont vécu.
L'ordre fécond et invariable sera le produit de la crise laborieuse
qui nous anéantit.[1]

It is clear that this theory of the destruction and renewal of
the existing order was familiar to Arnold, and not unsympathetic to him; as a figure to convey at least a symbolic truth,
it was certainly attractive.

The ideas in these first poems of Arnold he will return to and
exploit more richly and more curiously in later volumes. But
already they are a clear presage of whither his thought was
tending, and what form it was taking. And repeatedly, in this
evolution—whether the thought mounts back to some early,
ancient source, or is the offspring of a more modern age, and
its modern problems—we shall see the intermediation of
Obermann.

1 *Ibid.* pp. 198–9.

CHAPTER VI

ORIENTALISM CONTINUED: ARNOLD AND ALFRED DE VIGNY: ARNOLD AND LECONTE DE LISLE

Some twenty years before Arnold, Alfred de Vigny had expressed ideas of a somewhat similar turn to those of the English poet; the resemblances are striking enough to suggest considerable sympathy in outlook between the two poets. A few of these resemblances deserve mention at this point. The stoicism, for instance, ascribed to Arnold's *Gipsy Child*, is clearly not unlike Vigny's, with its stress on disdain and disillusionment. But in general the type of stoicism we find in Arnold has a more sentimental, more gentle, and more wistful cast of thought, than Vigny's proud renouncement.

Certain affinities of feeling undoubtedly exist—certain sympathies in thought and style which are inherent in the classic and patrician temper of both poets. But Arnold never approaches Vigny's thorough-paced pessimism—a pessimism which, though modified in after life, remains Vigny's most characteristic attitude. The impassivity behind which Vigny took shelter bears some resemblance to Arnold's resignation, but it is of a much more negative and defiant character, being less perhaps the result of a reasoned philosophy of life, than the heritage of a certain soldierly and aristocratic tradition, which had imposed silence, where it did not enforce conviction; Vigny's stoicism was in fact a device employed to mark his thinly-veiled contempt for creation and the Creator. While extremely original, the bent of his mind was definitely more *raide* and more uncompromising than Arnold's. His image, for example, of the race of men as confined in a prison house from which, at mysterious intervals, and for unknown purposes, they are taken away one by one, is a conception more bitter and mocking than occurs in Arnold, pessimistic as the latter may be at times. Despite his independence of thought, Arnold was no sardonic critic of creation. Vigny, on the other hand, would have man accept his destiny, if not with disdain, at least with phlegm, obeying his gaoler, but judging him in his heart.

In contrast with this is Senancour's doubt, which is without disdain; and his stern protest, that if we are to be destroyed, let us at least act so that this is an injustice—if we must die, 'périssons en résistant!'[1] This virile strain is far more in the manner of Arnold than the resigned *hauteur* with which Vigny accepts his destiny.[2]

Arnold, moreover, never regarded Nature, as Vigny constantly did, in the light of a foe. Though sometimes she might seem to him but an indifferent spectator of man's suffering, yet at times too, she offered him no niggardly measure of inspiration and solace.

What resemblances there are between Arnold and Vigny are due in the first place to certain general intellectual affinities, and the reaction of these to a similar *Zeitgeist*; and probably also to their reading of *Obermann*, by which what sympathies they had in common were confirmed. Vigny almost certainly knew Senancour,[3] and much in *Obermann* must have appealed to him

1 'C'est de nos fortes résolutions que quelque effet subsistera peut-être. . . . Périssons en résistant, et, si le néant nous est réservé, ne faisons pas que ce soit une justice' (*Obermann*, xc, vol. ii, p. 231)—a saying which compares well with the words of Addison's Portius, son of Cato:

　　''Tis not in mortals to command success,
　　But we'll do more, Sempronius,—we'll deserve it'.

2 For Vigny, 'L'espérance est la plus grande de nos folies'; an attitude far more cynical than that expressed in Senancour's saying: 'La vie n'est qu'un laborieux mouvement d'espérance'.

3 For the probable influence of Senancour on Vigny, see J. Merlant, *Sénancour*, pp. 275–80.

as to Arnold. But Arnold's reading of *Obermann* was independent of Vigny's reactions—the English poet would not
need to go to Alfred de Vigny for ideas and sentiments he had
tapped at their source.

Nevertheless, certain resemblances of thought and detail
occur that are at the least singular. In the *Mont des Oliviers*,
which appeared in June 1844 in the *Revue des Deux Mondes*—
a periodical of which Arnold would seem to have been a regular
reader at this time, probably in consequence of his enthusiasm
for George Sand, who was among its leading contributors—
these are very marked. In this poem Alfred de Vigny puts into
the address of *Jésus* to the 'divin père' the following lines:

> *Mal et Doute!* en un mot je puis les mettre en poudre;
> Vous les aviez prévus, laissez-moi vous absoudre
> De les avoir permis.—C'est l'accusation
> Qui pèse de partout sur la Création...
>   —Ce qui dure et ce qui doit finir;
> Ce qu'a mis le Seigneur au cœur de la Nature,
> Ce qu'elle prend et donne à toute créature;
> Quels sont, avec le Ciel, ses muets entretiens,
> Son amour ineffable et ses chastes liens;
> *Comment tout s'y détruit et tout s'y renouvelle,*
> Pourquoi ce qui s'y cache et ce qui s'y révèle;
> Si les astres des cieux tour à tour éprouvés
> Sont comme celui-ci coupables et sauvés;
> *Si la Terre est pour eux ou s'ils sont pour la Terre;*
> Ce qu'a de vrai la fable et de clair le mystère,
> D'ignorant le savoir et de faux la raison;
> *Pourquoi l'âme est liée dans sa faible prison;*
> *Et pourquoi nul sentier entre deux larges voies,*
> *Entre l'ennui du calme et des paisibles joies*
> *Et la rage sans fin des vagues passions,*
> *Entre la léthargie et les convulsions;*
> Et pourquoi pend la Mort comme une sombre épée
> Attristant la Nature à tout moment frappée....

Tout sera révélé dès que l'homme saura
De quels lieux il arrive et dans quels il ira.[1]

The resemblance here to some of Senancour's ideas is not fanciful; including the quotation from Martin, the philosopher of *Candide,* also referred to by Senancour, and the oriental notion of destruction and renewal. It is difficult to avoid the inference that Vigny's orientalism, like Arnold's, came to him at least in part through the intermediary of *Obermann.* But this fact, important as it is, seems yet insufficient to account for the near verbal resemblances between this poem and two or three of Arnold's, in particular *Obermann Once More, The Buried Life,* and *A Summer Night.*

The 'Mal' and 'Doute' of the first line may for instance have suggested the twin ills, 'doubt' and 'woe', to which Arnold refers in *Obermann Once More*:

> ...And palsied all our word with doubt,
> And all our work with woe.

But we have already seen these words coupled in *Lélia.*

The idea of the imprisoned soul, 'l'âme liée dans sa faible prison', may have been taken from Senancour, as well as those concerning the cosmic cycles, man's illusory importance on earth, and the dilemma in which he finds himself, placed between the alternatives of weariness and passion, of 'la léthargie' and 'les convulsions'. These ideas are all to be found in Arnold— some we have seen, and some we shall see—but they appear to have come to the English poet from Senancour, not from Vigny. On the other hand, the phrase 'nul sentier entre deux larges voies' seems a possible source of Arnold's idea:

> Is there no life, but these alone?
> Madman or slave, must man be one?[2]

1 Alfred de Vigny: *Les Destinées,* in *Poésies Complètes,* pp. 179–80; Garnier, Paris, 1925.   2 *A Summer Night.*

Above all, the concluding lines of Vigny's address:

> Tout sera révélé dès que l'homme saura
> De quels lieux il arrive et dans quels il ira,

recall very strikingly Arnold's conclusion to *The Buried Life*:

> And then he [man] thinks he knows
> The hills where his life rose
> And the sea where it goes.

And here at least the resemblance does not seem fortuitous. It is certain, however, that if this is a case of direct borrowing, Arnold has made something very much more graceful out of the idea, by his beautiful, figurative use of language, than Vigny's austere expression.

It is possible again that the image of the prison that Arnold employs in *A Summer Night* (see p. 171) owes something to Vigny as well as to Senancour. In *A Summer Night* the English poet writes:

> *For most men in a brazen prison live,*
> Where, in the sun's hot eye,
> With heads bent o'er their toil, they languidly
> *Their lives to some unmeaning taskwork give,*
> Dreaming of nought beyond their prison-wall...
> And while they try to stem
> The waves of mournful thought by which they are prest,
> *Death in their prison reaches them,*
> *Unfreed, having seen nothing, still unblest.*

And in the *Mont des Oliviers*, Vigny also, as we have seen, speaks of 'l'âme liée dans sa faible prison'.

But a more interesting passage on this subject occurs in Vigny's *Journal d'un Poète*, in an entry dated 1832:

Dans cette prison nommée la vie, d'où nous partons les uns après les autres pour aller à la mort, il ne faut compter sur aucune promenade, ni aucune fleur.. ...Il est vrai que vous ne savez pourquoi vous êtes prisonnier et de quoi puni; mais vous savez à n'en douter quelle sera votre peine: souffrance en prison, mort après. . . .

Voici la vie humaine.

Je me figure une foule d'hommes, . . . saisis dans un sommeil profond. Ils se réveillent emprisonnés. Ils s'accoutument à leur prison *et s'y font de petits jardins. Peu à peu, ils s'aperçoivent qu'on les enlève les uns après les autres pour toujours. Ils ne savent ni pourquoi ils sont en prison, ni où on les conduit après et ils savent qu'ils ne le sauront jamais.*

Cependant, il y en a parmi eux qui ne cessent de se quereller pour savoir l'histoire de leur procès, et il y en a qui inventent les pièces; d'autres qui racontent ce qu'ils deviennent après la prison, sans le savoir.

Ne sont-ils pas fous?

Nous ne sommes pas sûrs de tout savoir au sortir du cachot mais sûrs de ne rien savoir dedans.[1]

But the *Journal d'un Poète* was not published until 1866: *A Summer Night* is of 1852. We can conclude from the resemblance only the accidental sympathy of two minds working on the same idea, possibly under the same influence, that of Senancour.[2]

A parallelism perhaps more striking exists between the thought of Matthew Arnold and that of Leconte de Lisle, many of whose poems seem like contemporary manifestations on the other side of the Channel of the same trend of influences that were affecting Arnold: here again it is partly their interest in

1 Alfred de Vigny, *Journal d'un Poète*, ed. Baldensperger. The Scholartis Press, London, 1928, pp. 63–4.
2 In a sympathetic article on 'Matthew Arnold and some French Poets' (in the *Nineteenth Century*, June 1926, vol. XCIX, no. 592, pp. 869–80), Mrs Carrol Romer delicately draws attention to some general resemblances between Arnold, Senancour, Vigny and Lamartine. Senancour's pessimism and insistence on self-knowledge, the predominance of idea over feeling in Vigny, and the elegiac note and love of Nature in Lamartine, are what, in her view, draw them near to Arnold.

Eastern thought that gives them the air of holding much in common. This had been a secondary influence on Vigny. But Leconte de Lisle's orientalism was, like Arnold's, a very much more philosophic affair, and deeply impregnated his thought.

In the first place, there is great apparent similarity between their attitudes to Nature. Many of Leconte de Lisle's poems on this subject seem to reflect Arnold's conception of a world,

> Which never was the friend of *one*,
> Nor promised love it could not give,
> *But lit for all its generous sun,*
> And lived itself, and made us live.[1]

Leconte de Lisle describes the impassivity of Nature in similar terms:

> La nature se rit des souffrances humaines;
> Ne contemplant jamais que sa propre grandeur,
> *Elle dispense à tous ses forces souveraines*
> Et garde pour sa part le calme et la splendeur.[2]

Again, seeking to interpret this calm, the English poet adjures his sister:

> Yet, Fausta, the mute turf we tread,
> The solemn hills around us spread,
> This stream which falls incessantly,
> The strange-scrawl'd rocks, the lonely sky,
> If I might lend their life a voice,
> Seem to bear rather than rejoice.[3]

He expresses the same thought in

> That general life, which does not cease,
> Whose secret is not joy, but peace.[4]

---

1 *A Wish.*
2 *Poèmes Barbares; La Fontaine aux Lianes.*
3 *Resignation.*   4 *Ibid.*

Leconte de Lisle, with greater stress on Nature's power to dissemble, has the same idea of her secret interior coldness:

> Pour qui sait pénétrer, Nature, dans tes voies,
> L'illusion t'enserre et ta surface ment.
> Au fond de tes douleurs comme au fond de tes joies,
> Ta force est sans ivresse et sans emportement.[1]

A critic,[2] describing Leconte de Lisle's Nature, selects traits that are easily recognisable as belonging also to Matthew Arnold's conception:

> Si la nature est *insensible et indifférente*,...au contraire, *la fraîcheur* qu'elle répand dans les sens, *le calme* qu'elle insinue dans l'âme ont une vertu bienfaisante...tout au moins pouvons-nous attendre de la nature *qu'elle nous affranchisse de notre individualité misérable*, et qu'elle nous fasse goûter par avance *l'inaltérable paix* qui est réservée aux hommes comme aux dieux.

Arnold, in spite of the indifference he in general ascribes to Nature, also sees in her this same 'healing balm', and selfless labour; to Wordsworth he attributed the power to interpret these for men:

> He laid us as we lay at birth
> On the cool flowery lap of earth,
> Smiles broke from us and we had ease....[3]

The wish he expresses on his imagined deathbed, so curiously similar to Obermann's, contains the same longing for release from self, for union with the infinite soul of the world which, with far more emphasis, was also Leconte de Lisle's.

> There let me gaze, till I become
> In soul with what I gaze on, wed![4]

---

1 *Poèmes Barbares; La dernière Vision.*
2 E. Estève, *Leconte de Lisle*, Paris, 1923, pp. 138–9.
3 *Memorial Verses.*
4 *A Wish.*

But although many ideas are held in common by the two poets, their reactions to the common oriental inspiration are fundamentally different; the differences are in effect more striking than the similarities. A scrutiny of these will aid us in defining more precisely the nature of Arnold's debt to the East.

Leconte de Lisle's borrowings from orientalism were dictated by his sympathy with one particular aspect of its thought, Arnold's with another. The latter went to Buddhism for its philosophical content, above all for its moral teaching: Leconte de Lisle, on the other hand, took, mainly from Brahmanism,[1] only the one metaphysical idea, that of the transcendent unreality of the sensible world.[2] The conception of Mâyâ, which dominates his oriental poems, ministered to his implacable hatred of a world and a society which had duped and ill-treated him. This desire for revenge is at the root of his acceptance of a theory which condemned as mere fatuity and vanity the world of visible appearance: the idea of its annihilation was for him, from this point of view, singularly agreeable.

Nothing of this fierceness appears in Matthew Arnold. The English poet was attracted to Buddhism by the solution it offered to the woes of desolate and distracted man. Not the proud indifference, or rather disdain, to which Leconte de Lisle aspired, but the power of renunciation, the sacrifice of desire—this was the idea caught so eagerly by Matthew Arnold. The resolution of the enigma of existence is set forth by Buddhism as attainable only thus. This is the moral aspect of its metaphysic—the ideal of renunciation and limitation of desire.

The sensuous seductions with which Eastern philosophy paints the world, and to which Leconte de Lisle yielded, even

1 E. Carcassonne, 'Leconte de Lisle et la philosophie indienne', in the *Revue de Littérature Comparée*, oct.–déc. 1931, pp. 618–47.   2 *Ibid.* p. 644.

while condemning them, find no counterpart in Arnold. This, the negative aspect of orientalism, is elaborated in the poems where the creole, turning to his childish memories, paints the mysterious and beautiful reflections of Mâyâ, the souls and things of the world of illusions. The sumptuous beauty of this world is dwelt upon even to the obliteration of its profoundly spiritual significance.[1]

Arnold was incapable of such an attitude. In those of his poems (*Mycerinus, The Sick King in Bokhara, Sohrab and Rustum*) where an Eastern theme is explicitly introduced, the setting, beautiful and in perfect keeping as it is, never over-powers the thought. Inspired not, as was Leconte de Lisle, by the *Bhagavata Paurana* or the Vedanta, but by the Buddhist poem, the *Bhagavad Gîtâ*, he took from it one or two philo-sophic ideas only—all the superficial adornments of Hindu thought he left aside.

Nor did he push his acceptance of the thought very far; certainly not to its extreme article, the conception of Nirvana. Though at times he expresses the desire to merge his soul in the Infinite, he does not seem to suggest the actual extinction of human personality;[2] in general he prefers vaguely to pre-figure the soul as having the power to enjoy a kind of immortality, acquired through lessons of control, endurance, self-abnegation and self-dependence. Such an idea has at least as many affinities with Western stoical doctrines as with oriental thought. If Senancour sometimes seems to lean to a desire to accept the thought of 'l'éternel oubli' which will engulf the soul in the end,[3] Arnold never goes so far. And even in *Obermann* the idea is more usually that of the soul merging in the eternal and finding

1 *Ibid*. p. 633.
2 See the concluding lines of *A Wish*.
3 *Obermann*, XI, vol. I, p. 56.

its place there.[1] It was left to Leconte de Lisle to fasten on, and expound with *éclat*, the conception of salvation as attainable through the absorption of individual existence into the universal essence.

Certain lesser ideas Arnold undoubtedly took from Buddhism, directed thereto, in all probability, by their occurrence in Senancour. With these he was not profoundly impressed; yet he permitted echoes of them to enter into his poems. Among them is that idea, already discussed, of the world as a scene of change from degeneration to regeneration. The conception of Nature as a cyclic process, and of the destruction and fermentation of the old order which precede rebirth, we have seen occurring at least once, in the *Epilogue* to *Haworth Churchyard*: a suggestion of the same idea, though the world is this time a spiritual world, appears in two poems, to be discussed later, the *Stanzas from the Grande Chartreuse*, and *Obermann Once More*. Arnold had certainly recognised the idea in *Obermann*, and most probably took it from Hinduism by way of Senancour.

In the oriental system, the Buddhist god Shiva incarnates the force which destroys when, in its phase of dissolution, the world is annihilated in order to suffer rebirth. Leconte de Lisle either did not comprehend or did not care to use the second half of the idea: his *Çiva* contents himself with acting as 'a kind of officer of justice, who operates on Mâyâ and exults in his revenge'.[2] The idea of any subsequent rebirth of such a world would have been extremely distasteful to him.[3]

1 Senancour seems to express the limit of hope in his saying: 'Dites qu'il est affreux à notre âme avide de n'avoir qu'une existence accidentelle; dites qu'il est sublime d'espérer la réunion au principe de l'ordre impérissable: n'affirmez rien de plus...' (*Obermann*, XLVIII, vol. II, p. 19).
2 E. Carcassonne, *op. cit.* p. 642.
3 This is evident from all the later pieces in *Poèmes Barbares*, *Solvet Seclum* (with its exulting 'Tu te tairas, ô voix sinistre des vivants'), *La Dernière Vision* and others; but is even more strongly apparent in his rehandling of the Edda in *La Légende des Nornes*. The original narrative in the Edda, despite its

Arnold has no such parallel notion of Shiva. The triumphant nihilism of this philosophy would not have appealed to his questioning, only half-sceptical spirit. Not only would he have rejected the notion—he actually subscribed to its contrary; and in his more optimistic moods we shall see him sharing with Obermann hope in the rebirth of a new spiritual order of things.

It is noteworthy that in his lifetime Matthew Arnold was anxious to explain away the identity of sentiments of the speakers in his poems with his own;[1] nevertheless, it is no longer daring to assume, as he assumed of Senancour, that his characters are his sincere mouthpieces.

The more striking expressions of his thought, and its profound impregnation with the ideas of Senancour, will appear in the examination of the later, often longer, and more important poems of 1852, 1853 and 1867.

---

gloomy tone, does conclude with offering a ray of hope—the golden age may return one day. Leconte de Lisle, deliberately ignoring this, makes his Skulda depict the earth as plunging heavily and finally to its doom in the black ocean. (See J. Vianey, *Les Sources de Leconte de Lisle*, Paris, 1908.) In *Solvet Seclum* there is a concluding passage in which occurs a hint of the idea of 'fermentation', applied to worlds fertilised by the unclean remnants of the globe and its inhabitants; but it is less emphasised as a prelude to rebirth than as a state in the disintegrating process of the living world. The dominating sentiment of Leconte de Lisle is undoubtedly exultation in the idea of its total extinction.

[1] Writing to reassure his mother on Nov. 16, 1867, he protested against the tendency of the *Contemporary Review*, the *Christian World*, and other similar periodicals to 'fix on the speeches of Empedocles and Obermann, and calmly say, dropping all mention of the real speakers, "Mr Arnold here professes his Pantheism", or "Mr Arnold here disowns Christianity"' (*Letters*, vol. II, *Works*, vol. XIV, p. 150).

CHAPTER VII

THUN AND THE BLÜMLISALP

A sweet and charming perfume of youth clings to the story we must now recount of the days following Arnold's life at Oxford.

In 1848, a year after his appointment as private secretary to Lord Lansdowne, Matthew Arnold had put into execution his long-cherished project of visiting Switzerland, and of making a literary pilgrimage to the scene of Obermann's wanderings. In the autumn of this year he made his way to Thun, the picturesque old town on the lake of the same name, which reposes placidly under the white shadow of the Bernese Alps.

For centuries Thun, once the Celtic Dunum, had slept tranquilly in its Alpine seclusion. At the beginning of the nineteenth century its mediaeval appearance was scarcely changed. Built on the right bank of the Aar, just beyond the point where it issues from the lake, at this time most of the town was grouped about the Castle of Zähringen-Kyburg, a twelfth-century, turreted building, with a marked and curious resemblance to the Temple, destroyed in Paris in 1811. The Castle of Thun occupied a conspicuous position on a small mamelon rising above the river, and, with the church and cemetery, dominated the landscape to a great distance. This higher part of the town was linked to the lower shops and houses by flights of partly covered steps of picturesque appearance. The old thoroughfares, then more numerous than to-day, presented a quaint aspect with their pavements placed above the shops lining the roads. Part of the town straggled across the wide stone bridge, or Sinnebrücke, to the Bälliz, an island which had been formed between the Aar as it issued from the lake and a kind of overflow or tributary which escaped just above the town and filled an ancient 'graben' or fosse during the melting of the snows. The flooding from these had been increased by the diversion into the lake of the Kander, a small river coming down the Kandertal from the Blümlisalp, from its original entrance into the Aar at a point below the town. The Sinnebrücke led straight to the island and to the Sinneplatz, where stood the Freienhof, an ancient hostelry dating from the middle ages, the first inn and the only one of repute, which the traveller encountered on entering the town. Here it was that Senancour must have stayed on his visits to Thun about 1790. Here horses were changed, boats were brought up to the landing-stage, and much merry bargaining in fish and eatables was done at the 'échoppe' which used to project over the river. Until 1807 a clock-tower, similar to the one which is still preserved in Berne, guarded the little square in front of the Freienhof.

The Freienhof itself retained its ancient character until 1780 when it was rebuilt. It retained, however, even after that date its singular interest, from its having been for ages the asylum of fugitives from the episcopal jurisdictions of Constance and Lausanne, the Aar constituting the boundary between these two sees. The Freienzimmer, which had housed the fugitives, remained a curiosity of the place, long after the Freienhof was converted into a hostelry.

Two covered bridges connected the Bälliz with the mainland on the other side of the town, here thinly populated. One bridge, used also as a sluice, led by an avenue along the lakeside to Scherzligen and the stately home of the Rougemonts at Schadau; the other, now the station bridge, to the Frutigen road which cut directly across a wooded strip of country plentifully shaded by tall Lombardy poplars. This road rejoined the lakeside not far beyond Schadau, continuing thereafter in the direction of Spiez, Frutigen, Kandersteg and the Gemmi: it was thus the main entrance into the town from the Oberland.

In the middle ages Thun had owned a certain importance from its position on the frontier of the two sees of Constance and Lausanne. But this traditional prestige had long since departed. For many years the town had relapsed into playing a relatively obscure rôle as capital, under Berne, of the Bernese Oberland.

Early in the nineteenth century, however, Thun unexpectedly began to enjoy a revived importance in the world. The three brothers Knechtenhofer had brought to Thun their enormous fortunes, amassed in the Emmental, and had conceived the idea of exploiting the resources of the picturesque, old-world town and its perfect situation beneath the eternal snows of the Blümlisalp, Mönch, Eiger and Jungfrau. Since the fall of the Empire and the consequent reopening of the roads and frontiers of the Continent, tourists had recommenced the invasion of Switzerland in increasing numbers. The English colonies of Geneva and Lausanne were again as populous as in the eighteenth century, and Chamouni and the Oberland became the scene of daring climbs.[1] It occurred to the Knechtenhofers that they might well turn their money to account and secure their own and the town's prosperity by fixing Thun as a fashionable tourist centre. The higher mountain resorts were already in process of exploitation by industrious Swiss *hôteliers*; Grindelwald was by this time famous through the presence of Elizabeth Grossman, 'la belle batelière de Brienz'; and the hotel on the Faulhorn, which was to receive Liszt and Mme d'Agoult in the first year of their flight, was already open in 1830.[2] But the lower towns had not as yet realised their opportunities. At

1 C.-E. Engel, *La Littérature alpestre en France et en Angleterre*, 1930, p. 143.
2 *Ibid.* p. 174.

this time Interlaken, the modern centre, which lies at the other end of the Thunersee between the twin lakes, was as yet simply an English colony, a 'sort of Swiss Harrogate', Murray calls it, and goes on to say that it has few sights or lions for the tourist or passing traveller. Lucerne itself was hardly developed. Thun seemed, for the purpose of the Knechtenhofers, an ideal site.

In the year 1830 the brothers constructed the first modern hotel in Thun,[1] on the edge of the hill which rises beside the river, some little distance below the point where the Aar emerges from the lake: this was the Hotel Bellevue. Further down, the Aar continues its clear course beyond the castle and town through wide green valley-meadows to Berne. The upper windows of the hotel commanded in the opposite direction a long view across the lake to the Bernese Alps, among which, dominating the stern crags of Niesen by their silvery whiteness, show the glacier-fields of the Blümlisalp. A little higher up the hill, within the hotel grounds, the Knechtenhofers built the English church which still stands there:[2] they sent, moreover, to Paris for a steamboat, which was brought in pieces by a French gentleman, a certain M. Rivet of Paris, and was assembled on the lake. The ceremony of launching the steamboat, first of its kind, which was to displace for ever the romantic 'barques' with their beautiful 'rameuses' whose praises Byron had so charmingly sung, took place at the Bächimatt (that is, the water-meadow), beyond the Bellevue, and the adjacent Hofstetten or *quartier des étrangers*, at the point where the Aar leaves the lake. This celebrated event took place in 1835, so that in 1848, when Arnold visited Thun, it was still something of a novelty to travel in the steamboat. There was even an organ installed on board for the delectation of the tourists,

1 H. Haas, *Die Entwicklung der Stadt Thun*, 1926, p. 51.
2 The first stone was laid in 1841 by the British Minister to the Confederation.

which played, among other favourites, the rousing melody of
'God Save the Queen'. The popularity of the piece led in time
to its curious modification; the instrument would sneeze just as
the last word was due to be pronounced, much to the good-
natured amusement of the natives.[1]

Visitors began to flock to the Bellevue, which stood, a
handsome double building with numerous dependencies, at the
birth of a gentle rise into orchards and waving grass, and a
steep pine forest beyond, sprinkled with walnuts and beeches.
A picturesque wooden chalet, built behind the private landing-
stage of the hotel, was united to the two main buildings by
covered passages on either hand, and served as a *Salle de
Réunion* for the assembled guests. A fountain played into a
large stone basin, set in the pleasant open grounds by the lakeside; and newly planted trees and young, fragrant shrubs
fringed the lawny walks.

Captain Knechtenhofer, who had inherited the property
from his uncles, had been in France, and boasted in later years
an intimate acquaintance with the Emperor Napoleon III himself. The French were charmed with the site as a summer and
autumn residence: they came in numbers to the Hotel Bellevue;
and the resort became fashionable by the sojourn of princes and
exiles of high birth. In the middle of the century, between 1840
and 1865, the Bellevue was at the height of its glory: during this
period there came to Thun as visitors the kings of Holland and
of Württemberg.

Several French families were already at this time established
there, for the most part in the Hofstetten, the quarter adjoining
the Bellevue. Among the most notable residents were the
Swiss-French family of de Rougemont, who had acquired the

1 I owe these interesting details and much of the foregoing information about
the early days of the Bellevue and Thun to Dr C. Huber, archivist of the city.

ancient château of Schadau situated outside the town, on the side of the lake directly opposite the Bächimatt. In the period 1846–8 they replaced the old castle by the magnificent structure which is now the property of the State. In 1848 the castle stood almost deserted: on this side of the Aar few other houses as yet existed and the Rougemonts' château rose alone in grounds reaching far down the lake, a kind of wonder to the inhabitants, with its elegant French spires and terraces. Adjacent was the ancient chapel of Scherzligen, said to be founded by Alsatian monks at the order of Pepin in the eighth century. Its spire rose white among the woods, and sharply defined against the fantastic peak of the Stockhorn. Apart from these buildings, the lakeside was still green and countrylike. A road wound its way from Thun to Schadau, occupying part of the lakeside now become a basin for the modern steamboat station. Further inland the important main road to Frutigen emerged from the covered Scherzligbrücke and ran through a picturesque country-side. At this time the avenue of poplars which had been planted, in the French fashion, to line the approach to the town, were in their full beauty, and were a striking feature to the traveller entering Thun from the south.

Such was Thun when Arnold came to stay at the Hotel Bellevue in 1848, then at the height of its fame as one of the most popular tourist resorts in Switzerland, and the natural centre for excursions into the Oberland. Poplars still fringed the road to Schadau; and the stately avenue on the Frutigen road had not yet been demolished to make room for the railway constructions of 1858. Above all, the most charming vestige of earlier days, the covered bridge across the river, was still awaiting replacement by the substantial stone bridge of the same year. Of this approach nothing exists to-day. Only the white swans still float with grace down the river; and the

unchanging snowfields glitter, as they have always done, beyond
the lake.

It was early September when Arnold arrived, probably
crossing from the lake of Geneva and Vevey 'by the beautiful
path over the Col de Jaman'[1] and through the Simmenthal to
Thun.[2] This was the spot which was to furnish the background
for the sentimental experiences, of widely differing kind, and
the formative experiences of Arnold's youth; and was to change
the whole current of his life and thought.

To the young man, descending one dry autumn eve into the
glamorous streets, the freshness of the little Swiss town must
have made England and Oxford and Fox How all very remote
and even momentarily unimportant. Life was really to be lived
at Thun; one had escaped here the familiar formal atmosphere
of the affectionate Victorian environment which closed him
round so utterly when he was in England. Here one was fresh

1 *Poems*, vol. I, *Works*, vol. I, p. 326, note 20 to *Obermann Once More*.
2 It is possible that Arnold projected this journey as early as 1846, when he
perhaps had his first sight of the lake of Geneva, and of the entrance to the
pass of the Dent de Jaman (but see p. 37). We do not discuss the possibility
of Arnold's having actually followed this route in 1846; if he did visit Thun
in this year it seems certain that he did not have then the experiences on which
the poems to 'Marguerite' are founded; for the bulk of these would surely
then have found their way into the volume of 1849. That he visited Thun in
1848 is, on the contrary, a fact established by his correspondence, and it seems
reasonable therefore to assume that it was in this year that he took the route
indicated in his note to *Obermann Once More*.
    How much of this interest in the Oberland can be attributed to an early
admiration of Byron, or was maintained in spite of it, it is not possible to say;
we are not concerned in this study with the extent of the English romantic's
influence on Arnold. Arnold himself complained that the vulgar Byronic
associations of the Lake of Geneva had spoiled the whole locality for him (in
a letter to Clough, September 29, 1848). It does not therefore seem likely that
Byron provided any suggestion for the present journey. We may merely note
that in his *Swiss Journal* Byron describes this route over the pass of the Dent
de Jaman, and mentions the playing of the Ranz des Vaches and other airs.
The scene of *Manfred* is situated in the Bernese Alps; the poet says that the
tragedy was partly composed on the Wengen Alp in full view of the Jungfrau
and within hearing of its avalanches. It is not likely, as we have said, that these
facts suggested Arnold's journey to him in the first instance; but if they did,
his interest must have received a very great increase from the added knowledge
of the Oberland's associations with *Obermann*.

and spontaneous in one's outlook; one's thoughts ran crystal-clear as this blue Aar, hurrying swiftly past the town; here was no one to chaff or look uncomfortable if one betrayed the feelings of melancholy or enthusiasm which were alternately stirred before this ancient beauty. The schooled and airy nonchalance to which one accustomed oneself in England seemed suddenly a small, insipid and intolerable thing. The young man felt an aching eagerness to express himself. The spirit of Obermann which had accompanied him silently since he had left Glion, seemed suddenly now to stir beside him. He felt his brow grow warm; and he looked towards the mountain heights where blew far and thin the winds alone able to cool it. For the first time he felt awake to the real elements of suffering in the life of Obermann: and his spirit offered itself to those troubled influences, eagerly receptive, and luxuriating in a melancholy which seemed perfectly in tune with some fibre in his own being.

In such a mood, we may suppose, and with feelings so heightened by the scenes of beauty around him, Arnold had betaken himself to the garden of the hotel; and there, among the fragrant oleanders which one may yet see blooming above the river, the young man had sought and found a lady, introduced to him no doubt earlier; a girl, occupied like himself with reading and musing among the flowers.

Of 'Marguerite',[1] who first and last was the passion of Matthew Arnold's boyhood, we know little: but that little is enough to shed enlightenment upon the pensive, charming

[1] By a strange coincidence, 'Madame Marguerite' was the name which Senancour affectionately gave his friend of later years, Madame Dupin, author of a novel, *Marguerite*, which received a notice in the *Revue des Deux Mondes*. The heroine, Marguerite, professedly a disciple of Obermann, is a kind of attenuated but more sentimental Lélia. See G. Michaut, *Senancour*, pp. 324–69 and particularly p. 360 and p. 367.

figure, which was to float ever afterwards through Arnold's dreams of youth.

We guess that she belonged to that society of aristocratic French visitors who had settled down to an indefinite sojourn at Thun; we gather that at this date she was young and unsophisticated, and very happy: a child, Arnold must have considered her, viewing her with eyes he fancied worldly-wise at the mature age of twenty-five.

We may picture Arnold at this age; the dark eyes, and the lashes which drooped over and hid their lively gaze—imparting thereby an indescribable softness to the face; the mouth, too large; the lips a little thick, as wearing an air somewhat petulant; and the brow, clear and luminous under the shade of the black hair which was never to go grey. A fine face, fresh and ardent, and yet mellowed by that indefinable expression which genius gives.

Arnold was tall and would overlook the brown head of Marguerite as they walked together. But she made up for her delicate build by a surprising agility; a dancing fay, Arnold thought her, and owning the joyousness of those irresponsible beings. The arch outline of her nose and chin was very French; French too the complete inconsequence with which she tied her mauve sunbonnet: no starched Victorian miss she, but a laughing fairy-like creature, 'a mere sprite of caprice' and winsomeness, with a pure ringing voice of exceptional sweetness to Arnold's ears. The pale cheek might flush for him, as she would toss back the light-brown hair; but it was in her eyes that he gathered his greatest joy; the lucent blue eyes which flashed and sparkled, or beamed with childlike tenderness, as she would put up a shy hand and, her mirth suddenly quelled, take gently the hand which he offered.

During the day they roamed about the lake, or explored the

THE AAR AT SCHERZLIGEN

Photo: A. Gurtner, Thun

Still glides the stream, slow drops the boat
Under the rustling poplars' shade;
Silent the swans beside us float—

The River

hillside behind the church, ascending to Jacobshübeli to gain the last fading light of the day upon the pearly summits. Or they took the steamboat which quaintly puffed its way to Hilterfingen and Oberhofen, where the fruit hung thick and reddening on the orchard slopes. When the novelty of these excursions was exhausted, it was still a pleasure to take a flat row-boat, and lying in the bottom lazily, watch the swans glide by with their doubles in the river; or upon the lake follow the changing shadows where they darkened its clear blue; or see with joy a ripple raised by their oars catch momentarily a reflected hue of purple from the mountains. Marguerite was as silent as her companion; on her too the vast spaces exercised their charm.

In the evening, when the candles were lit and the lustres gleamed in their subdued light, Marguerite came shyly to Matthew, and together they perused the pages of Ugo Foscolo's *Lettere di Jacopo Ortis*,[1] of which a translation had but just appeared in the preceding year[2]—the work of that solitary, unhappy genius, who, like Byron, his friend, and Rousseau, had dragged a rebellious heart into voluntary exile and who had died, far from his Italian home and friends, in London, actually at Turnham Green; strange destiny for the translator of Swift, and author of the Italian *Werther*! As they read, the scenes of exile passed before their eyes—the green Euganeans, and the excursions to Arquà and the house of Petrarch with the gentle Teresa; and then Albenga, whence Ortis had fled to escape his fatal passion, with its grassy valley-floor above the Mediterranean and hill-slopes starred with the blue hepatica. . . . So the

---

1 See the sub-title to the poem *To Marguerite* in the edition of 1852.
2 *Jacques Ortis* [traduit] par Alexandre Dumas, *précédé d'un essai sur la vie et les écrits d'Ugo Foscolo*: Paris, 1847. The concordance of dates leads us to assume that they read *Ortis* in this translation. (The first edition of this translation was issued in 1839.)

two talked, taking the exquisite pleasure of youth in sorrows it only dimly fathoms. Nor was Arnold's interest out of keeping with his feelings then; the tale of love, and a certain affinity between Ortis' history and that of Obermann, drew from him more perhaps than a passing curiosity. For Ortis, as Sainte-Beuve pointed out,[1] belongs to the society of René and Obermann and of all those spirits who are, in the words of M. de Rémusat, 'tormented at once by the need and the powerlessness to feel and believe'.[2]

But what Arnold chiefly took from this reading was a dispirited sense of the inner loneliness of man, not merely of the man of genius, like Foscolo, but of man in general.[3] To him it seemed, looking at the frivolous crowds about him, as though he and his companion had withdrawn to some quiet refuge beyond their turmoil. And yet more than once, this consciousness of their mutual sympathy was troubled by a sense of desolation, that his loneliness was more complete than he fancied. But this was no more than a transitory feeling, which afterwards seemed to bind them the more closely together.

The happiness of these days was to remain only a little longer. Matthew Arnold had duties to return to in London; but before he resumed these he had still to fulfil his project of crossing the range which divided him from the Rhône valley: by this means he would cover more than half the ground of Obermann's wanderings; and look down upon the Valais, where Obermann had first fixed his home.

Before leaving Thun, however, he had resolved on making the more accessible ascent of the Faulhorn, a favourite pilgrimage at this time. The little white hotel at the top, where Liszt and Madame d'Agoult had stayed soon after its opening,

1 *Chateaubriand et son groupe littéraire*, 1878, p. 349, note 2.
2 Ch. de Rémusat, *Passé et Présent, mélanges*, 1847, vol. I, p. 119.
3 See *To Marguerite in returning a volume of the Letters of Ortis.*

was still a novel and attractive goal to visitors, who at this season of the year went up from Grindelwald with their guides and mules in great numbers.

The path began by skirting a wood; somewhat higher it ran beside the shores of a strange little lake, the Bachalpsee or High Pasture Lake, in whose waters Arnold looking back could see the reflected snows of the Schreckhorn, the Peak of Terror, and the Finsteraarhorn, monarch of the central Alps. At a little chalet by the way a kindly dame had refreshing loganberries for sale. From this point Arnold and his guide continued the long ascent to the summit, which looks down upon the turquoise waters of the Brienzer- and the Thunersee and far away over the Swiss plateau.

Returning from this ascent, Arnold's next thought was to cross the Tschingel glacier direct to Kandersteg:[1] this he knew to be a very beautiful route, and an interesting glacier-excursion; in addition, it would have been a short cut to the Gemmi, whither Arnold was bound.[2] The traveller this way goes by the valley of Lauterbrunnen under the great cliffs of Mürren on the right, and the glistening wall and hanging glaciers of the Jungfrau and her sister peaks on the left. From the top of the pass the descent is by the gently sloping Kanderfirn behind the Blümlisalp, and so into the Gasterntal, surely the most savage, if it is not quite the loneliest, of Alpine valleys. Uninhabited in winter, its only exit to the world below is through the narrow *klus* by which the Kander escapes before its mad course down to the lake of Thun. Here at Kandersteg, just below the *klus*, is the beginning of the route over the Gemmi.

Arnold did not take this short cut but returned from the

1 Judging from a reference in a letter to Clough.
2 Murray says quaintly of this route: 'The day's journey may be shortened by passing the night at the Steinberg; the accommodation is of course wretched, and the tourist would probably be unable to sleep' (p. 88).

Faulhorn, in all probability by Interlaken and Spiez. From Spiez he went on up the Kandertal, passing the famous little Blue Lake with its highly mineralised waters, lying among the fir trees under the famous ruined castle, to Kandersteg, and its bare green meadows. Here, above a little valley that opens out on the left, he could look up at the shining peaks of the Blüm- lisalp. A short distance beyond the village the path mounted among the fir trees on the steep ascent to the Gemmi. After a time he came out once more into the sunshine: on the mountain shelf where he stood he now overlooked the lonely Gasterntal, which appeared like a great rift lying under the giant Balmhorn and the jagged cliff of the Doldenhorn, the latter's saw-like teeth of rock in scalloped outline against the sky.

In the mysterious bottom of the valley a stretch of trackless forest lay devastated by a recent avalanche; mighty trees, broken and tossed about like bits of matchwood, had fallen in wild attitudes: the spot seemed one where the forces of Nature were alive in their primitive savagery.

On he climbed, higher and higher up the bare and lonely alp, where the only sounds, hushed and almost lost in the deep silence, were the distant tinkle of musical cow-bells, and now and again the roar of a hidden torrent, falling from the glacier of the Altels. Arnold and the guide sat down for a few moments outside the little inn at Schwarenbach, where they drank goats' milk and doubtless heard the story of Werner's gloomy tragedy, *The 24th of February*, and of the traveller murdered here one awful night of storm. The muddy and almost empty Daubensee was soon behind them; and they stood at the summit of the Gemmi, gazing, in that crystalline air, at the vast and jumbled array of peaks and glaciers around them. Here, Arnold, shading his eyes, had his first view of the Pennine Alps in the south. From beneath his feet the Rhône valley fled in a white haze.

At this point the path begins to descend the cliff in zigzags to Leukerbad, by a mule-track trodden for centuries, whose dust, Arnold fancied, had stirred more than once under Obermann's feet. All had spoken to him of Obermann as he had climbed the Gemmi: here was surely a site befitting the Ranz des Vaches! At Leukerbad he thought again of Obermann, recalling his adventure with the fair traveller hither.[1]

From Leukerbad the route followed a long and narrow valley. In half a day Arnold had descended from the level of the glaciers to the vineyards and cornfields of Leuk and Visp. At Brig he saw the castle of the Stockalper with its gilded cupolas; from thence a day's march across the Simplon brought him to Domo d' Ossola. Something in the air here impressed him as more grand and more monarchical than the republican atmosphere of Switzerland; so he reported to Clough. This was on the 27th of September.

On the following day the rain had set in. Relinquishing his project of pushing further south, he hired a 'char' and began the return journey; between Iselle and the top of the Simplon the profound gloom of the Gorge of Gondo struck him particularly. That night he probably slept at Brig. It had been raining all day and was still raining when he reached Leukerbad at last. At the hotel a wood fire was burning in the grate: Arnold was a little sad.[2] He had missed the Tschingel glacier, that was a source of annoyance, and momentarily he felt querulous and inclined to think Swiss scenery overrated. But some other ache he felt also within him. On one thing he was resolved, to return to England speedily; but before doing so he would go back to the Bellevue, for just one night. He did not conceal his motive, either to himself or to Clough; his heart was resolutely set on seeing Marguerite again, at least once before

1 *Obermann*, vol. I, Letter VI.   2 See the Letter to Clough, Sept. 29, 1848.

his return.[1] Then the memory of the Aar and its clear waters rose suddenly before him, alluring beside the muddied torrents in that dismal rain. . . .

Marguerite's joy at seeing him again seemed a confirmation to Arnold of her affection: did he then seek to bind her; and was she evasive? Shall I not see you again next year, her surprised eyes seemed to enquire; and she nodded her head resignedly at her lover's foolish haste.

And as Matthew turned sorrowfully away towards England and all the old familiar occupations he must resume, he strove for one moment to rescue from oblivion, that he might retain it during their long year of parting, the pale face turned to his; a little pouting which has now vanished; a murmur stifled quickly, a sudden frank seriousness beaming in the eyes—no misgiving there such as he himself could not but feel; only an 'angelic' 'tenderness'.[2]

Arnold was never to be the same again after that journey to Switzerland. When his first volume of poems came out, in February of the following year, his family felt a shock of astonishment.[3] The sisters examined their brother: his mother looked grave. It was evident that Matthew was no longer the gay irresponsible member of the family who had sometimes even seemed to do violence to their moral upbringing. Either he had changed suddenly, or they saw for the first time a side of him hitherto undetected. Mary, the second sister, was inclined to think they had not been mistaken in the past.[4] Some

1 'To-morrow', he says, in the letter just cited, 'I repass the Gemmi and get to Thun: linger one day at the Hotel Bellevue for the sake of the blue eyes of one of its inmates. . . .'
2 *A Memory Picture.*
3 Mrs Humphry Ward, *A Writer's Recollections*, p. 45.
4 In August, 1849, she wrote to her brother: 'I think you would be struck by the change in Matt since you last saw him; I do not mean any great change

THE HOTEL BELLEVUE, THUN, *ca.* 1840

'To-morrow I repass the Gemmi and get to Thun: linger one day at the Hotel Bellevue for the sake of the blue eyes of one of its inmates. . . .'

ARNOLD to CLOUGH, *September 29, 1848*

new influence was at work in Matt, though she hesitated to say
so: she preferred to call it a moral evolution operating within
him. Matt had developed a sense of responsibility and earnestness which really imposed respect. The family remained, in
spite of this explanation, still vaguely surprised: the poems
were a little too intense; the melancholy a little too deep to be
sincere—perhaps some degree of poetic artifice had entered
there...?[1]

in opinions or even in character so much as a growth, so it seems to me, in
self-discipline giving the impression of his living under and more continuously
following his convictions—and that his convictions are strengthening and
becoming more and more a consistent guide—I seem to have entered very
abruptly upon this subject...'.

And again, in an earlier letter to her sister, Jane Arnold, she says: 'These
poems have made me feel to know him better than I ever did before and expect
much more from him—they have given me as it were a look into his mind,
revealing experiences which I should not have expected, an earnestness and
reality—a more individual struggling with life and a keener consciousness of
responsibility than I should have at all expected'. (From two letters in the
possession of Miss Ward, in part quoted by Mrs H. Ward in her *Recollections*.)
1 Mrs H. Ward, *op. cit.* p. 45.

CHAPTER VIII

'MARGUERITE' POEMS: THUN REVISITED

No poetic artifice could disguise the truth and sincerity of at least two of the poems of 1849. *To my Friends who Ridiculed a Tender Leave-taking*, later and better known as *A Memory Picture*, and another poem of great beauty, *The Voice*, enshrine the memory of Marguerite in verses delicately lyrical. It is likely that they were hurriedly added to the volume just before it went to press. In the cool December following his autumn passion their composition must have warmed Arnold's sinking spirits.

Something a little more outspoken in these two poems than in any others of the 'Marguerite' group may account for the curious fate they afterwards suffered at their author's hand. *The Voice*, appearing first in February 1849, was not reprinted until 1877. The history of *A Memory Picture* is more varied, and is worth our attention here.

In 1849 this poem appeared under the long title, *To my Friends who Ridiculed a Tender Leave-taking*;[1] each verse then had the very frank concluding couplet:

> Ere the parting kiss be dry,
> Quick, thy tablets, Memory!

which the late Professor Saintsbury found a little intimate.

In Arnold's second volume of 1852, all the poems being new, it naturally does not reappear. In 1853, in the volume known as *First Series*, which is for the most part a selection from the two preceding volumes, with some of the 'Marguerite' poems

1 It is impossible that the friends referred to were Clough, Walrond and Wyndham Slade, as M. Bonnerot thinks (in 'La Jeunesse de Matthew Arnold': *Revue Anglo-Américaine*, août 1930, p. 525). Arnold was actually writing to Clough of his visit to Thun in September 1848; and appears to have been quite alone on this tour. If Walrond or Wyndham Slade had been with him it is inexplicable that he should make no mention of them in a letter to Clough, their common friend.

of 1852 judiciously omitted, it is placed first of the group called *Switzerland*, and has now the simple title *To my Friends*: the concluding words *Who Ridiculed a Tender Leave-taking* are omitted in the index but are preserved as a sub-title on p. 171 where the poem occurs. In the second and third editions of this series, that is, in 1854 and 1857, the title continues to be so written. In the last named, however, the concluding couplet of each stanza now reads much more coolly:

> Ere the parting hour go by,
> Quick, thy tablets, Memory!

and so these lines are written in all subsequent volumes.

In the first collected edition of 1869, the title is completely changed, and the poem bears the innocuous *en-tête* of *A Memory Picture*; it is, however, still placed at the head of the *Switzerland* group. In the selected edition of 1878 it is isolated in a separate part of the volume, and thenceforward is so placed in subsequent editions, dissociated (like *A Dream* of 1853) from the *Switzerland* poems.

The theme is the story we have already told, of Arnold's parting with Marguerite: here we have the first description of Marguerite's grace and charm, her coyness and nonchalance combined, and the concluding revelatory couplet—whose realism alteration could not obscure but only served to stamp with more convincing truth. Yet such is the pleasing delicacy and freshness of the sentiment that the poem might seem no more than a tribute to an outgrown and passing lover's fancy were not the more mournful accent of *The Voice* there to persuade us otherwise.

Marguerite's voice was of a specially sweet and musical quality, at least to Arnold's ears. In the poem called *Parting*, of 1852, one of the most beautiful stanzas is that in which he likens the call of Marguerite to some lovely nature-sounds:

But on the stairs what voice is this I hear,
Buoyant as morning, and as morning clear?
Say, has some wet, bird-haunted English lawn
Lent it the music of its trees at dawn?
Or was it from some sun-fleck'd mountain-brook
That the sweet voice its upland clearness took?
     Ah! it comes nearer—
     Sweet notes, this way!

The Voice, of 1849, is the lament of the lover who hears again in memory those 'melancholy tones so sweet and still', those 'lute-like tones' which had sounded on his ear in the 'bygone year'. The moon 'lancing' her light on the whirling waves, the tears that fall and burn, the wild rose on the wall, sunbeams on a ruin, music in sadness—by these symbols the poet tries to convey their beauty.

It is a curious fact, and perhaps worthy of mention here, that to Obermann also the voice of a loved one had been the most potent part of her influence. Many are the passages which reveal the power of sound upon him—the music of a torrent in mountain silences, 'the song of a bird on a sultry evening',[1] these things were the delight of Obermann, and yet they were enjoyed less for their physical beauty than for their rich suggestiveness and interior meaning. And above all other sounds in its power to charm and hold him was the voice of a fair woman. Obermann has the most exquisite touches where he describes the grace of womanhood, and the deeper spiritual beauty of a woman beloved.

Une grâce qui entraîne tout, une éloquence douce et profonde, une expression plus étendue que les choses exprimées, l'harmonie qui fait le lien universel, tout cela est dans l'œil d'une femme. Tout cela, et plus encore, est dans la voix illimitée de celle qui sent. Lorsqu'elle parle, elle tire de l'oubli

1 *Obermann*, xv, vol. 1, p. 71.

les affections et les idées; elle éveille l'âme de sa léthargie, elle l'entraîne et la conduit dans tout le domaine de la vie morale. Lorsqu'elle chante, il semble qu'elle agite les choses, qu'elle les déplace, qu'elle les forme, et qu'elle crée des sentimens nouveaux. La vie naturelle n'est plus la vie ordinaire: tout est romantique, animé, enivrant.[1]

The first glimpse we have of the meeting of Obermann and the lady he forlornly loved, Madame Dellemar,[2] is in the lovely setting of Lucerne's shores, where it is her voice which crowns, and even seems to deepen, the perfect tranquillity of the scene.

C'était en mars: j'étais à Lu✳✳. Il y avait des violettes au pied des buissons, et des lilas dans un petit pré bien printanier, bien tranquille, incliné au soleil du midi. La maison était au-dessus, beaucoup plus haut. Un jardin en terrasse ôtait la vue des fenêtres. Sous le pré, des rocs difficiles et droits comme des murs: au fond, un large torrent, et par-delà, d'autres rochers couverts de prés, de haies, et de sapins! Les murs antiques de la ville passaient à travers tout cela: il y avait un hibou dans leurs vieilles tours. Le soir, la lune éclairait; des cors se répondaient dans l'éloignement; et la voix que je n'entendrai plus....[3]

'La voix que je n'entendrai plus': this is the theme of Arnold's first, tentative, vaguely sorrowful love-poem.

> O unforgotten voice, thy accents come,
> Like wanderers from the world's extremity,
> Unto their ancient home!

The mystery of Matthew Arnold's love for Marguerite remains unsolved. What real motive separated the two, whether it was Marguerite's petulance,[4] or Arnold's self-sacrifice, is

[1] *Obermann*, XL, vol. I, p. 154.
[2] This lady had an original who played a similar rôle in Senancour's life—the baronne Walckenaër.
[3] *Obermann*, XI, vol. I, pp. 59–60.
[4] If *Urania* has a touch of Marguerite, one may judge her standards were too exacting for Arnold. We shall never know Marguerite's point of view.

obscure. On Marguerite rests in all likelihood the reproach of Arnold's unsuccessful suit, for such poems as the young man was to write in her honour bespeak a true and strong passion. Yet, from the concluding lines of *The Voice*, it would seem that there was an element of discipline, or repression, in it, as though Arnold had consciously striven to resist the spell; and that either he had already suspected Marguerite's capacity to love, or was persuaded of some other obstacle to his loving her.

> In vain, all, all in vain,
> They beat upon mine ear again,
> Those melancholy tones so sweet and still.
> Those lute-like tones which in the bygone year
>   Did steal into mine ear—
> Blew such a thrilling summons to my will,
>   Yet could not shake it:
> Made my tost heart its very lifeblood spill,
>   Yet could not break it.

Be this as it may, in September 1849, precisely a year after his first visit, Arnold returned to the Continent, travelling probably by Boulogne, Amiens and the Rhine—the same route which he had taken on his return in 1848;[1] and thence to Switzerland and Thun.

> Again I see my bliss at hand,
> The town, the lake are here.
> My Marguerite smiles upon the strand,
> Unalter'd with the year.
>
> I know that graceful figure fair,
> That cheek of languid hue;
> I know that soft, enkerchief'd hair,
> And those sweet eyes of blue.[2]

---

1 For this route see *The Letters of Arnold to Clough*, p. 91; for the conjectured itinerary south in 1849 see *On the Rhine*, which appeared first in 1852.
2 *Meeting*, originally called *The Lake*.

There is a hint of the existence of some pre-arrangement of this meeting in the words attributed to Marguerite in *A Memory Picture*, where she lightheartedly and confidently assures her lover that

> Some day next year, I shall be,
> Entering heedless, kiss'd by thee.[1]

It seems more than probable that Marguerite spoke here with knowledge.

At the Bellevue Hotel the experiences of the preceding year were revived. The rambles were resumed, and again the two visited together the church and castle, trod the winding paths on the surrounding hills, and rested on some upland point where the full beauty of the glorious panorama lay outspread before them. The autumn leaves fluttered listlessly from the trees and lay in yellow patches undisturbed, until some sudden gust, herald of wan days to come, would blow them giddily away. The shining snows glinted in the morning sunshine: in the evening their pearly hue was dulled as the sun sank beneath a ridge of cloud.

The evening light was sympathetic to Arnold: the autumn had descended on him as on the world without. A change had taken place in his companion since their parting of the previous year.

> We were apart; yet, day by day,
> I bade my heart more constant be.
> I bade it keep the world away,
> And grow a home for only thee;
> Nor fear'd but thy love likewise grew,
> Like mine, each day, more tried, more true.

---

[1] Note that Marguerite is already tutoying Arnold. In *The Terrace at Berne*, when in Arnold's thought she escapes from the 'lauriers-roses' and greets him with the delighted cry, ''Tis thou!', he is obviously translating her real words —'C'est toi!'.

The fault was grave! I might have known,
What far too soon, alas! I learn'd—
The heart can bind itself alone,
And faith may oft be unreturn'd.
Self-sway'd our feelings ebb and swell—
Thou lov'st no more;—Farewell! Farewell![1]

On September 23rd he had unburdened himself of his dis-illusionment to Clough: 'My dearest Clough, these are damned times—I am here in a curious and not altogether comfortable state: however to-morrow I carry my aching head to the mountains, and to my cousin the Blümlisalp'.[2]

For in the crisis which followed Arnold had turned as by instinct to the peace and consolation of the mountains.

Blow, ye winds! lift me with you!
I come to the wild.
Fold closer, O Nature!
Thine arms round thy child.

To thee only God granted
A heart ever new—
To all always open,
To all always true.

Ah! calm me, restore me;
And dry up my tears
On thy high mountain- platforms,
Where morn first appears;

Where the white mists, for ever,
Are spread and upfurl'd—
In the stir of the forces
Whence issued the world.

For the first time he understood the spell-binding power of the mountains with his heart, no longer with his head, and, like

1 *Isolation: To Marguerite.*
2 *The Letters of Arnold to Clough*, p. 110.

THUN AND THE BLÜMLISALP

Photo: A. Gurtner, Thun

Ye storm-winds of Autumn!
Who rush by, who shake
The window, and ruffle
The gleam-lighted lake;
Who cross to the hillside

Thin-sprinkled with farms,
Where the high woods strip sadly
Their yellowing arms—
Ye are bound for the mountains!
Ah! with you let me go....

Parting

Obermann, forgot their cold indifference before the greater
coldness of man. The journey up the Kandertal of the preceding
year came into his mind, and the irresistible desire was on him
to flee and bury his sorrow there:

> There to watch, o'er the sunk vale,
> The frore mountain-wall,
> Where the niched snow-bed sprays down
> Its powdery fall.
> There its dusky blue clusters
> The aconite[1] spreads;
> There the pines slope, the cloud-strips
> Hung soft in their heads.
> No life but, at moments,
> The mountain-bee's hum.
> —I come, O ye mountains!
> Ye pine-woods, I come![2]

But before turning his face to the Blümlisalp's everlasting peaks,
he looked back not once, but twice or thrice, on his vanishing
love.

> Forgive me! forgive me!
> Ah, Marguerite, fain
> Would these arms reach to clasp thee!
> But see! 'tis in vain.[3]

Now that this sorrow had him in thrall, the landscape wore
a changed aspect as he pursued his way. He was following
on Obermann's steps as of yore; but his apprehensions were
now sharpened; the stirring of sympathy he had long felt for
the solitary dweller of the Oberland suddenly, as he pushed
ever higher, grew and expanded into a deep and compassionate
understanding.

---

1 Not the true aconite, but *Aconitum napellus*, the *Blauer Eisenhut* or Common
Monkshood, whose bluish-violet perianth unfolds in the late summer from the
foot of the mountains up to a height of ten thousand feet.
2 *Parting*.   3 *Ibid*.

It was thus, through experience of loss and desolation, that Matthew Arnold came to his true and unique appreciation of Obermann.

The poet's love for this 'Daughter of France'[1] can in no sense be regarded as the first link in the chain of his long interest in French literature: nor can it be said to be responsible for any renewed preoccupation with it. But it is undeniable that the experience added a colour and a background to his appreciation that no intellectual understanding could have given. It may have, in general, furnished him with a new and more intimate reason for his interest in French civilisation. But its most important result was a profound effect on his character, leading to that enhanced and poignant sympathy for Obermann that controlled all his attitude henceforth. Indeed, some striking occasion was needed for a young Englishman, with Arnold's abilities and prospects, an Oxford graduate and Fellow, with all the flush of youth and promise upon him, to have flung himself—as he did at this moment—upon a mode of thought so hopeless, fatalistic and unprogressive as Obermann's: one which could offer only the austere consolations of a Marcus Aurelius for its highest prize, and the desperate end of an Empedocles for its sole solution.

But from Marguerite to Obermann, as from Thun to the Baths of Leuk, the way seemed naturally marked.

Whatever of melancholy bitterness he had felt before, passed away from him and was lost, as Arnold crossed the wonderful Gemmi and stood again on the spot, breathing of memories of Obermann, the lonely Baths of Leuk. It was here, with the majestic view of the valley beneath him, the mighty stair-cut way behind, and the deserted baths before him, that Matthew Arnold, vaguely comprehending in his own sorrow all the ills

1 *The Terrace at Berne.*

of the age, turned to the consolation of Obermann. While he stayed here, he took the decisive step into a new way of being; he grew to a spiritual stature beyond anything he had before known. It was in this hour that with peculiar vividness he saw, in the vision of the inward eye, the solitary of Imenström seated before him; and, turning the pages of *Obermann*, his mind held converse with the mind of the dead.

—I await no longer better days to come. The months change, the years succeed each other: in vain all things renew themselves; I remain the same. In the midst of what I have desired, I lack for everything; I have gained nothing, I possess nothing, slowly and silently melancholy consumes my days. *Whether the vain desires of life cause me to forget the world of nature, or the useless need to enjoy brings me back to its shadow*, always I am surrounded by emptiness, and each season as it passes seems to stretch it further about me. No friend has lightened my heaviness through the long-continuing mists of winter. The spring came to Nature, but not to me. The life-giving days brought awakening to all beings; me only their untamed fire wearied without reviving; I was a stranger in a joyous world. And now the flowers have fallen; the very lily has faded; the heat wanes, the days grow longer, and nights more beautiful. Happy season! The fair days are without meaning for me, the soft nights to me are bitter. Peace under the shadows, breaking of waves, silence, moon, birds singing in the night, sentiments of my early years, what have you become!

The shadows have remained: they appear before me, they pass, to and fro, into the distance; a moving cloud wearing a hundred pale tremendous forms. Vainly do I seek to begin with calm the night of the tomb, my eyes do not close. These shadows of life reappear without ceasing—they move about in silence, approach and recede, are engulfed to reappear. I see them, but I hear nothing; they are thin vapour; I seek them and they are no more. I listen, and call; I do not hear my own voice, and I am left in an intolerable void—alone, lost, uncertain, oppressed with anxiety and amaze, in the midst of wandering shadows, in impalpable, silent space.

Impenetrable Nature! thy splendour overwhelms and thy benefits consume me. What to me are these long days? Their light begins too soon; their burning noon crushes me; and the piercing harmony of their celestial even-tide brings weariness to the ashes of my heart: the spirit which sleeps in its ruins has shivered with the movement of life.

The snows are melting on the mountain-tops, *the stormy mists roll in the valley*: unhappy that I am! the skies are alight, earth matures; sterile winter remains within me. Soft light of the dying sun, shadows of the everlasting snow! And that man should have only bitter joys! *when the torrent rolls in the distance* amid the universal silence, when the chalets close for the peace of night, and the moon mounts over the Velan![1]

So reading, and in a similar setting, Arnold was to conceive the stanzas in memory of the author of *Obermann*:

> In front the awful Alpine track
> Crawls up its rocky stair;
> The autumn storm-winds drive the rack,
> Close o'er it, in the air.
>
> Behind are the abandon'd baths
> Mute in their meadows lone;
> The leaves are on the valley-paths,
> The mists are on the Rhone—
>
> The white mists rolling like a sea!
> I hear the torrents roar.
> —Yes, Obermann, all speaks of thee;
> I feel thee near once more!
>
> I turn thy leaves! I feel their breath
> Once more upon me roll;
> That air of languor, cold, and death
> Which brooded o'er thy soul.

1 *Obermann*, LXXV, vol. II, pp. 147–8.

He read on:

No sooner had I left behind the days of childhood, so much regretted, than I imagined, and felt, a real life; but I have found only fantastic sensations: I saw beings, where there are only shadows; *I desired harmony and found only contradictions.* Then I grew heavy-hearted; a hollowness invaded my heart, desires without bound consumed me in silence and *the weariness of life was my sole feeling at the age when one is* [*only*] *beginning to live.*

Arnold had imagined much the same fate to be the lot of his Gipsy-Child, whom he had apostrophised in terms that seem like a memory of these words of Obermann:

—Thou hast foreknown the vanity of hope,
Foreseen thy harvest—yet proceed'st to live.

All objects testified to me [continued Obermann] of that full, universal felicity of which the ideal image is moreover within man's own heart, and yet the natural means [to which] seem effaced from nature. As yet I reached towards only undefined sorrows; but when I saw the Alps, the shores of the lakes, the silence of their chalets, the permanence and uniformity of time and things, I recognised isolated traits of that dimly conceived nature. I saw the moon's reflections on the schistose rocks and the wooden roofs; *I saw men without desires;* I trod the short mountain grass; *I heard accents of another world.*

I came down the mountains to earth;—there it faded, that blind faith in the absolute existence of beings, that illusion of regular relations, perfections and positive enjoyments—radiant conjectures which beguile the youthful heart; but at which he must mournfully smile whom greater depths have chilled, or a greater age has matured.

Change without term, action without aim, universal impenetrability—behold all that is known to us *of this world where we reign.*

An invincible destiny effaces our dreams; and what does it bring in return to that void which still must be filled? Power grows wearisome; pleasure eludes us; fame is reserved for our ashes; religion is a system of the unhappy; *love wore indeed the colours of life*, the shadow grows, the rose pales, it falls, and it is universal night.[1]

Fly hence, poor wretch, whoe'er thou art,
Condemn'd to cast about,
All shipwreck in thy own weak heart,
For comfort from without!

A fever in these pages burns
Beneath the calm they feign;
A wounded human spirit turns,
Here, on its bed of pain.

Yes, though the virgin mountain-air
Fresh through these pages blows;
Though to these leaves the glaciers spare
The soul of their white snows;

Though here a mountain-murmur swells
Of many a dark-bough'd pine;
Though, as you read, you hear the bells
Of the high-pasturing kine—

Yet, through the hum of torrent lone,
And brooding mountain-bee,
There sobs I know not what ground-tone
Of human agony.

Is it for this, because the sound
Is fraught too deep with pain,
That, Obermann! the world around
So little loves thy strain?

Some secrets may the poet tell,
For the world loves new ways;
To tell too deep ones is not well—
It knows not what he says.

1 *Obermann*, LXXV, vol. II, pp. 148–9.

LEUKERBAD

Scene of the *Stanzas in Memory of t'e Author of 'Obermann'*
Photo: E. Gyger, Adelboden

Though to these leaves the glaciers spare
The soul of their white snows....

Yet, of the spirits who have reign'd
In this our troubled day,
I know but two, who have attain'd,
Save thee, to see their way...

Too fast we live, too much are tried,
Too harass'd, to attain
Wordsworth's sweet calm, or Goethe's wide
And luminous view to gain.

And then we turn, thou sadder sage,
To thee! we feel thy spell!
—The hopeless tangle of our age,
Thou too hast scann'd it well!

Immoveable thou sittest, still
As death, composed to bear!
Thy head is clear, thy feeling chill,
And icy thy despair.

Arnold continues, and now his thought travels over the causes of this unrest of Obermann's; for in his own aspirations he had recognised the same division of interests that had troubled Obermann:

Ah! two desires toss about
The poet's feverish blood.
One drives him to the world without,
And one to solitude.

These contradictory desires in Obermann, as we shall see also in Arnold's Empedocles, were constantly arising and annulling each other. 'Whether', he says in one of the pages Arnold was reading, 'the vain desires of life cause me to forget the world of nature, or the useless need to enjoy brings me back to its shadow, always I am surrounded by emptiness....'

The only solution of this conflict is through renunciation:

> He who hath watch'd, not shared, the strife,
> Knows how the day hath gone.
> He only lives with the world's life,
> Who hath renounced his own.

> To thee we come, then! Clouds are roll'd
> Where thou, O seer! art set;
> Thy realm of thought is drear and cold—
> The world is colder yet!

But even in that austere region of sacrifice Obermann had found, and was able to impart, the momentary joy he had tasted in presence of the eternal order; when he had

> Heard accents of the eternal tongue
> Through the pine branches play.

'Et moi aussi', he says, 'j'ai des momens d'oubli, de force, de grandeur.... J'abandonne les soins de ce qui passe, et ces pensées du présent déjà perdu. Je m'arrête étonné; j'écoute ce qui subsiste encore; je voudrais entendre ce qui subsistera: *je cherche dans le mouvement de la forêt, dans le bruit des pins, quelques-uns des accens de la langue éternelle....*'[1] Yes, despite thy sadness, O Obermann [Arnold continues], thou hast pleasures still and balm to offer us, as when thou, on summer nights,

> Listen'd, and felt thyself grow young!
> Listen'd and wept—Away!

The tone of the young poet grows more sorrowful as he proceeds:

> Away the dreams that but deceive!
> And thou, sad guide, adieu!
> I go, fate drives me; but I leave
> Half of my life with you.

---

1 *Obermann*, XLVIII, vol. II, pp. 19–20.

We, in some unknown Power's employ,
Move on a rigorous line;
Can neither, when we will, enjoy,
Nor, when we will, resign.

I in the world must live; but thou,
Thou melancholy shade!
Wilt not, if thou canst see me now,
Condemn me, nor upbraid.

For thou art gone away from earth,
And place with those dost claim,
The Children of the Second Birth,
Whom the world could not tame...

There without anger thou wilt see
Him who obeys thy spell
No more, so he but rest, like thee,
Unsoil'd!—and so, farewell....

Farewell! Under the sky we part,
In the stern Alpine dell.
O unstrung will! O broken heart!
A last, a last farewell!

The return route to England lay naturally through Thun.
Nor did Arnold resist the last transient pleasure of seeing
Marguerite again.

He had been away three or four days. Animated with returns
of despair and exhilaration he travelled fast, reaching Spiez
before nightfall: from here he pushed on to Thun. He has left
a picture of the calm approach by night.

My horses's feet beside the lake,
Where sweet the unbroken moonbeams lay,
Sent echoes through the night to wake
Each glistening strand, each heath-fringed bay.[1]

1 *A Farewell.*

Along the Frutigen road he hastened. The entrance to the town drew near:[1]

> The poplar avenue was pass'd,
> And the roof'd bridge that spans the stream;
> Up the steep street I hurried fast,
> Led by thy taper's starlike beam.[2]

> I came! I saw thee rise!—the blood
> Poured flushing to thy languid cheek.
> Lock'd in each other's arms we stood,
> In tears, with hearts too full to speak.

For a very little while, it seems, the old fluctuations of hope and despair revived in Arnold.

> Days flew;—ah, soon I could discern
> A trouble in thine alter'd air!
> Thy hand lay languidly in mine,
> Thy cheek was grave, thy speech grew rare.

1 Note that Arnold would approach Thun by this road if arriving from Montreux by the Simmenthal, whose exit lies between the Niesen and the Stockhorn, opposite Thun. This is the itinerary he probably did follow in 1848 (see above, chap. VII, p. 98). But we have preferred to associate the events described in *A Farewell* with his return from Leukerbad in 1849, rather than with his return to Thun from England in this year. The poem *Meeting* undoubtedly refers to the latter event and to his re-finding of Marguerite on his first arrival on this second visit to Thun. *A Farewell* would seem to describe another set of incidents, and so we have placed it a little later in the history of this episode. It is true that in his letter to Clough of September of this year (*Arnold's Letters to Clough*, p. 111) he mentions his intention of trying to see *how soon* he can leave the Bellevue on his return from Leukerbad, while in the poem he says 'Days flew . . .'. Giving Arnold full credit for his intentions, we may add that it is not perhaps necessary to desire exact correspondence in every detail between the events of the poems and the real happenings on which the poems are founded. Moreover, as elsewhere pointed out, the evidence of *On the Rhine* (published in 1852) suggests that Arnold returned to Thun in 1849 by the same route as he left it in 1848—that is, by Cologne and the Rhine, a perhaps more natural route than the roundabout excursion by the Simmenthal.

(One must deprecate the suggestion that *On the Rhine* was written in the year of his wedding-tour, as late as 1851.)

2 Originally written in 1852:

> 'Lit by thy taper's star-like beam'.

THUN AND THE BERNESE ALPS, *ca.* 1840

My horse's feet beside the lake,
Where sweet the unbroken moonbeams lay,
Sent echoes through the night to wake
Each glistening strand, each heath-fringed bay.
The poplar avenue was pass'd,
And the roof'd bridge that spans the stream;
Up the steep street I hurried fast,
Led by thy taper's starlike beam.

A Farewell

The melancholy reflections that followed led at last to re-cognition of the truth.

> Each on his own strict line we move,
> And some find death ere they find love;
> So far apart their lives are thrown
> From the twin soul which halves their own.
>
> And sometimes, by still harder fate,
> The lovers meet, but meet too late.
> —Thy heart is mine!—*True, true! ah, true!*
> —Then love, thy hand! *Ah no! Adieu!* [1]

The time had come to leave Thun, and for Arnold to see, as he half-humorously wrote to Clough, how soon he could ferociously turn towards England. In reviewing his farewell to Marguerite afterwards, there escapes a note of resignation, as though he saw in her a being inevitably not destined for him; beyond his reach, a soul charmed by some special benignant breath of Nature—almost the spirit of Nature herself, freely dispensing, like Nature, herself and her joys impartially to all. Her intellectual comradeship, her pleasure in his society, these, he now understood, were the manifestations of a being naturally generous, friendly, gay and free. The world, to such souls

> may homage make,
> And garlands for their foreheads weave;
> And what the world can give, they take—
> But they bring more than they receive.
>
> They shine upon the world! Their ears
> To one demand alone are coy;
> They will not give us love and tears,
> They bring us light and warmth and joy.
>
> It was not love which heaved thy breast,
> Fair child!—it was the bliss within.
> Adieu! and say that one, at least,
> Was just to what he did not win. [2]

1 *Too Late*; originally intended by Arnold to form the conclusion of *Longing*, perhaps the saddest of these poems.
2 *Euphrosyne*; originally called *Indifference*.

From Thun Arnold travelled north with a heavy heart. Some bitter lines he wrote then, commemorating this dark hour. He would forget Marguerite, banish her image from his mind. He would do this so utterly and completely, so lost would her memory be—that one day, should chance's revolutions bring them face to face again, he aged and changed, she perennially fair, her grey eyes scanning him would be perceived with vague surprise; her brown locks viewed with pleasure unalloyed in their loveliness, unspoiled by sad memory.[1] So Arnold formulated his heroic desire; but unsuccessfully. Already on his way south by the slow-flowing Rhine, he had declared:

Vain is the effort to forget.
Some day I shall be cold, I know,
As is the eternal moonlit snow
Of the high Alps, to which I go—
But ah, not yet, not yet. . .

Ah, Quiet, all things feel thy balm!
Those blue hills too, this river's flow,
Were restless once, but long ago.
Tamed is their turbulent youthful glow;
Their joy is in their calm.[2]

For Obermann also the struggle towards serenity was similarly mixed with a mournful, backward-looking resistance.

'Quand la passion de toutes choses, quand ce besoin universel des âmes fortes a consumé nos cœurs, le charme abandonne nos désirs détrompés et l'irrémédiable ennui naît de ces cendres refroidies. . . . Durant l'orage l'espoir soutient. . . mais si le calme lui-même vous fatigue, qu'espérerez-vous alors. . . ?'[3]

There is an element of tragedy in this effort to attain a forgetfulness which is only half-desired, an insensibility which brings more anguish than despair itself. And we have in Arnold

---

1 *Separation.* 2 *On the Rhine.*
3 *Obermann*, XLI, vol. I, pp. 165 and 167.

the further anomaly of his invoking Marguerite, the very author
of his trouble, to aid him to escape it:

> I struggle towards the light; and ye,
> *Once-long'd-for storms of love!* [1]
> If with the light ye cannot be,
> I bear that ye remove.
>
> I struggle towards the light—but oh,
> While yet the night is chill,
> Upon time's barren, stormy flow,
> Stay with me, Marguerite, still! [2]

Something irresolute, and infinitely sad, remains in this
appeal: years were to pass before Arnold could sincerely desire
the extinction of his passion.

Once, one conjectures, he tried to imagine Marguerite as
dead: it seems likely that she is the one for whom the beautiful
elegy, *Requiescat,* [3] was written. The rose associated with the
latter was also, it may be remembered, the symbol of the New
Sirens; the yew which the poet forbids her, that of the seeker
after light.

Marguerite might well have represented the rose in Arnold's
life; her charm had led the poet to a life of sensibility and
passion; and had drawn him aside from the austere intellectualism to which his reason pointed him. Moreover, if the
one mourned in *Requiescat* be not Marguerite, it is strange that
the poet should desire his death with hers. Already, in a poem
addressed to Marguerite, he had made her with him participant
of the calm life of the stars and heavens:

> How sweet, unreach'd by earthly jars,
> My sister! to maintain with thee
> The hush among the shining stars,
> The calm upon the moonlit sea!
>
> How sweet to feel, on the boon air,
> All our unquiet pulses cease! [4]

[1] A reminiscence, without doubt, of Chateaubriand's 'orages désirés' (*René*).
[2] *Absence.*   [3] Of 1853.   [4] *A Farewell.*

Now he repeats the same desire:

> In quiet she reposes;
>   Ah, would that I did too!

And lastly, the mirthfulness and glee of this unknown were pre-eminently qualities of Marguerite—one of those beings described in *Euphrosyne*, who, by their joyousness, for ever 'shine upon the world'.

In *Requiescat* he says again 'Her mirth the world required'.

It would not seem hazardous, therefore, to identify this unknown dead with Arnold's lost love.

But the memory of Marguerite had not died. His thought of her was nourished by dreams that often came at night—less often perhaps as time flew on. But the invitation which his heart had first offered to the dream had nothing of faintness in it; the beautiful poem, *Longing*, was written then:

> Come to me in my dreams, and then
> By day I shall be well again!
> For then the night will more than pay
> The hopeless longing of the day.
>
> Come, as thou cam'st a thousand times,
> A messenger from radiant climes,
> And smile on thy new world, and be
> As kind to others as to me!
>
> Or, as thou never cam'st in sooth,
> Come now, and let me dream it truth;
> And part my hair and kiss my brow,
> And say: *My love! why sufferest thou?*
>
> Come to me in my dreams, and then
> By day I shall be well again!
> For then the night will more than pay
> The hopeless longing of the day.

Ten years had passed away since last he saw her, and Arnold once again found himself near the Oberland. Travelling with his wife from Strasbourg to Geneva in 1859, he set foot in Berne.[1] His wife was sick: Arnold was wandering alone on the terrace above the curling river and great bridge of Berne. He looked back on the course of the river, on the wide valley to the south-east down which it came; beyond, in low faint outline glimmered the topmost peaks of the Bernese Oberland, among them the white Blümlisalp, far and small. Not seventeen miles away from him lay Thun, unchanged beside its lake.

And Marguerite? In his thought he saw her, also unchanged: she was walking in the garden of the hotel as of yore: the oleanders, now in bright midsummer bloom, half hid her slender figure: she emerged, she saw him, she started in joyful surprise: he heard her voice, with its soft French accent, pronounce the words, 'C'est toi!'...

The river flowed quietly past the garden, past the landing-stage; the swans glided by as of old; the light played on the lake: and Marguerite's glance rested on him: that glance of

> Eyes too expressive to be blue,
> Too lovely to be grey.[2]

Perhaps a sigh burst from Arnold. He started up: he walked along the terrace. He was mistaken; Marguerite no longer existed for him. The gulf that had separated them in the past yawned again and deeper between them. Caught up in the turmoil of her light-hearted companions, her way of life was not as his.

And now, looking up towards the mountains, a mist came and settled between his eyes and them. He was alone; why seek

1 This we conjecture from the date of the poem, and from the itinerary referred to in *Letters*, vol. I, *Works*, vol. XIII, pp. 125–30.
2 *On the Rhine.*

to probe the past, or carry it into the future? The truth was written in his heart: he had met, and missed, the 'twin soul' which halved his own.

> Like driftward spars, which meet and pass
> Upon the boundless ocean-plain,
> So on the sea of life, alas!
> Man meets man—meets, and quits again.[1]

> I knew it when my life was young;
> I feel it still, now youth is o'er.
> —The mists are on the mountain hung
> And Marguerite I shall see no more.[2]

1 Originally written in 1867: 'Man nears man, meets, and leaves again'.
2 *The Terrace at Berne.*

CHAPTER IX

'MARGUERITE' POEMS CONTINUED: *TRISTRAM AND ISEULT*

Whether because Arnold was chagrined by their poor reception, or because he had become discontented with them himself, the 1849 volume of poems was quickly withdrawn from circulation. The latter reason probably influenced him quite as much as the first. The change that had overtaken the poet since the composition of the greater part of his first volume might well have caused him to regard with impatience utterances so little expressive of his new and deeper outlook.

His engagement in 1850 to Miss Frances Lucy Wightman, and subsequent happy married life, could not alter the past; but it required him to show a little more circumspection in his personal utterances. A lifelong practice of delicacy and reserve was to end in their almost complete *embrouillement*: it is the more surprising that he frankly revealed so much in the volume of 1852, which appeared only one year after his marriage. Many of the poems must have been written some time before this event; and it is possible that their appearance was deferred on account of it. Nevertheless, by venturing to include them in the 1852 volume Arnold must have trusted much to the ambiguity of the facts. At least there is no hint that the publication of some of the saddest love-poems in English literature, by a man in the first year of young married life, occasioned rebuke, or more than surprise, among his friends.

In subsequent editions Arnold made many changes in the rearranging, renaming, and rehandling of these poems. But in the volume of 1852 the arrangement is transparently simple: a logical order controls it.

The volume is divided into three sections, of which the first is taken up entirely by the philosophical poem, *Empedocles on Etna*: the second consists of a series of lyrics, significantly terminated by a longer narrative poem, *Tristram and Iseult*. The last section, apart from the poem *A Farewell*, consists of smaller pieces grouped together by reason of some concordance of interior meaning. The first and last sections are the subject of the next three chapters.

The poems in the middle section, practically without exception, relate to the experiences of Arnold's stay in Thun. This section begins with a group including four poems which appeared afterwards under the title *Faded Leaves* in the volume of 1855 (known as *Second Series*): they are *The River*, *Too Late*, *On the Rhine* and *Longing*. In 1855 a fifth and new poem, *Separation*, was added; and in the first collected edition of 1869, the *Faded Leaves* group so reappears in its definitive form.[1]

Sandwiched among this group in 1852 are two poems, *Excuse* and *Indifference*, which, if we judge by their themes, seem to have had their titles confused, *Indifference* better suiting the content of the poem *Excuse*, and *vice versa*. This misnomenclature was retrieved, and a certain impersonal touch secured to the poems, by their renaming as *Urania* (= *Excuse*)

1 The theory, upheld by Hugh Kingsmill (*Matthew Arnold*, 1928), L. Bonnerot and A. Harris (articles cited), that these poems should be grouped with *Calais Sands* as referring to Arnold's wife, is improbable. The topography of *The River*, clearly that of Thun, and the epithets 'arch' and 'mocking', specifically those of Marguerite (see *A Memory Picture* and *Parting*), would seem to preclude this interpretation. Nor does there appear to be any real inconsistency in the physical portraits of the heroine of the different poems. In the *Switzerland* series alone Marguerite's eyes vary in colour from 'blue' in *Meeting* to 'grey' in *Absence*. The 'radiant climes' of *Longing*, moreover, surely points to Switzerland and Marguerite. Indeed, no love-story so sad as is recorded in *Faded Leaves* had the quick and happy issue which the above theory would require.

and *Euphrosyne* (= *Indifference*) in the first collected edition of
1869. From their position among the poems subsequently
known as *Faded Leaves* they may be regarded as most closely
associated with this group. Both poems clearly refer to Marguerite—Grace and Muse at once incarnate for Arnold; we
have already referred to *Indifference* in elucidating the problem
of the poet's relations to her. They do not, any more than the
other members of the *Faded Leaves* group, occur in *Poems:
A New Edition* (*First Series*), of 1853; but they reappear, still
under their original titles, in the *Second Series* of 1855, discreetly
divided by one other poem from *Faded Leaves*. It seems certain
that the subsequent titles of 1869, *Urania* (Muse of the Heavens,
the disdainful one) and *Euphrosyne* (Joyousness, one of the
three Graces), were an effort at readjustment as well as possible
concealment.

Following these poems without a break in the 1852 volume
is the handful of lyrics that was later separated into a group and
entitled *Switzerland*: they appear here in the following order:
The Lake, Parting, Absence, and finally, *To Marguerite, in
returning a volume of the Letters of Ortis*. In *First Series* of the
next year (1853) these poems were grouped for the first time
under the heading *Switzerland*, and two others added—*To My
Friends*, which had first appeared in 1849, and *A Dream*, which
occurs here for the first time. (It will be remembered that
Requiescat also appears in this volume for the first time.) The
poem *A Farewell* which, despite its philosophical ending, undoubtedly belongs to this group—although separated at its
original appearance in 1852, possibly because of its strong local
colour—is omitted in the volume of 1853, but reappears in the
second edition of *First Series* in 1854. In 1869 it takes its place
definitively in the *Switzerland* group.

It is clear that the arrangement of this group long caused its author hesitation and embarrassment. In *New Poems* (of 1867) it naturally does not reappear; but one new poem in the collection, *The Terrace at Berne*, is obviously a belated member, and is made the eighth and last poem of the group when it again makes its appearance in the first collected edition of 1869. In this edition *Switzerland* is the *en-tête* for the following poems:

(1) *A Memory Picture* (so called for the first time. In all preceding editions this poem appeared as *To My Friends*).

(2) *Meeting* (the new title of the poem called in 1852 and 1853 *The Lake*).

(3) *Parting.*

(4) *A Farewell.*

(5) *Absence.*

(6) *Isolation: To Marguerite.*

(7) *To Marguerite: continued.*

(8) *The Terrace at Berne.*

The next-to-last two poems appear to have caused Arnold much uncertainty. *To Marguerite: continued* is the original poem *To Marguerite in returning a volume of the Letters of Ortis*, entitled *To Marguerite*, simply, in 1853. *Isolation: To Marguerite* dates only from the third edition of *First Series*, 1857, where it first appeared, called *To Marguerite*; while the poem previously appearing under that title was transitorily called *Isolation* in this edition.

It is noteworthy that *A Dream*, appearing in the *Switzerland* grouping of 1853, was not reprinted till 1881; and then no longer in association with this group, to which it certainly belongs.

A Dream, with more truth than fancy, revives a memory of Marguerite in the Alpine setting where the poet had first seen her. In this poem occurs one of Arnold's favourite images, that

THE SALLE DE RÉUNION AT THE HOTEL BELLEVUE
as it appears to-day

Photo: A. Lytton Sells

Conjectured site of the poem, *A Dream*

of life regarded as a stream, on which man is borne onward resistlessly from the lonely fastnesses in the mountains whence it issues, to the flat peneplain, 'bristled with cities', and the wide ocean which receives him.

'Was it a dream?' The river seems here to be the Aar; at least the banks bordered with pines, and the Swiss chalets and chestnuts on each side are those of some Alpine valley: the scarlet-berried ash, and the golden gourds lying on the stone-strewn roof suggest that the season is autumn. The poet and his companion are gliding on the upper reaches of the stream; in the grounds of the Hotel Bellevue at Thun, it will be remembered (see chap. VII, p. 96), stood a wooden chalet, the *Salle de Réunion*, not more than three chains from the river's bank: steps on each side led from the garden to a brown wooden balcony, intertwined with wistaria. By these steps Marguerite might have emerged with her companion, Olivia, whom the poet mentions here for the first time; or she might have passed through one of the three French windows leading from the room where were gathered the guests of the hotel.

From the boat on the river the two white forms were seen to speak and beckon; but now the travellers had passed the chalet, and had breasted the rapids below the town. At last the Rhine received them; here great cities stood on either hand; and passing these, they were engulfed by the sea.

The remaining members of the middle section of the 1852 volume are *Destiny*, *Human Life*, *Despondency*, *Sonnet* (later called *Youth's Agitations*), *Self-Deception*, *Lines Written by a Deathbed* and *Tristram and Iseult*.

The first of these, *Destiny*, was never reprinted in Arnold's lifetime. The thought is an oft-repeated echo of Obermann, a paraphrase of two of Obermann's characteristic laments, the regret for waning capacities, here the capacity to love; and the

torture of unappeased desire. The poem is short, of two stanzas
only.

> Why each is striving, from of old,
> To love more deeply than he can,
> Still would be true, yet still grows cold?
> —Ask of the Powers that sport with man!

The same fatalism pervades *Obermann*. Man to its author
also is but the 'jouet lamentable d'une destinée que rien
n'explique'.[1] 'Me voici', he says, 'le jouet de la force qui nous
brisera tous.'[2]

> They yoked in him for endless strife,
> A heart of ice, a soul of fire;
> And hurl'd him on the Field of Life,
> An aimless, unallay'd Desire.

How often had Arnold read in *Obermann* the same thought.
'Je sens, j'existe', says Senancour, 'pour me consumer en désirs
indomptables.'[3] 'Le tourment du cœur *insatiable* [unallay'd]
est le mouvement aveugle [aimless] d'un météore errant dans
le vide où il doit se perdre....'[4]

It is probable that Arnold's version of the same sentiment
was inspired by the revulsion of feeling which followed his
parting from Marguerite.

Human Life is undoubtedly a sad little reminder of that
episode. The image of man, as a vessel labouring 'on life's
incognisable sea', and the exhortation

> Let us not fret and fear to miss our aim,
> If some fair coast have lured us to make stay,

seems an allusion to the siren invitation of love: that Arnold

1 *Obermann*, XLI, vol. I, p. 165.   2 *Id*. XC, vol. II, p. 233.
3 *Id*. LXIII, vol. II, p. 73.   4 *Ibid*.

had a grievous sense of his lost opportunities the concluding
stanza shows:

—So we leave behind,
As, charter'd by some unknown Powers,
We stem across the sea of life by night,
The joys which were not for our use design'd;
The friends to whom we had no natural right,
The homes that were not destined to be ours.

This is the fatalistic note again: the attitude which seems to
have determined his relinquishment of Marguerite, and in which
he constantly seeks consolation for her loss.

Despondency, with its expression of profound sadness, is a
fitting pendant to the *Switzerland* series. The *Sonnet*, later called
Youth's Agitations, in the now habitual vein, deplores the
waning of life and youth and love. We have already seen
(chap. v, pp. 62–4) how this thought is the special Arnoldian
variant of the melancholy of Obermann. The wish to have the
agitating desires of youth restored to him, even their racking
pains, in age and coldness, is the familiar turn which Obermann's
thought was always taking.

Shall I not joy youth's heats are left behind,
And breathe more happy in an *even clime?*—
Ah no, for then I shall begin to find
A thousand virtues in this hated time!

So also the 'climat fixe'[1] for which Obermann longed—the
physical background and symbol of the moral peace and
stability he desired—once attained, brought dismay and a new
melancholy. 'Nos jours', he says, with rare understanding,
'que rien ne ramène, se composent de momens orageux qui
élèvent l'âme en la déchirant; de longues sollicitudes qui la
fatiguent, l'énervent, l'avilissent; *de temps indifférens qui l'arrêtent*

1 *Obermann*, XIV, vol. I, pp. 68–70.

dans le repos s'ils sont rares, et dans l'ennui ou la mollesse s'ils ont de la continuité.'[1]

In *Youth's Agitations*, Arnold anticipates his frame of mind in the latter state—the discontent he fancies will be his in middle life, the dread at relaxing his hold on the vital enjoyments and even sufferings that at that distance will seem the things of most value in life; and when he will be left to

> sigh that one thing only has been lent
> To youth and age in common—discontent.

Over Obermann in youth, the same shadow and dread had passed.

'Mais quelle destinée que celle où les douleurs restent, où les plaisirs ne sont plus! Peut-être quelques jours paisibles me seront-ils donnés; mais plus de charme, plus d'ivresse...et je n'ai pas vingt-un ans! et je suis né sensible, ardent!'[2]

And again, with his own moving beauty of language, stressing the memory of a lost happiness, he says, 'Le songe du bonheur a passé avec leurs ombres dans la mort de l'homme et des siècles. ...Je ne cherche point à justifier ce cœur brisé qui ne conserve dans ses ruines que *l'inquiétude de la vie*'.[3] 'J'ai les *tourmentes* de la jeunesse, et n'en ai point les consolations.'[4]

The reflection in Obermann is occasioned by grief for the loss of that 'Madame Del**' whom he had loved in earlier years. And the 'passions' and 'heats' that Arnold imagines himself regretting—the 'passions' and 'heats' of his adolescence—can we believe that those associated with his stay at Thun are not among them?

The poem *Self-Deception* is less personal, and revives the

---

1 *Obermann*, LV, vol. II, note to p. 53.
2 *Id.* IV, vol. I, pp. 28–9.
3 *Id.* LXXXIX, vol. II, pp. 223–4.
4 *Id.* XV, vol. I, p. 72.

questioning note characteristic of Arnold. In the couplet
towards the end—

> We but dream we have our wish'd-for powers,
> Ends we seek we never shall attain—

one is reminded of the lines of wonder in which Obermann
expressed his view of incomprehensible Man: 'S'il est une chose
dans le spectacle du monde qui m'arrête quelquefois et quelquefois m'étonne', he says, 'c'est cet être qui nous paraît la fin de
tant de moyens, et qui semble n'être le moyen d'aucune fin; qui
est tout sur la terre, et qui n'est rien pour elle, rien pour lui-
même; qui cherche, qui combine, qui s'inquiète;...dont la
nature est l'activité, ou plutôt l'inquiétude de l'activité;...et
qui, toujours emporté d'illusions en illusions, n'a pas, ne peut
pas avoir autre chose, et ne fait jamais que rêver la vie'.[1]

By what strange process of self-deception do we ascribe to
ourselves an end to gain and powers to achieve it? asks the poet
wistfully.

> And on earth we wander, groping, reeling;
> Powers stir in us, stir and disappear.
> Ah! and he, who placed our master-feeling
> Fail'd to place that master-feeling clear.

The faltering question of the concluding lines of this poem
only just escapes sinking under a persuasion of its utter futility:

> Ah! *some* power exists there, which is ours?
> Some end is there, we indeed may gain?

The *Lines Written by a Deathbed* existed in this form only
in the 1852 edition, in subsequent editions being broken up
into two parts, of which the first was incorporated into *Tristram
and Iseult,* and the second became the poem *Youth and Calm.*
This poem falls into line with those others which reiterate the

1 *Id.* LXXI, vol. II, pp. 136–7.

regret for the lost 'bliss' of youth; the resigned ending is familiar:

> Calm's not life's crown, though calm is well.
> 'Tis all perhaps which man acquires.
> But 'tis not what our youth desires.

Tristram and Iseult, the last poem in the central section of the 1852 volume, follows immediately after the collection of short lyrics we have been discussing; at first sight it might seem irrelevantly there placed.

The original inspiration of the poem was, Arnold told Clough, an article on the subject of Fauriel's work on *Les Poèmes Gallois et les Romans de la Table Ronde* by Théodore de la Villemarqué, in the *Revue de Paris* of 1841.[1] It was at Thun that Arnold had come across this copy of the review. Writing to his old tutor, Mr Hill, in November, 1852, he says: 'I read the story of *Tristram and Iseult* some years ago at Thun in an article in a French Review on the romance literature: I had never met with it before, and it fastened upon me: when I got back to England I looked at the *Morte d'Arthur* and took what I could, but the poem was in the main formed, and I could not well disturb it. If I had read the story first in the *Morte d'Arthur* I should have managed it differently'.[2] In view of this letter we may conclude that *Tristram and Iseult* was planned and, for the most part, composed in 1848 or 1849. For what reason Arnold was attracted to the legend of these unhappy lovers might appear a matter for conjecture, although it is easy to assume that it was his own experience that had predisposed the poet to sympathy. Not for nothing, in that case, is this poem made the climax of the group of lyrics we may call the 'Marguerite' poems: not for nothing are *Empedocles* in the first

1 *Third Series*, vol. XXIV, pp. 266–82 and 335–48.
2 Letter to Mr [Herbert] Hill, Derby, Nov. 5, 1852. Published by R. E. C. Houghton in the *Times Literary Supplement*, May 19, 1932.

section, and the 'Obermann' poems in the third, hung about this central theme of love and death.

We leave hypothesis and approach certainty as the story of *Tristram and Iseult* progresses and we read on to the third part of the poem, that apparently inconsequent extension of the main theme, in which are elaborated the fancies of the 'young, surviving Iseult'. This section, beautiful as it is, and even superior in style to the earlier portions of the poem, is so lacking in coherence with the whole that it appears almost like an afterthought;[1] it is probable, in fact, that it was added after the composition of the main part of the poem, between 1849 and 1852. This would account for the improved style of the passage, and its apparently detached air. Moreover, it is practically certain that in the coda where Iseult tells the story of Merlin and Vivien, Matthew Arnold was drawing, for the portrait of Vivien, on his remembrance of Marguerite.

It may have been merely to allay Clough's suspicions regarding the true inspiration of the poem that Arnold furnished him with the information about La Villemarqué; for to the article mentioned he owed probably, as we shall see, little more than the suggestion. The story of Merlin and Vivien he professed, moreover, to have drawn from Malory; and yet this source too provided not much more than a few bare facts, which Arnold freely altered. The re-creation of Merlin's sleep, which substitutes for Malory's rather hyperborean conception of the wall and living tomb, a ring of daisies for a prison, is Arnold's own invention. Neither the character of Merlin nor that of Vivien, receives anything from the brief objective statements of the *Morte d'Arthur*. In fact, Malory's most important contribution to Arnold's poem is its last line; here indeed the

1 '. . . with regard to the conclusion of *Tristram and Iseult* the story of Merlin, of which I am particularly fond, was brought in on purpose to relieve the poem which would else I thought have ended too sadly' (Arnold, *letter quoted*).

debt, though small, is unmistakable. In the *Morte d'Arthur*,[1] the story reads: 'She was ever passing weary of him'. In *Tristram and Iseult* Arnold has it: 'For she was passing weary of his love'.

In another poem, *The Church of Brou*, we shall see Arnold taking, even more conspicuously, a borrowed phrase and from it coining a lovely ending for his own purposes.

We have noted that the closing pages of *Tristram and Iseult* do not maintain the unity of the whole proper to such an attempt in narrative verse. Yet it is to be questioned whether Clough was not unduly severe in his criticism of this circumstance in the article he wrote for the *North American Review*.[2] Clough had offered to review Arnold's two first volumes as a service to his friend; in his remarks, however, he shows himself hardly serviceable, or even indulgent. And yet Clough, if he had reflected, must certainly have held the key to the composition of the poem, or at least of its last part. Clough, of all his friends, had received Arnold's largest confidence, and the particular mood and episode to which the poem is linked were, as we have seen, known to Clough. It is possible that it was this very knowledge which occasioned his severity—some reason there must have been for the ironical turn his criticism takes. If this were so, one might read into his admonitions nothing more than a wish to rally his friend on a weak point; shake him from his languor and unrest and heartsickness, into a more desirable state of mind.

What, however, would have been salutary if addressed to Arnold in a personal letter, was certainly damaging when given the publicity of a noted Review. Arnold treated Clough otherwise, reserving his earnest, often severe, criticism of the elder poet for his private ear; while to the world at large he paid him

1 Bk. IV, chap. I, p. 91.   2 Vol. LXXVII, no. 160, July 1853.

noble tribute. His conclusion to the *Lectures on Translating Homer*, and the beautiful elegy which enshrines their college friendship, redound as much to Arnold's generosity as to Clough's virtue.

Clough's querulousness, therefore, seems a little misplaced and unjust. The 'faint, musical mumble' of 'Iseult's dreamy memories' and 'perplexed thought', which Clough professed left him with the vaguest possible notion of their author's meaning, were, he well knew, of no light import; but the very faithful reflections of Arnold's then perturbed soul, the envelope in which he delicately covered his sad, unrestful passion.

From an examination of Arnold's poem and the article mentioned by La Villemarqué above, it will appear that nothing much more than the idea of the subject of *Tristram and Iseult* was taken from the latter. As for the story of Merlin and the fay Vivien, a mere mention only of it is made in this article, on p. 267.

The poem opens with a description of Tristram on his death-bed, attended by his wife, Iseult of Brittany. The circumstances by which Tristram, convoying Iseult of Ireland to the court of King Marc, drinks with her of the love-potion; their fatal passion, separation, Tristram's wanderings and other details in La Villemarqué, are made no use of by Arnold. Moreover, in the versions to which La Villemarqué refers,[1] Iseult of Ireland arrives in the end too late to do more than fall and expire on her lover's dead body. Arnold uses none of this antecedent history, but makes his main theme out of the events of Tristram's death-bed. Part I is devoted to Tristram's retrospective fancies. In Part II Iseult of Ireland arrives (*not* as in La Villemarqué) in

---

[1] La Villemarqué mentions Bérox, Thomas, and Chrétien de Troyes, the three principal authors who have told the story in verse, and the prose version of Luc du Gast; he refers also to Raimbaud d'Orange, the first troubadour to give the story.

time to receive his dying salutation: their dialogue, and the description of the chamber of death with the two lifeless forms, take up the whole of Part II.

Part III is devoted to Iseult of Brittany, and to the tale of Merlin and Vivien, which engrosses nearly the whole of this section.

Now when Arnold spoke of the sources of his poem, he omitted to mention to Clough another article of La Ville-marqué's which he may well have seen. In this article the story of Merlin and Vivien is given in a passage which has undeniable resemblances to Arnold's account. The passage occurs in La Villemarqué's *Visite au Tombeau de Merlin,* and is as follows:

Lors commença Merlin à deviser, et la damoiselle moult grande joie en eut, et lui montra plus grand semblant de l'aimer qu'elle n'avait fait auparavant, et tant qu'un jour advint qu'ils s'en allaient main à main par la forêt de Brocélian, et ils trou-vèrent un buisson d'aubépine qui était tout chargé de fleurs, et ils s'assirent à l'ombre des aubépines, sur l'herbe verte, et jouèrent, et Merlin met son chef au giron de la damoiselle, et elle le commença à tatonner, tant qu'il s'endormit; puis se leva, et fit un cercle de sa guimpe autour du buisson et autour de Merlin, et commença ses enchantemens tels que lui-même lui avait appris, et fit neuf fois le cercle, et par neuf fois l'enchante-ment, et puis s'alla seoir auprès de lui, et lui mit la tête en son giron, et quand il se réveilla, il regarda autour de lui, et lui fut avis qu'il était enclos dans la plus forte tour du monde, et lors dit à la dame: Madame, déçu m'avez, si vous ne demeurez avec moi; car nul n'a pouvoir de défaire cette tour, fors vous. Bel ami, dit-elle, j'y serai souvent, et de ce lui tint-elle parole; car depuis ne faillit guère nuit et jour qu'elle n'y fût.[1]

1 *Le roman de Merlin,* xve siècle, quoted by Théodore de la Villemarqué in the 'Visite au Tombeau de Merlin', *Revue de Paris,* Second Series, vol. XLI, 1837, pp. 52–3. Professor H. F. Lowry (*op. cit.* p. 137, note 3) points to this article as a possible source, without, however, going further into the matter. He also mentions in this connection Louandre's 'L'Enchanteur Merlin', in the same review (Third Series, vol. XVI, 1840, pp. 109–22); and on p. 120 a passage

The resemblances between this story and Arnold's will be clear enough. In both versions the lovers proceed to the forest of Broceliande,[1] and seat themselves beneath a hawthorn bush (a thorn in Arnold); Merlin sleeps, and Vivien traces a circle about him with her wimple, nine times, in the magic way the secret of which she has gleaned from Merlin. The latter's imprisonment within a walled tower is the traditional version, also adopted by Malory; Arnold, as we have already pointed out, discarded this idea in favour of a fancy of his own. He further pleased his own purpose by substituting, in place of the faithful Vivien who stays beside her prisoner, a wayward Vivien (as in Malory) who, having enchanted her lover for her own sweet pleasure, thereby escapes his bondage.

We have now seen the extent of Arnold's borrowings from avowed and unavowed sources; it remains to enquire how far he was drawing, in this third part of the poem, on his own psychological experiences, and memories of Marguerite.

Before the tale of Merlin and Vivien begins, Iseult is pictured in her lonely hall among her children and her women; or worn with sorrow, roaming the heaths and cliffs of her native Brittany. For, the poet says, she is happy now to live so. Suffering has no power to take away delight in what once gave delight, nor sorrow to wear Iseult's spirit, so that she should no longer bear the company of her husband's hound, or to hear the tales she once loved that Breton granddames tell. These things remain her joy. For we retain the power to be moved, and soothed, with all our pain, so long as our spirits are guarded from the world, and the world's hot feverish breath. In short, Iseult,

occurs very similar to the one quoted above. The resemblances of detail to Arnold's version are, however, lacking. Other possible suggestions, not mentioned by Lowry, may have come from La Villemarqué's *L'Enchanteur Merlin*. Quinet's *Merlin L'Enchanteur* is of much later date (1860).

1 It is of some interest to note that Quinet places the scene of Merlin's enchantment, by a patriotic prejudice, in his birthplace, the plain of Bresse.

much as Obermann before her, is the exponent of the wilting effect of the world's touch on the soul.

And the poet here reiterates his rebellion; renewing as ever the complaint of Obermann—the complaint of one who fiercely struggles to retain his sensitive response to life, who, aching with the need to feel, is yet condemned to see the spring of feeling and of love run dry.

At this point the poet breaks off his lament. The world, he adds, is not alone among the influences that operate to change and fade out lives. Other forces there are, which act on us as fatally. What other forces are these? A thought, it may be, which enslaves us: or a fit of passion—of ambition, revenge or love—these also have the power to make our souls curl up and dry, and turn our lives to shadow and to dream.

So Obermann, 'all passion spent', was wont to insist on the dream-like quality of his life. Musing on the loss of Madame Del∗∗, 'J'étais destiné', he says sadly, 'à n'avoir que le songe de mon existence'.[1]

And among these consuming forces Arnold, like Obermann, also places the force of love, the theme of his poem. Later, his anguish grown less forlorn, Arnold will attribute to love the power to heal, to touch, and even to open the locked soul. For the moment he thinks only of its cruel power to subjugate. See, he says, the tyranny and unrest of passion, how it holds us in thrall! See how man struggles in vain against its charm; in vain strives to possess it, only to be overcome by its enervating power, by its 'unnatural overheat' which burns men up; how it will send men posting over the world, without ease. . . .

What tale, Arnold resumes, did Iseult tell her children under the hollies one winter's day?

She told them [runs the answer] a light and fanciful tale,

1 *Obermann*, LXXXIX, vol. II, p. 222.

which once happened in the forest-glades of Broceliande. She told them the tale of Merlin and Vivien.

The false fay was on her white palfrey, and Merlin beside. And together they drew near to the lone sylvan glades one April day, when the forest air came to loosen the fay's brown locks; her eyes shone blue and mocking, and fixed on Merlin, her prize. And he, before the morning spell in her face, at the sound of the voice 'buoyant as morning, and as morning clear', as Arnold says elsewhere,[1] forgot his craft and work and learning, and all that could divide them, and saw only the 'witching fair' creature beside him; the 'lovely brown hair'[2] and the mocking blue eyes; and then for evermore, there he made himself her slave, to do with as she willed.

And coming a little further to an open glen, where the brushwood ceased, and the white thorn began, and squirrels played, and the woodpecker made his 'weird, chipping sound', Merlin and Vivien stopped for a while; and looked upon the white anemones starring the turf and primroses running out from behind the dark underwood.

'We will halt here', said Merlin, and Vivien nodded. Then, sitting down, Merlin fell into a sleep: and Vivien took the wimple, or kerchief, from her head, and waved it nine times round. And so she made a little circle about her prisoner, of white marguerites from the fields.

> And in that daisied circle, as men say,
> Is Merlin prisoner to the judgment day;
> But she herself whither she will can rove—
> For she was passing weary of his love.

So ends the story of *Tristram and Iseult*.

And so we leave Merlin to sleep, surrounded by the symbol of repose, the marguerite of the field.

1 *Parting.*   2 *Separation.*

'Two flowers there are', says Obermann in the concluding passage of his confessions, 'which somehow breathe of peace and are alike nearly scentless; but which, by some kind of enduring grace, are dear to me beyond words. By the memories they awake, they bind me to the past, and seem in so doing to point to a happiness to come. These simple flowers are the cornflower and the tardy daisy-flower, the marguerite of the fields.

'The cornflower is the emblem of country life and must be seen in the corn, by farm or homestead, the cock crowing, the peasant on the road. . . .

'The violet and the marguerite are rivals. They bloom together, they have the same simplicity. The violet pleases at first sight; the marguerite comes to be loved only with the years. One is to the other as a portrait to a bust. The violet calls up the purest sentiment of love; so it shows itself to the pure in heart. But in the end such love, so sweet and so alluring, is only an incident, though a happy one, in life. It fades. But the peace of nature is prolonged to the end; and of this calm repose, the marguerite is the sign.'

'Should I', continues Obermann, 'arrive one day at old age, still full of thought, but having renounced converse with man; should I then have a friend to bear away my last farewell to earth; then let my chair be placed on the short mountain-grass, and there in the sun beneath the measureless sky, let the tranquil marguerite bloom beside me, so that, in quitting this transitory life, I may seem again to recover something of the infinite illusion.'

CHAPTER X

'OBERMANN' POEMS OF 1852: *EMPEDOCLES ON ETNA*

The subject of the title-poem of the volume of 1852, *Empedocles on Etna*, was perhaps suggested by a reference, in Sainte-Beuve's essay of January 1832 on *M. de Sénancour*, to 'Empédocle à l'Etna'. In the course of an examination of *Obermann*, the critic had observed:

L'athéisme et le fatalisme dogmatique des *Rêveries* ont fait place à un doute universel non moins accablant.... À la conception profonde et à la stricte pratique de l'ordre, à cette fermeté voluptueuse que préconise l'individu en harmonie avec le monde, on croirait par moments entendre un disciple d'Épictète et de Marc-Aurèle; mais néanmoins Épicure, l'Épicure de Lucrèce et de Gassendi, le *Grajus homo*, est le grand précédent qui règne. Dans son pèlerinage à la Dent du Midi, assis sur le plateau de granit, au-dessus de la région des sapins, au niveau des neiges éternelles, plongeant du milieu des glacières rayonnantes au sein de *l'éther indiscernable*, vers le ciel des fixes, vers *l'univers nocturne*, Oberman [sic] me figure exactement ce sage de Lucrèce,[1] qui habite

Edita doctrina sapientum templa serena;

temple en effet, tout serein et glacé, éblouissant de blancheur et semblable à un sommet neigeux que la lumière embrase sans jamais le fondre ni l'échauffer. S'il s'élançait, s'il disparaissait alors, ce serait presque en Dieu, comme Empédocle à l'Etna.[2]

The history and reflections of the disappointed philosopher

---

1 We may note that Matthew Arnold since 1846 had contemplated a tragedy on the subject of Lucretius, which was never written, owing (according to him) to his feeling that Tennyson had anticipated him. (See *Letters*, vol. ii, *Works*, vol. xiv, p. 80.)

2 Sainte-Beuve, *Portraits Contemporains*, vol. i, pp. 164–5.

and physician of Agrigentum have in fact much in common
with the spiritual experiences of Obermann: the very exclama-
tion of despair which Obermann addressed to the world might
have issued from the lips of the elder philosopher: 'Vivez, vous
que peut tromper encore un prestige heureux; mais moi,
fatigué de ce qui peut égarer l'espoir, sans attente et presque
sans désir, je ne dois plus vivre....'.[1]

But, though Obermann sometimes seemed to entertain the
possibility of suicide as a solution of his weariness, and even
established a strong plea for its justification in certain circumstances,[2] the weight of despair and hopelessness within him
never brought him to the point of desiring to terminate life and
its still hidden possibilities. There is a pathetic truth in his
remark: 'Nous sommes de pauvres insensés quand nous vivons;
mais nous sommes si nuls quand nous ne vivons pas!'[3]

Once indeed, wandering in the glades of Fontainebleau, he
had savoured the thrill and terror of a death self-inflicted. He
had been reading the romance *Phrosine et Mélidor*:

Je l'ai parcouru [he says], j'en ai lu et relu la fin. Il est des
jours pour les douleurs: nous aimons à les chercher dans nous,
à suivre leurs profondeurs, et à rester surpris devant leurs
proportions démesurées; nous essayons, du moins dans les
misères humaines, cet infini que nous voulons donner à notre
ombre avant qu'un souffle du temps l'efface.[4]

...Le jour finissait, il n'y avait point de lune; il n'y avait
point de mouvement; le ciel était calme, les arbres immobiles.
Quelques insectes sous l'herbe, un seul oiseau éloigné chan-
taient dans la chaleur du soir. Je m'assis, je restai longtemps;
il me semble que je n'eus que des idées vagues. Je parcourais la

---

1 *Obermann*, XLI, vol. I, p. 164.   2 *Ibid.* p. 167.
3 *Obermann*, LXXVIII, vol. II, p. 162.
4 For the same idea, of a perception which seems to announce the immortal
in man, see again where he says, speaking of the suffering of a dying friend:
'Il faut qu'un tel abîme de misères touche aux perceptions de l'immortalité'
(*Obermann*, XXXVIII, vol. I, p. 140).

terre et les siècles; je frémissais de l'œuvre de l'homme. Je
reviens à moi, je me trouve dans ce chaos; j'y vois ma vie
perdue; je pressens les temps futurs du monde. Rochers de
Righi! si j'avais eu là vos abîmes![1]

Less of a 'fearful joy', and more of melancholy pervade
other reflections on the same subject; writing from Lyons, he
says:

Je revois le triste souvenir des longues années perdues.
J'observe comment cet avenir, qui séduit toujours, change et
s'amoindrit en s'approchant. Frappé d'un souffle de mort à la
lueur funèbre du présent, il se décolore dès l'instant où l'on
veut jouir; et laissant derrière lui les séductions qui le mas-
quaient et le prestige déjà vieilli, il passe seul, abandonné,
traînant avec pesanteur son sceptre épuisé et hideux, comme s'il
insultait à la fatigue que donne le glissement sinistre de sa
chaîne éternelle. Lorsque je pressens cet espace désenchanté où
vont se traîner les restes de ma jeunesse et de ma vie, lorsque
ma pensée cherche à suivre d'avance la pente uniforme où tout
coule et se perd, que trouvez-vous que je puisse attendre à son
terme, et qui pourrait me cacher l'abîme où tout cela va finir?
Ne faudra-t-il pas bien que, las et rebuté, quand je suis assuré
de ne pouvoir rien, je cherche au moins du repos? Et quand
une force inévitable pèse sur moi sans relâche, comment
reposerai-je, si ce n'est *en me précipitant moi-même?*[2]

The somewhat staccato utterances of Arnold's Empedocles,
ascending the pass to the crater into which he will precipitate
himself, resume many of Obermann's ideas; nor is it fanciful
to see the outline of Senancour's creation plainly re-emerging
in Arnold's. A close scrutiny of the poem will quickly reveal
this correspondence.

Meditating, within hearing of the delicate songs of Callicles
in the vale below, the philosopher reviews the destiny of men
on earth. Man's partial vision, his transitory span here below,

---

1 *Obermann*, XV, vol. I, pp. 71–2.   2 *Id.* XLI, vol. I, pp. 157–8.

and its accompanying doubts and fears, is the theme of the first few lines:

> The out-spread world to span
> A cord the Gods first slung,
> And then the soul of man
> There, like a mirror, hung,
> And bade the winds through space impel the gusty toy.

> Hither and thither spins
> The wind-borne, mirroring soul,
> A thousand glimpses wins,
> And never sees a whole;
> Looks once, and drives elsewhere, and leaves its last employ.

Obermann has a similar image to convey the partial and ephemeral character of man's knowledge:

> Ces conceptions étendues qui rendent l'homme si superbe et si avide d'empire, d'espérances et de durée, sont-elles plus vastes que les cieux réfléchis sur la surface d'un peu d'eau de pluie qui s'évapore au premier vent? Le métal que l'art a poli reçoit l'image d'une partie de l'univers; nous la recevons comme lui.... Ces conceptions, dont l'immensité surprend notre faiblesse et remplit d'enthousiasme nos cœurs bornés, sont peut-être moins pour la nature que le plus imparfait des miroirs pour l'industrie humaine....[1]

> The Gods laugh in their sleeve
> To watch man doubt and fear,
> Who knows not what to believe
> Since he sees nothing clear,
> And dares stamp nothing false where he finds nothing sure.

'Pourquoi donc, ô hommes qui passez aujourd'hui! voulez-vous des certitudes? et jusques à quand faudra-t-il vous affirmer nos rêves pour que votre vanité dise: Je sais?'[2]

The philosopher continuing, now addresses himself to Pausanias, his companion to the heights, chiding him for his

1 *Obermann*, XLVIII, vol. II, pp. 18–19.   2 *Ibid.* pp. 4–5.

curiosity in the miracle of healing which he (Empedocles) has just performed. But first he asserts the impossibility of judging whether we are indeed wind-driven by fate, or independent of it. Is this, Pausanias, so?
And can our souls not strive,
But with the winds must go,
And hurry where they drive?
Is fate indeed so strong, man's strength indeed so poor?

On this point Obermann too had professed doubt. 'Je ne dis pas [he says] que le hasard produise les choses humaines; mais je crois qu'elles sont conduites, au moins en partie, par une force étrangère à l'homme.'[1] He concludes: 'S'il n'y avait pas une force morale qui modifiât ce que nous appelons les probabilités du hasard, le cours du monde serait dans une incertitude bien plus grande'.[2] To this conclusion Empedocles will also come.

'Be not, then, fear's blind slave!' the philosopher counsels his friend, for the wise man 'veut marcher entre la défiance et la témérité'.[3] He agrees that it is the lack of harmony between the world and Pausanias and himself which has occasioned their unhappiness; in the words of Obermann, 'nos misères viennent surtout de notre déplacement dans l'ordre des choses'.[4]

The remedy for this is self-examination (stanza 11). 'C'est dans l'indépendance des choses, comme dans le silence des passions, que l'on peut s'étudier.'[5]

The various solutions proffered by sophists and others are rejected (stanza 12).

The sophist sneers: Fool, take
Thy pleasure, right or wrong.
The pious wail: Forsake
A world these sophists throng.
Be neither saint nor sophist-led, but be a man!

1 *Obermann*, XLIII, vol. I, pp. 179–80.   2 *Ibid.*   3 *Obermann*, I, vol. I, p. 2.
4 *Id.* II, vol. I, p. 11.   5 *Id.* I, vol. I, p. 8.

'Que me feront', says Obermann likewise, 'les sophismes d'une philosophie douce et flatteuse, vain déguisement d'un instinct pusillanime, vaine sagesse des patiens qui perpétue les maux si bien supportés, et qui légitime notre servitude par une nécessité imaginaire?'[1]

And as Empedocles exhorts his friend: 'Be neither saint nor sophist-led, but be a man!' so Obermann also counsels: 'Ne t'isole point de l'ensemble du monde; regarde toujours l'univers, et souviens-toi de la justice. Tu auras rempli ta vie, tu auras fait ce qui est de l'homme'.[2]

> Once read thy own breast right,
> And thou hast done with fears;
> Man gets no other light,
> Search he a thousand years.
> Sink in thyself! there ask what ails thee, at that shrine!

(stanza 14).

'Vis en toi-même....L'intelligence ne trouve qu'en elle-même l'aliment de sa vie: sois juste et fort. Nul ne connaît le jour qui doit suivre: tu ne trouveras point de paix dans les choses; cherche-la dans ton cœur....*Ce que tu crains est vain*, ce que tu désires est vain. Une seule chose te sera bonne, c'est d'être ce que la nature a voulu.'[3]

For why, asks Empedocles, must man be ever disputatious, full of murmuring against fate, and of consequent unhappiness? It is that he has an excessive idea of his title to happiness, and his place on earth (stanzas 15–17).

Man only makes himself foolish, according to Obermann, when he so over-estimates his importance in the scheme of things. There is no justification for it in Nature. It is true that 'ces lois de l'ensemble, ce soin des espèces, ce mépris des individus, cette marche des êtres est bien dure pour nous qui

---

1 *Obermann*, XLI, vol. I, p. 158.   2 *Id*. Manuel, vol. I, p. 113.
3 *Ibid*. p. 112.

sommes des individus'; he adds, 'j'admire cette providence qui taille tout en grand, mais comme l'homme est culbuté parmi les rognures! *et que nous sommes plaisans de nous croire quelque chose!*' [1]

'But we are all the same—the fools of our own woes!' Empedocles continues:

> Man errs not that he deems
> His welfare his true aim,
> He errs because he dreams
> The world does but exist that welfare to bestow.

But 'Une destinée indomptable efface nos songes.... Mutations sans terme, action sans but, impénétrabilité universelle: voilà ce qui nous est connu *de ce monde où nous régnons*'.[2] Empedocles bows to the same conclusion:

> *We mortals are no kings*
> *For each of whom to sway*
> *A new-made world up-springs,*
> Meant merely for his play;
> No, we are strangers here; *the world is from of old.*

In the next stanzas Empedocles reproaches man with not observing the laws of the world and his being. Instead of conforming to the order of things as they are, man is for ever trying to build about himself an illusory *milieu*, yielding to an inner tendency to anticipate, to imagine, and combine, factitious events of his own creation, discordant to the true environment in which he must live, as though 'man possessed some inner contradiction which rendered him incapable of happiness'.[3]

> We—as some rude guest
> Would change, where'er he roam
> The manners there profess'd
> To those he brings from home—
> *We mark not the world's course*, but would have *it* take *ours.*

1 *Obermann*, XLV, vol. I, p. 202.   2 *Id.* LXXV, vol. II, p. 149.
3 J. Merlant, *Sénancour*, p. 62.

'J'ai cru nécessaire de changer les choses avant de changer
moi-même', says Obermann,[1] but 'nul individu ne saurait
arrêter *le cours universel*, et rien n'est plus vain que la plainte des
maux attachés nécessairement à notre nature.'[2]

> The world's course proves the terms
> On which man wins content.

'Que lui servirait de vouloir davantage, de résister à la force
du monde?'[3]

> We would have inward peace,
> Yet will not look within. . .

> We do not what we ought,
> What we ought not, we do,
> And lean upon the thought
> That chance will bring us through.

But 'other existences there are, that clash with ours'.

In a world governed by such apparent hazard, 'il ne me
reste', says Obermann, 'qu'à m'observer bien moi-même pour
écarter de cette direction générale toute impulsion particulière
qui pourrait s'y mêler, pour me conserver toujours simple et
toujours droit, au milieu des perpétuelles altérations et boule-
versemens que peuvent me préparer l'oppression d'un sort
précaire et les subversions de tant de choses mobiles'.[4]

The element of chance in our lives, operating either as the
forces of Nature, or the deeds of other men, may indeed annul
all our efforts. But instead of resigning himself to this, and still
pressing onward as best he may, man must needs invent gods
on whom to rest the blame of his frustrated efforts: and further,
not content with this, must next feign kind gods to console him,
and finish the task he himself is unequal to. For man, in his
egotism, has attempted to gain a wisdom not destined for him,

---

1 *Obermann*, I, vol. I, p. 8.   2 *Id.* XLI, vol. I, p. 160.
3 *Ibid.*   4 *Obermann*, IV, vol. I, p. 27.

and to survey all the fields of knowledge; but fruitlessly. Just as, 'il n'y a pas d'autre morale pour nous que celle du cœur de l'homme', so also '[il n'y a pas] d'autre science ou d'autre sagesse que la connaissance de ses besoins, et la juste estimation des moyens de bonheur. Laisse', continues Obermann, addressing wayward man, 'laisse la science inutile et *les systèmes surnaturels, et les dogmes mystérieux*...ce que ton intelligence ne discerne pas bien, cela ne lui fut point destiné'.[1]

Empedocles next turns to the demands of youth, its aspirations to pleasure and delight, and the gradual mining of the senses with age, and the soul with discontent.

> Again.—Our youthful blood
> Claims rapture as its right;
> The world, a rolling flood
> Of newness and delight,
> Draws in the enamour'd gazer to its shining breast.

'Jeune enchantement d'un cœur qui croit au bonheur!' Obermann also had known it.

But, instead of moderating the desires of youth with the passing of years and the opportunities for their gratification, we grow ever more eager in their quest, 'still hungrier for delight as delights grow more rare'. And at last, the world not satisfying us, we turn to illusions, and

> feign a bliss
> Of doubtful future date,
> And, while we dream on this,
> Lose all our present state.

In the same way Obermann had interrogated 'la multitude que flétrit la misère, et les privilégiés que l'ennui opprime; ils m'ont dit: Nous souffrons aujourd'hui, mais nous jouirons demain'.[2]

---

1 *Id*. Manuel, vol. I, p. 113.   2 *Obermann*, XLI, vol. I, p. 164.

But is life here indeed so worthless, ask both philosophers,
that we must confine all hopes to another world—'relegate to
worlds yet distant our repose', in the words of Empedocles.
'Sans l'espérance et la terreur de la vie future, vous ne recon-
naissez point de mobile; mais la tendance à l'ordre ne peut-elle
faire une partie essentielle de nos inclinations.... N'est-ce rien
de vivre dans le calme et la sécurité du juste?' asks Obermann.[1]
And again he says,

Il faut se hâter de prouver aux hommes qu'indépendamment
d'une vie future, la justice est nécessaire à leurs cœurs; que pour
l'individu même, il n'y a point de bonheur sans la raison.... Si,
laissant dans le doute ce qui n'a jamais été prouvé, ils rappe-
laient les principes de justice et d'amour universel qu'on ne
saurait contester; s'ils se permettaient de parler des voies in-
variables du bonheur; si, entraînés par la vérité qu'ils sentent...
ils consacraient leur vie à l'annoncer de différentes manières...
pardonnez, ministres de certaine vérité, des moyens qui ne sont
précisément les vôtres; considérez... que les miracles modernes
ont fait beaucoup rire, que les temps sont changés.... [2]

The thesis of this argument is one the poet will expand in his
later religious writings. Meanwhile, Empedocles points to the
man who enjoys life as it is given him on earth.

> Is it so small a thing
> To have enjoy'd the sun,
> To have lived light in the spring,
> To have loved, to have thought, to have done;
> To have advanced true friends, and beat down baffling foes...?
>
> Not much, I know, you prize
> What pleasures may be had,
> Who looks on life with eyes
> Estranged, like mine, and sad;
> And yet the village churl feels the truth more than you,

1 *Obermann*, XLIV, vol. I, p. 195.
2 *Ibid*. pp. 191–2.

Who's loath to leave this life
Which to him little yields—
His hard-task'd sunburnt wife,
His often-labour'd fields,
The boors with whom he talk'd, the country-spots he knew.

Much in the same strain, 'Vous seuls', says Obermann, 'savez remplir votre vie, hommes simples et justes, pleins de confiance et d'affections expansives, de sentiment et de calme, qui sentez votre existence avec plénitude, et qui voulez voir l'œuvre de vos jours! Vous placez votre joie dans l'ordre et la paix domestique, sur le front pur d'un ami, sur la lèvre heureuse d'une femme'.[1]

The philosopher on Etna's slopes concludes:

I say: Fear not! Life still
Leaves human effort scope.
But since life teems with ill,
Nurse no extravagant hope;
Because thou must not dream, thou need'st not then despair!

To this point Obermann could not always follow him. ' Quand tout échappe jusqu'aux rêves de nos désirs. . . que nous restera-t-il et que sommes-nous?'[2] he asks sadly.

The song of Callicles now interrupts Empedocles, and its lyric beauty is refreshing after the somewhat depressing reflections of the philosopher.

The second act takes place on the summit of Etna; here Empedocles holds his last soliloquy on man and destiny, and here he divulges the real reason for his weariness of life.

Alone!—
On this charr'd, blacken'd, melancholy waste,
Crown'd by the awful peak, Etna's great mouth,
Round which the sullen vapour rolls—alone!

1 *Obermann*, XLVI, vol. I, p. 210.   2 *Id.* LXXXIX, vol. II, p. 227.

...I
The weary man, the banish'd citizen...
Whose banishment is not his greatest ill,
Whose weariness no energy can reach
And for whose hurt courage is not the cure—
What should I do with life and living more?

No, thou art come too late, Empedocles!
And the world hath the day, and *must break thee*,
Not thou the world.

'Me voici', says Obermann, 'le jouet de la force *qui nous brisera tous.*'[1]

Empedocles continues:

With men thou canst not live,
Their thoughts, their ways, their wishes are not thine;
And being lonely thou art miserable,
For something has impaired thy spirit's strength,
And dried its self-sufficing fount of joy.
Thou canst not live with men nor with thyself—
O sage! O sage!—Take then the one way left...
Before the soul lose all her solemn joys,
And awe be dead, and hope impossible,
And the soul's deep eternal night come on.[2]

And continuing after another interlude of song from Callicles, in praise of Apollo, Empedocles invokes the latter:

Where shall thy votary fly then? back to men?—
But they will gladly welcome him once more,
And help him to unbend his too tense thought,
And rid him of the presence of himself,
And keep their friendly chatter at his ear,
And haunt him, till the absence from himself,
That other torment, grow unbearable;
And he will fly to solitude again,
And he will find its air too keen for him,

---

1 *Obermann*, XC, vol. II, p. 233.
2 'Et voici l'éternelle nuit' (*Obermann*, LXXV, vol. II, p. 149).

And so change back; and many thousand times
Be miserably bandied to and fro
Like a sea-wave...and only death
Can cut his oscillations short, and so
Bring him to poise. There is no other way.

We recognise the same oscillations between the world and
solitude that Obermann had suffered; to whom also neither had
brought satisfaction.

'Soit que les vaines sollicitudes de la vie me fassent oublier
les choses naturelles, soit que l'inutile besoin de jouir me
ramène à leur ombre, le vide m'environne tous les jours.'[1]

He too had felt himself out of harmony with society, and yet
its absence to be an intolerable source of loneliness. 'Je n'aime,
il est vrai, que la nature; mais c'est pour cela qu'en m'aimant
moi-même je ne m'aime point exclusivement, et que les autres
hommes sont encore, dans la nature, ce que j'en aime davantage.'[2]

'Je voulais savoir enfin', he adds, 'si mon existence est
étrangère dans l'ordre humain, ou si l'ordre social actuel
s'éloigne de l'harmonie éternelle, comme une sorte d'irrégularité ou d'exception accidentelle dans le mouvement du
monde.'[3]

The result of the enquiry was completely disillusioning. This
man, by instinct sociable, found himself out of harmony with
his fellows, and their society exhausting and unbearable.

'J'interrogeai mon être, je considérai rapidement tout ce qui
m'entourait; je demandai aux hommes s'ils sentaient comme
moi; je demandai aux choses si elles étaient selon mes penchans,
et je vis qu'*il n'y avait d'accord ni entre moi et la société, ni entre
mes besoins et les choses qu'elle a faites.* Je m'arrêtai avec effroi,
sentant que j'allais livrer ma vie à des ennuis intolérables, à des
dégoûts sans terme comme sans objet.'[4]

---

1 *Ibid.* p. 147. 2 *Obermann*, IV, vol. I, p. 24.
3 *Id.* VII, vol. I, p. 44. 4 *Id.* I, vol. I, p. 4.

Empedocles might have addressed Obermann in the terms he applied to himself:

> With men thou canst not live,
> Their thoughts, their ways, their wishes are not thine.

The same inner loneliness that had overcome Empedocles fell also upon Obermann, crying: 'Je suis seul; les forces de mon cœur ne sont point communiquées; elles réagissent dans lui, elles attendent: *me voilà dans le monde, errant, solitaire au milieu de la foule qui ne m'est rien*'.[1]

Like Empedocles, seeking in isolation some inner source of strength, he is overcome by bitterness in the end.

> Je vais vivre comme au hasard...heureux si dans le temps que j'abandonne, je parviens à préparer un temps meilleur; si je puis choisir, pour ma vie future, les lieux, la manière, les habitudes, régler mes affections, me réprimer, et retenir dans l'isolement et dans les bornes d'une nécessité accidentelle ce cœur avide et simple, à qui rien ne sera donné; si je puis lui apprendre à s'alimenter lui-même dans son dénûment, à reposer dans le vide, à rester calme dans ce silence odieux, à subsister dans une nature muette.[2]

It is perhaps the mark of a diseased soul to desire calm, and be unable to support it. Obermann, retreating to the loneliness of Nature, was to find with a revulsion of feeling 'ce silence absolu' 'plus sinistre encore'![3]

But in Obermann the sharpened sensibilities had not been entirely mortified by the intellect. Empedocles, more courageous or more desperate than Obermann, will end the dilemma by death: he will no longer suffer a life in which he has lost all joy. But before taking the final leap to death he recalls, in a beautiful passage, the days when life still had happiness to offer him,

---

1 *Obermann*, XXII, vol. I, p. 91. 2 *Id.* IV, vol. I, p. 30.
3 *Id.* XXII, vol. I, p. 91.

when there had still been pleasure for him 'in the delightful commerce of the world'.

What days were those, Parmenides!
When we were young, when we could number friends
In all the Italian cities like ourselves,
When with elated hearts we join'd your train,
Ye Sun-born Virgins! on the road of truth.
Then we could still enjoy, then neither thought
Nor outward things were closed and dead to us;
But we received the shock of mighty thoughts
On simple minds with a pure natural joy...
We had not lost our balance then, nor grown
Thought's slaves, and dead to every natural joy.
The smallest thing could give us pleasure then—
The sports of the country people,
A flute-note from the woods,
Sunset over the sea;
Seed time and harvest,
The reapers in the corn....

Before this antagonism between the heart and intellect was born, Obermann had tasted a similar joy.

'Jeune enchantement d'un cœur qui croit au bonheur, qui veut ce qu'il désire, et ignore la vie! Simplicité de l'espérance, qu'êtes-vous devenue? *Le silence des forêts, la pureté des eaux, les fruits naturels, l'habitude intime nous suffisaient alors.* Le monde réel n'a rien qui remplace...ce premier songe de nos premiers printemps.'[1]

But now that glow and light of life had failed.

This heart will glow no more; thou art
A living man no more, Empedocles!
Nothing but a devouring flame of thought—
But a naked, eternally restless mind!

'L'homme purement intellectuel ne fut jamais qu'un fantôme',[2] says Obermann soberly.

1 *Id.* XLVI, vol. I, p. 214.   2 *Id.* LXIII, vol. II, p. 81.

Even the stars above Empedocles seem to him momentarily to have shared in the general decline, and to have outlived some former delight:

> Weary like us, though not
> Weary with our weariness.

But no, gazing on their unblemished, perennial life, Empedocles recants:

> No, no, ye stars! there is no death with you,
> No languor, no decay! languor and death,
> They are with me, not you! ye are alive—
> Ye, and the pure dark ether where ye ride
> Brilliant above me!

And Obermann: 'Quelle majesté sublime dans une nuit douce, calme, éclairée! Quelle grandeur!...On ne saurait comprendre la nature, à la vue de ces astres immenses dans le ciel toujours le même'.[1]

'I only', continues Empedocles,

> Whose spring of hope is dried, whose spirit has fail'd,
> I, who have not, like these, in solitude
> Maintain'd courage and force, and in myself
> Nursed an immortal vigour—I alone
> Am dead to life and joy, therefore I read
> In all things my own deadness.

'Profondeurs de l'espace, serait-ce en vain qu'il nous est donné de vous apercevoir? La majesté de la nuit répète d'âge en âge: malheur à toute âme qui se complaît dans la servitude.... Comptons pour peu de chose ce qui se dissipe rapidement. Au milieu du grand jeu du monde, cherchons un autre partage: *c'est de nos fortes résolutions que quelque effet subsistera peut-être.*'[2]

1 *Obermann*, XVI, vol. I, p. 72.
2 *Id.* XC, vol. II, p. 231.

In the moment of death, this conviction, of some faint, spiritual immortality reserved for him also will descend on Empedocles:

> I know—
> ...it hath been granted me
> Not to die wholly, not to be all enslaved.
> I feel it in this hour. The numbing cloud
> Mounts off my soul; I feel it, I breathe free....

Thus Empedocles, not hopelessly, springs to meet his extinction.

Penetrated as Arnold was by the ideas of Obermann, it was inevitable that many of them should find their way into the long philosophic poem of *Empedocles*. It is, nevertheless, still with some surprise that one is obliged to recognise how very forcibly the character and thought of Obermann are recalled in *Empedocles*. Indeed, it might be said of the Sicilian philosopher of Arnold's version, as Vigny said of his *Moïse*, that he is truly 'plus moderne qu'antique'![1]

---

[1] In a letter to Mademoiselle Camilla Maunoir, December 27, 1838. A figure to outward seeming far removed from the cold, solitary hero of *Empedocles*, and yet in whom certain traits announce a resemblance, is that of Benjamin Constant. Constant indeed belongs securely to this group of tortured souls, of restless spirits suffering the agonies of tedium and disenchantment. Like Obermann, and Arnold's Empedocles, 'he could not live with other men, and he could not live alone'. (See Anatole France, 'Le Journal de Benjamin Constant', in *Œuvres Complètes*, vol. VI, *La Vie Littéraire*, p. 68.) In one mood he would exclaim: 'Solitude! Solitude!...I cannot describe my joy at being alone'; and in the next breath: 'In reality I can dispense with nothing'. Like Obermann, a refined epicurean, he desired 'all joys, those of the great and those of the humble'; and when he found frozen old age approaching he burst into the same kind of frenzied lament at the passing of the years of passion. *Adolphe* and the *Journal* contain the history of this fevered soul who, like Arnold in youth, and even more audaciously than René, so ardently 'longed for storms'. Such words were 'signs of the times'.

CHAPTER XI

POEMS OF 1852 CONTINUED: ASCETICISM AND STOICISM

In the shorter poems of the remaining third section of the volume of 1852, many of the ideas we have noted in *Empedocles* reappear; but others are added, and those that are repeated are cast in settings variously beautiful, so that a possible danger of monotony is converted into merely a grave consistency. We shall not err, therefore, in pointing out these shades in thought and expression as they are exhibited here, our consideration receiving its own unity by its constant reference to the thought of Senancour.

Memorial verses, the first poem of the section, are in honour of Wordsworth, whose feeling for Nature had passed naturally to the child brought up in nearness and devotion to him. What is stressed in this tribute is Wordsworth's healing power, and, above all, his reviving influence on spirits withered by the world.

Courage, the next of these poems, is an expression of the stoical spirit which the young poet had made his ideal, and after which in the end he did not strive in vain. This poem, like *Destiny*, was never reprinted in his lifetime,[1] perhaps wisely, for the style is undistinguished. For the sake of the thought, however, and to show Arnold's early admiration for two exemplars of the stoic doctrine, the Roman Cato and the English Byron, it will deserve full quotation here:

1 It is, however, included in the excellent edition of Arnold's poems in the World's Classics Series published by the Oxford University Press, with an introduction by Sir A. T. Quiller-Couch.

Courage

True, we must tame our rebel will:
True, we must bow to Nature's law:
Must bear in silence many an ill;
Must learn to wait, renounce, withdraw.

Yet now, when boldest wills give place,
When Fate and circumstance are strong,
And in their rush the human race
Are swept, like huddling sheep, along;

Those sterner spirits let me prize,
Who, though the tendence of the whole
They less than us might recognise,
Kept, more than us, their strength of soul.

Yes, be the second Cato prais'd!
Not that he took the course to die—
But that, when 'gainst himself he rais'd
His arm, he raised it dauntlessly.

And Byron! let us dare admire
If not thy fierce and turbid song,
Yet that, in anguish, doubt, desire,
Thy fiery courage still was strong.

The sun that on thy tossing pain
Did with such cold derision shine.—
He crush'd thee not with his disdain—
He had his glow, and thou hadst thine.

Our bane, disguise it as we may,
Is weakness, is a faltering course.
Oh that past times could give our day,
Join'd to its clearness, of their force!

The ideas of the first two or three stanzas are familiar echoes now. And the appeal of the last is one which Obermann, in rare brave moods, had also made.

'La force est la loi de la nature: la puissance c'est la volonté: l'énergie dans les peines est meilleure que l'apathie dans les voluptés', says the author of the *Manuel de Pseusophanes*;[1] and elsewhere Obermann reports with approval the saying: 'Nous n'avons peut-être reçu la vie présente que pour rencontrer, malgré nos faiblesses, des occasions de remplir avec énergie ce que le moment veut de nous'.[2]

Self-Dependence, which follows *Courage*, reads almost like a poetic rendering of the first few pages of *Obermann*. The 'air-born voice' invoked in the last verse is perhaps that of Senancour himself, and not of Nature or the impersonal spirit, to whom the first stanzas appear to be addressed—Senancour, in whom Arnold had in truth heard 'long since, severely clear', the cry that now breaks from his own heart: 'Resolve to be thyself!'

For this is the counsel which Senancour had given on the eve of his departure for the mountain-valleys:

Soyons d'abord ce que nous devons être.[3]

Weary of myself, and sick of asking,
  What I am, and what I ought to be,

says the poet, almost repeating the words of Obermann; and turns in this mood of dejection to interrogate the sea and stars, and seek an answer from them:

'Ye who from my childhood up have calm'd me
Calm me, ah, compose me to the end...'.

From the intense, clear, star-sown vault of heaven,
Over the lit sea's unquiet way,
In the rustling night-air came the answer:
'Wouldst thou *be* as these are? *Live* as they.

Unaffrighted by the silence round them,
Undistracted by the sights they see,
These demand not that the things without them
Yield them love, amusement, sympathy'.

1 *Obermann*, Manuel, vol. I, p. 112.   2 *Obermann*, XCI, vol. II, p. 238.
3 *Id.* I, vol. I, p. 7.

Obermann, dreaming of the quiet mountain retreat, whither his childish memories called him, had already sought and received the same answer. The conviction of a self-dependent inner life as the first necessity of a contented and liberated mind is summed up in his words: 'La vie réelle de l'homme est en lui-même, celle qu'il reçoit du dehors n'est qu'accidentelle et subordonnée.... Les différences positives du sort ne sont pas les causes principales du bonheur et du malheur des hommes'.[1]

And Obermann describes his abandonment of a too exacting attitude towards the world of external things and men: the *jour d'irrésolution* which preceded his decision was *un jour de lumière*. 'J'ai joui', he says, 'pour la première fois de la conscience de mon être... forcé d'être quelque chose, je fus enfin moi-même; et dans ces agitations je trouvai une énergie, d'abord contrainte et pénible, mais dont la plénitude fut une sorte de *repos* que je n'avais pas encore éprouvé.'[2]

Thus the calm which Arnold desired, entered into Obermann; as the stars, 'unaffrighted' and 'undistracted' by passion, seemed to Arnold to possess this power to confer repose, so man, by following their example, would receive it.

'Ainsi', says Obermann, '*employer toutes ses forces à propos, et sans passion comme sans crainte*, ce serait être pleinement homme.'[3]

For this is the life Nature has prescribed to him who seeks her balance and repose.

> ... With joy the stars perform their shining,
> And the sea its long moon-silver'd roll;
> For self-poised they live, nor pine with noting
> All the fever of some differing soul.
>
> Bounded by themselves, and unregardful
> In what state God's other works may be,
> *In their own tasks all their powers pouring*,
> These attain the mighty life you see.

1 *Id.* 1, vol. 1, p. 5.   2 *Ibid.*   3 *Obermann*, XCI, vol. 11, p. 238.

Obermann with Arnold had realised the inspiring example of Nature. 'Profondeurs de l'espace', he addresses them passionately, 'serait-ce en vain qu'il nous est donné de vous apercevoir?'[1]

And so he too exhorts his fellow-men, much as Arnold counsels himself: 'Soyons d'abord ce que nous devons être. . . . Ainsi, quoi qu'il arrive, et sans sollicitations étrangères, nous disposerons des choses, non pas en les changeant elles-mêmes . . . mais en maîtrisant les impressions qu'elles feront sur nous . . . ce qui maintient davantage notre être en le circonscrivant'.[2]

For it is only 'dans l'indépendance des choses, comme dans le silence des passions, que l'on peut s'étudier'.[3] So Obermann asserts, and so Arnold entitles his poem *Self-Dependence*, summing up in one word the train of Obermann's reflections: 'Je dois rester, quoi qu'il arrive, toujours le même et toujours moi, . . . tel que je me sens, tel que je veux être, tel que je suis dans cette vie intérieure, seul asile de mes tristes affections'.[4]

> O air-born voice! long since, severely clear,
> A cry like thine in mine own heart I hear:
> 'Resolve to be thyself; and know that he
> Who finds himself, loses his misery!'

A Summer Night contains the same yearning for the peace of Nature, and the possession of his own soul. The psychological motive is the return of the sadness that assails the poet in his struggle to forget what he has resigned, who feels himself

> Never by passion quite possess'd
> And never quite benumb'd by the world's sway.

'Qui suis-je donc', Obermann had asked, in the same dilemma, 'quel triste mélange d'affection universelle et d'indifférence pour tous les objets de la vie positive?'[5]

---

1 *Obermann*, xc, vol. ii, p. 231.   2 *Id*. i, vol. i, p. 7.   3 *Ibid*. p. 8.
4 *Obermann*, iv, vol. i, p. 27.   5 *Ibid*. p. 23.

Two melancholy alternatives only seem open to man; that which is offered by a life circumscribed and calm; and that to which he is drawn by an illusory sense of his own powers and a goal to win.

We have seen how Vigny was obsessed by the same sad sense of contradiction,[1] asking

> pourquoi l'âme est liée dans sa faible prison;
> Et pourquoi nul sentier entre deux larges voies,
> Entre l'ennui du calme et des paisibles joies
> Et la rage sans fin des vagues passions.

> Is there no life, but these alone?
> Madman or slave, must man be one?

asks Arnold in *A Summer Night*.

The same opposition, and even the same image, had struck Obermann. 'C'est le propre de *l'insensé*', he says, 'de prétendre lutter contre la nécessité. Le sage reçoit les choses telles que la destinée les donne.... Que lui servirait de chercher à éviter *des chaînes?*'[2] And again, 'Malgré sa liberté apparente, [l'homme] ne peut pas plus produire au dehors des actes de sa vie que celui qui consume la sienne dans un cachot'.[3]

> For most men in a brazen prison live,
> Where, in the sun's hot eye,
> With heads bent o'er their toil, they languidly
> Their lives to some unmeaning taskwork give,
> Dreaming of nought beyond their prison-wall.
> And as, year after year,
> Fresh products of their barren labour fall
> From their tired hands, and rest
> Never yet comes more near...
> Death in their prison reaches them,
> Unfreed, having seen nothing, still unblest.[4]

1 See chap. VI, pp. 82 and 84.   2 *Obermann*, XLI, vol. I, p. 160.
3 *Id.* XLIII, vol. I, p. 179.
4 As in Vigny's *Journal d'un Poète*, pp. 63–4.

And the rest, a few,
Escape their prison and depart
On the wide ocean of life anew.
There the freed prisoner, where'er his heart
Listeth, will sail...
Awhile he holds some false way...
And then the tempest strikes him; and between
The lightning bursts is seen
Only a driving wreck...
Still bent to make some port he knows not where,
Still standing for some false, impossible shore.
And sterner comes the roar
Of sea and wind, and through the deepening gloom
Fainter and fainter wreck and helmsman loom,
And he too disappears, and comes no more.

What are we to do with our lives then, asks Obermann
sadly; 'végéter stupidement...ramper énervé dans la bassesse
de l'esclave ou la nullité de la foule....Ainsi, jouet lamentable
d'une destinée que rien n'explique, l'homme abandonnera sa vie
aux hasards et des choses et des temps. Ainsi...il se hâte d'un
pas riant et plein d'audace vers la nuit sépulcrale'.[1]

At the conclusion of *A Summer Night*, a kind of solution is
proposed by the invocation of Nature's example, 'untroubled
and unpassionate', to man.

Plainness and clearness without shadow of stain!
Clearness divine!
Ye heavens, whose pure dark regions have no sign
Of languor, though so calm, and, though so great,
Are yet untroubled and unpassionate;
Who, though so noble, share in the world's toil,
                    ...you remain
A world above man's head, to let him see
How boundless might his soul's horizons be,
How vast, yet of what clear transparency!

1 *Obermann*, XLI, vol. I, p. 165.

And remembering Obermann, making his ascent to the region of perpetual snows on the Dent du Midi, we are recalled to that lonely figure, solitary before the *néve* fields, and how he found, as he says, in the 'ciel immense', and the 'air plus fixe' of that altitude an 'ordre' and 'harmonie' within himself, like that he felt without. There it was that, momentarily, Obermann had had the rare sensation of discovering his true self.[1]

So the English poet invites man similarly to find an escape, a widening of his 'soul's horizons', in the contemplation of the clear, untroubled heavens. But while Arnold ceases on this more optimistic note, it is characteristic of Obermann, returning from his glimpse of a freer life, that he should say sorrowfully: 'En redescendant sur la terre habitée, je sentis que je reprenais la longue chaîne des sollicitudes et des ennuis'.[2]

The Buried Life, the poem next in order in this volume, is one of Arnold's most beautiful and expressive pieces; in inspiration it repeats the same sense of inner loneliness as had overcome the poet when reading *Ortis* with Marguerite; when he had sadly realised how it is ordained our souls must always dwell in isolation. And though, on moonlit nights, when the song of the nightingale sounds and the breath of spring is in the air, there is an impulse, not faint but strong and full of yearning, to believe that the shores of the world were meant to be united, and 'parts of a single continent'; yet it is not so:

> A God, a God their severance ruled!
> And bade betwixt their shores to be
> The unplumb'd, salt, estranging sea.[3]

In these lines the poet had confessed to Marguerite his melancholy sense of their estrangement. The same difficulty in establishing a way between their two minds then, is the theme

---

1 *Id.* VII, vol. I, p. 44.
3 *To Marguerite: continued.*   2 *Ibid.* p. 49.

here in *The Buried Life*. And, in this poem, it gives rise to other sad reflections, on the barriers set between man and his fellows, and even the concealment in which a man's inmost identity seems to lie cloaked from his very self.

> Alas! is even love too weak
> To unlock the heart, and let it speak?
> Are even lovers powerless to reveal
> To one another what indeed they feel?
> I knew the mass of men conceal'd
> Their thoughts, for fear that if reveal'd
> They would by other men be met
> With blank indifference, or with blame reprov'd;
> I knew they lived and moved
> Trick'd in disguises, alien to the rest
> Of men, and alien to themselves—and yet
> The same heart beats in every human breast!

There is a shadow of the same sadness in Obermann's desire that men should live transparent lives, their thoughts known to other men, and uncertainty banished from the earth.

'Si les hommes sont presque tous dissimulés', he says, 'si la duplicité des uns force au moins les autres à la réserve, n'est-ce pas une nécessité qu'ils joignent au mal inévitable que plusieurs cherchent à faire aux autres en leur propre faveur, une masse beaucoup plus grande de maux inutiles.'[1] 'I should be happy', he says a little further on, 'if men's thoughts were known.'[2]

But in life this is not given us. The stream of our being, in Arnold's thought, pursues its 'indiscernible' way, hidden not only from others, but even from ourselves; while we are unceasingly harassed by distractions that almost obscure the unity of our real self.

> Fate, which foresaw
> How frivolous a baby man would be—

---

1 *Obermann*, XIV, vol. I, p. 69. 2 *Ibid*. p. 70.

By what distractions he would be possess'd,
How he would pour himself in every strife,
And well-nigh change his own identity—
That it might keep from his capricious play
His genuine self, and force him to obey
Even in his own despite his being's law,
Bade through the deep recesses of our breast
The unregarded river of our life
Pursue with indiscernible flow its way;
And that we should not see
The buried stream, and seem to be
Eddying at large in blind uncertainty
Though driving on with it eternally.

This is strangely like the saying of Obermann, that he must
escape the contentious atmosphere of society and seek in solitude
his 'vie réelle'. 'C'est une nécessité', he says, 'que l'homme
naturel soit sans cesse altéré, en respirant cette atmosphère
sociale si épaisse, si orageuse, si pleine de fermentation, toujours
ébranlée par le bruit des arts, le fracas des plaisirs ostensi-
bles. . . .'[1]

In an effort to recover himself Obermann had retreated to
the heart of Nature: for there only 'l'homme retrouve sa forme
altérable mais indestructible'; there 'il respire l'air sauvage loin
des émanations sociales; son être est à lui comme à l'univers:
il vit d'une vie réelle dans l'unité sublime'.[2]

But the stupefying power of the world can be combated in
another and a gentler way. Obermann had known it; and
Arnold fancied he had.

'L'harmonie qui fait le lien universel', says Obermann,
thinking of the woman he had loved, 'tout cela est dans l'*œil*
d'une femme. Tout cela, et plus encore, est dans la *voix* illimitée
de celle qui sent. . . .'

1 *Obermann*, VII, vol. I, p. 43.   2 *Ibid*. p. 44.

Under this melting influence the barriers had seemed to fall away for Arnold too.

Only—but this is rare—
When a belovéd hand is laid in ours,
When, jaded with the rush and glare
Of the interminable hours,
Our eyes can in *another's eyes* read clear,
When our world-deafen'd ear
Is by the tones of a *loved voice* caress'd—
A bolt is shot back somewhere in the breast,
And a lost pulse of feeling stirs again.
The eye sinks inward, and the heart lies plain,
And what we mean, we say, and what we would, we know.
A man becomes aware of his life's flow,
And hears its winding murmur. . .

And an unwonted calm pervades his breast.
And then he thinks he knows
The hills where his life rose,
And the sea where it goes.

In other, but still beautiful words, Obermann had spoken of the power of love to awaken and reveal hidden or forgotten truths:

Une grâce qui entraîne tout, une éloquence douce et profonde, une expression plus étendue que les choses exprimées, l'harmonie qui fait le lien universel, tout cela est dans l'œil d'une femme. Tout cela, et plus encore, est dans la voix illimitée de celle qui sent. Lorsqu'elle parle, elle tire de l'oubli les affections et les idées: elle éveille l'âme de sa léthargie. . .la vie naturelle n'est plus la vie ordinaire. . . .Là, assise en repos. . .elle nous emporte, elle nous précipite avec elle dans le monde immense et notre vie s'agrandit de ce mouvement sublime et calme. Combien, alors, paraissent froids ces hommes qui se remuent tant pour de si petites choses! [the thousand nothings of the hour] dans quel néant ils nous retiennent, et qu'il est fatigant de vivre parmi des êtres *turbulens et muets*![1]

1 *Obermann*, XL, vol. I, p. 154.

To this influence of love, the world's power to benumb the soul, to silence the 'airs, and floating echoes' of that 'infinitely distant land' where it dwells, had yielded. But the influence was, for Obermann as for Arnold, only of love as it came to them in memory, and contained elements sorrowful as well as calming. Obermann had lost the one who had brought to him this ideal sympathy, and it is the very sense of its preciousness and rarity that heightens his regret.

'Elle sentait comme moi', he says in a despairing passage, 'une même langue nous était commune: sont-ils si nombreux ceux qui s'entendent?' [1]

And so even the calm of the passions he had longed for beyond all else seemed, in his loneliness, but a sad possession. 'La paix elle-même est un triste bien', he says, 'si on n'espère point la partager.' [2]

To the English poet and lover of Marguerite, the same sentiments—the desire for freedom from passion, and the shrinking from the solitude involved by this renunciation, are combined; in the thought of the peace he will have 'in the eternal Father's smile' [3] is contained the lingering hope that for him and his love communion in repose will be theirs at last. This is the conclusion of *A Farewell*:

> And we, whose ways were unlike here,
> May then more neighbouring courses ply;
> May to each other be brought near,
> And greet across infinity.
>
> How sweet, unreach'd by earthly jars,
> My sister! to maintain with thee
> The hush among the shining stars,
> The calm upon the moonlit sea!

1 *Id.* LXXXIX, vol. II, p. 223.   2 *Id.* XV, vol. I, p. 76.
3 *A Farewell.*

How sweet to feel, on the boon air,
All our unquiet pulses cease!
To feel that nothing can impair
The gentleness, the thirst for peace—

The gentleness too rudely hurl'd
On this wild earth of hate and fear;
The thirst for peace a raving world
Would never let us satiate here.

The theme of *The Buried Life* is woven round an image which occurs so often in Arnold that it is almost to be regarded as part of his philosophy of life, if, in a broad sense, he may be said to possess one. This is his image of life as a current or stream which flows silently within man, or on which he is ceaselessly borne along—a piece of Heracleitan metaphysic which Arnold may well have received from Senancour.

The image takes slightly different forms in different poems. In *The Buried Life*, the current appears as the course of man's inner life; in *A Dream* it is represented as the 'river of Life', in *The Future* as the 'river of Time'; and it occurs as 'life's stream' in *In Utrumque Paratus*, as the 'stream of life' in *Progress* and in *To a Gipsy Child*. In two other poems, *A Summer Night* and *Self-Dependence*, the image is of man borne by the flow of ocean waters. But always the picture is the same, of a flow or course of water bearing man onward.

The idea is perhaps no more than a general one, sprung from the familiar consciousness of the passage of time. But it is singularly in keeping with the general stoical character of Arnold's thought that it should contain this element. It will be remembered that the notion of flux is cardinal to stoic doctrine. 'One can never step into the same river twice', Heracleitus had said; and the Stoics had been quick to seize on this idea for their own purposes, 'the flux of all things and the vanity of life' being ideas that readily lent themselves to association.

Senancour, we have seen, took over the idea from Montaigne, and was chiefly occupied with the thought of his own place in this universal movement. At one time he desires to maintain the integrity of his self in independence, and in despite of it; and again he appears to resign himself to swim with the tide, but only in order to maintain another kind of unity in continuity. 'Ainsi est agitée, au milieu de l'air, la cime d'un arbre trop flexible; et, si vous la regardez à une autre époque, vous la verrez céder encore, mais céder de même.'[1]

'Je dois rester toujours le même et toujours moi', is a characteristic utterance. But, considering unity under another aspect than that of changeless identity, 'la mobilité qui me caractérise', says Obermann, '...est constamment une grande inconstance'.[2] And he recommends[3] that we do not resist the perpetual movement of life, but that we commit ourselves to it with confidence. First let us take up our place as befits our nature, 'puis livrons-nous au cours des choses, en nous efforçant seulement de nous maintenir semblables à nous-mêmes', so that, as Arnold says, we shall not

seem to be
Eddying at large in blind uncertainty,
Though driving on with it eternally.

The idea of the world-current as time, and of the essence of life as duration, is the aspect of this thought which Bergson has made familiar in our time in the form of a new theory of knowledge.

Obermann, seated before his mountain torrent, had inevitably speculated on the same idea. To his mind the movement of the water resembled the flight of time, with something eternal in

1 *Obermann*, XC, vol. II, p. 232. 2 *Ibid.* p. 231. 3 *Obermann*, I, vol. I, p. 7.

its flow which contrasted with the intermittent sounds of humanity that floated out towards him from the distance.

Je me trouvais placé [he says] au détour de la vallée, entre les rocs d'où le torrent se précipite, et les chants que j'avais moi-même ordonnés; ils commençaient au loin. Mais ces bruits de fête, le simple mouvement de l'air les dissipait par intervalles, et je savais l'instant où ils cesseraient. Le torrent au contraire subsistait dans sa force, s'écoulant, mais s'écoulant toujours, à la manière des siècles. La fuite de l'eau est comme la fuite de nos années. On l'a beaucoup redit, mais dans plus de mille ans on le redira: le cours de l'eau restera, pour nous, l'image la plus frappante de l'inexorable passage des heures.[1]

In *The Future*, the last number of the volume of poems we are discussing, Matthew Arnold uses the simple poetic form of this fancy; Time is envisaged as a river and man the wanderer upon it. On this image he embroiders a familiar accessory thought, of the contrast between the life of the mountains and that of the plains, and the differing fates of man according as he belongs to the rise of the stream in the silent uplands, or to its issue on the populous plains—which latter spot represented for Arnold the point which our civilisation has reached to-day.

> This tract which the river of Time
> Now flows through with us, is the plain.
> Gone is the calm of its earlier shore.
> Border'd by cities and hoarse
> With a thousand cries is its stream.
> And we on its breast, our minds
> Are confused as the cries which we hear,
> Changing and shot as the sights which we see.

It is here, 'sur les terres basses', that Obermann, sighing, had also complained of man, consuming 'sans en jouir, sa durée inquiète et irritable'. In such an environment it is a necessary

1 *Obermann*, XC, vol. II, p. 230.

consequence that man should be 'sans cesse altéré'. 'Jamais le silence n'a été connu dans les vallées tumultueuses', he says in the beautiful passage describing his ascent of the Dent du Midi; 'ce n'est que sur les cimes froides que règne cette immobilité, cette solennelle permanence que nulle langue n'exprimera, que l'imagination n'atteindra pas.'[1]

But in Arnold, the hope that man will one day 'drink of the feeling of quiet again' is not abandoned. The river of Time, winding its way on to the great Ocean, renews in its last phase the hush of its early days; and, while the current freshens at contact with the outer waters, peace descends again on the soul of man, floating out under the stars to the murmurous sea.

1 *Id.* vii, vol. i, p. 47.

CHAPTER XII

OTHER POEMS OF 1852: NATURE IN ARNOLD AND SENANCOUR

The beautiful poem in memory of the author of *Obermann*, whose place and source of inspiration we spoke of in describing Arnold's travels in the Alps, divides *The Buried Life* from the next poem in the section, *Consolation*. *Consolation*, a short-stanza'd, unrhymed poem, contains further reflections on the passage of time, which flows on impartially through our happy or our distressed hours. There is surely here a reminiscence of Lamartine, in the image of the 'two young, fair lovers', who

> Where the warm June-wind,
> Fresh from the summer fields
> Plays fondly round them,
> Stand, tranced in joy,
>
> With sweet, join'd voices,
> And with eyes brimming:
> 'Ah', they cry, 'Destiny,
> Prolong the present!
> Time, stand still here!'

The prayer is Elvire's, gliding with Lamartine by night over the 'harmonious waves' of the Lac du Bourget:

> O temps, suspends ton vol! et vous, heures propices,
> Suspendez votre cours!
> Laissez-nous savourer les rapides délices
> Des plus beaux de nos jours![1]

'For the unhappy, hasten; for us who are joyous, stay a little....' But already, as she spoke, the dawn had broken, and dissolved the beauty of the night.

[1] *Le Lac.*

To Matthew Arnold, recognising that such favour shown to the happy must only prolong the wretchedness of the mourner, there is consolation in the swift passage of time.

The *Lines Written in Kensington Gardens*, with their peaceful imagery of birds and quivering grass and rural life, again recall the idea of escape from the world, 'which roars hard by', into the universal calm of Nature. The poet strikes gently the note of vague pantheism which Obermann in his happiest moods had before him sounded.

> I, on men's impious uproar hurl'd,
> Think often, as I hear them rave,
> That peace has left the upper world
> And now keeps only in the grave.
>
> Yet here is peace for ever new!
> When I who watch them am away,
> Still all things in this glade go through
> The changes of their quiet day...
>
> Calm soul of all things! make it mine
> To feel, amid the city's jar,
> That there abides a peace of thine,
> Man did not make, and cannot mar.

All through Obermann's thought runs the same desire. He, too, longs to flee from the vain fermentation of the 'atmosphère sociale' and its baneful influences. And he, like Arnold, had clung to his vision of the 'calme universel',[1] enveloping the workings of Nature, as an antidote to the sterile 'agitation des terres humaines'.[2]

But both Arnold and Obermann were not satisfied to desire this repose and submission for themselves only. It is charac-

---

1 *Obermann*, VII, vol. I, p. 45.   2 *Ibid.*

teristic of both that they should have a yearning for fellow-feeling and sympathy with other men.

> The will to neither strive nor cry,
> *The power to feel with others give.*[1]

This unworldly wish places Arnold with those of whom Obermann wrote—and among whom he also desired to be counted—who 'ne peuvent être bien qu'au milieu des hommes contens, *qui se sentent dans tout ce qui jouit et souffre*, et qui ne sauraient être satisfaits d'eux-mêmes que s'ils contribuent à l'ordre des choses et à la félicité des hommes'.[2]

For how should life be happy, says Obermann again, 'sans accord avec les choses, et passée au milieu des peuples souf-frans?'[3] The possession of the faculty of sympathy is here assumed, which requires happiness to be universal, before it is possible. It is part of the definition of 'culture' which Arnold was later to plead for, that it should be not an individual, but a *general* social movement, to perfection and happiness.

The last two of the *Lines Written in Kensington Gardens* return to another oft-repeated thought of Obermann, pro-longing, as it were, the very echo of his sadness:

> Calm, calm me more! *nor let me die*
> *Before I have begun to live.*

The thing which Obermann dreaded, and which is the chronic source of his weariness, is the impending sense of such a death in life. In one of his most beautiful letters, which we are sure Arnold had closely perused because of certain verbal echoes in his *Stanzas in memory of the author of 'Obermann'* (see chap. VIII), there occurs the striking passage in which

---

1 In Shelley's idealistic philosophy (as elaborated in *Prometheus Unbound*) the hope is obscurely hinted at, that evolution may be holding in reserve for man the possibility of attainment of a sixth sense, more spiritual than the other five—that of sympathy with his fellow-creatures.

2 *Obermann*, XLIV, vol. I, p. 190.   3 *Id.* VII, vol. I, p. 45.

Obermann describes how his youth was filled with dreams of living a 'real life'; which, however, eluded him on the very threshold of life; and how, to his despair, the weariness of life had been his portion at an age when one is only beginning to live. In his own words, 'Dès que je sortis de cette enfance..., j'imaginai, je sentis, une vie réelle; mais je n'ai trouvé que des sensations fantastiques: je voyais des êtres, il n'y a que des ombres...alors le vide creusa mon cœur..., et l'ennui de la vie fut mon seul sentiment *dans l'âge où l'on commence à vivre*'.[1] It is surely this kind of death in life, and not physical death, of which Arnold is dreaming in the quiet glade where he lies at ease, and which he prays to have averted:

> Nor let me die
> Before I have begun to live.

For the 'ennui de la vie' of which Obermann speaks was a kind of cessation of being. At the end of this letter he explains the feeling in a mournful piece of imagery. Like the fir tree placed by chance on the swamp's edge, he too at first reared himself up proudly, as its brother the forest-tree—vain energy! Its roots submerged in ooze suck up only fetid waters; the stem weakens. The summit, unresisting in the water-laden winds, droops dejectedly; the fruit, rare and poor, falls into the mud and uselessly perishes. 'Languissant, informe, jauni, vieilli avant le temps et déjà incliné sur le marais...sa vie a cessé longtemps avant sa chute': long before its fall, its life has ceased.[2] Of himself, he says also, 'My end is missed, my life is lost and sterile; it is already stricken with death'.[3]

We have seen, and shall see again, Matthew Arnold taking a meaning phrase from another's thought to round off harmoniously his own.

---

1 *Id.* LXXV, vol. II, pp. 148–9.   2 *Ibid.* p. 150.
3 *Obermann*, XLIII, vol. I, p. 181.

Following the *Lines Written in Kensington Gardens* is a characteristic little piece, *The Second Best*. The classic ideal of moderation, and *le juste milieu*, was in accord with Arnold's deepest instincts, however his sensibility might rebel on occasion. The poem as a whole, with its rather disenchanted expression, is redeemed from banality by the distinction of the thought, particularly of the last stanzas:

> No small profit that man earns...
> Who each day more surely learns

> That an impulse, from the distance
> Of his deepest, best existence,
> To the words, 'Hope, Light, Persistence',
> Strongly sets and truly burns.

Is there here a reminder of Senancour's saying in the *Rêveries*, with its expression of an ideal hardly less modest than Arnold's:

'La vie n'est qu'un laborieux mouvement d'espérance'— 'Life is but a painful movement of hope'; the hope that, laboriously conceived, had come to Senancour 'one day of light'?[1]

The idea of 'persistance', or 'permanence', or 'constance', we know to be a typical concept in *Obermann*. So clearly is this so, that, according to Sainte-Beuve, as we have seen, if one word might appropriately be singled out to represent the pervading thought of any writer, for Senancour that word would be 'permanence'.[2]

---

1 *Obermann*, I, vol. I, p. 5.
2 Michaut, in the *Notice Bibliographique* to his critical edition of *Obermann*, objects that Senancour designedly changed or omitted this word from his writings in three places in *Obermann*, as though he did not wish to give it the prominence of an habitual concept. On the other hand, the innumerable cases in which the word is retained, and indeed made the kernel of many passages —a core round which to group ideas of harmony or contrast—are significant. It was evidently an early obsession. 'Triste et indéfinissable opposition', he

Nature essentiellement méditative [says Sainte-Beuve], il a surtout visé au juste et au vrai...il s'est consacré avec une rigueur presque ascétique à la recherche du solide et du *permanent*. Chaque écrivain a son mot de prédilection, qui trahit ...chez celui qui l'emploie, un vœu secret ou un faible....La devise...de Senancour est assurément *Permanence*. Cette expression résume sa nature. L'élévation dans la permanence, c'est la maxime favorite qui domine et abrite en quelque sorte sa vie....Son idée se trahit constamment sous la forme morale; c'est tout au plus si de loin en loin il la couronne de quelque grande image naturelle.[1]

It is a striking testimony to the affinity between Arnold and Senancour to discover a modern critic making use of words very much like Sainte-Beuve's, to apply to Matthew Arnold.

'The deepest passion of his life', says this writer,[2] 'was for what is permanent in the human mind and the human heart.' And again, 'The careful reader of these letters [to Clough] will see Arnold's constant effort to live by what is permanent, to seek some principle by which he can possess his spirit'.

In both Arnold and Senancour the idea of permanence is primarily a moral conception; an ideal to which each aspires, but which he does not find in the commerce of his own, feverish kind. And both, alike disappointed by the world, turn to Nature, whose changeless purity and 'permanence silencieuse'[3] appear to them like a symbol of the moral peace they desire.

says in the *Rêveries* (ed. J. Merlant, 1910, p. 16) '*du tout permanent et sublime à l'individu souffrant et mortel*'. In *Obermann*, in the one case where the word 'permanence' is suppressed, it was probably omitted as unnecessary, as stressing a word which Senancour may have felt he had used only too often— for reasons of style, in short [Letter xxxviii]. In the case where 'permanence' is replaced by 'persévérance' [Letter i], the latter word is applied not to a state of things, as generally, but to a 'sage'; and might well be considered more fitting as an epithet applied to character. In Letter lxx he significantly changed it to 'constance'.

1 *Portraits Contemporains*, vol. i, pp. 162–3.
2 H. F. Lowry, *op. cit.* Introduction, p. 36.
3 *Obermann, Troisième Fragment*, vol. i, p. 149.

In *Revolutions* the thought is again that of the instability of
human things. The poet concludes with the hope that the cycles
of rise and decline will at last terminate with the 'word' and
'the order, which God meant should be'; and for which the
changes were the inevitable preparation. The idea is perhaps no
more than vaguely reminiscent of the Eastern notions discussed
at an earlier stage in this study.

Two important poems, *The Youth of Nature* and *The Youth
of Man*, are concerned with the relation of Nature to man, and
provide us with Arnold's reflections on a problem that had, very
much in the same way, occupied Obermann also.

In *The Youth of Nature*, the transitory life of man, even of the
man of genius (Wordsworth), whose power had seemed
actually to confer immortality on the senseless things of Nature,
is wistfully affirmed.

> Nature is fresh as of old,
> Is lovely; a mortal is dead.

The Spirit of Nature, to whom the poet addresses himself,
with a yearning to have this conviction denied, reveals herself
and corroborates it. The poet asks,

> For, oh! is it you, is it you,
> Moonlight, and shadow, and lake,
> And mountains, that fill us with joy,
> Or the poet who sings you so well?
> Is it you, O beauty, O grace,
> O charm, O romance, that we feel,
> Or the voice which reveals what you are?
> Are ye, like daylight and sun,
> Shared and rejoiced in by all?
> Or are ye immersed in the mass
> Of matter, and hard to extract,
> Or sunk at the core of the world

Too deep for the most to discern?
Like stars in the deep of the sky,
Which arise on the glass of the sage
But are lost when their watcher is gone.[1]

This is pure subjective idealism; we have already seen Arnold refuting the notion in the *Lines Written in Kensington Gardens*:

When I who watch them am away,
Still all things in this glade go through
The changes of their quiet day.

To the question addressed her the 'Mighty Mother' returns answer, and herself asserts her eternal changelessness, her inexhaustible resources and life-giving power, to the passing shade of man.

When your great ones depart, will ye say:
'All things have suffered a loss,
Nature is hid in their grave?'

She concludes, and there is compassion, but also something relentless and unswerving, in her conclusion:

Race after race, man after man,
Have thought that my secret was theirs,
Have dream'd that I lived but for them,
That they were my glory and joy.
—They are dust, they are changed, they are gone!
I remain.

The Youth of Man continues and completes the thought of the first poem by introducing the point of view of arrogant man, who asserts his supremacy over cold and inanimate Nature. Two lovers, in the spring and pride of life, are supposed to speak:

1 For this image, see the reference, in chap. x, to *Obermann*, XLVIII, vol. II, p. 19.

We are young, and the world is ours;
Man, man is the king of the world!
Fools that these mystics are
Who prate of Nature! for she
Hath neither beauty, nor warmth,
Nor life, nor emotion, nor power.
But man has a thousand gifts,
And the generous dreamer invests
The senseless world with them all.
Nature is nothing; her charm
Lives in our eyes which can paint,
Lives in our hearts which can feel.

Now this hesitation between a conception of Man which would give him, in spite of all his frailty, so immense an advantage over Nature; and the other, of his complete subjection to her, is a constant preoccupation with Obermann. In moments of exceptional exaltation he had assigned to man and man's consciousness, the supreme control of things and matter. At such times, he had upheld the claim that 'la pensée seule conserve, transforme et accroît la réalité';[1] the power of thought alone fills reality with life and continuity. With this conviction, he writes: 'La moralité de l'homme, et son enthousiasme, l'inquiétude de ses vœux, le besoin d'extension qui lui est habituel, *semblent annoncer que sa fin n'est pas dans les choses fugitives*; que son action n'est pas bornée aux spectres visibles; que sa pensée a pour objet les concepts nécessaires et éternels'. It would appear, he says again, that it is man's purpose in the universe to refine and elaborate matter, give it energy and an organised being, power, perfection, and fertility.[2] And, in presence of one of his loved Alpine scenes, he will make the truth tally with his desire, and impute to Nature no more than the power to reflect the sentiments and consciousness of man.

1 J. Merlant, *Sénancour*, p. 105.   2 *Obermann*, XLII, vol. I, p. 176.

'Monts superbes', he begins, apostrophising the natural objects round him, 'écroulement des neiges amoncelées, paix solitaire du vallon dans la forêt, feuilles jaunies qu'emporte le ruisseau silencieux! que seriez-vous à l'homme si vous ne lui parliez point des autres hommes? *La nature serait muette, s'ils n'étaient plus*....La nature sentie n'est que dans les rapports humains, et *l'éloquence des choses n'est rien que l'éloquence de l'homme.* La terre féconde, les cieux immenses, les eaux passagères ne sont qu'une expression des rapports que nos cœurs produisent et contiennent.'[1]

To this claim, Obermann does not seriously hold for long. 'Ces conceptions étendues', he says, with a sad sense of relinquishment, 'ces conceptions étendues qui rendent l'homme si superbe et si avide d'empire, d'espérances et de durée, sont-elles plus vastes que les cieux réfléchis sur la surface d'un peu d'eau de pluie qui s'évapore au premier vent?'

> —Like stars in the deep of the sky,
> Which arise on the glass of the sage,
> But are lost when their watcher is gone.

And so, 'Hommes d'un jour', says Obermann, 'qui projetez en vieillissant, et qui raisonnez, pour un avenir reculé quand la mort est sur vos pas, *en rêvant des illusions* consolantes dans l'instabilité des choses, n'en sentirez-vous jamais le cours rapide? ne verrez-vous point que votre vie s'endort en se balançant, et que cette vicissitude qui soutient votre cœur trompé ne l'agite que pour l'éteindre dans une secousse dernière et prochaine?'[2]

With this sense of our mortality heavy on him Arnold begins *The Youth of Man*:

1 *Id.* XXXVI, vol. I, p. 132.
2 *Id.* XLI, vol. I, p. 159.

We, O Nature, depart,
Thou survivest us! this,
This, I know, is the law.
Yes! but more than this,
Thou who seest us die
Seest us change while we live.

The last three lines express the same melancholy truth that
Obermann had observed. 'Si la vie de l'homme'—so he concludes the passage above—'était perpétuelle, si seulement elle
était plus longue, *si seulement elle restait semblable jusque près
de sa dernière heure...*! Mais y a-t-il quelque permanence dans
la vie?'

Not in the life of man, assuredly. But in Nature, yes, its
presence there is a sign indubitable and clear even to our obscure
vision. Looking up at the majesty of the calm, quiet, luminous
sky, Obermann had the same sensation as Arnold of enduring
Nature. 'Il y a là une permanence qui nous confond: c'est
pour l'homme une effrayante éternité. Tout passe; *l'homme
passe, et les mondes ne passent pas!*'[1]

In vain the lovers protest, in Arnold's poem, their scorn and
independence. Nature is represented as remaining mute, years
passing, changes coming, and the young lovers changing too,
and recognising with tears, that they have grown old, while
Nature has endured young. If they could retrace the years and
call back the past, they would, with undeluded eyes, now
acquiesce with Obermann: 'Je ne fais point de sermens, je ne
fais point de vœux; je méprise ces protestations si vaines, cette
éternité que l'homme croit ajouter à ses passions d'un jour'.[2]

For the passing of life, in the course of the ages, is the story
of a day, soon told: 'Ce voile ténébreux, ces rafales orageuses,
ces lueurs pâles, ces sifflemens à travers les arbres qui plient et

---

1 *Obermann*, XVI, vol. I, p. 73.   2 *Id.* LXXXIX, vol. II, p. 226.

frémissent, ces déchirements prolongés...; voilà le matin de la vie: à midi, des tempêtes plus froides et plus continues; le soir, des ténèbres plus épaisses, et la journée de l'homme est achevée'.[1]

This melancholy assurance of the brevity of life has turned men often enough to indulgence in sensibility or epicurean pleasures. Nor was Arnold at first exempt from some longings and indecision on this score. But it is proof of the moral ascendency Senancour exercised over him, that he was not long in discarding these in favour of a more ascetic ideal, like that towards which Senancour was to work in later life, and which already we see him struggling to gain in *Obermann*. But in *Obermann* the gain is not yet complete; Arnold is in advance of Senancour here, and a remnant of early hedonism makes the latter's utterance a little faltering beside the firmer temper of Arnold.

And yet in Arnold also, this temper is not at times without its wayward impulse to weakness and regret. *Morality* and *Progress*, the last two poems still to be considered in the volume of 1852, show this mingled strength of purpose and depression.

Morality begins with a bold exhortation to courageous action and perseverance. But the poem soon allows to peep through the old undercurrent of discouragement. To the poet, struggling with such difficulty to accomplish so little, the spectacle of Nature's serene achievement contains reproach and even blame.

> With aching hands and bleeding feet
> We dig and heap, lay stone on stone...
> Then, when the clouds are off the soul,
> When thou dost bask in Nature's eye,
> Ask, how *she* view'd thy self-control,
> Thy struggling, task'd morality—
>> Nature, whose free, light, cheerful air,
>> Oft made thee, in thy gloom, despair.

1 *Id.* xi, vol. i, p. 59.

And she, whose censure thou dost dread,
Whose eye thou wast afraid to seek,
See, on her face a glow is spread,
A strong emotion on her cheek!
　'Ah, child!' she cries, 'that strife divine,
　Whence was it, for it is not mine?

'There is no effort on *my* brow—
I do not strive, I do not weep;
I rush with the swift spheres and glow
　In joy, and when I will, I sleep....'

This attribution to Nature of what man would fain share but
which seems denied him—a calm, or even joyful, spirit in
labour—is not new in Arnold: Obermann had seen Nature in
an identical light, and it is hard to think that an idea so sympathetic to Arnold was not one of the first he had seized on in
reading Obermann. 'She, whose censure thou dost dread', had
also made her reproach to Obermann; 'sa paix', 'son apparente
immobilité' for him too had seemed like 'un reproche à notre
maladive inquiétude'.[1]

　'Ah, child!' she cries, 'that strife divine
　Whence was it, for it is not mine?'

says the World-Mother to Arnold, chiding our restless humanity. And Obermann had felt the same implied rebuke in
her presence. Once during a voyage on the lake by night, this
consciousness had overcome him in a quite special way; he
describes the scene, how the nightingale had been singing its
melody of olden times, 'ce chant des nuits heureuses', and how
he (Obermann) gliding over the lake, had had that revelatory
glimpse of celestial worlds in action, which in truth came to him
often enough in these moods. Nature then seemed to him *too*

---

1 J. Merlant, *Sénancour*, p. 113.

beautiful, 'trop belle', he says, and the elements—water, earth and night—too happy, 'trop heureuses'. It was as though their beauty and happiness were filled with reproach for a heart unquiet like his; as he expressed it in his own mystical way, 'la paisible harmonie des choses fut sévère à mon cœur agité'— 'the serene harmony of nature was a rebuke to my restless heart'.[1]

And stricken profoundly with her majesty, he exalted her in his heart above his own mean strivings: 'Nature impénétrable', he says, 'ta splendeur m'accable'.[2] But instead, like Arnold, of taking a lesson from this majesty and calm of natural things, Obermann was oppressed and discouraged. 'La navrante harmonie de leurs soirées célestes fatigue les cendres de mon cœur.' 'The piercing harmony of their celestial eventides brings weariness to the ashes of my heart.'

This reproach of Nature to man, less acute and less sorrowful in the English poet than in Obermann, was vivid enough to Arnold's consciousness for him to place it repeatedly in his poems: we have seen it before in *Self-Dependence* and in *Quiet Work*, in *The Lines Written in Kensington Gardens*, and in *Empedocles on Etna*. All these poems repeat the message of Nature to Obermann; with this difference, that the pessimism of Obermann is mitigated in Arnold, and that what to the French romantic was sometimes a source of impotence and gloom was to Arnold a vindication of that spiritual life of the Universe, in whose truth and reality he would never come to disbelieve.

Progress, the last of the poems left to be discussed (*The Future*, the final piece in this volume, has already received mention in another connection), contains an anticipatory frag-

1 *Obermann*, LXIII, vol. II, p. 72.
2 *Id.* LXXV, vol. II, p. 148.

ment of the thought Arnold worked out in detail in his later religious writings. The idea of tolerance, of all religious conceptions containing a germ of divine truth, and the need of seizing on this truth to fortify the soul, to enable us 'to think clear, feel deep, bear fruit well', was an idea already current in the middle of the century; and nowhere more so than in France. The French had in fact taken from German religious criticism ideas which, inaccessible to all but specialists, would have been lost without their renewed life under the less austere and more persuasive Gallic touch. The movement had been initiated by the appearance of Dr Kreuzer's treatise on the symbolism of the religions, and its translation during the period 1825 to 1849 by Guigniaut. But before this date, Benjamin Constant in 1824, and Edgar Quinet in 1841, had popularised the more important of Kreuzer's ideas. In brief, the principal of these was an affirmation of the value of the religious sentiment in all religions. In Quinet's words, 'in our historical review of religions'— 'dans ce pèlerinage à travers les cultes du passé. . . , *nous n'irons pas. . .nous railler* de la misère *des dieux abandonnés*: au contraire, nous demanderons aux vides sanctuaires *s'ils n'ont pas renfermé un écho de la parole de vie*; nous chercherons dans cette poussière divine. . .quelque débris de vérité'. Evidence, to be adduced later, will seem to indicate that the *Génie des Religions*, from which these words are taken, was not unknown to Arnold.

In Leconte de Lisle, and more conspicuously in his friend Louis Ménard, the idea had become apt for poetical treatment. According to Ménard, 'pour l'intelligence qui embrasse dans leur harmonie les révélations successives du divin, chaque affirmation de la conscience humaine est un des rayons de l'universelle vérité'.[1]

1 *Les Rêveries d'un païen mystique: Le Banquet d'Alexandrie.*

It is not surprising then to find Arnold expressing this sentiment in his own way:

> Children of men! the unseen Power, whose eye
> For ever doth accompany mankind,
> Hath look'd on no religion scornfully
> That men did ever find.

'Nous n'irons pas...nous railler...des dieux abandonnés.'

The lesson Arnold characteristically drew from this conviction was the necessity of cherishing the precious element which in the last resort lay within all these different religious creeds, 'the ray of universal truth' of which Ménard speaks.

> Leave then the Cross as ye have left carved gods,
> But guard the fire within!

And thus Arnold upholds the substance of Ménard's saying, 'Un peuple qui a renié ses dieux est un peuple mort'.[1] We cannot despise the central truth which has given all religions, present and past, their hold over human nature—their common power to sustain and purify the flagging, dust-soiled soul.[2]

Of Senancour's anticipation of this thought, his plea that men establish their faith on something more spiritual than dogma or superstition, we shall have to speak later in another connection.[3] Only here let us mention that the *épigraphe* Arnold

---

1 *Les Rêveries d'un païen mystique: Le Voile d'Isis.*
2 A question unsolved is that concerning the possibility of influence from Arnold upon Louis Ménard. Ménard in exile, on the eve of the Second Empire, had passed from Belgium to England on more than one visit: in 1852, the year of publication of *Empedocles on Etna and other Poems*, he was living in Soho for a time (H. Peyre, *Louis Ménard*, Newhaven, 1932, p. 86). Did he see this book, and, if so, take from it the idea for an Empedocles of his own? [Other parallels between Quinet, Arnold and Ménard will appear during the consideration of Arnold's religious writings.]
3 We can do no more here than refer to the frequent occurrence of this thought in *Obermann*, and its undeniable similarity, extended even to the manner of expression, to the same idea in Renan and in Arnold. In Letter LXXXI (vol. II, p. 184) Obermann speaks decisively of this necessity, '*de ne plus fonder sur ce qui s'écroule [notre] asile moral*'; so that when with the course of time

will choose to place, beside a longer quotation from Bishop
Butler, on the title-page of his great work in defence of religious
inwardness—*Literature and Dogma*—will be a saying from his
favourite *Obermann*.

men come to despise those lesser religious ideas now habitually received with
the higher, they may perceive '*qu'elles peuvent très-bien être séparées sans que
l'oubli de l'une entraîne la subversion de l'autre*'. (See also above, p. 157.)

Words and idea are almost those of Renan, writing fifty years later. 'La
religion', he says, 'de nos jours, ne peut plus se séparer...de la culture de
l'esprit. J'ai cru la servir en essayant de la transporter dans la région de
l'inattaquable, au delà des dogmes particuliers et des croyances surnaturelles.
Si celles-ci viennent à crouler, il ne faut pas que la religion croule...' (Preface to
the *Essais de Morale et de Critique*, pp. ii–iii).

Arnold's adaptation of this sentiment in *Literature and Dogma* is better
known: 'Culture then, and literature are required, even in the interest of
religion itself (*Works*, vol. VII, p. 387)....The sanction of Christianity, *if
Christianity is not to be lost along with its miracles*, must be found elsewhere
(p. 147)'.

CHAPTER XIII

POEMS OF 1853: *THE SCHOLAR-GIPSY, PHILOMELA, THE CHURCH OF BROU*

Obermann would have gladly lived the life of a Scholar-Gipsy. For a little while, in his Fontainebleau days, his way of living, his hopes and still fresh aspirations, perhaps brought him nearer the contentment of ideal fancies than he would ever be again. Like one of the primitive wood-folk, he roamed the glades by night, trod the sandy hollows marked by the track of a doe or hare in flight, or watched the sad moonlight playing on the ravaged white bark of the birch tree; then, as the dawn broke, plunged into the deeper wood.[1]

But Obermann never really cared for flat scenes and smooth horizons; where, as it seemed to him, a mere accident to the vegetation, or some other passing feature, could change the whole character of the landscape. In the Alps the feeling for permanence, denied in the low-lying forest, was satisfied.

It is pleasant to reflect that Arnold, however deeply sharing this feeling, nevertheless set many of his loveliest poems in English scenes, and was, by his affection for the intimate, beautiful details of Nature, still within the long tradition of English poetry. 'A green thought in a green shade' was his often enough, as well as the sublimer reflection provoked before some wondrous Alpine scene; and delicate impressions received from playing breezes, the shining back of a swallow, the sound of a punt rope unrolling—these 'shy to illumine' others, to him as to his Gipsy Scholar, remained always a source of 'the fugitive and gracious' light they both had sought.

1 *Obermann*, XI, vol. I, p. 58, and XIX, vol. I, p. 76.

The Scholar-Gipsy would seem, then, to be of purely English and Oxford inspiration. Yet we cannot fail to notice traits in this wanderer that make him kin with the Alpine Obermann. His love of retirement, his relinquishment of the world, his fancied immunity to death and languor, all place him beside the ideal figure of Senancour's dreams. Both Arnold and Senancour, indeed, were joined in their common desire to substitute truth for vagueness, fixity for wavering, resolution for vain unrest; and to this wished-for state, the Gipsy Scholar had seemed to hold the clue. Both suffered from the emptiness of an age which had lost faith, which knows no creed to which the heart and reason alike can give assent; and here again the Scholar-Gipsy had comfort to offer. For he had lived untroubled by such doubts: long since he had opened his heart to receive the awaited divine spark.

In this character of the Scholar-Gipsy the poet thus personified his own ideal hopes; and it would seem, some of Senancour's also. But where Arnold was strong, and Senancour weak, was in their different manner of reaching to their ideal. Obermann was apt to lose the form and even the meaning of his desires in mystical, unending reverie. Matthew Arnold understood, as the argument in *The New Sirens* showed, the necessity of crystallising ideas out of fluid dreaming. He knew, indeed, by experience just how far he could mellow thought with sentiment; and at what point the latter would become mere aimless divagation; while the overcharged reflection of Obermann had in it some unreasonable element which often sent it wandering down by-paths of vague feeling; and there, unreconciled and still repining, was lost.

Arnold's melancholy is more often under control; and like the delicate light-vibration that reveals the essential symmetry at the heart of amorphous matter, so his 'sad lucidity of soul' reaches continually into and penetrates the mass of formless sentiment.

This keen perception in Arnold, and his greater gift of creative expression, are what give him his immeasurable advantage over Senancour, whose sad lot it was, as George Sand pityingly said, to have been conceded the temperament, without the full *faculties*, of great genius.

The Scholar-Gipsy dates from 1853. In this year also appeared another poem which seems in part inspired by a memory of Obermann; this is *Philomela*.

The ancient myth of the nightingale might seem beautiful enough to have alone suggested the idea of the poem. But the poet, pacing the dewy lawn he describes beside the tranquil Thames, may well have had another image in his mind, of a past night like this one, when the moon had silvered the branches of a mountain-birch tree as she now whitened the cedar on the lawn. In night and dew and moonshine, he may have remembered how Obermann had also listened to the nightingale, placing 'de loin en loin' in the unquiet calm, its solitary song, 'unique et répété, ce chant des nuits heureuses, sublime expression d'une mélodie primitive, *indicible élan d'amour et de douleur*, voluptueux comme le besoin qui me consume; simple, mystérieux, immense comme le cœur qui aime'.

'Song of happy nights, sublime expression of an old-world melody, *untold impulse of love and pain*, beautiful like consuming desire; simple, grand, full of mystery like love.'[1]

[1] *Obermann*, LXIII, vol. II, p. 72. This passage had struck George Sand too. In the *Lettres d'un Voyageur* (VI, à Éverard, 22 avril 1835), describing a night in the garden at Nohant, she says: 'Les grands sapins élèvent leurs masses noires et vagues dans l'air grisâtre. La nature n'est pas belle ainsi, mais elle est solennelle et parle à un seul de nos sens, celui dont le rossignol parle si éloquemment à un être créé pour lui. Tout est silence, mystère, ténèbres...il semble que tout se taise pour écouter et recueillir avidement cette voix brûlante de désirs et palpitante de joies que le rossignol exhale. *O chantre des nuits heureuses!* comme l'appelle Obermann....O Dieu! mon Dieu, je suis encore si jeune!'

Hark! ah, the nightingale—
The tawny-throated!
Hark, from that moonlit cedar what a burst!
What triumph! hark!—what pain!

O wanderer from a Grecian shore, . . .
Still nourishing in thy bewilder'd brain
That wild, unquench'd, deep-sunken, *old-world pain*—
Say, will it never heal?
And can this fragrant lawn . . .
And moonshine, and the dew,
To thy rack'd heart and brain
Afford no balm? . . .

Listen, Eugenia—
How thick the bursts come crowding through the leaves!
Again—thou hearest?
Eternal passion!
Eternal pain!

We shall return to Arnold's fondness for the images which were also Obermann's favourites, a little later.

Among the other contents of the *New Edition* of 1853 (afterwards to be known as *First Series*) appeared a poem which Arnold had founded on a passage in Edgar Quinet. This was Quinet's *Des Arts de la Renaissance: L'Église de Brou*, in the volume of his *Mélanges* of 1839.[1] Quinet's article had already appeared in separate form as the introduction to a small volume of verses, written in honour of the church at Brou, and entitled: '*L'Église de Brou*, poème, par M. G. de Moyria, précédé d'une introduction par M. Edgar Quinet; suivi de stances sur le même sujet, par MM. L. Bruys et X. Marmier' (Bourg, imp. P.-F. Bottier, 1835).

[1] This discovery was made by Professor Ch. Cestre, who discusses it in 'The Church of Brou de M. Arnold', *Revue Germanique*, 1908, pp. 526–38; he, however, makes no mention of the original French poem of the same name. See also Sir E. Cook, *Literary Recreations*, pp. 294–6.

Arnold does not appear to have used this French poem, which is a somewhat ecstatic narrative of the events surrounding the lives of Marguerite de Bourbon and Marguerite d'Autriche, the two women who instigated the building of the church. Of Marguerite d'Autriche, the heroine of the poem, Matthew Arnold certainly ignored the real history, for he brings her as a bride to Savoy straight from the court of Vienna. But in fact Marguerite of Austria before her arrival in Savoy had already been affianced, and almost wed, to Charles VIII of France. The match not taking place, the King of Aragon was next selected as her husband. On her way to Spain she had nearly perished at sea, and it was at this moment that she is supposed to have fastened to her arm a casket containing the words:

> Cy git Margot, la gentil damoiselle
> Qu'eut deux marys, et si mourut pucelle.

But Margot lived after all to wed, first the King of Aragon, and then Philibert de Savoie, at whose death she resolved to carry out the project of her predecessor, Marguerite de Bourbon, to build a church to enshrine her husband's remains. It is with this part of the story that Quinet's introduction is concerned, and it is consequently to this episode that Arnold confines his poem.

Quinet had been brought up in the vicinity of Bourg-en-Bresse, where the Church of Brou is situated, and, in his account, he was drawing directly upon his early memories. But the circumstances of the building of the church, which Arnold was to make his theme, were not given in very great detail; and the poet, using these somewhat slight indications, embroidered on them facts which were not always in accord with the reality.

Following Quinet, Arnold omits to name Philibert II, the duke who had met his death while hunting and occasioned the building of the church; contenting himself with referring to him as 'Savoy's duke'.

With characteristic enthusiasm for Alpine scenery, Arnold next proceeded to place the burial-place of the Dukes of Savoy in the mountains, ignoring, or not troubling to ascertain, that they were Counts of Bresse as well as Dukes of Savoy, and that Bourg actually stands amid no mountains, but in a flat country of forest and swamps. Quinet gives a short description of this country, the 'Dombe', a land 'triste et malfaisante', where even the daylight falls with 'une mélancolie infinie', while at night the sinister will-o'-the-wisps alone lighten the darkness.[1]

Arnold, in haste or indolence, did not observe these details, and discovering his mistake later,[2] attempted to disguise the precise local reference of *The Church of Brou* by omitting two parts (in the *New and Complete Edition* of 1877) and renaming the third, *A Tomb among the Mountains*; the difficulty was at last only solved by a frank claim for poetic licence and the republication of the poem in its original form, in 1881.

But Quinet had none the less furnished Arnold with many authentic details. Curiously enough, some of these details occur immediately after the long descriptive passage about the plain of Bresse, which, if Arnold had heeded it, would have saved him from his uncomfortable mistake. The picturesque description of the 'sandall'd palmers', and of the working train of 'Flemish carvers, Lombard gilders', and 'German masons', was derived from information supplied by Quinet.[3] So too the mention of the duchess's old architect is merely a translation of

1 In G. de Moyria, *L'Église de Brou*, introduction par M. Edgar Quinet, p. 12. (This introduction is reprinted in *Œuvres Complètes d'Edgar Quinet*, 1877–82, vol. VIII, *Premiers Travaux*, pp. 291–308.)

2 That the mistake was made unintentionally is clear from his remark to Oscar Browning, referred to by Sir E. Cook (*op. cit.* p. 295, note).

3 In G. de Moyria, *L'Église de Brou*, introduction par M. Edgar Quinet, p. 14.

her 'vieil architecte', referred to by Quinet.[1] And at the beginning of Part III the description of the young prince who will
never again arise to ride and hunt all day, and come home
benighted to his waiting lady, seems founded on the dream
attributed to Marguerite of Austria in Quinet's version—of the
day when she will rest beside her husband, '*quand les fanfares
ne sonneront plus pour la chasse, quand son époux sur son cheval
fougueux ne poursuivra jamais le sanglier dans la forêt, et qu'elle
n'attendra plus en vain jusqu'à la nuit*. . .'.[2]

Arnold's lines recall this passage:

> So rest, for ever rest, O princely Pair. . .
> *Where thou,* young Prince! *shalt never more arise*
> From the fringed mattress where thy Duchess lies,
> On autumn-mornings, *when the bugle sounds,*
> And ride across the drawbridge with thy hounds
> *To hunt the boar* in the crisp woods till eve;
> And thou, O Princess! shalt no more receive. . .
> The jaded hunters with their bloody freight
> *Coming benighted to the castle-gate.*

The grandeur of the apostrophe to the kingly pair, which
constitutes the third part of Arnold's poem, is due to an
intrinsic beauty of sentiment and diction that can hardly at any
point be called derived. Nevertheless the paragraph in which
Quinet had evoked the dreams of the sleeping marble pair
supplied not only the germ and sequence of the thought, but,
above all, the harmonious last line of Arnold's lyrical address.

In Quinet the dreams are carried on as a dialogue between
the duke and his lady,

qui dorment *leur sommeil de marbre* [dans le silence de la nef
déserte]. Qui pourrait raconter leur songes *plus blancs que
l'albâtre des tombeaux? Quand leurs froides paupières se soulèvent,*
ils voient les arceaux sur leurs têtes, *la lumière transfigurée des*

1 *Ibid.* p. 19.   2 *Ibid.*

vitraux, la Vierge et les Saintes immobiles à leurs places; et ils pensent en eux-mêmes: c'est ici l'éternité. Et *quand le vent* fait gémir les portes, ils murmurent entre eux: Qu'avez-vous, mon âme, pour soupirer si haut? et *quand la pluie creuse le toit sur leurs têtes, ils se disent: Entendez-vous aussi sur votre dais la pluie de l'éternel Amour?*[1]

The vision of the smiling saints, the cold stone eyelids raised to regard them, the vaults above, and the transfigured light of the stained glass—these reappear in Arnold. And the thought of the royal pair, awakening to an imagined eternity, and listening to the wind, and to the rain bringing its message of love, is also repeated in Arnold:

—So rest, for ever rest, O princely Pair!
In your high church, 'mid the still mountain air,
Where horn, and hound, and vassals, never come.
Only the blessed saints are smiling dumb,
From the rich painted windows of the nave,
On aisle and transept, and your marble grave....

So sleep, for ever sleep, O marble Pair!
Or, if ye wake, let it be then, when fair
On the carved western front a flood of light
Streams from the setting sun, and *colours bright*
Prophets, transfigured Saints and Martyrs brave,
In the vast western window of the nave;
And on the pavement round the Tomb there glints
A chequer-work of glowing sapphire-tints,
And amethyst, and ruby—*then unclose*
Your eyelids on the stone where ye repose,
And from your broider'd pillows lift your heads,
And rise upon your cold *white marble beds;*
And, looking down on the warm rosy tints,
Which chequer, at your feet, the illumined flints,
Say: What is this? we are in bliss—forgiven—
Behold the pavement of the courts of Heaven!

1 E. Quinet, in *op. cit.,* pp. 20–1.

Or let it be on autumn nights, *when rain*
Doth rustlingly above your heads complain
On the smooth leaden roof...
And the wind washes through the mountain-pines.
Then, gazing up 'mid the dim pillars high,
The foliaged marble forest where ye lie,
Hush, ye will say, *it is eternity!*...
And, in the sweeping of the wind, your ear
The passage of the Angels' wings will hear,
And on the lichen-crested leads above
The rustle of the eternal rain of love.

Dost thou not also hear upon your dais, say the duke and his lady in Quinet's version, the rain of eternal Love?

Among the poems of 1849 had appeared one of which the inspiration had seemed too beautiful and too purely ideal for us to seek in it a local or a personal reference: this is *The Forsaken Merman.*[1] Yet it may perhaps without trifling be noticed how the poet had here introduced a name, which had long enjoyed his exceptional favour—that of 'Margaret'; not perhaps insignificantly linked in the poem with the theme of desertion. In *The Church of Brou* we see the name again appearing—it is true here with an historical justification: Marguerite is the lonely princess who superintends the building of the monument which is to contain herself and her noble husband. If Arnold had known more of the history of this incident, he need not have let go another occasion to introduce the word, and have called the duke's mother, who bore in fact the name of Marguerite de Bourbon, the 'Duchess Maud'. Or was it with intent that he chose to reserve the name for the faithful wife of the dead duke?

[1] For the possible source of the theme of *The Forsaken Merman* from Danish or German folklore, see the article of Ch. Cestre cited above, p. 526.

CHAPTER XIV

POEMS OF 1853 CONTINUED:
SOHRAB AND RUSTUM

A light is thrown on Arnold's attitude to his sources, and the extent to which he believed himself obliged to them, by the *Note* written to *Sohrab and Rustum* on its second appearance in 1854. From this *Note* we learn that *Sohrab and Rustum*, the first poem in the *New Edition* of 1853, owed its original inspiration to a passage of Sainte-Beuve's in his review of Jules Mohl's translation and edition of the *Livre des Rois* (Shāhnāma, or 'Book of Kings') by the Persian poet Firdousi, or Ferdousi.[1]

'Le plus célèbre épisode du poëme', says Sainte-Beuve, in the course of his analysis,[2] 'et qui est de nature à nous intéresser encore, a pour sujet la rencontre du héros Roustem et de son fils Sohrab.' He continues: 'C'est une belle et touchante histoire qui a couru le monde, qui a refleuri dans mainte ballade en tout pays, et que bien des poëtes ont remaniée ou réinventée à leur manière, jusqu'à Ossian dans son poème de *Carthon* et jusqu'à Voltaire dans sa *Henriade*. Voltaire n'avait pas lu assurément Ferdousi, mais il a eu la même idée, celle d'un père, dans un combat, aux prises avec son fils, et le tuant avant de le reconnaître'.

The peculiar interest of such a situation, and its aptness for a new poetic treatment, struck Matthew Arnold also; reading this passage, he did not hesitate to avail himself of the invitation it offered to contribute yet another version of the story. The

1 Lundi, 11 février, 1850. Sainte-Beuve, *Causeries du Lundi*, vol. 1, pp. 332–50.
2 *Ibid*. p. 343.

Note which he added to his poem, in the year of its second appearance, was provoked by an attack on its originality.

The beginning of this *Note* artlessly recapitulates the story of *Sohrab and Rustum* as told in Sir John Malcolm's *History of Persia*; this fragment was retained and appeared in editions of the poem subsequent to 1857. The second and much longer part of the *Note*, that which gives the summary of his obligations to Sainte-Beuve, was never reprinted. Arnold no doubt considered the acknowledgment it contained more than sufficient; nevertheless there is a certain incriminating quaintness in the discretion which dictated his later silence on the point. The matter was explained away honourably; what need therefore to multiply the chances of the question being raised again by perpetuating the explanation of it? So he may plausibly and justly have reasoned.

After the introductory excerpt from Sir John Malcolm's *History of Persia*, the poet had continued:

M. Sainte-Beuve, also, that most delightful of critics, in a notice of an edition of Ferdousi's great poem by M. Mohl now in course of publication at Paris, containing the original text and a prose translation, gives an analysis of this episode, with extracts from M. Mohl's translation, which I will quote at length: commencing from the point where Rustum leaves Tehmineh, the future mother of Sohrab, before the birth of her child; having given her an onyx with instructions to let the child wear it in her hair, if a girl, and on his arm, if a boy. Of M. Mohl's book itself I have not been able to obtain sight.

Arnold then adduces a long quotation from Sainte-Beuve, of which we give an abbreviated account as follows:

After his sojourn with the Turks, Rustum sets forth on his horse *Raksch*, and returns to Iran, where he hears only at long intervals of his child and its mother. The child's growth to manhood is attended by prodigies of valour; until at last one day, learning the name of his illustrious father, he resolves to seek him out. He is placed at the head of an army of Turks, and proceeds to challenge the Persian host. The king appeals to Rustum, who has at this point a premonition of the identity of the young warrior: 'il a l'idée d'abord que ce pourrait bien être son fils; mais non: ce rejeton de sa race est trop enfant, se dit-il. ...Roustem arrive pourtant; mais, mal accueilli par le roi, il entre dans une colère d'Achille, et il est tout prêt à s'en retourner dans sa tente'.

In Arnold's version, it will be remembered, Rustum is likewise presented as sullen in his tent and full of wrath against the king:

> Aloof he sits
> And sullen, and has pitch'd his tents apart.

He is, however, prevailed upon to accept the challenge, as in Sainte-Beuve's version, by the taunt that by his behaviour he will give colour to the insult that he dare not face a younger rival and imperil his name.

> Take heed, lest men should say:
> Like some old miser, Rustum hoards his fame,
> And shuns to peril it with younger men.

'On ne le fléchit', says Sainte-Beuve, 'qu'en lui représentant que s'abstenir en une telle rencontre, ce serait paraître reculer devant le jeune héros.' Then follows an incident in which Rustum introduces himself secretly into the Turkish camp, and sees, though unknown to him, his son. This incident is not reproduced by Arnold; nor another in which Sohrab in his turn demands of a prisoner the names of the chieftains in the opposing host, hoping to hear the name of his father, Rustum. The name is, however, withheld from him. 'Mais *Sohrab a beau ouloir forcer le secret, la fatalité l'emporte.*'

This prevailing idea, of a fatality guiding our destinies,

whose decrees are not to be withstood, was acceptable to
Arnold, and perhaps, indeed, determined his choice of the
theme:

> For we are all, like swimmers in the sea,
> Poised on the top of a huge wave of Fate,
> Which hangs uncertain to which side to fall.
> And whether it will heave us up to land,
> Or whether it will roll us out to sea,
> Back out to sea, to the deep waves of death,
> *We know not, and no search will make us know;*
> *Only the event will teach us in its hour.*

The description of the hand-to-hand encounter between
father and son engrosses the next few pages of Sainte-Beuve's
account:

> Roustem est appelé; il arrive, il se trouve seul en présence de
> son fils, et le duel va s'entamer. *La pitié, tout à coup, saisit le*
> *vieux chef, en voyant ce jeune guerrier si fier et si beau:*
> 'O jeune homme si tendre!' lui dit-il,[1] 'la terre *est sèche et*
> *froide, l'air est doux et chaud.* Je suis vieux; *j'ai vu maint champ*
> *de bataille,* j'ai détruit mainte armée, et je n'ai jamais été battu.
> ...Mais j'ai pitié de toi et ne voudrais pas t'arracher la vie. *Ne*
> *reste pas avec les Turcs; je ne connais personne dans l'Iran qui ait*
> *des épaules et des bras comme toi'.*

Arnold's version follows this passage very closely; the old
warrior is seized by compassion in the same way at the sight
of the young man.

> *And a deep pity enter'd Rustum's soul*
> *As he beheld him coming; and he stood,*
> And beckon'd to him with his hand, and said:—
> '*O thou young man, the air of Heaven is soft,*
> *And warm, and pleasant; but the grave is cold!*
> Heaven's air is better than the cold dead grave.
> Behold me! I am vast and clad in iron,

[1] It is not clear in Arnold's quotation of this speech that it is an extract made
by Sainte-Beuve from M. Mohl's translation of the poem.

And tried; and *I have stood on many a field*
Of blood, and I have fought with many a foe—
Never was that field lost, or that foe saved.
O Sohrab, wherefore wilt thou rush on death?
Be govern'd: *quit the Tartar host,* and come
To Iran, and be as my son to me,
And fight beneath my banner till I die!
There are no youths in Iran brave as thou'.

After this speech Sainte-Beuve continues the narrative:

En entendant ces paroles qui semblent sortir d'une âme amie,
le cœur de Sohrab s'élance, il a un pressentiment soudain; il
demande ingénument au guerrier s'il n'est pas celui qu'il cherche,
s'il n'est pas l'illustre Roustem. Mais le vieux chef, qui ne veut
pas donner à ce jouvenceau trop d'orgueil, répond avec ruse qu'il
n'est pas Roustem, et le cœur de Sohrab se resserre aussitôt;
le nuage qui venait de s'entr'ouvrir se referme, et la destinée se
poursuit.

The corresponding passage in Arnold's poem is rendered as
follows:

So he spake, mildly; Sohrab heard his voice,
The mighty voice of Rustum, and he saw
His giant figure planted on the sand,
      . . .hope filled his soul,
And he ran forward and embraced his knees,
And clasp'd his hands within his own, and said:—
'Oh, by thy father's head! by thine own soul!
Art thou not Rustum? Speak! art thou not he?'
    But Rustum eyed askance the kneeling youth,
And turn'd away, and spake to his own soul:—
    'Ah me, I muse what this young fox may mean!
False, wily, boastful, are these Tartar boys. . .'.

And Rustum, suspecting the young man of a vainglorious
desire to prate at some future date of his encounter with himself,
denies his identity; and by Arnold, too, the course of events is

attributed to some incognisable Fate. Sohrab, provoked by the accusation of boastfulness, is stirred to ire, and to consummate his destiny.

We resume the narrative as given by Sainte-Beuve: In the contest which now ensues, first swords and then clubs are used, when the swords are broken; 'nous sommes en plein âge héroïque'. At the end of the first day Rustum realises with astonishment that he has at last met his equal, 'presque son maître, et de sentir son cœur défaillir sans savoir pourquoi. Le second jour, au moment de reprendre la lutte, *Sohrab a un mouvement de tendresse*, et la nature, près de succomber, fait en lui comme un suprême effort. En abordant le vieux chef, il s'adresse à lui *le sourire sur les lèvres . . .*'.

In Arnold's version also, spears are soon replaced by clubs; Rustum seizes his club, but Sohrab avoids the blow and so has Rustum at his mercy; but now he hesitates and his heart misgives him.

And now might Sohrab have unsheathed his sword . . .
But he look'd on, and smiled, nor bared his sword.

He speaks:

'*Are they from Heaven, these softenings of the heart?*'

Sainte-Beuve at this point in the narrative now proceeds to quote Mohl's translation of the speech in which Sohrab implores Rustum to put up his club and sword, and seat himself with him on the ground, and with wine and talk celebrate their comradeship.

'Jette cette massue et cette épée de la vengeance, jette tout cet appareil d'un combat impie. *Asseyons-nous tous deux à terre, et adoucissons avec du vin nos regards courroucés. Faisons un traité, en invoquant Dieu, et repentons-nous dans notre cœur de cette inimitié. Attends qu'un autre se présente pour le combat,* et apprête avec moi une fête. Mon cœur te communiquera son

amour.... Puisque tu es né d'une noble race, fais-moi connaître ton origine; ne me cache pas ton nom, puisque tu vas me
combattre: *ne serais-tu pas Roustem?*'

In a similar way Arnold's Sohrab addresses his father:

'No, when I see thee, wrath forsakes my soul.
Thou say'st, thou art not Rustum; be it so!
Who art thou then, that canst so touch my soul?...
O thou old warrior, let us yield to Heaven!
Come, plant we here in earth our angry spears,
And make a truce, and sit upon this sand,
And pledge each other in red wine, like friends...
There are enough foes in the Persian host,
Whom I may meet, and strike, and feel no pang;
Champions enough Afrasiab has, whom thou
Mayst fight...
But oh, let there be peace 'twixt thee and me!'

To revert to Sainte-Beuve's summary:

Roustem, par sentiment d'orgueil, et *soupçonnant toujours une
feinte* de la part d'un jeune homme avide de gloire, dissimule
une dernière fois, et, dès ce moment, le sort n'a plus de trêve.
Toutes ces ruses de Roustem... tournent contre lui; il finit par
plonger un poignard dans la poitrine de son fils, et ne le
reconnaît que dans l'instant suprême.

Rustum in Arnold's poem responds with similar indignation
to the young warrior's proposal:

...While he spake, Rustum had risen,
And stood erect, trembling with rage...
...at last these words broke way:—
'Speak not to me of truce, and pledge, and wine!
Remember all thy valour; *try thy feints*
And cunning! All the pity I had is gone...'.

And the contest is resumed, and described with some elaboration by Arnold, until the moment when Rustum fatally pierces
his son's side. The revelation that he has slain his own son is at

last made, and the proof of it established by means of the seal pricked on Sohrab's arm. And now it is for the young man to console his father, in words heavy with the sense of fatality that fills these heroes of olden time, and reconciles them, uncomplaining, to their destiny.

Le jeune homme meurt avec résignation [concludes Sainte-Beuve], avec douceur, en pensant à sa mère, à ses amis, en recommandant qu'on épargne après lui cette armée qu'il a engagée dans une entreprise téméraire:

'Pendant bien des jours [he says, and here Sainte-Beuve is again quoting from his original] je leur ai donné de belles paroles, je leur ai donné l'espoir de tout obtenir; car comment pouvais-je savoir, ô héros illustre, que je périrais de la main de mon père?... Je voyais les signes que ma mère avait indiqués, *mais je n'en croyais pas mes yeux. Mon sort était écrit au-dessus de ma tête, et je devais mourir de la main de mon père. Je suis venu comme la foudre, je m'en vais comme le vent*; peut-être que je te retrouverai heureux dans le ciel'.

Ainsi parle en expirant cet autre Hippolyte, immolé ici de la main de Thésée.

This is the conclusion of Arnold's quotation from Sainte-Beuve; and in the speech which he similarly attributes to the dying Sohrab, he freely uses this ending, as follows:

'Father, forbear! for I but meet to-day
The doom which at my birth was written down
In Heaven, and thou art Heaven's unconscious hand.
Surely my heart cried out that it was thou,
When first I saw thee . . .
. . . but Fate trod those promptings down.
. . . *Fate, Fate engaged*
The strife and hurl'd on me my father's spear . . .
. . . *for like the lightning to this field*
I came, and like the wind I go away—
Sudden and swift, and like a passing wind.
But it was writ in Heaven that this should be'.

'Mon sort était écrit au-dessus de ma tête', says the poem. And remembering his mother, and entreating for the safety of his host, Sohrab dies, as in the original poem, promising peace to his father, when he shall at last have returned 'home over the salt blue sea'.

Arnold follows up his extract from Sainte-Beuve's review with some striking comments of his own on plagiarism, and with these the *Note* is concluded:

A writer in the *Christian Remembrancer* [he adds] (of the general tenour of whose remarks I have, assuredly, no right to complain) having made the discovery of this notice by M. Sainte-Beuve, has pointed out the passages in which I have made use of the extracts from M. Mohl's translation which it contains; has observed, apparently with blame, that I 'have not thought fit to offer a single syllable of acknowledgment to an author to whom I have been manifestly very largely indebted'; has complained of being 'under some embarrassment from not being sure how much of the treatment is Mr Arnold's own'; and, finally, has suggested that 'the whole work of M. Mohl may have been used throughout, and the study of antiquity carried so far as simply to reproduce an ancient poem as well as an ancient subject'.

It would have been more charitable, perhaps, had the reviewer, before making this good-natured suggestion, ascertained, by reference to M. Mohl's work, how far it was confirmed by the fact.

The reader, however, is now in possession of the whole of the sources from which I have drawn the story of *Sohrab and Rustum*, and can determine, if he pleases, the exact amount of my obligation to M. Mohl. *But I hope that it will not in future be supposed, if I am silent as to the sources from which a poem has been derived, that I am trying to conceal obligations, or to claim an absolute originality for all parts of it.* When any man endeavours to 'remanier et réinventer à sa manière' a great story, which, as M. Sainte-Beuve says of that of *Sohrab and Rustum*, has 'couru le monde', it may be considered quite certain that he has not drawn all the details of his work out of his own head. The reader is not, I think, concerned to ask, from what sources these have been drawn; but only how the whole work, as it stands, affects him. *Real plagiarism, such as the borrowing without acknowledgment of passages from other English poets— real dishonesty, such as the endeavouring to pass off the mere translation of a poem as an original work—are always certain enough to be discovered.* I must not be led on, from defending the morality of my imitation, to defend at length its aesthetics; but I cannot forbear adding, that it would be a most unfortunate scruple which should restrain an author, treating matter of history or tradition, from placing, where he can, in the mouths of his personages the very words of the old chronicle, or romance, or poem (when the poem embodies, as that of Ferdousi, the tradition of a people); and which should lead him to substitute for these any 'eigene grossen Erfindungen'. For my part, I only regret that I could not meet with a translation from Ferdousi's poem of the whole of the episode of *Sohrab and Rustum*; with a prose translation, that is: for in a verse translation no original work is any longer recognisable. I should certainly have made all the use I could of it. The use of the tradition above everything else, gives to a work that naïveté, that flavour of reality and truth, which is the very life of poetry.

We have not been disarmed by Arnold's frank invitation to the reader to 'determine. . . the exact amount of [his] obligation to M. Mohl'; this, and the more important debt to Sainte-Beuve, we have sufficiently pointed out. It is evident from these that we are not here in presence of any pervasive thought-influence. The borrowed matter is in fact limited for the most part to details of narration or description; for the idea of the theme can be justly conceded to be a universal property, and to attempt to recreate the atmosphere appropriate to it, though on the basis of suggestions from the original, is only what the poet has a natural right to claim. His adherence, for instance, to the idea of a fatality pursuing his personages is a necessary piece of imitation if the tone of the original story is to be preserved: incidentally the fact that this idea was also in accord with Arnold's own convictions is proof how far these always controlled his borrowings. The only serious criticism, indeed, that may be made of this particular practice is in the nature of a regret, shared by the poet himself, that his sources should have been utilised in such a very indirect way, as by reference to Sainte-Beuve's second-hand version.

Thus Arnold is not to be censured for having plagiarised ideas, or even words and phrases, from Sainte-Beuve; but—if for anything—for the cursory and negligent way in which he collected them; in particular, for having failed to discriminate, in his borrowings, between elements so disparate as Sainte-Beuve's summary of the poem and the extracts from Jules Mohl's translation of it. But, in fact, this easy manner of getting his material will prove almost a habit of Arnold in later life. The critic in the *Christian Remembrancer*, if he had known the poet better, would never have suspected him of putting himself to the trouble of searching out the original work on which Sainte-Beuve's review was founded. We shall have more particular occasion to refer to Arnold's habit of collecting his material, when we come to discuss the influence of his French masters on the later prose works—a habit dictated partly no doubt by carelessness, to a greater amount by the pressure of time and occupations; but, above all, by an almost uncritical and quite unreserved admiration of those masters.

Lastly, the claim is not perhaps to be disputed, that the reader can have no interest in the degree of originality of a piece of literature, but only in its aesthetic completeness; more disputable, perhaps, is the extent to which an author is justified in preserving, as his own, literal words and phrases, in the form in which they occur in his sources. Arnold has somewhat airily explained away these specific borrowings. He has done better to base their morality on the success of his re-creation, than on his denial of the need of any scrupulous acknowledgment. The poet's own contention is, indeed, his best apology, that the use of such borrowed material is justified in an author, provided that it is made contributory to the beauty of the whole. And that this proviso has been complied with, in the case of *Sohrab and Rustum*, no one will wish to dispute.

CHAPTER XV

NEW POEMS (1867): THE LANGUAGE AND IMAGERY OF ARNOLD AND SENANCOUR

In 1867 Matthew Arnold brought out the first edition of his *New Poems*. At the head of this volume appeared, for the first time as a whole since its publication in 1852, that poem which ranks with *Obermann* as one 'in which', as its author said, 'the suffering finds no vent in action; in which a continuous state of mental distress is prolonged, unrelieved by incident, hope, or resistance; in which there is everything to be endured, nothing to be done',[1]—*Empedocles on Etna*.

In *Thyrsis*, the succeeding poem, the Gipsy Scholar, who had wandered a little out of Arnold's life in recent years, again passes over the hillside into the poet's view, and lays a benedictory hand on the long mute pipes. And at that touch, the hoarse shout of the city dies away, and the youth-loving spirit of the wanderer, with its message of 'unconquerable hope', invades the poet's soul again, where he lies crying in mournful memory of that other companion of his quest, his dead friend Clough.

Thyrsis had appeared before its publication in 1867, in the July number of *Macmillan's Magazine* of the preceding year. The poem *Saint Brandan*, which follows, is much earlier, having been first printed in 1860.

Saint Brandan appears to have been inspired by a remark of Renan's,[2] in his essay on *La Poésie des Races Celtiques*, a fruitful

1 Preface to First Edition of *Poems* (1853), in *Irish Essays, Works*, vol. XI, p. 273.
2 As pointed out by Lewis F. Mott in 'Renan and Matthew Arnold', *Modern Language Notes*, Feb. 1918, vol. XXXIII, no. 2, note to p. 71.

source of inspiration to Matthew Arnold in other ways, to be elsewhere discussed. Arnold had met Renan for the first time the year before (1859), and refers to the meeting, and to the *Essais de Morale et de Critique* (which had just appeared, and in which this essay occurs), in a letter to his sister of December 24 in this year. Speaking of the characteristics of the Celts, Renan had instanced their kindliness and sympathy for weaker beings; he continues: 'Ce sentiment est un des plus profonds chez les peuples celtiques. Ils ont eu pitié même de Judas. Saint Brandan le rencontra sur un rocher au milieu des mers polaires: il passe là un jour par semaine pour se rafraîchir des feux de l'enfer; un drap qu'il avait donné en aumône à un lépreux est suspendu devant lui et tempère ses souffrances'.[1]

Saint Brandan is again mentioned[2] in company with a list of heroes including Arthur, Perceval and Merlin, as forming part of the spiritual legacy of Celtic literature to civilisation. The incidents of Arnold's ballad-poem closely correspond with the story as told by Renan, with the slight difference that the mercy extended to Judas is reduced from a sojourn in the snows of one day a week, to one hour a year. Nor is Judas allowed, by Arnold, the leper's cloak suspended before him to mitigate his sufferings; the holiday in the snows is the sufficient reward of his one charitable deed. On the other hand, apart from the poetic handling and development, there is very little elaboration of the legend as given by Renan. It seems unlikely, therefore, that Arnold had recourse to any other informant.

Three Sonnets on Rachel remind us of Arnold's early enthusiasm for her acting in French classical drama.

Two other sonnets, *Worldly Place* and *Anti-Desperation*,[3] resume and repeat Arnold's now firmly held ideal of the virtue

1 E. Renan, *Essais de Morale et de Critique* [1859], ed. 1929, pp. 394–5.
2 *Ibid.* p. 416.   3 Later entitled *The Better Part*.

of a pure life led for its own sake. The concluding line of the first of these poems is the conclusion also of Obermann's reflections: 'The aids to noble life are all within'.

The inspiration of this poem is a saying of Marcus Aurelius, whom Obermann also knew and admired. But while respecting the elements of grandeur, even of heroism, in the philosophy of the 'imperial sage', Obermann had drawn back, with characteristic wavering, from its complete acceptance.

'To sigh, yet not recede; to grieve, yet not repent', was a frame of mind to which he had not attained. One autumn Obermann had stayed a few weeks at Lyons, aiding the grape-pickers on the estate of a friend: he had found then, he says, in the simple occupations of that life a peace of mind and even a gentle contentment that more ambitious pleasures had failed to give. And for a little while, as he pushed his barrow of fruit to and fro between the trellised vines, and tasted at the close of day the still-warm milk poured for his supper, he had meditated on this humble way of living, and the possibility of finding happiness in a *milieu* so restricted. For 'I have seen', he says, 'the vanity of life, and in my heart I bear the principle of mighty passions, of the social sentiment, and of the philosophic order. I have read Marcus Aurelius without surprise—and comprehend the difficult virtues, even the heroism of the monastery. But,' he says, 'all this can animate my soul; it does not fill it. My barrow, with its fruit, sustains me better. . . .' [1]

Obermann, indeed, rarely attained to the attitude of finality and submission that distinguished Marcus Aurelius. Nor was the philosophy of resignation, as practised by the 'imperial sage', altogether Arnold's ideal. Matthew Arnold's final moral outlook involves a similar quest for renunciation and inwardness —qualities he had found Obermann seeking too—but it con-

---

[1] *Obermann*, IX, vol. I, p. 52.

tains also a challenge to effort and attainment which is not in
Marcus Aurelius, and which, perhaps, the latter hardly needed.
Nevertheless, this presence of effort makes Arnold's creed a
little more positive and bracing than that of Aurelius, to whom
submission had seemed to come easily, and to whom ac-
quiescence had not seemed difficult, nor inward purity a
sacrifice.

In *Anti-Desperation*, or *The Better Part*, the poet reiterates
Obermann's scorn of the weak hope of reward, or com-
pensation, in another life. Make the most of this one, is the
conclusion Arnold draws, the precept being taken, as by the
Cyrenaics, in its highest moral sense.

The whole of this group of sonnets is animated by the single
idea, the need of cultivating our inward and spiritual life.
Immortality, in another strain, repeats the summons to the
'here-now', and to the perfecting of our lives as we must live
them on earth. Is it nothing, Obermann had also asked, to live
life here on earth rationally and virtuously? is not such a mode
of living its own *raison d'être*? Why, then, must we for ever
seek to make appeal to another life, as though this earthly one,
lived according to the dictates of our higher instincts, were not
beautiful and justified of itself?[1] Later, Arnold will define immortality as life 'in the eternal order, which never dies',[2] 'la réunion au principe de l'ordre impérissable', Senancour calls it.[3]

In the beautiful poem of *Dover Beach*, by thought and image
alike, we are plunged back into the heart of the shadowy world
of Obermann. Indeed, although so typical of Arnold, *Dover
Beach* bears the trace of influence from at least two other
sources.

The precise fancy, of the poet left stranded on the shore from

1 *Id.* XLIV, vol. I, p. 195, and also p. 193.
2 'A Comment on Christmas', in *Irish Essays*, *Works*, vol. XI, p. 323.
3 *Obermann*, XLVIII, vol. II, p. 19 (and see above, p. 66 and p. 89).

which the sea of Faith has long withdrawn, is not indeed Obermann's, but Sainte-Beuve's.[1]

Sainte-Beuve's youth, which only with difficulty can be uncovered from beneath the thousand accretions that form his better-known maturity, was beset with the romantic longings of his age; religion and faith had withdrawn their stay from him, as from so many young and ardent spirits of those days, and 'Joseph Delorme' for a short space took his place beside the Adolphes, Manfreds, Werthers and Renés of the day. 'Joseph Delorme', though buried deep under the cosmopolitan critic, never forgot his debt to 'Obermann'.

At Aigues-Mortes in 1839 he had written: 'Mon âme est pareille à ces plages où l'on dit que Saint Louis s'est embarqué: la mer et la foi se sont depuis longtemps, hélas! retirées....'.[2]

From this bare image Arnold constructed his own vision of the receding sea:

> Listen!...
> The Sea of Faith
> Was once, too, at the full...
> But now I only hear
> Its melancholy, long, withdrawing roar,
> Retreating, to the breath
> Of the night wind, down the vast edges drear
> And naked shingles of the world.

The poem of *Dover Beach* begins with all the moon-gilded, mysterious beauty of an Obermannesque night.

> The sea is calm to-night.
> The tide is full, the moon lies fair
> Upon the straits;—on the French coast the light
> Gleams and is gone; the cliffs of England stand,
> Glimmering and vast, out in the tranquil bay.

1 This suggestion I owe to Prof. Irving Babbitt; see *The Masters of Modern French Criticism*, p. 104.
2 Sainte-Beuve, *Portraits Littéraires*, *Pensées*, vol. III, p. 540.

Come to the window, sweet is the night air!
Only, from the long line of spray
Where the sea meets the moon-blanch'd land,
Listen! you hear the grating roar
Of pebbles which the waves draw back, and fling,
At their return, up the high strand,
Begin, and cease, and then again begin,
With tremulous cadence slow, and bring
The eternal note of sadness in.

It was this image of the expiring wave, and its analogy with
the perpetual death and renewal of things that Sainte-Beuve had
precisely singled out in his exposition of the *Rêveries* of
Senancour, to illustrate the mood of the disillusioned sage, and
his meditations on the world of things and men: 'Souvent au
sein des montagnes', says the dreamer, 'quand les vents en-
gouffrés dans leurs gorges pressaient les vagues des lacs solitaires, je recevais du perpétuel roulement des ondes expirantes
le sentiment de l'instabilité des choses, et de l'éternel renouvellement du monde'.[1]

Arnold had read this description in Sainte-Beuve.[2] But he
had also read for himself the account of a scene very similar in
Obermann.

Once when Obermann was wandering on the banks of the
Thièle, he describes, in a passage Arnold was fond of quoting,
how he left the house and went by night along the greeny-
coloured waters of the river, to where it flows out of the lake
of Neuchâtel, and down a certain slope to the sandy shore of
the lake, 'où venaient expirer les vagues. *L'air était calme....*
Tous reposaient, les uns dans l'oubli des travaux, d' autres dans
celui des douleurs. *La lune parut*: je restai longtemps. Vers le
matin, *elle répandait sur les terres et sur les eaux l'ineffable*

1 *Rêveries sur la nature primitive de l'homme*, ed. J. Merlant, 1910, vol. I, p. 45.
2 Sainte-Beuve, *Portraits Contemporains*, vol. I, p. 158.

mélancolie de ses dernières lueurs. La nature paraît bien grande lorsque, dans un long recueillement on entend *le roulement des ondes sur la rive solitaire, dans le calme d'une nuit encore ardente et éclairée* par la lune qui finit'.[1]

And speaking of another night on the lake of Geneva Obermann again describes the white light of the moon, and the sound of the waves rolling back the innumerable pebbles on the lake-shore: 'Le lac est bien beau, lorsque la lune blanchit nos deux voiles;... quand les vagues se brisent;... quand elles font entendre au loin leur roulement sur les cailloux innombrables....'.[2]

The association, in the first passage, of the night, the calm, the moon, the dying waves, the cadence of their roll upon the shore, and the fact that this passage is twice quoted by Arnold[3] are too striking for the similar natural theme and setting of *Dover Beach* to be a mere coincidence. And the reflections which assail Obermann, of a melancholy message in this moon-lit loneliness, before which he seems to shrink and grow old, is paralleled in Arnold by the 'eternal note of sadness' he finds in these sounds of night.

> The sea is calm to-night.
> The tide is full, the moon lies fair
> Upon the straits...
> Only, from the long line of spray
> Where the sea meets the moon-blanched land
> Listen! you hear the grating roar
> Of pebbles which the waves draw back....
> Begin, and cease, and then again begin,
> With tremulous cadence slow, and bring
> The eternal note of sadness in.

---

1 *Obermann*, IV, vol. I, p. 22.
2 *Id*. LXI, vol. II, p. 69.
3 In the article on *Obermann* in *The Academy*, Oct. 9, 1869, p. 3; and in the essay on Amiel in *Essays in Criticism*, Second Series, *Works*, vol. IV, pp. 224–5.

It is not only that the image, reaction and thought of Obermann are so often and so strikingly reflected in Matthew Arnold; there is in Arnold the repetition of a hundred little details which are dear also to the imagination of Obermann. One would say that the English poet had steeped himself in the enchantment of Obermann, had caught his peculiar atmosphere, reproduced the very overtones which sound out from moment to moment in Obermann and enrich the dominant strain. The *timbres* of their songs are indeed the same. Or, if their wood-notes must be held to differ, it is but as the sighing note of the flute differs from the reedier voice of the hautbois. So deeply are their souls attuned that the same air of autumnal dream, of moon-silvered darkness, song of nightingale, and breath of wind in leaves, is diffused around and enters into both.

We have noticed Obermann's preference for closing seasons, fading lights, the changes of autumn, the romance of the dying day, and of the moonlit night. 'Les paysages éclairés par la lune sont ceux qu'il sait le mieux mettre en musique', says one of his critics.[1] The same subdued and silvery tones are also Arnold's favourites. How often is the moon by her presence contributory to his most beautiful images! She lights the hollow caverns of the sundered isles, and gives them unquiet yearnings: the nightingale's song is the symbol of these, and on another moonlit night this bird is again the mingled expression of love and pain in *Philomela*, as she is of the restless loving heart in *Obermann*.[2]

The Scholar-Gipsy emerges by night to rest on the 'moonlit pales', and hearken to her song. And the hush and calm of bliss shared with Marguerite are those of the star brooding over a moonlit sea. The 'moon-blanch'd street' of the deserted town of Cette where the poet wanders with a heart full of sad

1 J. Merlant, *Sénancour*, p. 109.   2 *Obermann*, LXIII, vol. II, p. 72.

memories of lost love, and the 'moon-blanch'd land' which the sea washes in *Dover Beach*, are not whiter than the sails of Obermann's tiny craft upon Lake Leman, 'lorsque la lune [les] *blanchit*'.[1]

The sea performs its 'long moon-silver'd roll' in *Self-Dependence* in a calm envied by man; and the 'main' is elsewhere (in *A Southern Night*) 'moon-charmed'. It is in the same 'lovely moonlight' that abides the pure, rarely visited, soul of man (*Palladium*).

In another way, besides this taste for cold lights, and fading beauties, Matthew Arnold resembles Obermann. This is their common and characteristic habit of turning to address objects in the Nature they are painting, when sudden pain overcomes them, or they are struck by some bewilderment or awe. Arnold's way of apostrophising, almost pleading with, stars, or night, or waters, in such moments, is not very like anything in Wordsworth, to whom his love of Nature in other ways unites him. Wordsworth takes the gracious spirit of Nature more often as a presence, a third Person, who is there and felt and spoken *of*, not often *to*.

Now this detail, apparently of only slight importance, is in its way, significant; it is a real index of one aspect of Arnold's genius, an aspect which differentiates him from Wordsworth who, though a greater poetic genius than Arnold, is nevertheless a less rare literary phenomenon. The gifts in which Wordsworth is eminent are his imagination, his insight, and humanity— qualities which, though carried to a high perfection in Wordsworth, are yet typical of the English genius. Arnold had these gifts too, in smaller measure; but what he had, in a degree Wordsworth had not, was a very great intellectual development. This, common enough in the domain of the scientist and

---

[1] *Obermann*, LXI, vol. II, p. 69.

philosopher, is rarer among English men of letters. And it is because of this endowment that Arnold is a more lonely figure than Wordsworth.

In a French *milieu*, among its numerous intellectual élite, he would have found more easily an environment sympathetic to him. In England, with its emphasis on practice, and on maintaining the inner life inarticulate, he suffered from a sense of spiritual isolation.

And this loneliness precisely reveals itself in the impulse to turn to and call upon the things of Nature, and make them his companions. So we get those appeals, half-oratorical, half-supplicatory, which often give Arnold's poetry an impassioned, quite *saccadé* utterance; entirely different from anything in Wordsworth. Wordsworth rarely has these sudden, passionate outbursts. The movement of his verse, at its best, is grave, noble and grand, as befits the contemplative or descriptive *genre*. When he communes with Nature, there is a tranquil contentment in the act; the spirit of Nature passes into his amidst a gentle calm. Arnold's poetry is grand; but it is also sad; and sadness is a source of weakness. It is also a source of isolation.

To some minds, the element of sadness which mines a strong intellect has a sharpness which fills them with pity. But to the majority, this is an element which alienates them; they turn from a thing so disturbing, to the faith and optimism which reassures, and knows neither doubt nor sadness. Wordsworth is not a robust optimist in the sense that Browning is; nevertheless there is far more cheerfulness and serenity in him than in Arnold. In Arnold the estranging element is only too visible.

Wordsworth's sympathy with and understanding of Nature do not make him therefore a figure remote from his fellows; rather they tighten the bond between him and them. But

Arnold, lost in his intellectual solitude, invoking the night and the stars, the heavens and the ocean, plunges into a world apart. The things which touch him are unmating things;[1] they symbolise his loneliness, and they are its companions.

In this way too Obermann had regarded Nature. It is exactly in his manner to apostrophise her, as Arnold does; to find the night and the stars sympathetic, and man a world away. He also, in his solitude, is driven to break silence, and address the stars, the heavenly depths—Nature herself, or the natural objects which are parts of her; even to address the qualities of these elements, as moral symbols of a greater reality than the bodies which shadow them.

We have insisted a great deal on the characters which unite Arnold and Senancour. None of these have seemed unimportant, even the detailed resemblances, in providing knowledge of the basis of Obermann's attraction for Arnold. Such parallelism as exists in their use of minor images—like that of the mirror of consciousness, of the river of Time; the symbolism of the plain and mountains, the love they held in common for the sound of running water,[2] for physical and moral purity; their fastidiousness in material and moral matters—perspectives beheld at the same angle, and a common general vision of life and reality—all show the bond that joined Arnold to Senancour with such an intense fidelity.

---

1 *Isolation: To Marguerite.*
2 See, for explicit references to this characteristic in Obermann, J. Merlant, *Sénancour*, p. 32; *Obermann*, v, vol. I, p. 35; III, vol. I, p. 15; IV, vol. I, p. 19, etc.: and in Arnold, *Letters*, vol. II, p. 54; *Letters to Clough*, p. 92, etc.

CHAPTER XVI

NEW POEMS CONTINUED:
OBERMANN ONCE MORE

Among the other members of *New Poems* that remain to be considered, *A Southern Night*, written in 1859 from Cette where Arnold was then on an official tour, contains, besides its personal expression of sorrow in his brother's death, an allusion to the earlier sorrowful episode which had ended in his separation from 'Marguerite'. The lapse of ten years had not changed the poet very much; his musings on the inhibitions and restraints of our modern age are of the old restless type.

It is perhaps in remembrance of a thought of Obermann that Arnold lightly censures the English for their feverish habit of travel; a reproof that we deserve as a nation, who

> ...see all sights from pole to pole,
> And glance, and nod, and bustle by;
> And never once possess our soul
> Before we die.

Obermann passes a similar stricture on himself. I would like to say, he observes, as I sit by my quiet fireside, 'I have been hither and thither, seen the sands, seas, and mountains, cities, and deserts; the tropical and northern skies, the Southern Cross and the Little Bear; the Equator and the poles...'.[1] But, he continues, having seen them, can I say I am less fanatical, less narrow-minded?[2]

Early Death and Fame was originally a fragment of *Haworth Churchyard*, first published in 1855, which Arnold, in view of its containing a favourable allusion to Harriet Martineau, and

---

1 *Obermann*, LXVIII, vol. II, pp. 125–6.   2 *Ibid*. p. 127.

from a dislike of having his ideas identified with hers, had been reluctant to republish in full. This fragment is inspired by the mood in which Arnold would doubtless have subscribed to the words of the song in *Old Mortality*:

> One glorious hour of crowded life
> Is worth an age without a name.

So Arnold reiterates:

> Heap up his moments with life!
> Triple his pulses with fame!

The central idea, of snatching at a too brief present, of drinking deep of life, of tasting emotion that is painful, rather than enduring a senseless apathy, is an idea we have noticed too often to need to press it here. It is the philosophy of life of which the New Sirens had been the exponents, and to which Obermann had lent himself so often; but with a tendency to ennoble the main conception, and substitute for mere epicurean joy, the intense appreciation of a life rich in moral, intellectual, and emotional values. For one whose life is short these joys must be concentrated and keen: so Arnold pleads for such a one:

> Fuller for him be the hours!
> Give him emotion, though pain!
> Let him live, let him feel: *I have lived.*

This is the counsel Obermann had drawn from the *Manuel de Pseusophanes*, that imagined work of Aristippus:[1]

Le présent est le temps. . . .
L'énergie dans les peines est meilleure que l'apathie dans les voluptés.[2]

And Arnold, with his appeal:

> Let him live, let him feel: *I have lived,*

was without doubt recalling the complaint of Obermann, who

---

1 *Obermann*, XXXIII, vol. I, p. 110.   2 *Id*. Manuel, vol. I, p. 112.

had been denied, by the strange fatality which governed his course on earth, this satisfaction.

Qu'un jour...je puisse dire à un homme qui m'entende: *Si nous avions vécu!*[1]

In *Growing Old*, and *The Progress of Poesy*, the poet gives, in the one case a personal, and in the other a more general, expression of his melancholy shrinking from the thought of advancing age, and an empty and faded life. The idea of the world's applause, which follows belatedly on achievement when we are only 'the phantom of ourselves', is reminiscent of a comment of Obermann's on the same subject, on the fame 'which is reserved for our ashes'.[2]

This idea, and the recurrence of the prison symbol, seem to associate the poem with others of the Obermann inspiration. Moreover, the general tenor of the poem *Growing Old* is very like that of a confession of Obermann, facing a similar prospect of dying youth.

I begin to feel, he says, writing from Fontainebleau in the autumn, that I am advancing in life. 'Ces impressions délicieuses, *ces émotions subites qui m'agitaient autrefois* et m'entraînaient si loin d'un monde de tristesse, *je ne les retrouve plus qu'altérées et affaiblies.* Ce désir que réveillait en moi chaque sentiment de quelque beauté dans les choses naturelles, cette espérance pleine d'incertitude et de charme, ce feu céleste qui éblouit et consume un cœur jeune, cette volupté expansive dont il éclaire devant lui le fantôme immense, tout cela n'est déjà plus....'[3]

> What is it to grow old?...
> Is it to feel our strength—
> Not our bloom only, but our strength—decay?...

---

1 *Obermann* XII, vol. I, p. 65.   2 *Id*. LXXV, vol. II, p. 149.
3 *Id*. XXI, vol. I, p. 80.

It is to spend long days
And not once feel that we were ever young;
It is to add, immured
In the hot prison of the present, month
To month with weary pain.

It is to suffer this,
And feel but half, and feebly, what we feel.
Deep in our hidden heart
Festers the dull remembrance of a change,
But no emotion—none.

In *The Last Word* a more courageous mood resumes sway.
The poem is one of Arnold's bolder expressions of stoical
endurance, or defiance. The disciple had caught his master's
message: 'Périssons en résistant'.[1] Obermann's melancholy
has too often a resigned and ineffectual element in it; words
like these reveal in him a less common strength and tenacity.
Arnold was not likely to be less responsive to these qualities
of sinew than to Obermann's more fantastic griefs and sadnesses.

Charge once more, then, and be dumb!
Let the victors, when they come,
When the forts of folly fall,
Find thy body by the wall!

The concluding pages of Obermann's confessions mildly
repeat this more heroic strain; there is little in the French writer
more characteristic of his attitude to the life from which he had
claimed so little.

We have already noticed the similarity between this last letter
of Obermann's and the poem *A Wish*. In both passages their
authors anticipate their last thoughts on an imagined death-bed.

'Si j'arrive à la vieillesse', says Obermann at the end of his
book, 'si, un jour, plein de pensées encore, mais renonçant à
parler aux hommes, j'ai auprès de moi un ami pour recevoir

1 *Obermann*, xc, vol. ii, p. 231.

mes adieux à la terre, qu'on place ma chaise sur l'herbe courte, et que de tranquilles marguerites soient là devant moi, sous le soleil, sous le ciel immense, afin qu'en laissant la vie qui passe, je retrouve quelque chose de l'illusion infinie.'[1]

A Wish records a desire much the same, the desire to be allowed to die in quiet, in freedom from the officious presence of friends and doctors, from all that has the taint of the ephemeral. Amid such calm and refreshment, the poet desires to be moved near the window, that he may gaze with dying eyes on the world of Nature without; and so take his leave of earth while his spirit wanders forth into that aerial world where beats 'the pure eternal course of life' he fain would share.

The image of the life-stream which bears us all away, is taken up in the next poem, the *Epilogue to Lessing's Laocoön*. This poem, in the course of a consideration of the different arts, asserts the greatest fitness of poetry to convey the moving current of our life. And the question is revived of the power of the highest poetry (rarer than music or painting of the same excellence) to interpret life, and to confer on it the unity which binds all its movement together.

For the poet 'looks before and after' as well as to the present, but from his survey he draws dejected conclusions. In *Baccha-nalia*, all the excitement and pleasure and achievement of the new age is represented as passing before his undazzled eyes; but in the carols and carousings he only sees what is of value that is left behind, what is delicately beautiful that is trampled down.

As George Sand had rebelled against the world's crude awards of praise and honour and sided with the weak and fallen, so the poet too feels pity, seeing

> The puissant crown'd, the weak laid low.

[1] *Id. Dernière Lettre*, vol. ii, p. 246.

Only in a momentary hush is the faint, sweet voice heard of those
> Delicate spirits, push'd away
> In the hot press of the noon-day.

Heine's Grave contains the well-known arraignment of England, 'the weary Titan', deaf and stiff and blind, staggering with misdirected energy on to her goal, or doom. And here the pantheistic doctrine of Spinoza is put to contribution to furnish a symbol, and Heine, the sardonic smile which momentarily flitted across the face of the Spirit of the World, takes his place with us all as moods of the Infinite,

> Of the Spirit in whom we exist,
> Who alone is all things in one,

or, in more philosophic terms, as modes of the attributes constituting the Infinite Substance which is God.

The philosophy of Spinoza, in which God is identified with the totality of things, is, in fact, a development of what the ancient Stoics had already held; with the difference that spirit or thought is placed by Spinoza on an equal footing with corporeality. This sort of pantheism, with its unifying principle of God, was likely to appeal to Arnold. But much else in Spinoza was of a kind to attract a high thinker like Matthew Arnold: he had felt, we must believe, something of the sublimer beauty that the cold, logical treatises of the seventeenth-century philosopher contain at their heart's core: 'In interpreting pantheism as an ethical enthusiasm of the Universe, he returns to the creed of Stoicism, and strikes the keynote of Wordsworth's highest poetry', says a modern critic;[1] and we may surely add, with even greater truth, that also of Arnold. By his identification of virtue with the intellectual love of God; and his insistence on the value of religion as a means of popularising

1 A. W. Benn, *A History of Modern Philosophy*, pp. 47–8.

moral truths, Arnold approaches unmistakably the standpoint of the Jewish philosopher. Such words, indeed, as the following, reveal in Spinoza a character essentially of a type to appeal to Matthew Arnold:[1]

If the way of salvation lay ready to hand, and could be found without great toil, would it be neglected by nearly everyone? But all glorious things are as difficult as they are rare.

It will be remembered in what terms the poet answered the American lady, in search of an easy perfection: 'Excellence is not common and abundant; on the contrary,...excellence dwells among rocks hardly accessible, and a man must almost wear his heart out before he can reach her'.[2]

The *Stanzas from the Grande Chartreuse* were first published in 1855, when Arnold's interest in Obermann was still comparatively new. The poem unwittingly recalls the frame of mind in which Louis Ménard, in so many ways a companion spirit to Arnold, had confronted a similar problem. For both poets, so much had had to be 'unlearnt, so much resign'd'. Before the deserted shrines, both had stood in solitary sadness, and grieved over the fallen stones which faith had set up, and broken faith cast down.

But while Ménard had hopefully tried to reconstruct a new religion from the most beautiful assembled remnants of the past, the English poet had no heart to give even to the fragments of forsaken creeds. In vain Byron's courage and Shelley's spiritual lament[3] had tried to inflame the dead hearts of the old

1 *Ibid.* p. 46.
2 'Milton', in *Essays in Criticism*, Second Series, *Works*, vol. IV, p. 43. We shall return to this interest of Arnold's in Spinoza when dealing with the Essays, in the volume which we hope to devote to Arnold's prose.
3 In a letter (which the author had the privilege of seeing), in the possession of the late Mr T. P. Arnold, of Hobart, Tasmania, Matthew Arnold, in response to a protest from his nephew, revised his well-known verdict on Shelley. No doubt he planned to do him greater justice in the second essay he projected on the subject, but did not live to complete (see H. F. Lowry, *op. cit.* p. 45, note 1).

votaries; the passing exhilaration of the new freedom had given place only to a feeling of emptiness, of fretful unrest, which had not even the dignity of sorrow, but only its cankered smart. With Obermann's eyes, Arnold saw the aftermath of the new emancipation as more bitter even than servitude: the core of unbelief, stripped of its melancholy but still beautiful trappings of idealism, had revealed itself rank and sterile. This truth Arnold had recognised in Obermann: to this sorrowful conclusion had the reading of Obermann's 'stern, sad page' brought the poet. From it he felt no escape:

> The eternal trifler breaks your spell;
> But we—we learnt your lore too well!

Haply, the poet continues—lit by a ray of hopefulness of which Senancour also, but more rarely, had had the glimpse,—a new world is to dawn in which wisdom and happiness will be reconciled. Until then, let the quiet shadow of some cloister receive me: let life be passed aloof, as in a forest glade. In the lone brakes of Fontainebleau and chalets by the Alpine snows, Obermann had consumed the age and its longings: me too, the poet says, will reverie, shade, and prayer fence round likewise, where

> In the high altar's depth divine,
> The organ carries to our ear
> Its *accents of another sphere*

—'*sons d'un autre monde*', as Obermann calls them.[1]

In *Obermann Once More*, the poem that closes this volume of 1867, is contained the proof, if proof were needed, of Arnold's long and unswerving fidelity to the 'master of his wandering youth'. It was composed many years after his first enthusiasm; twenty years had passed away since then, and though Arnold had felt, travelling from time to time near some

1 *Obermann*, LXXV, vol. II, p. 149.

spot sacred to the name of Obermann, his interest and affection constantly renewed, even to himself it is doubtful if he had rendered the full account due to that early influence. Indeed, he had fancied, on bidding Obermann adieu at the Baths of Leuk, that he was really about to give him up; that, by entering the life of the world, he was in fact renouncing the master. But the resolution was taken too late—not by a word, a gesture, a mere attitude, could Arnold shake off an influence that had so deeply penetrated him, so subtly informed his own genius: the roots had by then sucked deep of the nourishment that, for nearly twenty years, they were to send aloft to leaf and bud and flower.

On more than one occasion during his subsequent wanderings abroad Arnold had not disguised from himself his objective. In 1857, on a visit to Switzerland with his wife, he had extended his journey from Lucerne to Zermatt expressly to pass by the Titlis and Grimsel, 'for Obermann's sake', as he wrote to his favourite sister.[1] At least two beautiful passages in *Obermann* must have been vividly present to him, as he passed up the arm of Lucerne to Stanstad, and on up the valley to Engelberg; over the Joch pass, up the Haslital, over the Grimsel—near where the Aar has its source—and down into the Rhône valley before the climb to Zermatt. For it was the Grimsel that Obermann had declared to be the perfect setting for the *Ranz des Vaches*.[2]

Si celui qui le joue le sent bien [he says], les premiers sons nous placent dans les hautes vallées, près des rocs nus et d'un gris roussâtre, sous le ciel froid, sous le soleil ardent. On est sur la croupe des sommets arrondis et couverte de pâturages. On se pénètre de la lenteur des choses et de la grandeur des lieux; on y trouve la marche tranquille des vaches et le mouve-

---

1 *Letters*, vol. I, *Works*, vol. XIII, p. 75.
2 *Obermann, Troisième Fragment*, vol. I, p. 147.

ment mesuré de leurs grosses cloches, près des nuages, dans l'étendue doucement inclinée depuis la crête des granits inébranlables jusqu'aux granits ruinés des ravins neigeux. Les vents frémissent d'une manière austère dans les mélèses éloignés; on discerne le roulement du torrent caché dans les précipices qu'il s'est creusés durant de longs siècles. A ces bruits solitaires dans l'espace succèdent les accens hâtés et pesans des Küheren, expression nomade d'un plaisir sans gaieté, d'une joie des montagnes. Les chants cessent; l'homme s'éloigne; les cloches ont passé les mélèses, on n'entend plus que le choc des cailloux roulans, et la chute ininterrompue des arbres que le torrent pousse vers les vallées. Le vent apporte ou recule ces sons alpestres; et quand il les perd, *tout paraît froid, immobile et mort.* C'est le domaine de l'homme qui n'a pas d'empressement.... L'air est froid, le vent a cessé avec la lumière du soir; il ne reste que la lueur des neiges antiques, et la chute des eaux dont le bruissement sauvage, en s'élevant des abîmes, semble ajouter à la permanence silencieuse des hautes cimes, et des glaciers, et de la nuit.[1]

The Grimsel and Titlis would always be associated in Arnold's mind with Obermann. During a second visit to Lucerne, in 1865, he speaks of the trees, the lake with its background of rich autumn colour, 'and, at the head of it all, the snowy line with Titlis, a mountain', he says in the primly affectionate way he used towards his mother, 'for whom Obermann has always given me a peculiar interest'.[2]

Arnold was perhaps thinking of that early letter of Obermann's, which had so struck George Sand by its pathos; where, after speaking sorrowfully of his empty and disappointed life, Obermann had gone on to describe how he had sought moral peace, and religious hope; how he had found neither, and had resigned himself never to have either—never to live, but always to expect to live; and had concluded:

1 *Obermann, Troisième Fragment*, vol. i, pp. 147–9.
2 *Letters*, vol. ii, *Works*, vol. xiv, p. 61.

Triste et vaine conception d'un monde meilleur! Indicible extension d'amour! Regret des temps qui coulent inutiles! Sentiment universel, soutiens et dévore ma vie: que serait-elle sans ta beauté sinistre? C'est par toi qu'elle est sentie, c'est par toi qu'elle périra.

Que quelquefois encore, sous le ciel d'automne, dans ces derniers beaux jours que les brumes remplissent d'incertitude, assis près de l'eau qui emporte la feuille jaunie, j'entende les accens simples et profonds d'une mélodie primitive. Qu'un jour, montant le Grimsel ou le Titlis, seul avec l'homme des montagnes, j'entende sur l'herbe courte, auprès des neiges, les sons romantiques bien connus des vaches d'Underwalden et d'Hasly; et que là, une fois avant la mort, je puisse dire à un homme qui m'entende: Si nous avions vécu! [1]

Arnold had understood the terrible desolation of Obermann's soul: very few perhaps have realised the aptness of the words he had used to describe Obermann, in 1849; with what care and exactitude they were chosen:

> Immoveable thou sittest, still
> As death, composed to bear!
> Thy head is clear, thy feeling chill,
> And icy thy despair

—'*froid, immobile et mort*'! [2]

Arnold was always to delight in these literary pilgrimages; never would he give up the habit; he remained at heart deeply and unalterably attached to the memory of Obermann; just as Switzerland continued to be the one country for him. [3]

1 *Obermann*, XII, vol. I, p. 65.
2 See above, p. 240.
3 In 1875, one cannot avoid noticing, this country is rather irrelevantly introduced into the poem entitled *Rome-Sickness*, included in a volume in memory of Emily Bliss Gould who died in this year. It is clear that Swiss scenes would always be Arnold's favourites, in spite of the fourth line of the first verse, which seems inspired by a sense of the proprieties simply, or at most the needs of the rhyme:

In 1858 he took with his friend Walrond a journey which practically retraced the steps of a famous adventure of Obermann's. This was the excursion to Aosta and the Great St Bernard.

The incident as described in *Obermann* was founded on a real experience of Senancour's.[1] A year before his marriage (in September 1790), Senancour had conceived the wild idea of climbing the Great St Bernard without a guide. The description of this climb is given by Obermann as follows:[2] 'J'allais à la cité d'Aoste et j'étais déjà dans le Valais, lorsque j'entendis un étranger dire, dans l'auberge, qu'il ne se hasarderait point à passer sans guide le Saint-Bernard'. Fired by this statement, Obermann says, 'Je résolus aussitôt de le passer seul'.

Leaving Martigny he pressed on to Liddes; a storm was brewing and snow fell as he reached Saint-Pierre, the last inhabited village on this side of the mountain. In summer the

> 'To daily tasks we set our hand
>   And oft the spirit, pent at home
> Breaks out and longs for Switzerland,
>   Longs oftener yet and pines for Rome.
>
> I pass'd to-day o'er Walton Heath—
>   The coming springtime's earliest stir
> Quicken'd and moved, a happy breath,
>   In moss and gorse and shining fir.
>
> Fortunate firs! who never think
>   How firs less curst by Fortune's frown
> O'er Glion fringe the mountain's brink
>   Or dot the slopes to Vevey down...'.

How much the thought of his early passion for Marguerite mingled with that of Obermann in this love of Switzerland cannot be determined. They were, indeed, linked memories. Perhaps when he spoke of retiring to Berne on a diplomatic appointment, as a vision haunting him one day (see *Letters*, vol. I, *Works*, vol. XIII, p. 35), the preference of influence in this obsession may be assigned to Marguerite, so inextricably bound up for Arnold with associations of the quaint, fresh Swiss capital. It is perhaps strange that Arnold should confess so much to his wife: but the fact is at least evidence of the strength of his early attachment.

1 See the *Notice Biographique* of Mlle de Senancour, published by G. Michaut, *Senancour*, pp. 83–6.

2 *Obermann*, XCI, vol. II, pp. 238–42.

gracious slopes would be covered with a flowery beauty, and
the snow-clad peaks screen the blue shadows at their base; but
now the snow had come down to the valley-pastures. In spite
of this, however, and undeterred by the cold and the half-
obliterated track, Obermann was determined to push on. Only
when the coming of darkness had complicated the situation did
he realise his danger. He now saw that he had lost the path; he
felt only an ice-track under his feet, and his limbs were rapidly
becoming rigid with the cold. Impossible to stop—there was
now the fear of complete numbness overtaking him. Powerless
to advance for fear of hidden crevasses, or to return to the lost
track, to await the day where he was would have been equal
madness. There was only one course to be taken, says Obermann
coolly relating the enterprise afterwards: he remembered to
have come some distance along a mountain torrent, the Drance,
which traversed the hamlets he had left behind. Now in the
great silence he listened for the roar of the torrent; to locate it
was his sole hope of salvation. He was not deceived; he pushed
into the darkness and came suddenly upon the sound of the
falling water. And now, despite the fierce aspect of the rocky
bed of the stream and its foaming sheets of spray, he took the
one course left him, and threw himself into the water. Then
began, as Mlle de Senancour relates, the struggle with the
elements and with death. Yet this combat for Senancour was
not devoid of a certain joy. The battle of life among mankind
had been more painful to him than this contest with the icy
water of the torrent. At one moment he thought his end indeed
near, as he dropped down a steep cascade; but a deep basin of
water beneath received him. Thus with eyes closed, and nails
and even teeth gripping the rocks that gave him a momentary
stay, he was whirled down the course of the torrent, and would
have passed Bourg-Saint-Pierre in the darkness and confusion,

had not a light, fortunately showing through a chink in a shutter (illicitly, according to Mlle de Senancour, for the curfew had long since sounded) revealed to him his whereabouts. It was at the village inn, where he was obliged to stay some days after his strange adventure, that he developed the fever which undermined his constitution and made Alpine life thenceforward an impossibility to him.

This incident, so striking in the facts and the relation, must surely have given an impulse to Arnold's desire to visit the locality. It must have been clearly present to him throughout his crossing of the Great St Bernard, which he undertook in the month of August 1858. Arnold missed his wife, and was undoubtedly a little sad on this journey.[1] From Geneva, the starting-point, he with his friend Walrond had gone on to Vevey, where he visited the Château de Blonay, and perhaps recalled some memories of Rousseau. From Vevey he went on by boat to Villeneuve, whence the train took him up the 'Valais-depth profound' to Bex. It is unlikely that his reflections at this point bore any resemblance to those in which Addison had indulged, in the preceding century, on just such a tour; and who had so much admired this valley, as providing a channel 'providentially cut in the rocks to guide the Rhône to the lake, and turn the water mills of the poor people of Geneva...'.[2] He might, however, have noticed with some pleasure the quaint costumes which, seventy years ago, were still distinctive of the different cantons; the women of the Valais would be yet wearing the low hat with its broad, encircling ribbon, to-day confined to markets, pageants or cabarets.[3]

Continuing the next day, Arnold crossed the Diablerets,

1 *Letters*, vol. I, *Works*, vol. XIII, p. 86.
2 Addison, *Remarks on Italy*, 1705: *Geneva and the Lake*.
3 Professor Bonney, 'The Alps from 1856 to 1865', in the *Alpine Journal*, Feb. 1917, vol. XXXI, no. 214, p. 33.

deeply impressed by the descent through the valley of the
Liserne. That night he slept at Sion, the capital of the district.
From Sion he went on to Visp, and at Zermatt climbed the
Riffel. The next day he began the climb over the St Théodule,
an easy pass, to Breuil, where he slept; and so on to Châtillon
and into the Val d'Aosta. From Aosta Arnold achieved his
purpose of climbing the Great St Bernard, where he slept on the
night of September 4. It was during the descent to Martigny
that he would pass the scene of Obermann's exploit, see the wild
course of the Drance, and stop, not unmoved perhaps, to admire
the beauty of the mountains from above Bourg-Saint-Pierre.

He now seems to have thought of visiting Chamouni. 'It
will be curious', he wrote to his sister on the 6th, 'if I again miss
Chamouni, which I have missed so often.'[1] But rain did in fact
prevent the fulfilment of a wish that was perhaps inspired by
the memory of George Sand's famous 'course à Chamouni';
of which, if he had not heard the story from her own lips, he
had undoubtedly read in the *Lettres d'un Voyageur*. Another
year was to pass, however, before Arnold was able to pay the
long-projected visit (1859).[2]

It was probably in 1865, when Matthew Arnold was again
in Switzerland, that he wrote *Obermann Once More*.

Arnold was at Vevey in September of this year;[3] he does not
seem to have gone abroad again before July 1867, the date of
its first publication. Moreover, according to the first lines of
the poem, it was twenty years since Arnold had last seen Glion,
the little village above Montreux where the scene of the poem
is placed. It was by Glion that the poet had passed on his first
visit to Thun in 1848. But Arnold had perhaps visited Switzerland before this, in 1846; the year that George Sand had almos

---

1 *Letters*, vol. I, *Works*, vol. XIII, p. 97.   2 *Ibid.* p. 130.
3 *Letters*, vol. II, *Works*, vol. XIV, p. 49.

certainly introduced him to Obermann. If so, he must assuredly have visited the Lake of Geneva in this year. And between 1846 and 1865 is approximately the twenty years' interval to which he refers in the opening line of the poem.

The east end of the Lake of Geneva would always have for Arnold its particular association with Obermann.

'C'est du côté de Rolle, qu'on admire le lac de Genève', Obermann says in one of his early letters;[1] 'pour moi, je ne veux pas en décider, mais c'est à Vevay, à Chillon surtout, que je le trouve dans toute sa beauté. Que n'y a-t-il dans cet admirable bassin, à la vue de la dent de Jamant, de l'aiguille du Midi et des neiges du Velan, là devant les rochers de Meillerie, un sommet sortant des eaux, une île escarpée, bien ombragée, de difficile accès.... Je n'irais pas plus loin.' Here was indeed the spot that Obermann had chosen, out of all Switzerland, to fix his last habitation. Here he had built the chalet he describes in Letter LXVIII; and it is from here, at 'Imenstròm' near Vevey, that the last of the confessions were written. He says of it, characteristically pessimistic:

Cette partie de la Suisse où je me fixe est devenue comme ma patrie, ou comme un pays où j'aurais passé des années heureuses dans les premiers temps de la vie. J'y suis avec indifférence, et c'est une grande preuve de mon malheur; mais je crois que je serais mal partout ailleurs. Ce beau bassin de la partie orientale du Léman, si vaste, si romantique, si bien environné; ces maisons de bois, ces chalets, ces vaches qui vont et reviennent avec leurs cloches de montagnes; les facilités des plaines et la proximité des hautes cimes; une sorte d'habitude anglaise, française et suisse à la fois;... cette longue plaine d'eau courbée, prolongée, indéfinie, dont les vapeurs lointaines s'élèvent sous le soleil de midi, s'allument et s'embrasent aux feux du soir, et dont la nuit laisse entendre les vagues qui se forment, qui viennent, qui grossissent et s'étendent pour se perdre sur la rive

1 *Obermann*, v, vol. i, pp. 32–3.

où l'on repose: cet ensemble entretient l'homme dans une situation qu'il ne trouve pas ailleurs.. . .

En vérité, c'est un lieu bien tranquille que cette gorge d'Imenstròm, où je ne vois au-dessus de moi que le sapin noir, le roc nu, le ciel infini.. . .[1]

As Matthew Arnold went on up the slope above Vevey, he looked across the lake, and his eye travelled far down the great, diminishing valley opposite him, with the snowy top of the Velan crowning the distance; it was the view that had most delighted Obermann. Nearer at hand, the lake, with its waters, turquoise-blue to the very shallows, where the little waves lapped and broke against the Castle of Chillon; the swathes of hay that the harvesters had piled up for the second or third time that year; the mellow smell of orchard and well-filled grange; and the burning heaps of chestnut-husks filling the air with their aromatic tang—all for Arnold was redolent of memories of Obermann. And above all, the eternal line of mountains overhead, the cone of Jaman, 'pale and grey' 'in the blue profound'—Jaman 'delicately tall, Above his sun-warm'd firs'—these spoke to his fancy as though he had but left them yesterday.

> Yes, I forget the world's work wrought,
> Its warfare waged with pain;
> An eremite with thee, in thought
> Once more I slip my chain.
>
> And to thy mountain-chalet come,
> And lie beside its door,
> And hear the wild bee's Alpine hum,
> And thy sad, tranquil lore!

The very image in which his thought had pleased itself on an earlier day, returned now. The dying wave, the receding tide, the ebb of faith he had witnessed in *Dover Beach*, the

1 *Id.* LXVIII, vol. II, pp. 122–3 and p. 129.

'sentiment of the perpetual instability of things' which Obermann had experienced beside the moonlit lake—these gave way
before the conviction of their eternal renewal, 'de l'éternel
renouvellement du monde'; before the vision of

> One common wave of thought and joy
> Lifting mankind again.

And as night fell, the shade of Obermann, with his mountain-
flower, and book in his breast, approached Arnold in a new
dream, scanning with pensive but keen gaze the face of his
disciple. And there, under the cone of Jaman, with the tall
yellow gentians nearly at their end and flowering over the grass,
and the pines rocking in the fading light, the spirit of Obermann
spoke and revealed to the poet the approaching birth of the new
world which he himself had not lived to see; the world which
was to be in accord with the innate harmony of things, the
world towards which the thwarted aspirations of Obermann
had agonised in vain. As he spoke, the icy despair of the sage
dissolved; his face was lit with hopefulness:

> O thou, who, ere thy flying span
> Was past of cheerful youth,
> Didst find the solitary man
> And love his cheerless truth—

> Despair not thou as I despair'd,
> Nor be cold gloom thy prison!
> Forward the gracious hours have fared,
> And see! the sun is risen!

> He breaks the winter of the past;
> A green, new earth appears.
> Millions whose life in ice lay fast,
> Have thoughts, and smiles, and tears.

> What though there still need effort, strife?
> Though much be still unwon?
> Yet warm it mounts, the hour of life!
> Death's frozen hour is done!

THE DENT DE JAMAN

Photo: Brügger, Meiringen

Ah, Jaman! delicately tall
Above his sun-warm'd firs—
What thoughts to me his rocks recall,
What memories he stirs!

Obermann Once More

And now the spirit added a last injunction, that the poet aid in this transformed world, to drive out the occasions of the doubt and woe which had sent him and his fellows to seek refuge in a palsied solitude; charging him:

> What still of strength is left, employ
> That end to help attain:
> *One common wave of thought and joy*
> *Lifting mankind again!* [1]

As he ceased to speak, a light appeared in the sky and glimmered over the lake; the silence was unbroken except by the mountain torrent heard far below; and as the haze opened above the valley, the spirit of Obermann vanished into the breaking day.

About the same time that Arnold was composing his first poems under the influence of Obermann, Sainte-Beuve, in his course of lectures on Chateaubriand delivered at Liége (1848–9), had devoted a long and eulogistic chapter to Senancour. In 1854 Arnold, now in touch with the critic, sent him his latest volume, anxious to have Sainte-Beuve's opinion on his first essay in criticism, the *Preface* of 1853, and also, perhaps, on his rehandling of the story of Sohrab and Rustum. Accompanying this volume was the earlier one of 1852 which contained the *Stanzas in memory of the author of 'Obermann'*. From Sainte-Beuve, in his home in the rue Mont-Parnasse, Paris, Arnold received a sympathetic and flattering letter of thanks.[2] And when the text of the lectures on *Chateaubriand et son groupe littéraire* was edited for publication in 1861, the chapter on

---

1 Originally written in 1867:
> 'What still of strength is left, employ,
> That end to help men gain:
> *One mighty wave of thought and joy*
> *Lifting mankind amain!*'

2 See *The Unpublished Letters of Matthew Arnold*, ed. A. Whitridge, p. 26 and pp. 68–70, where the letter is given *in extenso*.

Senancour was a little longer than as first planned in 1848: it now concluded with a reference to the secret adherents of Senancour, 'not indeed numerous, but religious in their way, and passionate: a posterity which will remain faithful'. And Sainte-Beuve names one: 'Un jeune poëte anglais, fils d'un bien respectable père, et dont le talent réunit la pureté et la passion, M. Mathieu Arnold, voyageant en Suisse et y suivant la trace d'Oberman, lui a dédié un poëme où il a évoqué tout son esprit et où, lui-même, à la veille de rentrer par devoir dans la vie active, il fait ses adieux au grand méditatif rêveur'.[1]

The *Stanzas in memory of the author of 'Obermann'* follow, translated in full by Sainte-Beuve's friend, the poet Lacaussade; with these words of Sainte-Beuve: 'Behold, upon this solitary tomb, its immortal funeral wreath'.

A word may be added in conclusion.

Complete as the above tribute is, and fittingly as it seems to close our knowledge of Arnold's love of Obermann, one more circumstance deserves relation here—perhaps more striking to us who read of it to-day when we consider that the compliment which it pays Arnold was privately expressed, and was, it seems, unknown to its subject.

In 1868 the aged Mademoiselle de Senancour, in retirement in Paris, was still faithfully guarding the reputation of her father. Sainte-Beuve, in his office as champion of Senancour, had been for many years in communication with her; it had indeed often been his lot to fan her passionate belief in the genius of her father; and this not merely from a feeling of personal respect for the child of Senancour, but because he sincerely shared her belief. Yet we cannot do less than appreciate the desire to convey a delicate pleasure to Mademoiselle de Senancour in reading the letter he addressed to her in August 1868. In

1 *Chateaubriand et son groupe littéraire*, Paris, ed. 1878, p. 364.

this note, which appears unsolicited, Sainte-Beuve informed Mademoiselle de Senancour of Matthew Arnold's second poem in honour of her father, in these words:

Si j'avais le plaisir de causer avec vous, je vous ferais voir chez un poète anglais, M. Matthew Arnold, de belles stances à la mémoire d'Oberman qui sont de l'année dernière.... Tout cela n'est pas sans doute ce que l'auteur lui-même ou sa fille pourrait écrire d'exact ou désirer de tout à fait vrai; mais la gloire n'est qu'un grand nuage doré, une sorte de mirage qui plane sur le paysage réel. Oberman vivra, le nom de Senancour ne sera jamais oublié.[1]

To value Arnold's poetry as it is serviceable to Senancour's greatness is an unusual way of regarding it. Yet it is likely that these words would have given more pleasure to Matthew Arnold than any direct flattery; it is likely that to him it would have counted hardly less to set at rest a solitary woman's fears for the illustrious name of her father, than to achieve a second immortality for himself by that name.

[1] *Nouvelle Correspondance de C.-A. Sainte-Beuve*, Calmann Lévy, Paris, 1880, p. 296.

CONCLUSION

It has been far from the purpose of this book to suggest that the resemblances we have shown to exist between Matthew Arnold and certain French writers can diminish Arnold's true greatness. From Senancour, the most important of these writers, he certainly took a multitude of ideas; but they sank into his personality and were assimilated there, as elements native to it. When subsequently they emerged under his pen, clothed in a new poetic form, and, as it were, refreshed by their reincarnation, they definitely had become Arnold's own. This was no ordinary sort of plagiarism, not even that kind of indebtedness of which Addison said: 'To borrow and better in the borrowing is no plagiarism'. We are here in the presence of something much more deep-seated—the refashioning of character under the influence of ideas acceptable and sympathetic to it.

From our review of Matthew Arnold's poetry it might seem that a very great amount is to be considered as the direct outcome of his reading of *Obermann*. But if so, it was not the *natural result* of such reading. Rare as is the appeal of *Obermann*, it is not limited to half a dozen readers merely. And of these readers, only one wrote the poetry of Matthew Arnold.

Arnold, indeed, went to Senancour because he found in him a kindred spirit, whose experiences, intellectual and sentimental, were strangely like his own. Thus there has been no question in our study of discovering sources, valueless in themselves, which acquire a kind of celebrity by their having furnished clues to the inspiration of a master. Senancour, though not a genius of Arnold's distinction, is a great poet in his own way, a subtle psychologist, and a philosophic writer of some calibre—

certainly a much more original thinker than Arnold; he had indeed the ideas which Arnold, generalising no doubt from an undue sense of his own deficiency, felt to be lacking in English writers. To Sainte-Beuve he was the 'true René', the ancestor of all the sad singing-birds of the French romantic era. But how few since Sainte-Beuve have realised this importance of Senancour—how few still appreciate his power, his originality, and above all, his poetic appeal! Senancour himself was eager to rest his title to the respect of future generations upon his work as a moral thinker; the fact remains, nevertheless, that it is primarily in the artistic greatness of his compositions that his genius lies. A writer of sympathy[1] has recently pointed out, what has often been forgotten or ignored, that Senancour was the first writer who thought of making the notation of his impressions of Alpine scenery a *literary* subject. This is his great distinction; in which, though he initiated the *genre*, he has not yet been surpassed. The transition to this very different way of regarding wild and rugged Nature from that which had prevailed a century before—an attitude summarised in Dr Johnson's complaint of mountainous scenery, 'which, by hindering the eye from ranging, forces the mind to find entertainment for itself',[2]—was made complete, and given its perfect expression, in Senancour. And side by side with Senancour, Arnold takes rank as perhaps the finest *poetic* interpreter of the Alps.[3] In this fact lies a large part of the secret of Senancour's attraction for Arnold. The spirit of the Alps is Arnold's muse, as it never

1 C.-E. Engel, *La Littérature alpestre en France et en Angleterre*, p. 104.
2 *Journey to the Western Islands.*
3 Despite the contrary view expressed by Sir William Watson. In *In Laleham Churchyard* Sir William says that Arnold is more fittingly at rest beside the Thames than by the Rotha, and 'summits lone and high'; he expresses it:

> 'Tis fittest thus! for tho' with skill
> He sang of beck and tarn and ghyll,
> The deep, authentic mountain-thrill
>   Ne'er shook his page....

was for Wordsworth. Wordsworth's descriptions of his Continental tours, in spite of some striking passages in the poems of his youth, make little contribution to our real understanding of Alpine loneliness and beauty; the intuition that divined the softer graces of the English Lake-country is lacking here.The fall of the avalanche 'thundering to dumbness' the wild mountain torrent was not like the soft voice of the Rotha to Wordsworth's ears: not on the cloud-strips hanging in the heads of the fir-trees, but on the cool flowery lap of earth, his pensive gaze was oftenest fastened, while his thoughts remained turned in on himself. But Arnold shared with Senancour the gift of plunging his personality into Nature, in a self-effacing way more complete than we find in Wordsworth. Wordsworth's love of Nature for the most part has not in it this strong pantheistic element. Sainte-Beuve remarked of Bernardin de Saint-Pierre and of Rousseau, that neither would have comprehended Senancour's abandonment of himself; in Nature, in spite of their sympathy, they had always distinguished a second Presence; and perhaps a third—that of God. And this is also Wordsworth's attitude. But Obermann, and Arnold, had sought to be only a kind of modification of the universal being; and, so entering the soul of Nature—which they often chose in its desolate and least human aspects—they were enabled to feel and interpret it in a way no one else had done. Not stopping at the mere reception of impressions, as Keats to some extent does, or even building on them a structure of beautiful abstract ideas, in the manner of Shelley, they took the impressions as fused in the light of their own intense personalities; and the qualities of which they saw the natural world was bearer—sublimity and purity—came to be, as it were, tokens of their analogues in an ideal moral world.

Perhaps in the foregoing study we may have seemed at times

to press resemblances, or to insist on borrowed ideas, where we were dealing merely with those which were the general currency of the age. But it has seemed worth while to point even to facts which were only a slender demonstration of our case, for these, by their suggestiveness, and above all, by their great number, have seemed to possess a cumulative weight of evidence which could hardly be disregarded.

Up to about 1855 and for brief spells later, Arnold was primarily a poet; and during this period the influence of Obermann overshadows all others. Where he has used other French writers—Quinet, Vigny, Lamartine, Renan or Sainte-Beuve—he has taken sparingly and with discrimination, and in his rendering of the borrowed idea or expression has in general transcended the original. But his penetration with the thought of Senancour is on a different footing: we believe, and it has been the intention of this book to show, that Arnold owed to Senancour at least as much as he himself stated, and far more than any of his critics have yet realised.

After 1860 Arnold, like Sainte-Beuve, began to devote himself to critical rather than to poetical writing, an evolution naturally determined by the intellectual quality of his genius. In a letter addressed to Madame de Solms Sainte-Beuve speaks of this change: 'Je connais Arnold,' he says, 'il nous aimait beaucoup dans sa jeunesse; il est allé voir George Sand à Nohant. C'était un Français et un romantique égaré là-bas'. He continues: 'Depuis il s'est marié, s'est réglé, et dans ses poésies il reste fidèle au culte des anciens et de l'art...'.[1]

In his later poetry indeed, by his returning classical bias, Arnold seems to withdraw more and more from his early romantic interests. As the fire of his youth and sentimental

[1] *Correspondence of Sainte-Beuve.* To Madame de Solms, 1860, quoted by A. Fryer Powell, 'Sainte-Beuve and Matthew Arnold', in the *French Quarterly*, Sept. 1921, vol. III, p. 153.

experiences sank lower, he turned less often to the sources that had kept it bright and living in the past; from that natural lyric inspiration he fell back upon a thoughtful and more self-conscious art: henceforth he would write little poetry with the pure spontaneous beauty of his first poems. The critical and intellectual instincts had triumphed in him.

But despite these changing interests, his attitude to French culture remained unchanged. If he sought something different in it now, his search was not less fruitful than of old: the new ideal which animated him he saw most clearly exemplified in the civilisation he preferred before all others. His own literary evolution, from romantic poet to critic, seems like a reflection of that of the man whom he now took as his master—Sainte-Beuve.

France, indeed, would never resign her dominion over him; she would maintain in his life her old rôle to the end. So, in this second period of Matthew Arnold's literary career, we shall find the influences from the Continent operating as strongly as ever; and, chief among these, France, continuing her constant function, of providing him with ideas, subjects and a model.

APPENDIX A

LINES WRITTEN ON THE SEASHORE AT EAGLEHURST, *July* 12, 1836

This poem was composed by Matthew Arnold in 1836, then aged thirteen years, when staying with his aunt at Eaglehurst, on the Isle of Wight. I am indebted to the kindness of Mrs Vere O'Brien for permitting its reproduction here for the first time, and for the following details.—An expedition of some kind having been planned by the family, it was found, at the moment of setting out, that the child Matthew was missing: after a search, the young poet was found sitting by the water, where he had written these lines:

Naiads were wont of old to dwell
Beneath the boundless Ocean's swell
And sport midst Halls of coral reared
Where winds and angry waters feared
To force their rushing way,
And crowned with sea-weed dance along
With bounding steps and mirth and song
While each perchance presided o'er
Some favour'd glen on wooded shore
    With mild and gentle sway.

What Naiad then—what Nymph presides
To shelter thee from winds and tides
To deck thy wooded cliff with flowers
To revel mid thy sea-girt bowers
And haunts, O Eaglehurst?
If Thetis self had deigned to prove
For some sweet spot peculiar love
Sure thou wert worthy of her sway
Thus cradled in thy quiet Bay
    By woodland fairies nurst.

What though the murmur of the sea
Beats gently on the sandy lea
And ever restless fills the ear
With sounds which it is sweet to hear
On many a quiet shore.
Yet here it seems as if the wave
Were struggling with the sand to lave
The foot of yonder wooded cliff—
And then a barrier firm and stiff
Opposed the Ocean's roar.
Still restlessly it struggles on
O'er sea-weed fair, o'er shell and stone
As though yon castled height looks down
And on the billows seems to frown
And bid the Invader go.
But other scenes than castled towers,
The flowery fields, the woods and bowers
Invite the Intruder onward still
But while his Fancy takes its fill
His waves must roll below.

These lines are interesting as a proof of Arnold's early poetic development; the idea is of course slight but the form is graceful. The Miltonic air is probably due to some unconscious imitation. It is inevitable that the youthful poems should not contain much hint of the thoughtful content which belongs to his later writings.

APPENDIX B

ARTICLE BY MATTHEW ARNOLD ON *OBERMANN*
[*The Academy*, October 9, 1869]

Obermann—Par De Senancour. Nouvelle Édition, revue et corrigée avec une Préface, par George Sand. Charpentier, Paris, 1863.

The most recent edition of *Obermann* lies before me, the date on its title-page being 1863. It is, I believe, the fourth edition which has been published; the book made its first appearance in 1804; three editions, and not large editions, have sufficed for the demand of sixty years.[1] Yet the book has lived, though with but this obscure life, and is not likely to die. Madame George Sand and Monsieur Sainte-Beuve have spoken in prose much and excellently of the book and its author. It may be in the recollection of some who read this that I have spoken of Obermann in verse, if not well, at least abundantly. It is to be wished, however, that Obermann should also speak to English readers for himself; and my present design is to take two or three points where he is most significant and interesting, and to present some of his deliverances on these points in his own words.

It may be convenient, however, that first I should repeat here the short sketch which I have already given elsewhere[2] of the uneventful life of the personage whom we call Obermann. His real name is Senancour. In the book which occupies us—a volume of letters of which the writer, calling himself Obermann and writing chiefly from Switzerland, delivers his thoughts about God, nature and the human soul—it is Senancour himself who speaks under Obermann's name.

1 Arnold seems not to have been aware that the edition under review was at least the third reprint of George Sand's edition of 1840; making a total number of editions of at least six at the time he was writing.
2 In the note to the *Stanzas in memory of the author of 'Obermann'*. Arnold says, in this note, of *Obermann*, 'The impressiveness of this production can hardly be rated too high'.

Étienne Pivert de Senancour, a Frenchman, although having in his nature much that we are accustomed to consider by no means French, was born in 1770, was trained for the priesthood, and passed some time in the seminary of St Sulpice, broke away from his training and country to live some years in Switzerland, where he married, came back to France in middle life, and followed thenceforward the career of a man of letters, but with hardly any fame or success. His marriage was not a happy one. He died an old man in 1846, desiring that on his grave might be placed these words only: 'Éternité, deviens mon asile'.[1]

Of the letters of Obermann, the writer's profound inwardness, his austere and sad sincerity and his delicate feeling for nature, are, as I have elsewhere remarked, the distinguishing characteristics. His constant inwardness, his unremitting occupation with that question which haunted St Bernard—*Bernarde, ad quid venisti?*—distinguish him from Goethe and Wordsworth, whose study of this question is relieved by the thousand distractions of a poetic interest in nature and in man. His severe sincerity distinguishes him from Rousseau, Chateaubriand, or Byron, who in their dealing with this question are so often attitudinising and thinking of the effect of what they say on the public. His exquisite feeling for nature, though always dominated by his inward self-converse and by his melancholy, yet distinguishes him from the men simply absorbed in philosophical or religious concerns, and places him in the rank of men of poetry and imagination. Let me try to show these three main characteristics of Senancour from his own words.

A Frenchman, coming immediately after the eighteenth century and the French Revolution, too clear-headed and austere for any such sentimental Catholic reaction as that with which Chateaubriand cheated himself, and yet from the very profoundness and meditativeness of his nature, religious, Senancour felt to the uttermost the bare and bleak spiritual

---

1 *Libres Méditations*, Soirée XXVIII, p. 410. The passage which is concluded by these lines is typical and striking. 'Le mal n'est qu'une discordance momentanée, la perfection doit appartenir à ce qui n'est pas soumis au temps: le doute, l'irrégularité, les vicissitudes peuvent attrister un lieu de passage; mais au-delà se retrouve la règle de la permanence. . . . Éternité, deviens mon asile!'

atmosphere into which he was born. Neither to a German nor to an Englishman, perhaps, would such a sense of absolute religious denudation have then been possible, or such a plainness and even crudity, therefore, in their way of speaking of it. Only to a Frenchman were these possible; but amid wars, bustle, and the glory of the *grande nation* few Frenchmen had meditativeness and seriousness enough for them. Senancour was of a character to feel his spiritual position, to feel it without dream of illusion, and to feel, also, that in the absence of any real inward basis life was weariness and vanity, and the ordinary considerations so confidently urged to induce a man to master himself and to be busy in it, quite hollow.

'People keep talking', says he, 'of doing with energy that which ought to be done; but amidst all this parade of firmness, *tell me then, what it is that ought to be done.* For my part I do not know; and I venture to suspect that a good many others are in the same state of ignorance.'

He was born with a passion for order and harmony, and a belief in them; his being so utterly divested of all conventional beliefs, makes this single elementary belief of his the more weighty and impressive.

'May we not say that the tendency to order forms an essential part of our propensities, our *instincts*, just like the tendency to self-preservation, or to the reproduction of the species? Is it nothing, to live with the calm and the security of the just?'

And therefore, he concludes, 'inasmuch as man had this feeling of order planted in him, inasmuch as it was in his nature, the right course would have been to try and make every individual man sensible of it and obedient to it'. But what has been done? Since the beginning of the world, instead of having recourse to this innate feeling, the guides of mankind have uniformly sought to control human conduct by means of supernatural hopes, supernatural terrors, thus misleading man's intelligence and debasing his soul. '*Depuis trois siècles, les résultats sont dignes de la sagesse des moyens.*'

What are called the virtues, 'are laws of nature as necessary to man as the laws of his bodily senses'. Instead of teaching men to feel this, instead of developing in them that sentiment of order and that consciousness of the divine which are the native possession of our race, Paganism and Christianity alike have tampered with man's mind and heart, and wrought confusion in them.

'Conquerors, slaves, poets, pagan priests, and nurses, succeeded in disfiguring the traditions of primitive wisdom by dint of mixing races, destroying memorials, explaining allegories and making nonsense of them, abandoning the profound and true meaning in order to discover in them absurd ideas which might inspire wonder and awe, and personifying abstract beings in order to have plenty of objects of worship. The principle of life—that which was intelligence, light, the eternal—became nothing more than the husband of Juno; harmony, fruitfulness, the bond of all living things, became nothing more than the mistress of Adonis; imperishable wisdom came to be distinguished only through her owl; the great idea of immortality consisted in the fear of turning a wheel, and the hope of strolling in a green wood. The indivisible divinity was parcelled with a hierarchical multitude torn by miserable passions; the fruit of the genius of primitive mankind, the emblems of the laws of the universe, had degenerated into superstitious usages which the children in great cities turned into ridicule.'

Paul at Athens might have set forth, in words not unlike these, the degradation of the Unknown God; now for the religion of which Paul was a minister:

'A moral belief was wanted, because pure morality was gone out of men's knowledge; dogmas were wanted which should be profound and perhaps unfathomable, but not by any means dogmas which should be absurd, because intelligence was spreading more and more. All religions being sunk into degradation, there was needed a religion of majesty, and answering to man's effort to elevate his soul by the idea of a God of all things. There were needed religious rites which should be imposing, not too common, objects of desire, mysterious yet simple; rites which seemed to belong to a higher world, and which yet a man's reason should accept as naturally as his heart. There was needed, in short, what only a great genius could institute, and what I can only catch glimpses of.

'But you have fabricated, patched, experimented, altered; renewed I know not what incoherent multitude of trivial ceremonies and dogmas, more fitted to scandalise the weak than to edify them. This dubious mixture you have joined to a morality sometimes false, often exceedingly noble, and almost always austere; the one single point in which you have shown sagacity. You pass some hundreds of years in arranging all this by inspiration; and your slowly built work, industriously repaired, but with a radical fault in plan, is so made as to last hardly longer than the time during which you have been accomplishing it.'

There is a passage to be meditated by the new Oecumenical Council! Not that Senancour has a trace of the Voltairean bitterness against Christianity, or against Catholicism which to him represented Christianity:

'So far am I from having any prejudice against Christianity, that I deplore, I may say, what the majority of its zealous adherents never think of deploring. I could willingly join them in lamenting the loss of Christianity; but there is this difference between us, that they regret it in the form into which it settled, nay, in the form, even, which it wore a century ago; whereas I cannot consider such a Christianity as that was to be much worthy of regret.'

He owns that religion has done much; but 'si la religion a fait de grandes choses, *c'est avec des moyens immenses*'. Disposing of such means, it ought to have done much more. Remark, he says, that for the educated class religion is one of the weakest of the motive-powers they live by; and then ask yourself whether it is not absurd that there should be only a tenth part of our race educated. That religion should be of use as some restraint to the ignorant and brutal mass of mankind, shows, he thinks, not so much the beneficence of religion as the state of utter confusion and misery into which mankind has, in spite of religion, drifted:

'I admit that the laws of civil society prove to be not restraint enough for this multitude to which we give no training, about which we never trouble our heads, which we bring into the world and then leave to the chance of ignorant passions and habits of low debauchery. This only proves that there is mere wretchedness and confusion under the apparent calm of vast states; that the science of politics, in the true sense of the term, is a stranger to our world, where diplomacy and financial administration produce prosperity to be sung in poems, and win victories to figure in gazettes'.

This concern for the state and prospects of what are called the masses is perpetually recurring with Senancour; it came to him from his singular lucidity and plain-dealing, for it was no commonplace with his time and contemporaries, as it is with ours. 'There are men', he says, and he was one of them, 'who cannot be happy except among men who are contented; who feel in their own persons all the enjoyment and suffering they witness, and who cannot be satisfied with themselves except they contribute to the order of the world and to man's welfare.' 'Arrange one's life how one will,' he says in another place, 'who can answer for its being any happier, so long as it is and must be *sans accord avec les choses, et passée au milieu des peuples souffrans?*' This feeling returns again and again.

'Inequality is in the nature of things, but you have increased it out of all measure, when you ought, on the contrary, to have studied to reduce it. The prodigies of your industry must surely be a baneful work of superfluity, if you have neither time nor faculties for doing so many things which are indispensable. The mass of mankind is brutal, foolish, given over to its passions; *all your ills come from this cause.* Either do not bring men into existence, or if you do, give them an existence which is human.'

But as deep as his sense was that the time was out of joint, was the feeling of this Hamlet that he had no power to set it right. *Vos douleurs ont flétri mon âme,* he says.

'Your miseries have worn out my soul: they are intolerable, because they are objectless. Your pleasures are illusory, fugitive; a day suffices for knowing them and abandoning them. I enquired of myself for happiness, but with my eyes open; I saw that it was not made for the man who was isolated: I proposed it to those who stood round me; they had not leisure to concern themselves with it. I asked the multitude in its wear and tear of misery, and the great of earth under their load of ennui; they answered me: We are wretched to-day, but we shall enjoy ourselves to-morrow. For my part, I know that the day which is coming will only tread in the footsteps of the day which is gone before.'

But a root of failure, powerlessness, ennui, there certainly was in the constitution of Senancour's own nature; so that, unfavourable as may have been his time, we should err in attributing to any outward circumstances the whole of the discouragement by which he is pervaded. He himself knew this well, and he never seeks to hide it from us. 'Il y a dans moi un dérangement', says he; 'c'est le désordre des ennuis.'

'I was born to be not happy. You know those dark days, bordering on the frosts of winter, when mists hang heavily about the very dawn, and day begins only by threatening lines of a lurid light upon the masses of cloud. That glooming veil, those stormy squalls, those uncertain gleams, that whistling of the wind through trees which bend and shiver, those prolonged throes like funeral groans—you see in them the morning of life; at noon, cooler storms and more steadily persistent; at evening, thicker darkness still, and the day of man is brought to an end.'

No representation of Senancour can, however, be complete without some of the gleams which relieved this discouragement. Besides the inwardness, besides the sincerity, besides the re-nouncement, there was the poetic emotion and the deep feeling for nature.

'And I, too, I have my moments of forgetfulness, of strength, of grandeur, I have desire and longings that know no limit. But I behold the monuments of effaced generations, I see the flint wrought by the hand of man, and which will subsist a hundred centuries after him. I renounce the care for that which passes away, and the thought of a present which is already gone. I stand still, and marvel; I listen to what subsists yet, I would fain hear what will go on subsisting; in the movement of the forest, in the murmur of the pines, I seek to catch some of the accents of the eternal tongue.'

Nature, and the emotion caused by nature, inspire so many beautiful passages in Obermann's letters that one is embarrassed to make a choice among them. The following, with which we will end our extracts, is a morning- and night-piece from the north end of the Lake of Neufchâtel, where the river Thièle enters the lake from Bienne, between Saint Blaise and Morat:

'My window had remained open all night, as is my habit. Towards four o'clock in the morning I was wakened by the dawn, and by the scent of the hay which they had been cutting in the cool early hours by the light of the moon. I expected an ordinary view; but I had a moment of perfect astonishment. The midsummer rains had kept up the waters which the melting snow in the Jura had previously swollen. The space between the lake and the Thièle was almost entirely flooded; the highest spots formed islands of pasture amidst the expanse of waters ruffled with the fresh breeze of morning. The waves of the lake could be made out in the distance, driven by the wind against the half-flooded bank. Some goats and cows, with their herdsman, who made a rustic music with a horn, were passing at the moment over a tongue of land left dry between the flooded plain and the Thièle. Stones set in the parts where it was worst going supported this natural causeway or filled up gaps in it; the pasture to which the docile animals were proceeding was not in sight, and to see their slow and irresolute advance, one would have said they were about to get out into the lake and be lost there. The heights of Anet and the thick woods of Julemont rose out of the waters like a desert island without an inhabitant. The chilly plain of Vuilly edged the lake on the horizon. To the south, this chain stretched away behind the slopes of Montmirail; and farther on than all these objects, sixty leagues of eternal snows stamped the whole country with the inimitable majesty of those bold lines of nature which give to places sublimity.'

He dines at the toll-house by the river-bank, and after passing the afternoon there, goes out again late in the evening:

'The moon had not yet risen; my path lay beside the green waters of the Thièle. I had taken the key of my lodging that I might come in when I liked without being tied to a particular hour. But feeling inclined to muse, and finding the night so warm that there was no hardship in being all night out of doors, I took the road to Saint Blaise. I left it at a little village called

Marin, which has the lake to the south of it. I descended a steep bank and got upon the shore of the lake where its ripple came up and expired. The air was calm; not a sail was to be seen on the lake. Everyone was at rest; some in the forgetfulness of their toils, others in the forgetfulness of their sorrows. The moon rose; I remained there hours. Towards morning, the moon shed over earth and waters the ineffable melancholy of her last gleams. Nature seems unspeakably grand, when, plunged in a long reverie, one hears the washing of the waves upon a solitary strand, in the calm of a night still enkindled and luminous with the setting moon.

'Sensibility which no words can express, charm and torment of our vain years! vast consciousness of a nature everywhere greater than we are, and everywhere impenetrable! all-embracing passion, ripened wisdom, delicious self-abandonment,—everything that a mortal heart can contain of life-weariness and yearning, I felt it all, I experienced it all, in this memorable night. I have made an ominous step towards the age of decline; I have swallowed up ten years of life at once. Happy the simple, whose heart is always young!'

There, in one of the hours which were at once the inspiration and the enervation of Senancour's life, we leave him. It is possible that an age, breaking with the past, and inclined to tell it the most naked truths, may take more pleasure than its predecessors in Obermann's bleak frankness, and may even give him a kind of celebrity. Nevertheless it may be predicted with certainty that his very celebrity, if he gets it, will have, like his life, something maimed, incomplete, and unsuccessful about it; and that his intimate friends will still be but a few, as they have hitherto been. These few will never fail him.

MATTHEW ARNOLD

APPENDIX C

FIVE UNPUBLISHED LETTERS FROM MATTHEW ARNOLD TO MADAME BLAZE DE BURY

The following letters, with their reference to the last volume of poems Arnold was to write, have their interest as belonging, for the most part, to his transitional period; and also as marking his association with a French family of some literary note in nineteenth-century Paris. The lady to whom they are addressed is the baroness Marie-Pauline-Rose de Bury, born Rose Stewart. She married a French diplomat and man of letters, Blaze de Bury, whose translation of Goethe's *Faust* (1840) is his best title to remembrance to-day. Three other works of his on German literature appeared in 1846, 1861 and 1868. He was a son of Castil-Blaze, a well-known personality in literary and dramatic circles of the first half of the nineteenth century. A musical critic of distinction, Castil-Blaze was responsible for the French libretto of *Der Freyschütz* which he adapted to the stage under the title of *Robin des Bois*. He wrote many successful *opéras-comiques*, among the best known being *Les Noces de Figaro*, an adaptation after both Beaumarchais and Mozart. By his friendship with Buloz he was intimately connected with the *Revue des Deux Mondes*, a connection maintained by his son. The 'paper' referred to in Arnold's letter of January 27, 1868, is the article by M. Henri Blaze de Bury on 'Guillaume Tell, pages d'histoire littéraire et musicale' which appeared in the *Revue* on December 15, 1867 (vol. LXXII, pp. 985–1000).

Castil-Blaze's son resumed the name of 'de Bury', to which he was entitled by his connection with the family of that name, descendants of Richard de Bury (bishop of Durham and tutor of Edward III), who wrote *Philobiblion*. His wife shared his interest in political and literary subjects, publishing studies on Molière, Racine and the French theatre. She also wrote some now forgotten novels, including *All for Greed* (1868), and *Love the Avenger* (1869). *All for Greed* ran during the winter of 1867–8 in *Saint Paul's*, and is the 'story' Arnold refers to below.

There is a certain humour in the scrupulously polite earnestness with which the English critic assures Madame de Bury that he cannot guarantee the publication of work not yet written.

Thomas Trevenen Penrose, the 'uncle' referred to in the first letter below, died on July 5, 1862. The adverse criticism of which Arnold speaks is probably that which was aroused by the lectures *On Translating Homer*, the series having just been concluded by *Last Words*; or possibly by his article on *The Twice-Revised Code* (March 1862).

Aylesbury—*July* 16 [1862].

Dear Madame de Bury

Your letter has just reached me here—had I been in London I should most gladly have accepted your invitation. The death of an uncle who was formerly my guardian obliged me about ten days ago to give up all my London engagements and to go into the country, and now I fear I shall not return to London till you have left it. I shall come and see however, when I return at the beginning of August, whether you are still to be found in Portugal Street. I am very glad you like my criticism, which has been, as possibly you have heard, vehemently *contested*. Believe me

Ever sincerely yours

MATTHEW ARNOLD.

Athenaeum, *Feb. 7th*, 1867.

My dear Madame de Bury

I had great pleasure in mentioning to the managers of Macmillan and the Cornhill your wishes about the notice of Cousin, and I will certainly, now that this notice is otherwise disposed of, mention to them your other projects. Your kind expressions do me and what I have written a great deal more honour than we deserve, but it is not my gratified vanity which induces me to make myself your intermediary with the editors, it is the conviction that in proposing your articles to them I am proposing to them what it is for their interest to take. Of this, however, they will insist on being themselves the judges, and I am perfectly certain they will say to me about these other papers as they did about the one on Cousin, that the project sounds well, that you are a good writer, etc. etc. etc., but that they will accept no article without first seeing it. But if you think fit to send either to Macmillan or to the Cornhill the papers you have named to me, I will undertake to have spoken to the editors about them before they arrive, and I should think there was little doubt of their being inserted, although I am, as

I have said and as I again assure you, perfectly powerless to procure a promise beforehand on this head.

I am sorry for the cause which makes you write, although I know that what you write I shall read with pleasure. I remain, dear Madame de Bury, very truly yours,

MATTHEW ARNOLD.

[Madame,
      Madame la baronne Blaze de Bury,
         rue de la Chaise, 9,
            Paris,
               France.]

2 Chester Square, *March* 17/67.

Dear Madame de Bury

You have not quite understood my suggestion. I recommend you to send the paper on Alfred de Vigny to Froude for 'Fraser'. I called at his house yesterday to speak to him about it, but he is out of town for a few days: however I am sure to have an opportunity of seeing him soon. And I have told Macmillan that I shall advise you to send the paper on French domestic life under Louis XV to *him*, though he will not enter into any engagement about taking it. But I think he will take it, though really, as I have before told you, my intervention in the matter has probably done harm rather than good.

Ever very faithfully yours

MATTHEW ARNOLD.

[Madame Blaze de Bury,
    9 rue de la Chaise,
        Paris
          France.]

The Athenaeum, *January 27th*, 1868.

Dear Madame de Bury

I have been away, and your letter addressed to me here has only just reached me. I am very glad you like my Cornhill disquisition[1]; when I see my criticisms of various kinds begin-

---

[1] 'Anarchy and Authority', in the *Cornhill Magazine*, January 1868.

ning to take hold here and there in England I often think of your having insisted on my critical qualities, years ago.

I have several times, as you know, spoken to Mr George Smith about your contributing to the Cornhill, but always, as I have told you, with one result: he speaks most civilly of you and your powers, declares that he will give his best attention to anything you may send him and that if suited to the Magazine it shall go in, and he will be most glad of it; but more than this I have never got from him, and never shall.

I have a weakness for novels and I daresay my judgements of them are indulgent—but I hear people who are, or think themselves, strict novel-critics speak favourably of your story in St. Paul's. Monsieur Blaze de Bury's paper in the Revue I had already seen, and thought it most interesting.

I will with pleasure send you my last volume of Poems. Considering that the Poems are mine, they may be said to have been popular.

> I remain, dear Mme de Bury,
>
> Very truly yours,
>
> MATTHEW ARNOLD.

[Madame Blaze de Bury   Grosvenor Hotel   Pimlico   S.W.]

Cobham, Surrey
Saturday [*June 11th*, 1881].

Dear Madame de Bury

I am quite sure you never either wrote or said anything to make me angry. I have been away for the Whitsun holidays, and have only just had your note: shall I call upon you on Tuesday at 3? if I do not hear, I shall conclude that I may.

> Most truly yours
>
> MATTHEW ARNOLD.

A. NOTE TO CHAPTER III: "A VISIT TO NOHANT." ARNOLD'S DIARIES OF 1846 AND 1847.

What Arnold did not mention in the account of his visit to Nohant was the extension of his journey from Boussac. It may be that this trip was not taken with the sole object of seeing George Sand, but was planned, from the outset, as an excursion to central France, and particularly to the Auvergne country, "the very heart and nucleus of old France," in his own words ("Auvergne, the kernel, as it were, of France," according to his father, who visited it in 1840), taking in Nohant en route. One can imagine him poring over "the great map," discussing the details of his journey beforehand, and perhaps reaching some sort of compromise over these; for Arnold did not set off alone; he had a companion to whom he refers as "J.P."

This was perhaps John Penrose, the cousin who had been assistant master at Rugby from 1839 to 1846, and so was there during the period when Arnold was teaching, from late February to mid April of 1845. John Penrose had only just left his post, and would be ready for an excursion of the kind. A little older than Arnold, he was a son of John Penrose the younger, his mother's brother.

When Arnold arrived at Boussac on July 1st, 1846 (and not August, as he says), he visited the Pierres Jomâtres (he must have skipped the description in *Jeanne*, or he would never have made the mistake of writing "Jaunâtres"), and saw the sunset at Toulx-Sainte-Croix; he gazed at "Puy and the high valley of the Loire," and wrote to George Sand.

But he did not immediately return to Boussac, as he implies in his *Essay*, but resumed his journey on July 2nd to

Montluçon in the Bourbonnais, and thence to Néris. On July 3rd he went on to Clermont Ferrand, and arrived the same day at Mont Dore, which he spells erroneously (following Madame de Sévigné) Mont D'or. After a visit to Lake Guéris, "J.P." left him on the 7th, presumably to return by a shorter route via Clermont or perhaps by the fashionable resort of Vichy, where the new Thermal Establishment had just been inaugurated. After "J.P.'s" departure, Arnold prolonged his stay, spending in all a week at Mont Dore and its environs. Perhaps inspired by the visit to the Lac de Guéry, he went to see Pavin to the south, and then round by La Tour d'Auvergne to Bort-les-Orgues in the Dordogne valley, where it was the thing to go and see the curious pipe-like formations. From Bort he returned to Mont Dore via Tauves on July 11th.

Everyone who has visited Auvergne knows the excitement of the approach to the shadowy blue line of its mountains, which appear to rise and loom clearer as one advances; knows also the pleasant sight of the scattered outlying farms, the quaint heaps of cottages that go for villages, the "southern air" of the whole region, with its ruins, churches, bastions and other memorials of devout and martyred France. The orchard-blossom around the farms would be over when Arnold arrived; and passed, too, was that early ripple of colour from sheets of golden broom, pink loose-strife and yellow king-cups, which runs over the spring grass.

No doubt his first act was to ascend the Mont Dore above the village and baths; this he strongly recommended his sister to do when she was contemplating a similar trip in 1855. From here he would get his most extensive view of the whole volcanic massif.

On the 6th, presumably still with "J.P.", he made the excursion to Lac Guéris (which he spells Guéry), an exquisite little lake lying to the north of Mont Dore. It is at a good height, over a thousand metres above sea-level, and is the result of a fall of basalt which has formed at this point a natural barrage. Arnold had a fondness for small lakes. When with Walrond at Breuil in 1858, he rambled about in search of some glacier tarns, marked on his map, and which are entered in his diary as the "lakes of La Balma". He also visited and bathed in a little lake above the village of Valtournanche the next day, and he and his wife were to rush past Lake Garda on their honeymoon; except for a stay overnight at the southern tip at Desenzano. Tennyson's later celebration of its beauties, in "Frater ave atque vale," would surely have exaggerated his distaste! He must have lingered, however, to gaze at "Guéry's" enchanting sleeping waters and its verge of sweet meadow-land; in contrast, above, at the basin of hills strewn with black boulders, where late-lurking snow had only just ceased to cast pale reflections into the blue lake. From here, too, he would have a good view of the Puy de Sancy to the immediate south; to the north he would glimpse the steep way up to the Banne d'Ordanche. On July 7th his companion left him, a pity, for it was the Lac Pavin, visited on the next day, the "Némi-like lake", as he described it to his sister, which most delighted him. To reach Pavin from Mont Dore he crossed the Col de la Croix-Saint-Robert, with another fine view of the region and the Puy de Sancy, and descended the low divide over a stretch of meadow-country, the Plateau de Durbise, to Besse, passing on the way Chambon-sur-Lac, Rocher de l'Aigle and Le Verdier.

Besse-en Chaudesse (a line of poetry is in the name, and Arnold was already, he fancied, feeling his poetic vocation) is an ancient agricultural town, with the remains of its early fortifications in a good state of preservation, and interesting for its fifteenth-century shops and houses, many of them built from the natural lava of the region. Arnold might have visited the Maison de la Reine Margot, where Marguerite de Valois is supposed to have stayed, or the Romanesque church of a much earlier date (but it is noteworthy that he never appears to have tried to see Saint-Nectaire).

From Besse he went round the south flank of the Puy de Sancy. The road turns south-east soon after leaving Besse, and the Lac Pavin is reached by a path on the left. This is his "Némi-like lake at the Cantal side of the Mont D'or". Almost circular, it is a typical crater-lake, strikingly sunk amongst forest-growth and scattered boulders, which contribute to its rather mysterious aspect (the name—Pavin, pavens—is the root of "épouvantable").

Immediately above it, to the south, rises the miniature Puy de Montchal, from which Arnold would have a magnificent circular view: the Monts Dore on the north-west; the Monts Dôme massed around the Puy de Dôme to the north; the valleys of Couzes and la Comté, and the Monts de Livradois and Le Forez to the north-east and east; and the Monts du Vélay to the south-east. In the foreground, to the south-west, Arnold had his best view of the Monts du Cantal.

From Pavin, Arnold skirted the Puy de Sancy, not turning aside for Condat-en-Fénicis, with its charming resort chalets, but continuing past the Lac Chauvet, Picherande, and Chastreix, to La Tour, where he spent the night.

"The old bourg of La Tour d'Auvergne" is a pretty place, not to be missed, Arnold says; it is surrounded by pastures, streams and cascades, and stands on the edge of the volcanic plain of the Artense, with its characteristic outcrops visible here and there. From La Tour a pleasant walk through pine-woods leads back to Mont Dore; but Arnold did not take this, preferring to strike across the plateau, via Bagnols, Cros and Lanobre, to Bort. This led him over the granitic plain which covers the area enclosed between the angle made by the confluence of the Dordogne and the Rhue. The Grande Rhue, augmented by the waters of the Rhue de Cheylade, which joins it where the gorge of the Rhue widens at Coindre above Embort, comes cascading over the Saut de la Saule, to join the Dordogne below Bort. Arnold must have greeted these rushing waters with joy, after his strange walk down the boulder-strewn plain, with its hillocks, moraines, fairy lakes and bogs, landmarks of a former glacier age. Rough crops, a few cattle and sheep (some of the blue cheese of Auvergne is produced here now) were the only signs of life as he pursued his way.

But at Bort-les-Orgues he was back in inhabited country. Bort is today a small town charmingly situated in the valley of the Dordogne. The Dordogne itself—resulting from the union of the torrents of the Dogne (D'afon) and the Dore, sister to that ubiquitous Dora, found (among other places) in French-speaking Aosta, which Arnold would follow down the valley five years later; and again, in his own Derwentwater and Lodore; with their headwaters in the Mont Dore group—is today disfigured by hydro-electric installations which Arnold was spared seeing. He probably made the tour of the basaltic organ-pipe formations and would have splendid views of both the Dordogne valley and the gorge of the Rhue from the Plateau des Orgues. The vast panorama of river, plain, and mountain, sank into his memory. It was from the first sight of this beauty that the poet of nature in him was confirmed, as he confessed to "K", forgetting perhaps those influences of his youth and boyhood received from Wordsworth in Westmorland.

He may have had a glimpse of the picturesque Château de Pierrefitte. He seems at all events to have slept in the village that night, the 9th, and very comfortably.

The next day he left Bort, and retraced his steps over the plain, seeing again the curious remains of its former glaciation. At Lanobre, where the path forks, Arnold took the more northerly route to Tauves, through scenery ever-changing and ever-changing perspectives. The broken terrain, river-gorges and mountain silhouettes must have deeply impressed him. From Tauves he rejoined the road to Mont Dore, re-entering the village from the north, on the 11th. There is no record of his visiting the Cascade de

Quereult, or Queureuich, which Clough was to see in the summer of 1861 during his stay at Mont Dore with the Tennysons.

On the 12th, Arnold had returned to Clermont. In one day he made the journey from Clermont to La Châtre; here, he says, he found the answer to his letter to George Sand awaiting him, and he called on her the next day, July 14th.

When he had stopped at the Eaux de Néris on his way south, the day after leaving Boussac, there is some piquancy in noting that he was preceding, by only a few days, the arrival there of another visitor, Madame d'Arbouville, a niece of Count Molé, and the close friend of Sainte-Beuve. She reached Néris on July 6th for a three weeks' sojourn to take the waters; and began writing almost immediately somewhat agitated letters to Sainte-Beuve (the first is dated July 8th), complaining of his silence, of the baths, and of the gambling and smoking habits of the male visitors (Matthew Arnold was fond enough of cards to have visited the casino too). Madame d'Arbouville's next letter crossed Sainte-Beuve's to her, of July the 12th. This coincidence with Arnold's presence on the spot has a certain interest, in view of the later fortunes of all three protagonists. Sainte-Beuve's and Madame d'Arbouville's letters were deemed worthy of collection after his death by his last secretary, Jules Troubat, who assembled them under the title "Le Clou d'or, petit roman imité d'*Adolphe*", for the *Nouvelle Revue* of September 1880.

Madame d'Arbouville was a cultivated woman, musical and widely read (she had read the novels of Lord Normanby, currently fashionable), and a poetess of sorts. She actually wrote a poem entitled "Resignation" for the *Revue des Deux Mondes*. At the moment of Arnold's visit to Néris, Sainte-Beuve had been for some time an assiduous frequenter of her salon. His letter of July the 12th is soothing, if a little flippant. On Arnold's return journey to Boussac, on July 13, he had to re-pass Néris, all unconscious of what the future was to hold in store for him in the way of friendships.

When he recommended his sister "K", in the letter referred to (of 25th April 1855), to go to Auvergne, in particular to La Tour and Clermont, he stated that he himself had never been as far as Issoire to the east, and this fact his diary bears out, indicating that his memory was not always unreliable. He speaks of the inns as good. However, he tried to dissuade Clough from going, probably fearing that the cold altitude would not suit him (see Arnold's *Letters to Clough*, p. 156); he suggested that if Clough did venture he should try "the Haute Loire above Puy" (Professor Lowry has not read the manuscript aright at this point and refers to "the Hanli Loui"); or Brittany, where Arnold acknowledges the inns are not so good (in 1859 he wrote disgustedly of his experiences of them when on an official tour of inspection).

Clough did, however, go to Mont Dore—he gives an unenthusiastic description of the village—and met Tennyson and his family there. He had arrived by a different route from Arnold's; via Clermont by diligence over Puy from the valley of the Allier. In company with Hallam Tennyson he visited the Cascade de Quereult; but was not well enough to go up the Pic, or Puy, de Sancy. Clough next went to Luchon via Tarbes in the Pyrenees, and was rejoined by the Tennysons. Subsequently he went to Dover to meet his wife, who accompanied him to Florence; where he was to die that November, in 1861.

There is a sad analogy here with the journey undertaken by Pauline de Beaumont. She also had gone to Mont Dore —against the advice of Joubert, her protégé, and thence to Rome, to rejoin Chateaubriand, just before her death in 1803. (Arnold, much later, in a flattering letter to Lady de Rothschild, could not resist comparing her to Madame de Beaumont, in Joubert's description!) To Néris, Chateaubriand also went in 1840 for the cure, and again in 1842, gaining, however, no more than a bad cold on each occasion in what he described as that "plus triste pays du monde"! Was Arnold perhaps aware of these associations when in 1861 he tried to dissuade Clough? For Dr Arnold, of course, Néris was not the equal of Harrogate!

In spite of the observation above, Arnold's memory was apparently not good, or he had mislaid his diary when he stated that he went on to Switzerland after his visit to Nohant. He went, in fact, straight back to Paris, and to London, and attended those two memorable performances of Rachel in *Phèdre* and in *Andromaque*, which he recalls in *The French Play in London*. The experience of seeing Rachel, almost certainly more than the plays themselves, had a magnetic effect on the impressionable youth; and it sent him back in December of the same year to Paris for an orgy of theatre-going.

The visit to Vevey and Glion, which, according to his statement in the essay on George Sand (see page 37, note 2), seemed to follow the excursion to Nohant, must be referred to another year. There seem to have been no journeys to Switzerland in 1845, 1846, or 1847. If it is referred to 1848, this date would not conflict greatly with his mention of the earlier visit in *Obermann once more* as occurring twenty years (a round number) before (see Note H). His diary entry "Begin Obermann", of October 1st, 1865, is made at Geneva. On January 20th of the following year, the entry "Obermann Once More" is erased, as though denoting the completion of the poem, which was subsequently published in 1867. It seems that the earlier visit to Glion was part of the tour which took him to Thun in 1848, when he probably approached Thun from the Valais. At all events, he did not make the journey to the Lake of Geneva and Glion in 1846; his diary is definite on this point. The climax of the Auvergne trip was London.

Possibly it was on the recommendation of George Sand that he returned to London to see Rachel. It would not be out of keeping that Sand should praise Rachel, and mention her London season to Arnold. At this time the two women were on very cordial terms. Rachel had succeeded George as Musset's friend, but this would arouse no resentment in George Sand, whose association with Chopin had replaced the earlier one.

On Monday, July 20th, Arnold saw Rachel for the first time, as Hermione in *Andromaque*, at the St James's Theatre. This was a repeat performance of the previous Saturday's. On the 22nd he attended what was a command performance of *Phèdre*, honoured by the presence of the Queen and Prince Albert. This was indeed a gala night. Rachel was received "with unbounded enthusiasm", according to the notice in the *Times*, and had to take repeated curtain calls at the close. *Les Plaideurs* was also billed for performance, but in the event it was replaced by *Le Bourgeois gentilhomme*; *Les Héritiers* was also given as a curtain-raiser. Truly an evening to stir the imagination.

On the following night, Rachel was to appear in *Virginie*, a modern tragedy on a subject taken from Livy, which had been specially written for her by Latour de Saint Ybars. It had not the success accorded to *Adrienne Lecouvreur*, also her own play, in 1849; nor did Arnold stay for it. He was at last on his way home. By the end of the month he was back at Fox How.

But, one assumes, he was already revolving the decision to return to France, if he had not actually taken it. Back to Paris, indeed, he was to go; arriving there on December 29th, 1846.

Paris, at the close of 1846, was in its usual state of gay ferment. The year that was passing had brought some tragedies to the world of art and letters (in London the suicide of Haydon had shocked his friends, including Elizabeth Barrett), but also many exciting events. When Arnold hastened home in July, he knew no doubt of Senancour's death in January, perhaps also of Toepffer's in Geneva, in the month preceding his call at Nohant. But did he also notice when passing through Paris any of the plays billed to appear that year? Among them was to be an adaptation of *Werther, Charlotte,* by Émile Souvestre and Eugène Bourgeois; it was first presented at the Vaudeville on July 25th. Another play billed to appear was Jacques Aragon's *Mademoiselle Lange,* also given at the Vaudeville Theatre.

Sainte-Beuve and Juste Olivier, preparing their joint *Sommaires des Chroniques parisiennes* for the *Revue Suisse* of that year, give news that reads very excitingly at this distance of time. One of the outstanding events in theatrical Paris in August was Jules Janin's translation of *Clarissa Harlowe* and its adaptation for the French stage by the trio, Dumanoir, Clairville and Gaillard, for the actress Rose Chéri at the Gymnase. It had been widely acclaimed by the public and noticed as a great success by Auguste Vacquerie, writing for *L'Époque.* Among other literary titbits, the "chroniqueurs" described Saint-Marc Girardin's call on Madame d'Arbouville; the publication of Béranger's memoirs, with some newly-written songs (it was probably owing to Sainte-Beuve's influence that Arnold at first ranked Béranger above Musset); and an article on "La Poésie slave" by Lacaussade, the creole from Réunion and future secretary of Sainte-Beuve; and also the translator of the *Stanzas in memory of the author of Obermann.*

In October, Philarète Chasles had put forward his candidature for election to the Academy; and he, with Sainte-Beuve, had resigned from the *Revue des Deux Mondes.* Curiously, Philarète Chasles had a review on July 13th in the *Journal des Débats* of Lord John Campbell's *Vies des Grands Chanceliers.* Arnold may have remembered seeing this review when he picked up or was offered the volume— in English, *Lives of the Chancellors*—when staying on May 5th, 1851, after the engagement party, at Hampton with his future father-in-law, Justice Wightman.

The question of Chasles's influence on Arnold it is hoped to discuss elsewhere. Arnold states that it was through Chasles that he first met Michelet, and perhaps he was introduced to him at one of the functions he attended during this winter in Paris. Rachel, it is known, frequented the salon of the first Madame Chasles.

Chasles had met Dr Arnold when working in London for an English publisher, James Valpy, in Chancery Lane, whose school text-books were probably used or consulted by Dr Arnold. There are one or two references to him in Chasles's essays. The fact that Matthew Arnold drew away from him to court Sainte-Beuve (was Arnold as fastidious as he is generally held to be in his friendships?) does not preclude some direct influence. Chasles's criticism of Shelley, for instance, reads very much like Arnold's lines:

> What boots it, Shelley! that the breeze
> Carried thy lovely wail away,
> Musical through Italian trees . . .

Chasles speaks of Shelley's "mélodie sans mesure" and likens it to the "nuage qui passe dans le ciel et se disperse sous le vent qui souffle". It is odd, by the way, to note Arnold's lines above, and set them beside his criticism of Keats for using archaisms; this is also precisely what Chasles finds fault with in Keats.

But of greater importance for Arnold was the collection and publication earlier in the year of Sainte-Beuve's first two volumes of *Portraits contemporains*, which included his articles on Béranger, as well as the famous two articles on Senancour of 1832 and 1833.

In December there appeared Jules Janin's letter in the *Journal des Débats*, giving the account of Rachel's supposed conversion and Rachel's reply. Arnold's diary entry for January 23rd, 1847 ("Janin, Rachel, Andromaque") may be a reference to this, or simply to Janin's notice of the performance.

Matthew Arnold's diaries for 1846 and 1847, which Alan Harris saw and used—perhaps when they were in John

Drinkwater's possession, as they appear to have passed to him from Browning, possibly at the sale of Browning's property in London in May, 1913—show that he left Oxford on December 24th, 1846. On December 27th he left London, and on the 28th he started at 6.30 a.m. from Folkestone for Paris. On December 29th he was in Paris to see Rachel in *Polyeucte*.

There appear to be no letters of Arnold's own available for this period; and the diaries, and some comments in the letters of Clough and his friends with Arnold's own back-glancing references, must be relied on for the reconstruction of the story of his stay in Paris. But these meagre data throw a very interesting light on his doings, and the picture accords well with what was latent and to be developed, and what was latent and to be suppressed, in the young Arnold's character, as one may conjecture it to be in these formative years.

During this winter he appears to have spent money lavishly, both on himself and in entertaining others. His expense-accounts for the journey and the stay in the French capital—prolonged until February 11th, 1847—show that he disposed of a very large sum indeed for the times. But even his entries of trivial items have a certain savour; there was the umbrella, for example, bought in London, where it was probably raining, and of course he had a new hat to protect—and perhaps had left his old umbrella in the train. There was also the opera-glass—for quizzing his favourite actresses?

Leaving out of account his rail- and steamer-fares and hotel-bills, he spent an inordinate amount on books and clothes, including hats, shoes and accessories; an enormous sum on "bonbons"—no doubt for a mysterious purpose of his own; on dinners (sixty francs on one occasion and fifty-five at the Café de Paris on another); on cabs and on theatre- and opera-tickets. The latter are small items when he seems to have gone alone; but at times he must have entertained a party of friends, to judge from the size of the entries. He also took French lessons, which cost him one hundred and eight francs. As he attended Lady Elgin's Embassy Ball, and the Opera Ball, dined out, played (and lost) at whist, his expenses mounted. He was, not surprisingly, laid up once or twice (notably after dining at the Café Löwenberg) and had to disburse something for medicines in consequence.

What is most interesting is the record of his attendances at the Théâtre Français and other theatres. In addition to seeing ten performances by Rachel, he frequented the Variétés, the Ambigu, the Gymnase, the Palais Royal, the Vaudeville and the Opera.

Pauline (or Marie-Virginie) Déjazet, "cette vive, bizarre et indéfinissable créature," in the words of Sainte-Beuve, had been playing at the Variétés since 1845, and Bouffé since 1843. These two actors, after Rachel, seem to have captured Arnold's fancy more than any others. Déjazet was an accomplished and experienced actress. She had begun her career as an interpreter of juvenile parts, among them the fairy in *La Belle au Bois Dormant* in 1811. On one of her provincial appearances she dropped the name Virginie and was thereafter known simply as Déjazet. She subsequently interpreted many men's parts, in plays by Scribe and others, and appeared at the opening of the Gymnase in 1821; where, however, Jenny Vertpré was a serious rival. She also played at the Nouveautés. Her mature acting caused the raising of some supercilious eyebrows, but her roguish and charming manner endeared her to the public. Gautier was one of her admirers and praised her performance, particularly in *La Gardeuse de Dindons* of 1845. By the end of her career she had appeared at nearly all the leading theatres in Paris, including the Palais Royal and the Gaîté. When a new theatre was built in 1854, her son became director, and it was known as the Théâtre Déjazet. On the opening night she played to a distinguished audience in the production of a play by Sardou.

Hughes-Marie-Désiré Bouffé had acted at the Variétés since 1843. He had appeared in London at the Haymarket (London's French Theatre) as early as 1831, and again in 1842, when he and Déjazet nearly stole Rachel's laurels. In 1831 he was acting at the Gymnase, and remained there, until engaged at the Variétés in 1843. But the star of the Gymnase in 1846, at the time of Arnold's visit, was Rose Chéri.

Rose Chéri, otherwise Marie Cizos, was later to marry Montigny, the proprietor of the Gymnase, in 1847. In 1848, when the theatre was converted into a hospital during the riots, "she, with many of her charming companions, were indefatigable in their attendance [on the wounded], showing," in Lord Normanby's words, "that they knew as well how to alleviate the real wants and sorrows of human life as to chase away its ennuis" (*Journal of a Year of Revolution*, Vol. II, p. 12, note).

Rose Chéri had also been on tour in London. She was playing there in June 1846, and it was precisely on June 22nd that Arnold had gone up to town to see his dentist. It seems likely enough that he at least heard about her then. She had made her regular début in Paris at the Gymnase in 1842, in the play *Estelle*. It had not caused any sensation. But chance favoured her, and in this same year she actually replaced Mademoiselle Nathalie in *Une Jeunesse Orageuse*; and with her charm had conquered audience and critics alike. Théophile Gautier saluted her talent, and Musset was so much impressed with her acting in *Clarissa Harlowe* that he went to see her thirty times running. One need not then feel surprise to note Arnold's assiduity; he went to see her play four times at the Gymnase, and surely at least once in *Clarisse Harlowe* (first given in August 1846). He certainly saw her in *Irène*, which he notes.

At the Palais Royal he attended a performance by Mademoiselle Nathalie; at the Vaudeville it was Madame Doche who was the attraction.

Madame Doche, born Marie-Charlotte-Eugénie de Plunkett in 1823 in Brussels, had made her début in 1837, and had married the composer Pierre Doche in 1839. Her most famous rôle was that of Marguerite in *La Dame aux Camélias*, which she created in 1852. She also had played at the Gymnase for a short period; but had returned to the Vaudeville, and was to remain there, apart from the usual tours in London, Brussels and Switzerland, until her retirement. She had a style of her own and was not in any sense a rival of Rachel. The two actresses appear to have felt a mutual esteem each for the other; thus Rachel gave her portrait to Madame Doche, inscribed simply "Rachel à Doche".

Rachel's career is too well known to be more than summarised here. Born in 1821 in Switzerland in the Canton of Aargau, she made her first appearance in Paris, also at the Gymnase, in 1837. The next year she appeared as Camille in *Horace* at the Théâtre Français; and from this time, until her health failed, her genius was universally acclaimed. The harshly-singing child had become the irresistible actress whose impersonation of the characters of French classical drama left her audiences spellbound. In 1849 *Adrienne Lecouvreur* was written for her by Scribe and Legouvé, and this was her greatest success in contemporary drama. There is no record of Arnold's seeing her in this year, although one might have expected him to pass through Paris with the intention of doing so. Her death at Le Cannet in 1858 was memorialised in his three sonnets. In 1859 he took stalls for himself and his wife at the Français—one wonders with what sensations.

Clough, in one of his letters, observed after Arnold's return to England: "Matt Arnold is just come back from Paris; his stay at the latter end seems to have been very satisfactory to him . . . [he] is full of Paris and the things of Paris—specially the theatres." He might have added: "and specially the Théâtre Français." This theatre appears to have been Arnold's favourite—"Rachel's Switzerland", he calls it, in a phrase that could sound oddly but is, in fact, from Arnold's pen, most revealing. This was where her high art reached its supreme expression; as, for others, a country like Switzerland could serve (see page 241).

Arnold went to see Rachel there ten times in all, and appears to have been completely subjugated by her. After *Polyeucte* on December 29th, the day of his arrival, he saw her as Hermione in *Andromaque* again, on the 31st, and so could compare her performance with his first sight of her in London on July 20th in the same rôle. On December 30th he saw Déjazet at the Variétés. On January 1st he was at the Français to see *Tartuffe*, with the actress Brohan as Dorine. Joséphine-Félicité-Augustine Brohan, born in 1824, had made her début in this part in 1841, following her famous mother, Susanne, in the same rôle. Arnold was always lacking in enthusiasm for Molière, and this appears to be the only representation he attended. On January 2nd he was present at *Horace*, with Rachel playing Camille. After Rose Chéri at the Gymnase on the 5th, he saw *Cinna* at the Français, with Rachel as Emilie, on the 6th.

On the 9th he was at the Ambigu; on the 11th at the Variétés to see Bouffé and (Virginie) Déjazet again. On the 12th he was at the Français to see *Judith*; and at the Variétés again on the 13th.

On the 14th he attended the Opera; and on the 16th he saw Rachel in *Horace* again.

On the 17th he was at the Palais Royal to applaud Mademoiselle Nathalie. Although he saw her only once, it is a guess if this was due to circumstances or because Arnold was less attracted to her.

Zaïre Nathalie, or Nathalie Martel, born in 1816, made her effective début at the Gymnase in 1838, after a series of smaller parts mainly at the Odéon and at the Théâtre St. Antoine. At this time she passed for one of the prettiest women in Paris. Slim and elegant, with large dark eyes, she could dance as well as act. Her favourite parts were light rôles in melodrama. In 1845 she left the Gymnase, where Rose Chéri replaced her; and after the season in London, which had now become classical, she returned to Paris and was engaged at the Palais Royal for two years. Among her popular successes was the part of Dorothée in *La Pêche aux Beaux-pères*; she appeared also in two revues, *Les Pommes de terre malades* in 1845, and *La Poudre à Coton* in 1846. Perhaps this last was the piece which Arnold witnessed. He had a fondness for the not-so-serious stage which he kept all his life. As late as 1885, when he was in Berlin, he went off with his English cronies from the Embassy to attend a popular theatre (in preference to seeing *Undine,* or *The Duchess of Gerolstein,* then being produced), where he saw *The Wild Cats,* "a broad, comic piece", in his own words.

But Mademoiselle Nathalie aspired to higher things, as she informed Jules Janin; and after a preliminary run of the old type of play at the Vaudeville, "elle s'est rangée", and she went on to perform in more serious drama. After 1849 she was to play the Countess in *Le Mariage de Figaro,* Madame Maréchal in *Le Fils de Giboyer,* Jocaste in *Oedipe Roi,* Madame Guérin in *Maître Guérin*—parts which would have been perhaps less to Arnold's taste.

At all events, on the 19th of January he was back at the Théâtre Français to see Rachel again, this time in *Le Cid.*

A couple of dinners and the Embassy Ball supervened; but on January 23rd he was to see *Andromaque* with Rachel a third time.

On Sunday the 24th he went out to Versailles, but returned in the evening to attend a performance at the Vaudeville. On the 25th he saw Rachel in Corneille's *Don Sanche.* On the 26th he was at the Vaudeville to see Madame Doche, playing perhaps in Gozlan's *Trois Rois, Trois Dames.*

For two consecutive nights he was again at the Gymnase, with Rose Chéri playing. On the 29th it was Rachel again, in *Phèdre.* After the Opera Ball he closed this breathtaking

month with an attendance at the Variétés, and noted seeing Déjazet and Bouffé again.

On the first night of February he saw Rachel's performance in *Marie Stuart*. The Variétés followed; the Vaudeville with Madame Doche; then he was back at the
Variétés for two nights running, with his two favourites
playing.

On February 6th he bought a copy of Béranger's songs
for Clough; what else he did is not recorded; but on Sunday the 7th he was at the Vaudeville again to see Madame
Doche. The next night he notes Rose Chéri in *Irène* at the
Gymnase, and on the 9th he saw Madame Doche again
at the Vaudeville. On February the 10th he saw Déjazet
again at the Variétés, playing opposite the actor Vernet.
As this attendance at the Variétés definitely belongs to
"the latter end of his stay", it must have been among the
"highly satisfactory experiences" to which Clough alludes.
No doubt Arnold's French, and his appreciation of French
acting, had improved after his almost frantic "appren-
tissage".

It is not clear whether this was the first time, on the
10th, that he had seen Charles-Edmé Vernet. The latter
had made an early début at the Variétés, as far back at
1807; and was an artist in the best tradition of French
acting. He was at the Variétés for over forty years, creating
one new rôle after another.

His acting was considered excellent and correct—rather
more in the conscious classical tradition than inspired;
but comedy parts he appears to have played to perfection.
Gautier wrote enthusiastically of his performance in the
rôle of Gaspard in *Le Père de la Débutante*, dating from
1838; and after his acting in *Madame Pinchon*, he declared:
"Vernet, ce comédien si naturel . . . [est] si parfait que nous
[le] préférons beaucoup à Bouffé." A. de Rochefort did not
rate him so highly in his "critiques"; he thought Vernet
"gai, sans esprit", and was otherwise more reserved in his
praise. It is a thousand pities that we have no record of

Arnold's preference; largely unsophisticated at this time, he might have given a more naïve but more sincere comparison of the two actors, before he had developed "the nice sense of measure" which enabled him later to condemn out of hand the great ladies who sought for soul and "found it in Madame Sarah Bernhardt".

This performance at the Variétés was his last fling. The next day he left Paris; on the 12th of February he was at Boulogne, crossing to Folkestone and reaching Oxford on the 13th. He reappeared among his friends in a state of jubilation. On the 14th and 15th Clough is writing about Arnold's holiday. Clough's published letters appear to be much cut, but the remaining contents leave little doubt that Arnold returned highly exhilarated by his adventure. Every night out for more than six weeks—"two months" he says in his essay on *The French Play*, pardonably exaggerating—seeing Rachel, whom he was never to forget, ten times; the handsome Madame Doche at least four times; the charming Rose Chéri also four times; Mademoiselle Déjazet nearly as often as Rachel! It was indeed a feast for a stage-struck boy.

Charlotte Brontë had shrunk from seeing one performance of Rachel's in 1842; Arnold had revelled in a dozen. When later he was to criticise *Villette* and express his distaste for its exhibition of passion (curiously insensitive to its style, more fitted, indeed, than his own to express a lyric view of life), he was revealing the change in himself. He disliked "Villette", as he disliked the poems of Elizabeth Barrett, possibly because it was written by a woman and he came to care less for women in professions; but mainly because it was too passionate and too personal for his taste. He had determined to thrust passion out of his own life, and had chosen to live in the world and to adopt its worldly tone. "I in the world must live," he declares.

But why, at the height of his powers and appeal—for these words occur in the first poem to *Obermann*—did he see the choice imposed on him? Why did "an invincible destiny have to efface his dreams?" Why did he accuse fate of forcing him to leave half of his life with Oberman; and let some undefined deity deprive him of 'Marguerite', or at least halt his pursuit of her? His genius poses these questions, but does not answer them. He had determined to forget; or to remember only as a man of the world recalls his youthful enthusiasms. He succeeded. As Sainte-Beuve said, "Il s'est réglé" (one must modify the view [see page 256] that Sainte-Beuve's own conduct of life offers an explanation, or a complete analogy. Sainte-Beuve was never a great poet). And to this deliberate choice, and to his success in adhering to it, we owe the formation of the urbane and brilliant critic who ousted the young and amorous, mercurial and restless poet (see pages 255 and 256).

It has seemed delightful to dwell on these early experiences of the young Matt Arnold. It was certainly at this time (see pages 7 and 8) the pure glamour of the stage, and the artists' personalities, which had conquered him. We need not take too seriously his later assertion that French actors are generally superior to the dramatists whose plays they are interpreting; or that Rachel overtopped Racine in intellectual power; but this exaggeration recalls to us the younger, more natural Matthew Arnold, sincere and boyish, rather than the later apostle of "culture". Deep in his heart, he assures us, he never forgot this other self entirely. He was certainly conscious in after years that he was playing a part; he speaks as though it were a forced necessity; and perhaps it was, to fill the blank caused by the dying poet. In the years to follow he was painfully to ransack his manuscripts and his imagination for more poems to publish. They were not forthcoming. But the first of the three sonnets to Rachel, which appeared in the volume of 1867, has a glancing reference to her birthplace in Aargau (he says "Aarau", confusing the town with the canton. She was actually born in the village of Mumpf), the valley-canton drained by the Aar; and it flings open suddenly, if momentarily, a door onto the poetic past. Arnold is back in spirit revisiting the world of his youth; the region of the Aar and the scene of his romantic love, and of the Sarine (alias the Saanen) which joins the Aar; and so perhaps of Senancour hovering over its "torrent". Surely Arnold briefly glimpsed these scenes again as he wrote; relived the days of his "fellowship of mood" with his "master", Senancour, and recalled "his flying span of cheerful youth"; as he made that curious analogy with the Théâtre Français, of Switzerland and the Rhine—into which flows the Aar from Thun and Berne.

If the name of the river Aar contains as its root the Celtic "arw", with its implications of ravage and violence, the site was symbolic, not for Rachel only, but for Matthew Arnold. How sharply—continuing to seek for roots!—could one make a contrast with the antithetical Thames, "the quiet river", associated with his marriage, and near which he rests quietly today (see page 253, note 3).

B. NOTE TO PAGE 58, AND PAGE 58, NOTE 3: *STANZAS FROM THE GRANDE CHARTREUSE.* ARNOLD'S DIARY OF 1851, "THE FOREIGN TOUR".

Although Oberman mentions his intention of visiting the Grande Chartreuse (in Letter LXXXII), there is no record of Senancour's having gone there. In a letter to Saussure, he speaks of having considered it as a place to retire to. It was of course, a recognised objective for travellers and sightseers, long before Dr Arnold's visit in 1830 with his brother-in-law, Trevenen Penrose, and the latter's wife. On this occasion, the party had gone on to Chambéry on July 17th and proceeded, by the Val d'Aosta almost certainly, to Varese, which they reached on July 24th. Here

they visited the Sacro Monte before continuing their journey to Venice. The return had been by way of the Tyrol
(Meran), and the Rhine, and included Dr Arnold's famous visit to the ageing Niebuhr at Bonn.

The Carthusian monastery was a "point de repère" in
the standard tour of the times. Thomas Gray, the friend
of Bonstetten, Wordsworth, and Ruskin among English
travellers; Stendhal and Lamartine among the French, have
all recorded their impressions. Chateaubriand, in Book IV
of the *Mémoires*, which Arnold was reading at this time,
describes a visit in 1805 with his wife and Ballanche, when
they were also caught in a rainstorm. (He went again in
1838).

In planning his wedding-tour in 1851, Arnold must have
had in mind an itinerary which would not overlap his previous trips to the Continent, with their, perhaps, too vivid
associations, especially with 'Marguerite'.

His fancy must have turned him away from these to a
journey which would include a spot no doubt a by-word
in the family, after Dr Arnold's enraptured description of
it as "certainly enough to make a man romantic".

One cannot agree, however, with the criticism which
attempts to connect the ideas of the poem with the circumstances of Arnold's wedding-tour. Arnold's mind had
long been pondering the poem's theme. His visit in 1851
with his bride can only very inconsistently be linked with
the main subject, and with the despairing image of himself as having "nowhere yet to rest [his] head". The ironic
description by one critic of the *Grande Chartreuse* as a
"poème de noces" is pointless.

Arnold had for years cherished the sad forebodings which
are the staple of the poem; and his reverence for Senancour, who personified these in his fancy, was also of long
standing. To show how he harboured old memories, and
how he would continue to dwell on the past and his
period of youth, is unnecessary here. But one may mention that the *Grande Chartreuse* was not published until

1855. In 1852 the poet was to note his reading of Senancour's *Libres Méditations;* and again in 1858 he was re-reading and annotating it, still under the spell of Senancour's thought and manner. In 1877 he is quoting Oberman's exquisite passage on death. It is certain that his mind brooded for long after his marriage on the allied interests of his youth. What occurred in 1851 enabled him to collect notes for a description of the site of the monastery, but the idea for the poem must have already been fully adumbrated; only some details and perhaps the formal presentation needed working up.

The topographical details naturally enhance the poem's interest. The Arnolds appear to have attended, in the conventual chapel, the "office de nuit" at midnight, and probably slept after this in the little Hotel du Désert. The verses which give an account of the service also describe the library and garden. There appears no ground here for the charge of discrepancy, levelled at Arnold by Tinker and Lowry, in this description with that of the concluding stanzas, where the imagery is transferred from the severe monastery:

> Where no organ's peal
> Invests the stern and naked prayer,

to a conventual abbey, in which

> The organ carries to our ear
> Its *accents of another sphere.* [my italics]

Arnold prepares the change of scene by a change of emphasis in the argument, as well as giving himself the chance of a literal translation of a line of Senancour's—"Sons d'un autre monde".

There is, again, no contradiction in his substitution of "desert" for "forest" in the last line. The meaning is clear for either word, but "desert" is an improvement, because the region surrounding the monastery was known to everyone as the "désert", and the word emphasises the note of desolation which pervades the poem. It gives also another vivid reminder of Senancour. Those critics who reproach Arnold for this apparent discrepancy fail to see that he was doubtless not thinking exclusively of the Grande Chartreuse and its "desert", but also of Oberman's "Imenstròm", which was his "désert" or his "chartreuse", as he variously calls it (see Note L). "Désert" is in fact a general term, probably from the Celtic *dysart*, a holy, retired place, and is so used by Senancour for any Alpine solitude, however situated. "Imenstròm", in the verdurous valley of the Vevayse, was his "désert", and so also was the region between Ermenonville and Chaalis where he took refuge in 1795, after his father's death and the realisation of his disastrous marriage. This particular desert is a vast region of hilly undergrowth and tortured birch-trees, reminiscent both of some parts of Switzerland and of the "lone brakes" of Fontainbleau. Arnold certainly read the passage which describes it in the *Réveries* for the year VIII. As an additional touch, there was in fact a deserted monastery at Chaalis. One need go no further to explain the apparent contradiction which critics, unfamiliar with the special meaning of the word, and particularly with Senancour's use of it, have expended much ingenuity to explain. In short, the French word simply designates a sequestered spot. The Jansenists' "désert" in the Vallée de Chevreuse had its garden and woodland. When, in the last scene of the *Misanthrope*, Alceste speaks of returning to his "désert", he means a well-appointed country mansion! In our time, the "desert" of Edgar Varèse's ballet-score is identified at one moment with life in a great city; and also with the desert in the soul.

Arnold may not have been aware of all these *nuances*, but he must certainly have understood the use of "desert" to express a place of retreat—even if in the heart of a forest! It is quite possible that he knew the passage in

Boileau's *Lutrin* in which "La Piété sincère, aux Alpes retirée, Du fond de son désert entend les tristes cris," etc.; Boileau takes the trouble to append a note to the effect that "La Grande Chartreuse est dans les Alpes."

The rest of the poem is a meditation on the plight of modern man. After invoking Byron, Shelley, and Oberman in verses which have the familiar melancholy ring, he turns to the Carthusians for some sort of comfort and hope for the future. The poem furnishes an excuse for re-introducing his well-worn reflections on Senancour. There is no evidence to support Tinker and Lowry's theory that the background motif of the poem is linked with the Oxford movement. Arnold had separated himself not so much, like his father, from Newman, Pusey and Keble, as, like Senancour, from Christian belief. The atmosphere is continental and the references to Senancour are textual.

The further stages of Arnold's honey-moon tour do not strictly belong to a study of his relations with France, but they may be associated with these insofar as France's intervention in Italian affairs was to be a later pre-occupation of Matthew Arnold. From this point of view, one has an excuse for following him and his wife on their interesting tour across the Sardinian Kingdom, to Novara, Milan and Venice, back to Milan, and thence hurriedly by way of Como, Lugano, and the St Gothard, to Lucerne, Strasbourg, and Paris.

Sardinia and the Lombardo-Venetian provinces had already been the scene of Dr Arnold's travels on at least five occasions between 1825 and 1841, which had included Padua and Venice. His son was thus again following in his footsteps, as he had done in Auvergne. Matthew Arnold would take his wife, as Dr Arnold had not always done, and he would have the additional pleasure of showing her Verona and Venice (he was reading *Romeo and Juliet* before he left, as well as *Delphine*—although *Corinne* would have fitted in better with Venice). For himself, he would be seeing the Graian Alps for the first time; and, what may have been the most important motive of all, he would get a glimpse of conditions in Italy after the insurrections of 1848 and the First War of Italian Independence.

How much he saw of these, and to what extent he was impressed, one can only gather from later references, for example, to the destruction in Milan as he first saw it; in a letter to his wife, on a much later visit, he speaks of the mutilated Cathedral and the statues thrown from their heights and niches, as all being restored.

The details of the 1851 tour are unfortunately not available, but the record of the exact route has been preserved, with a few scant notes, in Matthew Arnold's diary for this year; of which Professor Arnold Whitridge has kindly allowed me to make a copy.

It is a tantalizing document, leaving so much to conjecture, even to the reasons, hazarded above, which prompted the choice of itinerary. For the first five days of the journey, some brief notes supplement the entries; but after the stay at Lyons on the outward journey there is little more noted beyond the bare indications of the overnight stopping-places of the young couple. But it is not fanciful to explain the route planned as satisfying several objectives, placing in the first rank a desire to show his wife some of the more romantic Italian cities, while at the same time making a dutiful pilgrimage in his father's footsteps, added to, perhaps, some private motive of expediency, as elsewhere suggested (see Note I). Arnold longed to exchange his post at the Education Office for a diplomatic career. He had hobnobbed with the Embassy set in Paris in 1846 and 1847, and his memories of Thun in 1848 and 1849 doubtless included brushing up against some French and English Embassy officials, accustomed to make of Thun a summer vacation centre. And now, in 1851, there was an interesting state of affairs in Italy, which might with advantage be looked into. A report on the spot might stand him in good stead, if any opening were to materialise in the political or diplomatic fields. This was not to be. Although, in later life, Arnold could not resist some literary incursions into politics, he was marked out, perhaps destined from birth, for a rôle in the educational world only.

On September 1st, 1851, a Monday, Matthew Arnold and his wife left Eaton Place, his father-in-law's town house, for London Bridge and Calais. It was a close night and there were "heaps of foreigners" on board the Channel steamer. They reached Paris at 9 a.m. on Tuesday on a rainy morning. After a hot bath and some shopping, they went to the Louvre; and the rain having cleared, they dined at the Trois Frères (Provençaux), a fashionable restaurant of that time, which Arnold had frequented in January 1847. Arnold afterwards strolled alone to the Rue du Bac; perhaps to evoke reminiscences of Chateaubriand who had died there, and whom he had been reading only the previous May. It does not appear that he called at No. 120, on Madame Mohl.

Before her marriage, as Mary Clarke, she had here received Lady Verney, Florence Nightingale's sister and a cousin of the future Mrs Clough. Since 1847, her salon had been much frequented. Here Arthur Stanley was to meet his future wife, Lady Augusta Bruce, the sister of Lady Charlotte Locker, at whose house Arnold dined with Swinburne. Monckton Milnes, the Bunsens and a host of visitors of distinction, French and foreign, many of whom Arnold would meet, came to her dinner parties. Lord Lansdowne was a frequent guest and perhaps it was he who gave Arnold his letter of introduction. Arnold could have met Chasles here, if not earlier; and through Chasles perhaps got in touch with Sainte-Beuve. But the diary makes no mention of a call on September 2nd. On Wednesday the travellers left at 10.30 for Chalon (in a later letter he reminds his wife how they nearly missed the train at the Gare de Lyons), following the Seine and passing

Fontainebleau, and then along the Yonne to Dijon, where
there was "a grand view". They continued by train to
Chalon, and here there was "a great crush". They stayed
overnight at the Hotel du Parc, and Arnold took his usual
solitary walk along the banks of the Saône after supper. As
the line then ceased at Chalon, at 7 a.m. they went off by
boat down the Saône to Lyons; passing Macon (where
Arnold was to unhook from the train for Geneva in 1858).
They arrived early and put up at the Hotel de l'Univers;
after lunch they went to the Observatoire. On Friday they
were up late; they went together to the junction of the two
rivers, where Arnold observed that the Saône was more
rapid than the Rhône. They visited Jean Jacques' grotto,
referred to in Chateaubriand's *Mémoires*, the Bank, and
the Hotel de Ville. After dining and seeing round the
Cathedral, Arnold again wandered off alone to a café near
the Theatre.

On Saturday they reached Grenoble, where they stayed
at the Hotel des Trois Dauphins; on Sunday, September
7th, they were at the Grande Chartreuse.

The massif of the Grande Chartreuse runs north and
south between Chambéry and Grenoble. The monastery,
which lies in a wooded hollow between parallel ranges,
was of more difficult access in 1851 than it is today, although tourists are no longer admitted to the monastery.
One now follows the main road (Route Nationale) direct
from Grenoble over the Col de Vence and the Col de la
Porte to Saint-Pierre de Chartreuse and thence to the
monastery further west. Matthew Arnold and his wife,
like Chateaubriand, seem to have taken a carriage to
Voreppe, a small town to the west, and there hired a
guide and mules. Their route was over the Col de la
Placette and across the Pont Demay to Saint-Laurent du
Pont, also called Saint-Laurent du Désert. Rain had fallen
and the meadows were starred with the autumn crocus.
From this point the mule-track made by the monks in the
early sixteenth century climbed steadily through the woods

above the torrent to the "Entrée du Désert", some two miles from Saint-Laurent. Limestone crags plumed with scanty foliage rose above them. "Not a precipice, not a torrent, not a cliff, but is pregnant with religion and poetry", Gray had declared, and Dr Arnold had admitted to the same impression. His son agreed apparently with these romantic pronouncements, although he arrived on a day of wind and rain and scudding mists. A little further on, and they had crossed the high bridge and were on the right bank of the "Guiers Mort".

Arnold might have spared another stanza to describe the "Dead Guiers", the Dead River, so-called to distinguish it from the "Guiers Vif", which cuts across the range further to the north. Long ago, so tradition has it, the stream had remained dry for a year, and only by the miraculous intervention of St Bruno himself was the water replenished and made to run again.

The Arnolds saw it in full spate as they continued their ascent. The Courrerie, once the house of the Procurator of the Convent, now came into view. Here it was necessary to turn left, and in another kilometre they came to an opening in the forest and beheld the monastery before them. This visit furnished Arnold with all the details for a picturesque setting of his poem, but little more.

From the Grande Chartreuse the shorter and easier way to Chambéry is to return to Saint-Laurent, and take the road via Les Echelles. This was probably their route, and they would then cross into Sardinian territory at the passage of the Guiers Vif. A possible alternative would have been to push on to Saint-Pierre d'Entremont and then follow the track over the high Col du Granier. In view of the weather, and the climb up, it is doubtful if they took this route.

Having seen Rousseau's "grotte" at Lyons, it is unlikely that Arnold failed to visit the picturesque villa of Les Charmettes, with its orchard and vineyard, which occupies so romantic a place in the *Confessions*. But Arnold had

ceased to make long notes in his diary after Lyons; a glance
at the later entries shows that they were written probably
one after the other at a single sitting, and the book was
closed abruptly, unblotted. On September 8th he has
noted simply the one word, "Chambéri". Perhaps the
house of Joseph and Xavier de Maistre, which is in Chambéry itself, was pointed out to him.

On Tuesday he again notes simply, "L'Hopital Conflans". One would now write Albertville.

Conflans, or Conflent, is that part of the town which
struggles over the left bank of the Arly, above the point
where it flows into the Isère. L'Hopital was the ancient
section on the right bank. In 1846 Charles Albert had
founded on this side of the river the new industrial town,
which is called after him and which today includes both
quarters of the old town. Perhaps the Arnolds visited the
Maison Rouge in Conflans, formerly the castle of the
Dukes of Savoy, which was being used at this time as a
hospice for pensioners.

Their route next day led up the Isère valley through
Moutiers to Bourg-St-Maurice. But they did not go on to
cross the Petit St-Bernard that day; instead they hired
mules to take them some nine miles up a side glen by
the torrent des Glaciers to the tiny Alpine hamlet of Les
Chapieux, then called by its local name of "Chapiu". Saussure has described Chapiu as "standing in a horrible situation at the bottom of a funnel", surrounded by lofty
mountains, "naked and savage". In 1855, four years after
the Arnolds' visit, the Rev. Seymour King and his wife also
passed a night here, sleeping in what they called "a miserable hut". It must have been slightly less uncomfortable
in 1851 when Arnold brought his wife there, and in fact
one wonders today at the adverse accounts given by the
earlier travellers. Just as Shelley, advancing up the Mon-
tanvert, was repelled by the wildness and gloom of a region
which is today a flowery haunt of tourists, so perhaps
Chapiu seemed severe and lonely to Saussure. What in-

duced Arnold to stop there can only be surmised. It may have been in fact the result of a desire to see the south-western end of the Mont Blanc range and the dazzling Aiguille des Glaciers, which rises robed in white at the head of the valley. Perhaps this view was known to Dr Arnold when he crossed the Little St-Bernard in 1825, Polybius in hand, and professed to see the very tracks of Hannibal. Or perhaps, through his wife, Arnold had been in touch with the young lawyer and future judge, Alfred Wills, who had come this way from Chamonix in 1850. The pass, the Col de la Seigne, over to the Val Veni to the Rifugio Elisabetta, is now well-trodden in summer, and, though treeless, is green with herbage, bright and shining in the clear air.

At Chapiu the Arnolds slept probably in the Hotel au Soleil, still standing hospitably open, with its walls more than a yard thick and its flagged and uneven flooring. It has today the air of a delightful French country inn, and could not have looked very different in 1851. But they might alternatively have stayed at the adjacent Hotel des Voyageurs (which was to become the Edelweiss, but is now closed) No doubt they went into the tiny chapel of St-Jacques near by and rambled up the gorge to the alpages beyond Séloges for a full view of the Aiguille and its glacier.

They must have risen early next day to descend the valley to Bourg-St-Maurice and catch the diligence to Aosta. The crossing of the Little St-Bernard could hardly have been achieved in less than seven hours. Whether or not this was Hannibal's route (and the theory that he approached the Alps by the Durance valley is favoured by some historians), it had for long been the principal highway between Savoy and northwest Piedmont. A diligence formerly went daily over the pass. The Roman road takes the hillside very steeply; the modern carriage-road ascends gradually in wide loops. Leaving Bourg-St-Maurice, the wedding-tour travellers passed the outlying village of Séez, where clearly visible was the great outcrop of white

gypsum, which Seymour King identifies with the "leukope-
tron ochuron" of Polybius; looking back across the Isère
valley, the huge mass of the Mont Pourri dominated their
view for a long time, its shadowy glaciers cradled between
the broken, sunny ridges.

At the summit of the pass a stone circle is all that remains of the temple where the Allobroges of the Tarentaise
fraternised with the Salassi of the Val d'Aosta, in pre-
Roman times. There were also vestiges of the foundations
of a Roman mansio, or hospice, which had been uncovered only a few years earlier, in 1837. Were the exploits
of Albert Smith of that summer in their mind as they now
glimpsed for the first time Mont Blanc, the monarch of
the Alps, with the top of the Peuterey ridge leaning wor-
shippingly towards him? (Albert Smith was a lighthearted
journalist on the staff of *Punch*, who had climbed Mont
Blanc in August and had worked up his adventure into an
entertainment which he gave at the Old Egyptian Hall,
London). From the long plateau at the top of the pass
there is a steep descent to La Thuile, where they would
no doubt have made a short stop to change horses. Arnold
and his wife must have been charmed by the torrent which
rushes past the village, and the white expanse of the Ruitor
with its level snows, now in full view. And as they continued to zigzag down to the Orrido gorge, the mass of
the Mont Blanc range burst into sight, visible from the
two Peuterey Aiguilles as far as the gap known today as
the Col des Hirondelles below the ridge of the Grandes
Jorasses—a sheer dazzling line of whiteness, even at that
late hour. The weather appears to have been good, and in
the autumn air the clear outlines of the great peaks have a
crystalline perfection lacking in any other season.

At Pré St Didier they must have baited again, and Arnold, if one may judge from the entry on the flyleaf of his
diary, half-considered turning up to Courmayeur, only
seven miles away. Courmayeur, nestling at the foot of
Mont Blanc—which, however, is invisible from the village,

as it is hidden by the Mont Chétif, crouched in front—was already well organised at this time as a tourist centre. Forbes had visited it in 1842; he described and drew the famous glacier of the Brenva, just out of view from the village. Other British climbers were beginning to explore the marvellous peaks of the Val d'Aosta, making many fresh ascents. Alfred Wills, William Matthews, Charles Hudson, John Ball, G. F. Hardy, Llewellyn Davies were all contemporaries of Arnold, and their exploits may have fired him later on to attempt a modest bit of climbing on his own account with his friend Walrond in 1858—at least sufficient to qualify him for membership in 1859 of the Alpine Club, founded in 1857.

In 1851 he may, therefore, have been tempted to leave the valley and go up to Courmayeur; perhaps also to Gressonay, further down the valley, for this resort is recorded too, on the flyleaf of his diary. No doubt in deference to his wife, however, the journey was continued from St Didier by diligence to Aosta, the provincial capital. The weather continued splendid, to judge from a reference in a later letter of Arnold's. After leaving Pré St Didier, the retrospective view up to Mont Blanc must have struck them as dazzling in the extreme. It is indeed even more beautiful from here than from many nearer viewpoints. The shining Ruitor on the south side of the valley is still just visible; to the southeast the pyramid of the Grivola can be seen. This was Arnold's last glimpse of the high Alps. Approaching Aosta, the Mont Emilius came into view ahead, and appeared to tower over the valley

At Aosta they put up at the Couronne, "a dirty inn", according to Arnold's later remembrance of it, but certainly a very picturesque one—with its old interior wall- and ceiling-paintings, its terrace and inner court, its ancient coach-house, and the quaint imitation Venetian arcading, which can still be seen today. But his wife was alarmed by "a great spider", which may have put them off. The more modern inn, the Mont-Blanc,- at the upper end of the town, where Arnold was to stay in 1858, was not yet built. (Jean Tairraz, the founder and landlord, was a noted alpinist. He was to climb the Grivola with J. Ormsby the following year, and the Grand Paradis in 1860 with J. J. Cowell.)

They did not leave Aosta until late the next day; so, however weary, they must certainly have taken a carriage and visited the more interesting sights in the town, including the Roman monuments. Aosta had remained, from its comparative isolation, one of the best preserved of the old garrison towns. Arnold and his wife could not have avoided seeing the remains of the walls which were only partially dismantled, and the Porta Praetoria and the Arch of Augustus, both dating from 24 B.C.; finally, the Theatre with its noble back drop silhouetted against the Grand Combin and the snowy Vélan.

The rectilinear streets still roughly coincide with those of antiquity, and driving would be very pleasant in 1851. Perhaps they visited the sinister "Tour du Lépreux", the scene of Xavier de Maistre's story, "Le Lépreux de la Vallée d'Aoste". Arnold does not name this work, but his mentor Sainte-Beuve had interviewed General de Maistre in Paris in 1839, and had reviewed the tales in the *Revue des Deux Mondes* in May of that year. With his wife as a companion, Arnold could hardly have missed a visit to the reputed birthplace of St Anselm in the Abbot's house, adjoining the Church of Sant'Orso, and thence passed into the exquisite romanesque cloisters. Arnold may also have been aware of Aosta's association with Bernard de Menthon, the patron of alpinists.

The next entry in the diary, for September 12th, indicates that they slept at Ivrea. According to a later remark of Arnold's it appears it was dark as they passed Châtillon, which is scarcely twenty-five kilometres down the valley from Aosta, so that it can be assumed they did not leave Aosta until late afternoon on the 12th. Arnold was later to cross the Saint-Théodule from Zermatt and see Breuil,

where he stayed at the then new Hotel du Mont Cervin
on the Jomein—still standing above the ultra-modern
hotels of today. On this occasion he had walked down
the charming Val Tournanche to Châtillon (see page 245).

The way down the Aosta valley from Châtillon to Ivrea
is full of interest, but it is doubtful if the travellers saw
much of it or could distinguish more than the rush of the
Dora Baltea and the dark shapes of the many feudal
strongholds that line the valley. Its later history and associations may have come to mind as they passed Fort Bard,
and perhaps visualised the famous defence put up by the
Austrian garrison in 1800, which had almost succeeded,
against Napoleon's army. Napoleon had put Marshal
Lannes in command of the van; the Marshal had crossed
the Grand St-Bernard on May 15th; on the 16th he was at
Aosta and had taken the village of Bard on the 21st. The
next day he had routed the Austrian troups at Ivrea and
crossed the Po at Belgiojoso. At Montebello, with only
five thousand men, he defeated fifteen thousand Austrians
—hence his title; he had given Napoleon the key to Italy.

Marshal Lannes's calm courage and excellent tactics
were again shown at Marengo. He was unfortunately
wounded in the Austrian campaign at Essling near Vienna
in 1809, and died as a result, leaving his wife, a Breton
lady, of almost Correggio-like beauty, according to the
Duchess d'Abrantès, with five children. His eldest son
was made duke and hereditary peer of France at the Restoration, and played an important rôle as the Duc de Montebello in the political and diplomatic spheres (Arnold
might have met him or his family at Thun; see Note I).

Matthew Arnold was "penetrated with admiration" for
Napoleon in 1848, when he mentions he is reading again
in Las Cases (the *Mémorial de Sainte Hélène*), to his
mother. He had also been rereading this book in February
of the present year, 1851.

At Pont St-Martin he and his wife would glimpse the
opening of the glen giving access to the Val de Gressonay,

a favourite haunt of Browning and Sarianna at a later date, but apparently never visited by Arnold.

At Ivrea they had reached the entrance to the valley, and as they passed between the two great moraines which encompass it on either side, would recall the vast glacier, over sixty miles long, which had carved out the Val d'Aosta in a former age. It must have been near midnight when they arrived. On the 13th, next day, they were at Milan.

From the date of this entry it can be concluded that they did not turn north before reaching Milan to visit Varese, as Dr Arnold had done in July 1830. Instead, they followed no doubt the main road through Vercelli and Novara, the scene of a disastrous encounter between Charles Albert and Radetsky in February 1849. Another entry on Arnold's flyleaf, "Arona", seems to indicate a plan to explore the Lago Maggiore on this or some later occasion.

From Novara onwards they could not fail to have been continually reminded of the War of Independence, by the scars and ruins it had left behind; and must have sensed the bitter disappointment which was its aftermath. The depression of the population in Piedmont and in Lombardy, their hopelessness and angry resentment, must have made the Arnolds wish to press on to brighter surroundings. The Ticino then formed the frontier between Sardinia and Lombardy, and here they had to produce their passports, "visés" for Austria—which small expense, one shilling, Arnold had noted in his accounts earlier in the year. (Arnold was always scrupulous in small money matters. In 1884, when he was in Indianapolis, the Hoosier poet, James Whitcomb Riley, noted with amusement the care with which he pocketed his few cents' change after the purchase of a newspaper). They continued their journey the same day to Milan, where they stayed for three nights.

What was Arnold's attitude at this time to the insurrection of 1848 and to the First War of Independence, which had ended only two years before?

It appears from his letters to Clough that he had followed the events of the "year of revolutions" with an interest mingled with scepticism. Unlike the member for
Halifax—as James Stansfeld became later, when Arnold
knew and met him on one of his inspection tours, and
again, through Forster, his brother-in-law, and Goschen,
an old Rugbeian—Arnold had apparently not joined the
People's International League. This was a group founded
in April 1847 and designed, among other ideals, to combat
the "insularity of the English". In 1851 a more limited
organization took its place, called the "Friends of Italy",
with David Masson, G. H. Lewes, and Professor Newman
among its members. Arnold always kept aloof from the
Pre-Raphaelite group and never joined in the circle of Mazzini's friends; unlike Swinburne, his own former admirer.
But Arnold's pamphlet of 1859 on the Italian Question,
by which he was to set great store, shows that he was gen-
uinely interested in the Italian struggle for freedom.

It would have been difficult in any event for an intelligent traveller in 1851, even on his honey-moon tour, not to
be pre-occupied with the Risorgimento, whether he sym-
pathised or not. The movement had been gathering
strength for years, ever since Napoleon had given the
Italians a taste for freedom and at least partial self-govern-
ment, as Paul Hazard has shown in his *La Révolution
française et les lettres italiennes*. If Mazzini was the ideal-
ist, Garibaldi the hero, and Turin the brain of the movement, the brunt of the unrest was borne by Milan and its
nobles and intelligentsia. The un-masking in 1820 of the
first conspiracy, the confessions, imprisonment, and torture
of the noble Count Confalonieri, Andryane, Pellico and
others in the Spielberg, from which they were to emerge
prematurely old and broken men—all this would be familiar history to Matthew Arnold. Still more recent was the
insurrection, of 1830 and 1831, in the Papal States, and
its suppression by the hated Metternich. But not even

Metternich could now quell the surge of new ideas and the rise of Italian nationalism.

By the latter part of 1847 the ferment was near boiling point. In 1848 the cause of liberty had had a brief triumph in the Papal States. First Sicily and southern Italy, then Milan, rose in rebellion. For five days the populace in Milan fought the Austrian garrison with a fury that compelled Marshal Radetsky to evacuate his troops. The King of Sardinia, Charles Albert, declared war on Austria. Venice declared itself a Republic, while both Padua and Vicenza threw off the Austrian yoke. In consequence, the whole of northern Italy except for the fortresses of the Quadrilateral was freed. Had Charles Albert been a competent general, he would have marched straight on to Vicenza and probably forced a decision. There had been a rising in Vienna; Metternich had fallen, and the Austrian government was in disarray. The Emperor had even offered to cede Lombardy first to the provisional government in Milan, then to Sardinia. Palmerston had recommended Charles Albert to accept the terms; the king, however, felt that it would be dishonourable to desert the Venetians; he procrastinated, giving the enemy time to bring up reinforcements, and was then worsted in July at Custozza and forced to retreat. England and France now prepared to mediate; but Radetsky, aware that General Cavaignac and Lord Normanby were conferring in Paris, hurried Charles Albert into signing an armistice.

His position was even now not hopeless. An offer to cede Savoy and Nice to the French would probably have brought them to his aid. Palmerston foresaw their almost certain future intervention, and suggested to Vienna it should abandon Lombardy—sound advice, but it was not taken. Radetsky was now again firmly entrenched in all the cities which he had lost, with the exception of Brescia and Venice. In March 1849 Charles Albert renewed the war, making a gallant effort to retrieve Lombardy, but he was decisively defeated at Novara, and obliged to abdicate, retiring to a Portuguese cloister.

The tide of success now turned in favour of the autocracies. Austrian and French armies advanced on Rome, which had for three months been a Republic ruled by Mazzini. The French occupied the city and re-installed the Pope, who had fled in October 1848. The Republic fell in July 1849, watched by Clough, who sent his impressions to Arnold.

[*Consolation*, written, according to Arnold's note, during the siege, alludes only briefly to Rome. Arnold is pre-occupied in this poem with what one suspects is a personal problem, and, at the heart of it, his involvement with 'Marguerite'.]

Venice, meanwhile, had been facing a longer siege, and in July the Austrian bombardment, plus famine and an outbreak of plague, compelled her to surrender on August 24th, 1849. Daniele Manin, the President, and a true patriot and statesman, escaped, to die in Paris.

But the cause of freedom was not lost. The savagery with which the rebellion had been suppressed had had the effect of exasperating still further the Italian patriots. Thus when Vicenza had been re-captured in June 1848, the scenes of violence were only surpassed by the brutalities to be undergone by Brescia in April 1849. Twenty-two thousand men supported by artillery were needed to break down the resistance of the Brescians, who were subjected to incredible atrocities. Houses were sacked and dismembered bodies thrown from the windows. But their heroic defence earned for the city the name she has ever since borne, the Leonessa d'Italia.

There is no evidence to show Arnold was much perturbed at the time. In a letter to Clough towards the end of June 1848 he had written: "I am divided between a desire to see those cursed poltroons the Lombards well kicked —and to have so ugly a race as the Germans removed from Italy." His remark about the Lombards must have resulted from false press reports, for nothing could have exceeded their bravery. Fundamentally Arnold seems to have known little about the Italians. When in September 1848 he crossed the Simplon and went as far as Domodossola, he confessed himself pleased with the "courtliness and kingliness of the buildings and people, as opposed to this land [Switzerland] of a republican peasantry".

Dr Arnold, grossly prejudiced in favour of the Germans, had not cared for the Italians, or even understood them. He had been delighted, when in Venice in 1830, to see German soldiers exercising authority in "what had once been the seat of falsehood and ignorance and cruelty"— a remark which shows he knew little of the history of the Serenissima. One may suppose that by 1851 Matthew Arnold had to some extent weaned himself of the parental prejudice, and realised that the Risorgimento was a serious fact to be taken into account, and also it might provoke French intervention in its favour. Some sympathy he must have felt by 1859, or he would not have written his pamphlet.

The fact is that his impressions of the Italian people varied from time to time; he was generally unstable in his opinions—"a reed", he calls himself on one occasion— about people and countries, even about France, his favourite, in later life. He liked the Piedmontese; "the rest wanted backbone, serious energy and power of honest work". He was flattered when in 1869 the Italian Government asked him to take Prince Thomas of Savoy into his household for the Prince's education at Harrow. And it was pleasant at Stresa, in 1880, to hobnob with the Prince's mother, the Duchess of Genoa, and her circle. At Rome in 1873 he was agreeably lionised at Story's Barberini palace, and turned a supercilious eyeglass on the young American, Henry James—who, had he known it, deserved his thanks as the author of the article in the *North American Review* on *Essays in Criticism*, which, he said to his sister in 1865, "I like as well as anything I have seen". (According to

Leon Edel, in *The Conquest of London,* this meeting took place at the end of February; but Arnold was on the Riviera at that date, and only on his way to Rome on March 16. James's own letter confirms the date as March 30th.) On an earlier occasion, when in Italy in 1865, Arnold expressed his dissatisfaction with the people, and the country—"My opinion of the Italians, from all I have seen of them, is very unfavourable"—but he had got no farther out of Italy than Chur, and run into a party of German women "talking loud in their hideous language", than he bitterly regretted the gracious Italians he had left. "You may imagine how my Italian family [whom he had picked up also at Coire] was a relief to me!"

He would perhaps never fully understand the Italians, nor appreciate, like Meredith, the heroic character of the Risorgimento. He did not think of them as a people; he tended to divide them whilst they themselves were striving for unity. He was not sentimental, he had not the intuitive sympathy of a woman like George Sand; nor the understanding of the Brownings; nor the knowledge of a Stendhal. His ideas on Italian art and architecture were primitive, and Italy's political future seemed to him dim. He could not foresee the birth of that modern Italy which has been the culmination of long, painful and heroic effort. But Arnold was not lacking in political sense; perhaps he had a subtler prescience and had come to share, with others of like vision, including Chateaubriand in his memoir on Germany of 1821, the forebodings of the example a united Italy might set to a divided Germany.

On September 13th, 1851, Arnold and his wife had reached Milan. As sight-seers pure and simple they certainly visited the Duomo, probably first of all. It is doubtful if its interior impressed them as much as it had done Shelley. They probably visited next the Ambrosian Library, and the church of Santa Maria delle Grazie to see Leonardo's Last Supper in the refectory; and surely, also, the Scala Opera House. This had always been the principal social centre of the city, and the presence of Austrian officers had been keenly resented there. Prior to the insurrection of 1848 it had been boycotted by the Italians, particularly by the wives of the aristocracy, to show their contempt. If Arnold had not heard about this, he could not ignore the material damage which the presence of the Austrians had caused during the desperate street fighting of March 1848, the "cinque giornate", when the whole population, from nobles to the common people, had fought the Austrians with every and any missile to hand—"to the last bottle", as Churchill would have said.

The Arnolds probably climbed to the roof of the Duomo, from where the Tyrolese troops had fired on the townsfolk below. Many of the statues had been shattered by gunfire, as well as those on the façade. In 1865, when Arnold re-visited Milan, he wrote to his wife of the white marble pinnacles "of that incomparable church", standing out against the blue sky, "as if they were going to take their flight into it". He continued, "a great deal has been done towards peopling the niches with statues, adding white marble fretwork on the roof, repairing etc. since you were here. It would fill you with delight to see it again."

One can infer that in 1851 it did not look its best, and was indeed in a sorry state. Perhaps Arnold chose a fine day, however, and at least they would have had the unchanging view—in favourable weather even affording a glimpse of the Monte Rosa.

Arnold visited the Brera in company with the Provveditore in 1865, when, although it was closed, the secretary had shown them around. "I saw the pictures to perfection. One gets very much interested in pictures", he says, and he refers in particular to Luini. From this one gathers that they had not gone to the gallery in 1851, and that an interest in painting, and in the history of art generally, was only a feature of Arnold's later development. The street architecture, the great houses, the gardens and the churches impressed him on his later visit very agreeably. But, although Milan was certainly less gay and brilliant in 1851, Arnold and his wife put in three nights and two full days there; and again stayed for two nights on the return journey. If their sojourn left them with mixed feelings, perhaps, at that age, pleasure predominated.

On Tuesday, September 16th, they resumed their journey, travelling "by mail poste" to Verona. The "poste" served at this time the same purpose as the Swiss "autopostale" of today, and carried travellers as well as letters and parcels. As Verona is about a hundred miles from Milan, the journey must have been wearisome, although the frequent change of horses would make it fairly rapid. The road ran through Brescia, where there could have been little temptation to linger and only meagre accommodation, if they had wished to stay there. The "Leonessa d'Italia" had been cruelly battered and must have presented in 1851 a piteous picture of desolation.

There is no record of their impressions as they passed Lake Garda. The beauty of Garda is very dependent on the weather. The satin-blue water, on a dull day, becomes a cold, grey expanse, that could appear very uninviting to Arnold, always more in love with the smaller type of lake.

At Verona they stopped off for two nights; and no doubt visited the house and "tomb" of Juliet, since *Romeo and Juliet* had been on Arnold's reading list for June. Verona is at all times a beautiful city. Its position on the Adige and superb mountain background are unique, even for an Italian city. Among its attractions for visitors are the great Roman amphitheatre, the Villa Giusti and its gardens, the great piazze, and the statues of Roland and Oliver in front of the Duomo. Some of these Arnold and his wife must have seen.

On Thursday the 18th they left Verona for Venice. Starting very early, their journey took them through the deep valleys that lead to Vicenza; on the way they would pass Montebello, the "Belmont" of the *Merchant of Venice*. Vicenza, one of the loveliest of Italian cities, had won additional renown for itself by its resistance to the Austrian assaults of 1848. Padua, the "many-domed", would be their next stopping place, for a brief halt only, as this day must have been one of their longest. They perhaps followed the Brenta, passing Byron's villa on the canal at Mira, unless their conveyance went by the upper road. In any case, no causeway then existed to Venice, and they had still to cross the lagoon, and traverse the Grand Canal to the Piazzetta.

Venice, where they spent four nights, was perhaps Mrs. Arnold's choice. Arnold's interests at this time were primarily in mountain scenery and literary associations. But more and more, he confided to his sister later, in his less active middle age, he used travelling to visit places marked by events of interest, and not for pure scenic reasons. Perhaps this attitude was initiated during his present tour, and was to grow on him, along with his later interest in art and architecture. Certainly, however, when he had the chance to visit Venice on another occasion, in 1873, and had actually taken a round ticket to include Venice, he was content to miss it.

In 1851 conditions after the siege must have been tolerable, or he would not have brought his wife so far. It would be pleasant to think that they stayed at the Danieli for the sake of George Sand; and saw the Lido, for the sake of Byron. But there is no hint of their movements in the diary or later correspondence. Presumably they did the stock sights, went about in gondolas, and sat in the Piazza to watch the sun-set light on the Duomo, turning its vivid mosaics into some fabric seen in a dream. They would be eating ices at Florian's at the time—not perhaps as good as the Neapolitan ones, for love of which Leopardi forsook his country lair, to return to die in Naples—but no doubt better than today's.

On the 22nd they left Venice, early as usual, since they

planned to reach the southern tip of Garda that night and sleep at Desenzano. They pushed on back to Milan the next day, and so certainly did not have time to take a boat on the lake and row out to Sirmione, for the sake of Catullus. They appear to have stayed at Milan until the morning of September 25th. On this day they set out for Cadenabbia. The Lombard plain would be beautiful, and the thinning leaves of the poplars and the bright maize fields more spring-like than autumnal. But they had stormy weather on the lake, and Cadenabbia's Grand Hotel was not then built, so that it is doubtful if they enjoyed Lake Como very much. At all events, they only stayed overnight, and went on next day to Bellinzona. For this journey they had to leave the lake at Menaggio and cross the fairy-like upland above Porlezza, passing on the way the exquisite little Lago di Piano. The narrow railway—now abandoned, although the tracks remain under the rank herbage—was not then running. From Porlezza the steamboat took them to Lugano.

From Lugano they probably went by carriage to Locarno and up the Ticino valley to Bellinzona, where they stayed the night. The next day they resumed their journey as far as Faido. From Bellinzona onward, apparently, it rained furiously; and at Bodio, near Biasca, Arnold was to recall his wife's pleasure at the sight of the many waterfalls.

Arnold had already seen the Simplon, and the approach to the St Gothard by the Val Leventina was perhaps the attraction of the latter route. He may have seen Ruskin's sketch of the pass. It is less gloomy and there are many lovely romanesque campaniles to be seen as one ascends the gorge. But, alas, they were to find it snowing at the top, and Arnold had to wait till 1880 to see the pass in its full summer beauty. At Faido, on Saturday, they slept at the Angel, still standing today. To cross the St Gothard and gain Amsteg by nightfall, they must have again risen early next day. Towards Airolo the valley opens out, and the torrent comes down from the west. Here the road climbs the mountain in steep zigzags. Travellers usually left the diligence and walked up, in good weather; between the first set of zigzags and the second, there is a level stretch which provides some respite for the toiling horses. Arnold recalled in 1880 "the place where the diligence came to grief when we were making the passage that snowy day, and I remembered the very spot, by one of the little lakes, where some cattle passed us." From the hospice at the summit, the road descends to Hospenthal, and to Andermatt, in its green hollow and banks of alpine plants. If the autumn had touched these, the meadows would be glowing with rich colour.

From here the descent is by the narrow Schollenen gorge, famous for its Devil's Bridge. Amsteg lies a little way down the Reusstal, near the foot of the Bristenstock. Dr Arnold, who had come this way in 1840, described and admired the Reuss valley, which is, however, more shut in and gloomy than the Leventina.

Arnold stayed at Fluelen in 1880, but the travellers in 1851 must have gone on by steamboat to Lucerne, where they spent two nights. On the 30th, Tuesday, Arnold's note reads "Righi-Kulm". The railway was not opened until 1871, and completed only in 1873, so that they must have gone up the Righi on mule-back. The summit had been for some time a popular belvedere, and there are few viewpoints in the world to rival it for sheer beauty.

On the first day of October, Arnold made his entry, curiously, in French: "diligence entre Lucerne et Bâle". However, he reverts to German on the 2nd, noting simply, "Strassburg", which they reached presumably by steamer down the Rhine.

On Friday, the third, he again makes his entry in French, "diligence entre Strasbourg et Paris".

Five nights in Paris followed. On October 8th they returned to Dover, and on the 9th they were at Eaton Place, to spend their last night at the Wightmans' town house.

On Friday they went on to Hampton, where Arnold probably left his wife. For on October 11th, Arnold "began inspecting with [Dr] Morell". According to Professor Lowry, who so interprets a remark made to his wife, he was by October 15th beginning to feel "adjusted" to the work. In fact, he was only just starting on it; his accounts show that he received £5.4.0 on October 19th for his "first week's inspecting". His remark may have been an instance of wishful thinking, an effort to make the best of the situation. He had been only four days at work, and the transition from the continent to Manchester, where he found himself on October 11th, must have given him a severe jolt. "With schools in the Pittener [sic, for "Potteries", surely, as he is writing from Derby] starting, and 2 [= twelve; Arnold writes "12". Lowry has taken the numeral 12 for a combination of the abbreviated style of and (&), badly formed, plus the numeral 2; making pointless Arnold's complaint of overwork] hours to inspect, tooth-ache and other incommodities I have been sore put to it," he writes to Clough—according to Lowry, shortly after December 19th, 1851. But this dating is another error; Arnold's account-book shows that he went on the 20th with his wife to Fox How to spend the first Christmas after his marriage with his mother. In subsequent years it was spent with the judge's family. The letter above should surely be dated January 1852. These mistakes and many misreadings of Arnold's manuscript call for a corrected version. [This applies also to the Mulhauser edition of Clough's *Letters*.]

He had indeed to set to work to repay the large sums he had borrowed all round from family and friends for the expenses of the year—nearly a thousand pounds, including £120 for "the foreign tour".

On the flyleaf of his diary for this year he had written out a column of names of six places abroad: Courmayeur, Aosta, Gressonay, Varallo, Arona, Milan. Aosta and Milan were visited on the wedding-tour. It is intriguing to speculate whether the other places had to be squeezed out of the itinerary, or were entered as possibilities for the future. He had only just missed seeing Courmayeur; Gressonay-Saint-Jean and Gressonay-la-Trinité were very near when he passed Pont Saint-Martin (Gressonay was to be a favourite resort of Browning and his sister). Varallo, with its Sacro Monte and the forty-five panels from the hand of Gaudenzio Ferrari and others, is in the Val Sesia, a popular haunt of tourists. The Arnolds visited neither Varallo, nor Arona, which is at the southern end of Maggiore. The greater part of their tour was spent in the Sardinian Kingdom, and in the region of Lombardy and Venetia embraced within the Austrian Empire. The return through Switzerland resembled a scamper rather than a leisured holiday. Accompanied as he was, Arnold could indulge few of his early enthusiasms.

One is impelled to ask again if there were not some special motive for the journey. It was not strictly their wedding-tour. (Arnold had gone with his wife to Alver and the Isle of Wight in June—spending more than £20—immediately after their marriage.) Did he, in fact, want to learn more about the Italian question; and, if so, was the journey undertaken disinterestedly, or for an ulterior motive? What say did his wife and her family have in the itinerary? The rush, the rough going, and many hardships were perhaps endured by Fanny Lucy for a purpose.

C. NOTE TO PAGE 59: "STAGIRIUS".

The title of this poem, which is dated 1844 in the manuscript and was published in February 1849, appears to have been taken, contrary to Arnold's usual practice, directly from Saint-Marc Girardin and not from Sainte-Beuve's article on him.

The latter's first "lundi", on the subject of Saint-Marc Girardin, had referred to "Stagyre" and placed him in the

René-Werther group; but this article appeared only in October 1849, in the *Constitutionnel*—the first to be written after Sainte-Beuve's return from Liège.

Arnold's letter to Clough of March [?], 1848, mentions his reading of Saint-Marc; and although the lecture to which he refers in his letter—on the rôle of the father in modern comedy—is not the one in which the mention of "Stagyre" occurs, there seems no escape from the inference that he took over the name directly to entitle his already-written poem. Following his usual practice, he did add a note on St Chrysostom, calculated to mislead the reader about the source of the title.

On its first appearance he used the gallicised form "Stagyre"; but he later altered this to what he presumably regarded as the Latin form of the name, "Stagyrus". Still later, he emended the spelling to "Stagirius".

The exact procedure which decides when a proper noun is to be quoted in its original form, and when incorporated into the language being used, is a delicate one, and varies with the language; the French being more prone than the English to bring the word into line with their own spelling and pronunciation. This was to cause Arnold some hesitation on a later occasion, when he wrote to Sainte-Beuve regarding "Virgile et Apollone de Rhodes", to whom Sainte-Beuve without comment referred in his reply as "Virgile et Apollonius de Rhodes"—Apollonius not having quite established for himself a place in the French language.

Arnold wrote excellent French, but occasionally made a slip, as in his translation of "agonie", in a passage quoted from G. Sand, in his *Essay* on her.

D. NOTE TO PAGE 84: "THE IMAGE OF THE PRISON". PASCAL, POPE, VIGNY, SENANCOUR AND ARNOLD.

The "prison" motif in Senancour, Vigny, Guérin, Ménard and other writers, and employed by Arnold in A *Summer Night*, could have come, notably by way of Pascal, from much earlier sources. In Pascal's version, "L'homme [est] dans son cachot ne sachant si son arrêt est donné". Arnold was probably already familiar with the image; just as, though owing much of the direct inspiration for his *Empedocles* to Senancour, he naturally used ideas which would already be known to him from his classical studies.

Presumably he recognised ideas in Senancour, Vigny and others, which these authors had derived from the *Pensées* —his reading of the *Pensées* is, however, noted only in 1852 (see page 50); he should have known also of Pope's ironical treatment of them in the *Essay on Man*. In Epistle III, Pope, deliberately paraphrasing Pascal, sets forth the concept of man as the part which is able to contain the whole—"un néant à l'égard de l'infini, un tout à l'égard du néant", as Pascal says. Senancour's view of men, "Dieux par la pensée, insectes pour le bonheur", is a variation on the theme, as are also Arnold's poems *Resignation* and *In Harmony with Nature* (see pages 75–76).

Appropriately, the opposition between contemplation and action, the notion of man as a creature torn between two extremes, between two ways of living, is an idea also collected by Pope for his *Essay* from the *Pensées*. It is not remarkable to find it one of the main themes of Senancour (see pages 44–45) and poignantly treated by Arnold (see page 63 and Chapter X). In this century, Israël Zangwill's *Dreamers of the Ghetto* has fastened on the theme of man in the same predicament. More recently, Stephen Spender has been drawn to ponder the issue, and to propose a solution—a period of retirement from time to time in some monastic retreat.

These pre-occupations are as old as philosophy, and nothing definite can be affirmed about their reappearance in writers of widely separated ages and nationalities. One cannot claim priority of source for any one thinker on these lines.

Most of the ideas and reflections embodied in Arnold's poetry are bound not to be original; it is their presentation and treatment which are that, and which justify a description of him as the "poet of thought". So, with regard to his use of the prison symbol, one cannot know if he drew it directly from Pascal; or, by way of Vigny, from Senancour. Monglond has shown that Vigny was definitely influenced by Senancour, so that the latter conjecture may well be the case.

It remains difficult to assess Arnold's precise indebtedness to Vigny. His borrowing for the conclusion of *The Buried Life* is almost textual:

> And then he thinks he knows
> The hills where his life rose,
> And the sea where it goes.

> Tout sera révélé dès que l'homme saura
> De quels lieux il arrive et dans quels il ira

L. Bonnerot has established the fact that Arnold had read Sainte-Beuve in a number of the *Revue des Deux Mondes* for 1844, which is the year when these lines appeared.

Quiller-Couch thought Arnold's lines above so typical that he used them to conclude the introduction to his edition of the Poems!

(This coincidence, and other findings published in 1935, in particular the textual borrowings from Senancour, reappear in K. Allott's edition. Many of my conjectures of the above date, from the accounts of Arnold's visits to Nohant and Thun, to details about the edition of Foscolo, which it is suggested Matthew Arnold read with 'Marguerite', are adopted by this editor.)

E. NOTE TO PAGE 96: "THE SWISS-FRENCH FAMILY OF DE ROUGEMONT".

Rougemont (Rothenburg) is near Gesseney (Saanen); it was at Gesseney, after Charles-Victor de Bonstetten's appointment as a member of the Council of Berne, his birthplace, that he went to reside when he was installed as magistrate in 1775; in 1779 he accepted the prefecture of Saanen. In 1787 he was removed to Nyon in the Pays de Vaud (when Gibbon was also sojourning in Lausanne).

In 1865, the year of *Obermann Once More*, begun at Glion, Arnold copied into his diary his favourite quotation from Bonstetten: "Rien ne sauve dans cette vie-ci que l'occupation et le travail"; it was to reappear significantly in subsequent years. It is not clear whether Arnold found it himself, or took it from Sainte-Beuve, who had written on Bonstetten many years before, in the twenties, in the so-called "Premiers Lundis".

F. NOTE TO PAGE 101: "THE GREEN EUGANEANS".

The Villa del Foscolo, at Feriole near Abano-Terme, was formerly the country-house of Federico Manfredini, "marchese e vescovo di Padova". Here Foscolo wrote many of the *Letters of Ortis*.

The villa is still standing (now the homestead of the Gottardo family) with its tiny chapel and huge granary; surrounded with its own orchards, vineyards and fields of corn. In the foreground is the rich plain of the Veneto, and beyond are the blue volcanic cones and massifs that make up the Euganean range. Not far to the south is Este, much overgrown since Shelley lived there in the Villa Capuccini, lent to him and Mary by Byron.

G. NOTE TO PAGE 111: "LU**".

The description given here is that of the pleasant setting of a garden in Fribourg, in the home of Mademoiselle Marie-Françoise Daguet's parents (André Monglond, *Le Journal intime de Senancour; Oberman*, vol. I., p. 93), situated above the Sarine, the "green river" of *Obermann Once More*, which at this point makes a sharp bend and falls abruptly enough to be identified as the "torrent" of the passage. By his confusion of place-names—for "Lu**" is certainly intended to hint at Lucerne, which (see Note H) he probably never visited—Senancour sought to throw a veil over the experiences of his youth, fearing to compromise the woman he loved and his own family.

It was her voice which first attracted Senancour to Marie-Françoise; it was, indeed, all he first knew of her; sounding on the night like a perfume from the balcony of her home. The story of his marriage, and its aftermath of bitterness, became mingled with that other passion which was to inspire the pages of *Oberman*, for "Madame Del **".

For it was also the sound of Madame Del **'s voice which had revealed to him his love for her. In the garden of the Faubourg Poissonnière, in the house which had come back to her husband's family after the Revolution, it is Madame Del **'s voice which he describes, in an exquisite passage, in the supplement which he wrote for the 1833 edition of *Oberman*. (The incident was re-told by his daughter, in a softened version, in her *Notice Biographique*.) There is little doubt that the experience, recalled more than a quarter of a century after the event, was as vivid to Senancour as the day on which it occurred.

"Madame Del **", or, as he completed the name in a

later letter, "Madame Dellemar"—with the last syllable echoing her real name—was Madame Walckenaer, the sister of his friend François Marcotte (who later assumed the name d'Argenteuil). This friendship had dated from their school days at the Collège de la Marche in the Rue de la Montagne Sainte-Geneviève. (Senancour was never at the Seminary of Saint-Sulpice, as Arnold states in his *Academy* article: see also Note H.) Marie-Jeanne-Antoinette-Joséphine Marcotte, six years younger than Senancour, had been married to her handsome cousin (he was painted by Greuze), the Baron Walckenaer, during Senancour's absence in Switzerland on the journey which had included his stay at Fribourg with the Daguets, and marriage to Marie-Françoise. When Senancour left Paris, Joséphine Marcotte had been a young girl living in the provinces, and only occasionally coming to the capital. With her widowed mother, the sister of Duclos-Dufresnoy, she had been brought to live in Paris in 1791, and affianced to the natural son of Duclos-Dufresnoy and a lady of noble birth. It was after his return from Switzerland in 1795, and his ill-assorted marriage there, that Senancour's affection for the young girl was turned into the deep passion for "Madame D**" which gave birth to the composition of *Oberman*.

His first recorded meeting with her after the return is described with his usual attempt at dissimulation. For the banks of the Saône, where the encounter is placed in *Oberman*, one must read the Seine, below the Champs Elysées between Passy and Sèvres, where Madame Walckenaer was in the habit of passing the spring months; and where Senancour came eventually to retire to die.

Senancour had made an attempt to return to Switzerland and his wife in 1798, but had been arrested in the Jura and obliged to go back to Paris. There he had been appointed tutor to two grandchildren of the old Comtesse d'Houdetot, who still kept up the circle of those intimates who remained to her—Saint Lambert and the Abbé Morellet had been among them. One of her other grandchildren had been adopted by their aunt, whose own daughter was married to the young Count Molé.

Such was the circle to which Senancour now had the entrée. He was accepted as a member of the household and was living at the hotel Beauvai, in the Faubourg St Honoré, at the time of his meeting with the Baronne Walckenaer.

It was not far, in those days, to the veritable country-side, and walks under the elms lining the alleys of the Champs Elysées, now almost deserted since the Revolution. Here his first meeting with Madame Walckenaer since his return to the capital took place.

Joséphine Walckenaer was no doubt much interested in her brother's young friend, and perhaps touched by the misfortunes which had dogged his career. But it is impossible to know whether she gave him more than pity and affection. Her husband was later to assist Senancour in trying to obtain financial help after his total loss of fortune. Senancour himself seems only to have realized the nature of his feelings on the day, somewhat later, when he came upon her unexpectedly on the stone terrace of her home in Paris, and heard her utter his name as he mounted the steps from the garden. It is a passage which is the very counterpart of the lines in *Parting*; when Arnold hears, with a mixture of joy and despair, the voice of 'Marguerite' above him on the stairs, and likens it to all those exquisite nature-sounds—only to be compared, amongst our English poets, with Meredith's similar, much later attempt to convey his impression of a young girl: "What my heart, first awaking, fancied the world was". "C'est pour l'amour", says Senancour, "que la lumière du matin vient éveiller les êtres et colorer les cieux; pour lui les feux de midi font fermenter la terre humide sous la mousse des forêts [this might be Robert Moore speaking, in *Shirley*]; c'est à lui que le soir destine l'aimable mélancolie de ses lueurs mystérieuses."

In spite of the life-long memory which he kept of her, Senancour did not yield to his passion (like Arnold in this, too) in the romantic manner of the school of René and Werther. With "une énergie latente", he resolutely withdrew from temptation; he writes of Madame Del ** in words which anticipate Matthew Arnold's expression of renunciation in *The Lake:* "Si Madame D** eût été libre, j'eusse trouvé le plaisir d'être malheureux à ma manière, mais elle ne l'était et *je me retirai*" (my italics). "Be counsell'd, and retire!", Arnold wrote. Elsewhere Senancour says, speaking in the third person, "Il y avait tellement d'analogie dans leurs goûts simples et purs . . ."; as Arnold, of himself and 'Marguerite', "The bent of both our hearts was to be gentle, tranquil, true."

But Senancour could not cast out her memory, and this, above all the memory of her voice, would always haunt him. In *l'Amour* (a book which is also on Arnold's reading list) it is her voice which he singles out above all her other characteristics. It was her voice which was mysteriously echoed in Marie-Françoise's singing, and with which he fell in love. In this passage, and in the garden-scene at Paris, Senancour, like Arnold in *Absence*, deliberately mingles his memories of the two women.

H. NOTES TO CHAPTER IV:
"THE AUTHOR OF *OBERMANN*,"
TO CHAPTER VII:
"THUN AND THE BLÜMLISALP,"
AND TO CHAPTER XVI:
"*OBERMANN ONCE MORE*."
ARNOLD'S DIARIES OF 1857 TO 1865.

The assumption has been that Arnold came to Thun in 1848 by way of Geneva and by Glion above Montreux, at that time approached from Vevey. But the possibility of an earlier visit to Glion arose, owing to his own misleading statement regarding a visit to Switzerland in 1846. Glion is the setting of *Obermann Once More*, begun in 1865, according to his diary; and in this poem Arnold refers to a twenty years' interval since his previous visit. The diaries for 1845, 1846 and 1847, now available, are silent about any journeys to Switzerland (see Note A), so that 1848 seems reasonably established as the date for this early visit to Glion. His note to the poem refers to the passage to Thun from Glion by the Col de Jaman and the Simmenthal; which virtually confirms the date and his route.

But if he thought, as doubtless he did, that by this way he was following in Senancour's tracks, he was, it now appears, probably mistaken (see page 99). His association of Leukerbad with Oberman, in the *Stanzas*, may be equally without foundation. If so, this does not invalidate the sources of his inspiration, which remain intrinsically unaffected; but the question is of interest in its own right (see particularly pages 39 and 40, page 105, and pages 116–118).

For the extent and sequence of Senancour's travels and sojourns in Switzerland, the best account is that given in A. Monglond's *Journal Intime d'Oberman*. In this delightful book the author traces and dates most of Senancour's itineraries, and in particular unmasks the deviations in *Oberman* (which he always spells with the one final 'n' of the first edition) from the factual events in the real life of Senancour.

In a discussion of Senancour's deliberate mystifications, of his changes in the true chronology of his travels and the events of his life (whilst retaining the authentic story of his inward evolution)—as when Lyons (see page 151) is substituted for Paris as the hero's birthplace—Monglond considers amongst other matters this very fact of the possibility of Senancour's having visited Thun, and the Haslital, and the Lake of the Four Cantons, or indeed of his ever having strayed much outside his favourite Jorat (see pages 239, 240 and 241).

Whilst one can today be certain about most of the places Senancour visited—and, despite its title, *Oberman* is primarily about France—the evidence regarding Thun and the Oberland is conflicting. Arnold, in associating the passes from the Valais, and particularly Titlis and the Grimsel, with Senancour, was perhaps deceived, as Senancour had wished to deceive his readers.

Monglond asks: "Par les lacs de Thoune et de Brienz, Senancour aurait-il gagné le pays de Hasli; de là Lucerne et le lac des Quatre Cantons [et] passé le Righi . . . ? C'est l'itinéraire", he adds, "suivi, à l'automne de 1797, par Elzéar de Sabran [the son-in-law of the Chevalier de Bouf-flers and the friend of Senancour, sharing his passion for the Alps] et sa mère; et, en sens inverse, par Ramond, en juin 1797." He goes on to state that there is one apparent piece of evidence for this, in a letter written under one of Senancour's pseudonyms, "l'Habitant des Vosges", in which he mentions "L'Under-walden, où moi-même j'ai vécu". But the confusion of imagery which surrounds his descriptions, particularly his setting of the passage on the Ranz, the merely fugitive allusions to the Grimsel and Titlis, his reference to a glimpse of the mountains of Hasli and Grindelwald (which he takes the trouble to mention were only seen from Thièle, whence he had come from Fribourg)—all suggest that the Swiss background of *Oberman* was a composition made up of literary souvenirs of the lakes of Neuchâtel, Lucerne, Brienz and the Léman, with his own striking and more precise memories, includ-ing his journey to Charrières near Saint-Maurice, his day on the Dent du Midi, and the continuation of his journey to Martigny and Etroubles filling out the picture.

The fact that one of Oberman's letters is dated from "Thoune" in itself proves nothing. It is sandwiched be-tween a letter from the Schwarzersee near Fribourg and one from Fribourg, and could have been simply suggested by the Sabrans' visit in 1795. Senancour nowhere describes the twin lakes, nor the view of the peaks of the Oberland.

In short, the references to, and descriptions which he gives of, Titlis and the Grimsel, and of the Oberland in general, do not seem the result of personal acquaintance. They could have been taken, Monglond thinks, in the form in which he gives them, from his reading of Ramond and Coxe, Saussure and Bourrit, perhaps dating from his boyhood, when he had the run of the wonderful library belonging to Marcotte's unfortunate uncle, Duclos-Dufresnoy, in the Rue du Faubourg Poissonnière. Monglond reproduces the engraving of the Grimsel by Dambon after the drawing by Le Barbier for the *Tableaux de la Suisse*, which adds all that Senancour needed, he considers, for his famous symbolic description of the Ranz des Vaches.

It is improbable that Senancour, after his first arrival in Switzerland and his visits to the historic sites on the Léman —Lausanne, Cully, Saint-Saphorin, Vevey, and Clarens, associated for him with *La Nouvelle Héloïse*; his journey up the Valais to Villeneuve and Chessel, his ascent of the Dent du Midi, and venture across the Grand St-Bernard to Etroubles above the Val d'Aosta—ever in fact travelled much beyond the Jorat. Contrary to Sainte-Beuve's statement in the *Portraits Contemporains*, he never resided at Etroubles. Sainte-Beuve, who came late on the scene, was an untrustworthy guide to Arnold's knowledge of Senancour, both as to the external events of his life and the assessment of his character (see page 253). Both he and George Sand, for instance, exaggerated Senancour's "énervement" and underestimated his "énergie secrète". They represented him as more discouraged than did Arnold, who, in some ways, understood Oberman more intensely than either of them.

Arnold seems to anticipate the description of him by our later critic as "déchiré entre les souvenirs d'un monde révolu et les aspirations de l'âge nouveau".

> Wandering between two worlds, one dead,
> The other powerless to be born.

The adventure of the Drance on the way to the Grand St-Bernard is proof of a certain hardiness. But this was Senancour's supreme effort. Unravelling the facts from their distortion in *Oberman*, Monglond has described his return to Saint-Maurice, where he spent the winter, and his journey to Fribourg, where he settled at Agy, and there met the Daguets. From this time he seems never again to have wandered far from the Jorat, the region of low Alps lying between Fribourg and the Lake of Geneva; except for a possible journey of later date when he may have accompanied, for part of the way, his friend Marcotte on the latter's appointment as Director of the Forestry Commission in Piedmont. In *Oberman*, the hero leaves his wooden chalet, built by workmen from Gruyère, and accompanies his friend as far as Saint-Branchier (Sembrancher), above Martigny.

It now seems very uncertain if Senancour carried out the project, described by Oberman, of exploring "nearly all the valleys between Charmey, Thoune, Sion, Saint-Maurice and Vevey", or even, in his search for the ideal site, the region between Vevey, Saint-Gingolph, Aigle, le Sépey, Etivaz, Montbovon and Sempsales. He refers to one of the passes, the Col de Sanetsch, between Gsteig and Sion, but it seems doubtful if he ever crossed it. At Saint-Saphorin, on the Geneva side of Vevey, he conjured up his "chartreuse", his "désert", the Imenstròm of his dreams, which was to combine all the advantages of an Alpine site with a southern type of vegetation! His two letters to Bernardin de Saint-Pierre and to Saussure (the latter unearthed by Mademoiselle Claire Engel at Geneva), in which he sought their advice on the subject, amusingly if pathetically list his desiderata.

It is possible that when at Neuchâtel, he wandered towards the Jura and the "pays de Motiers", associated with Rousseau; as Matthew Arnold recalled when travelling in 1871 with his family. In subsequent journeys between Paris and Fribourg—Senancour took his young wife back to Paris from Fribourg to meet his parents after his marriage in 1790—the obvious way would have been through the Val de Travers.

After the failure of his marriage and his return to Paris in 1794–5—and not "in middle life", as Arnold says in his article; Senancour was twenty- five at the time—he was not able to see Switzerland again until 1802, when he rejoined his wife at Lausanne and took her back to Fribourg. From 1802 he was domiciled at the Château de Chupru, at a reasonable distance from his in-laws, in an attempt to re-knot his broken marriage. In 1803 he had returned to Paris; in 1804 his two children rejoined him there. He never went back to Switzerland, as far as is known.

When in 1857 Arnold went with his wife and family abroad, he expressed the hope that he could include a sight of Titlis and the Grimsel "for Obermann's sake". But the diary for 1857 shows that the plan had to be abandoned owing to the illness of his eldest son, the delicate little Tom, who had been left in Paris (see page 239). Arnold and his wife went only as far as the Baur-au-lac in Zürich, which they used as a base for short excursions on the lake and to the Wallensee and Bad Ragaz. They returned to Bâle and Paris via Lucerne, when they might just possibly have had a glimpse of Titlis. In October 1865 Arnold mentions seeing "the snowy line of Titlis" when at Lucerne with his family. This followed the journey to Geneva and Glion, when he had the inspiration to write *Obermann Once More*, described below.

But the Grimsel Arnold was not to see until his journey of 1871, when he took his family abroad on a kind of wedding-anniversary tour. They travelled via the Jura to Thun and Interlaken, and this time Arnold went at last over the Grimsel and down to Brigue. They stayed at Belalp, and continued down the Valais to Leuk, whence they returned to Thun by Leukerbad. Much of this route clearly recalls the first visits to the Oberland of 1848 and 1849. Arnold this time broke a little new ground by visiting the Wengern

Alp, with its Byronic associations, from Thun; but the main novelty was the Haslital and the crossing of the Grimsel.

There seems a kind of insensitivity in Arnold's make-up that led him to wish to repeat, in circumstances so different, the experiences of his younger, more romantic period. But it is certainly additional proof of the powerful influence which the past continued to exert on him (see Note B).

Is it possible to gain more information about Arnold's probable visit to Glion in 1848 from the account of his movements, in reverse, in 1865? But these are rather mysterious, and pose another question.

His diary for 1865, where he notes "to Geneva" on Sunday, October 1st, has the further entry for this day, "begin Obermann" (that is, *Obermann Once More*). But the poem appears to be written *at* Glion, some distance away.

There is no further clue in the diary to his movements, either immediately before or after this date; but on September 30th, the day preceding, he is writing to William Forster, from Berne, to say he expects to be at the Baur-au-lac, Zürich, within eight or nine days; so that his tour—an official one for the Schools Inquiry Taunton Commission—evidently included the plan to put in some time elsewhere before going on to Zürich. There are no entries in the diary after October 2nd until November; but in an earlier letter from Vienna, of September 22nd, he mentions that he expects to be at the "Hotel du Rhin" [?] at Geneva, and hopes to see the Swiss Rothschilds there (travelling back past the lakes of Ischl, the scene of the 1849 tour with Slade). Earlier still, on August 21st, he had written to George von Bunsen to say, "I shall be at Vevey in September." This sounds like a reference to a stay, not to a fleeting excursion.

But, as he was writing from Berne on September 30th, had he already been to Vevey and returned? Or could he

have got round to Vevey and roamed about Glion on the
30th, and started on the poem next day at Geneva?

He could have reached Vevey directly from Berne via
Lausanne; and he could have left Berne on September
30th, after writing his letter to William Forster; he often
wrote letters by early morning candle-light. The records
of visitors to the Trois Couronnes, which might have confirmed a stay at Vevey either overnight on September 30th
or slightly earlier, at some time after September 22nd, are
completely lost.

If he went straight to Geneva, he might have taken the
boat to Vevey, as he did when with Walrond, and returned
the same day after visiting Glion; the entry "to Geneva"
being placed first seems to indicate he was there first and
began the poem afterwards (unless it means "return to
Geneva"). But this conjecture rules out the plan referred
to, of a stay in Vevey in September. He may indeed have
made some preliminary notes, after arriving in Geneva on
October 1st, and made a leisurely excursion to Vevey and
Glion later in the week. But the opening stanzas of *Obermann Once More* give the reader the positive impression
that he is actually at Glion to compose them; nor does
this further conjecture tally with the plan to be at Vevey
in September.

One thing is clear, that he had had other chances to see
Glion again, between his earlier visit, of whatever date,
and 1865. In 1858 he had stayed at the Trois Couronnes,
Vevey, with Walrond, but had then gone on directly to
Bex. In 1859, also, he had come from Strasbourg to Bâle
and Berne, and thence to Geneva and Vevey, rushing in
a visit to Martigny, the Col des Montets and Chamonix,
and back to Geneva (see page 245). He went back to
Geneva on July 17th, via Lausanne, crossing out the entry
"Glion". Arnold had planned to include "Neufchâtel" and
"Fryburg" on the return journey; but, in the event, he saw
neither—so full of reminiscences of Senancour. (He also
ruled out the return to Paris by Châteauroux, La Châtre,

and Nohant, and went direct by Lyons). His wife was with him, and this may have made a difference to his feelings and choice of route.

It thus seems impossible and is perhaps irrelevant to use the journey of 1865 to make any further inferences about his route to Thun in 1848; or vice-versa. If in 1848 he went on from Glion by the Simmenthal, he was probably not in Senancour's tracks. For this he should have gone by Gruyère, Bulle, and Fribourg. The time-element and other considerations probably precluded any journey to Glion by the passes from Berne in 1865; when the present "MOB" trains were not yet running to Vevey and Montreux. By October 24th, 1865, he was, at all events, back at Zürich, although it is not clear when he had arrived. According to his own statement, he is there for the third time that year, and he has been to Lucerne (evidently since his stay in Geneva), and seen Titlis and Pilatus, as stated above, with his family (who had rejoined him; one imagines he was alone at Geneva, Vevey and Glion). He appears to have just returned from the Lucerne trip, made therefore from Zürich, so that his stay in the Pays de Vaud cannot have been long. But he has Oberman still very much in mind, speaking affectionately of the Titlis.

As postulated in Chapter VII, Arnold's first visit to Thun seems to have been inspired by his eagerness to explore a part of Switzerland which he believed to be associated with Senancour—the Oberland, Oberman's own country. The identification seems to have been taken for granted, not only by Arnold. But the name, "Oberman", occurs only once in the whole book—in its title! Monglond is inclined to think it was simply a translation of "surhomme" (see page 40 and page 40, note 1). Arnold was in reality on surer ground, it is now clear, when he pictured Oberman gazing up the Valais at the breaking dawn and the snowy Vélan. He apparently did not know, what Sainte-Beuve learnt only just before his death, of Senancour's special connections with Fribourg.

Other motives there may have been for Arnold's choice of Thun as a centre. We have referred to it as a natural centre for many popular excursions. It would most probably be known to him by its proximity to the Chevalier Bunsen's chalet at Berne, who had welcomed his friend Lake there in 1839 and 1840. It could have been more recently suggested to him by Clough's visit in 1843, with Burbidge and Walrond. Returning in October from Italy, the three friends had crossed the Simplon, gone up the Rhône and over the Grimsel to Thun. They continued their journey from Thun to Berne and Bâle, and down the Rhine homewards—travel by the water-route at this time, if slow, being the most comfortable and most favoured. This route may have been in Arnold's mind as normal for his return journey, rather than going back via Geneva, as he had come. (In 1858 he was to explore with Walrond more of the east end of the Lake of Geneva, including Vevey and the Château de Blonay, where Shelley's cousin, Medwin, lived for a time. On this occasion Arnold did the pass of the Diablerets from Bex to Sion down the Valley of the Liserne; see pages 244 and 245).

There were still other precedents for Arnold's choice of Thun. Granted that the desire to explore the Oberland was his chief motive, he may have been also influenced by the earlier presence there of an old friend, the Reverend Henry Wall. There may actually have been some connection between Balliol and the English chaplaincy—now abolished—at Thun, as Henry Wall, a Balliol scholar, held it in 1845. He was Wykham professor of exegetical logic at Oxford from 1849, and was a contemporary of Tait and Lake. He and his sister were certainly at Thun in 1845, and Arnold was in friendly touch with him in March 1849 (see Note I).

Finally, Thun, as a popular haunt of tourists, at this time was one of the main asylums for the many exiles who had the means to escape from the disturbed Paris of 1848. If there were a possibility that Arnold had known 'Marguerite' before this visit, then he might have expected to find her in 1848, as well as in 1849, installed in Thun at the Bellevue. "Inmate", the word he uses about her, is also his term for Prince Thomas of Savoy, staying in his own house at Harrow. It is even not impossible that Arnold went to see her in 1850, when he is known to have returned to Switzerland in the summer, after his first repulse from Judge Wightman, with the object of making a despairing last bid for 'Marguerite', or to say goodbye. Why, otherwise, has the diary for 1850 also disappeared?

There are more definite indications about his route to Thun in 1849 (see page 112 and page 124, note 1). From a letter of Shairp to Clough, dated July 1849, it appears that Arnold was planning to visit the Tyrol in September of that year with his young friend Wyndham Slade. In two letters, of September 12, 1865, and of August 28, 1883, which Arnold wrote subsequently to Slade, there are references to this journey. Arnold almost certainly went on from Ischl and Salzburg to Switzerland by way of Innsbruck, Landeck and Zürich. His letter to Clough of 1849 is dated from Leukerbad at the end of September, whence he returned to Thun; October was no doubt spent, at least in part, at Thun; but by the 29th he was back at Fox How, as he was at home to forward a letter from Clough to his brother Tom on that date.

This journey of 1849, the arrival at Thun, and return there after the excursion to Leukerbad, must have been inspired on this occasion mainly by the presence of 'Marguerite' at the Bellevue. But Arnold's experience of love, and Senancour's melancholy ascendancy over him, were inextricably mixed motives for this journey. His escape to the mountains may have been due to the impulse to seek consolation in Oberman's mystic presence there, as much as to despair over 'Marguerite' (see Note L).

To Slade he wrote in after years as though the tour, at

least the part in the Tyrol, had been wholly delightful, but this must have been due to the attitude he had bent himself to; the letter to Clough, written at the time, tells a different tale. And the poems of this period, the nearest in which he came to sincere self-expression, are also among his saddest. Here too he draws close to Senancour; whose *Oberman* is a prose-poem in which a profound interpretation of nature is allied to the expression of a sorrow similar to Arnold's, and of an equally stoic attitude.

I. NOTE TO CHAPTER VIII:
" 'MARGUERITE' POEMS: THUN REVISITED."

In addition to their treatment in this chapter, I have set out what is known and what may feasibly be conjectured regarding the arrangement and inspiration of the love-lyrics in an article on 'Marguerite', printed in the *Modern Language Review*, vol. XXXVIII, no. 4, October 1943. Their re-grouping and re-titling is summarised there, with the reasons for regarding the original appearances of the poems as decisive for their interpretation.

There are still critics who would like to separate the love-poems into the two artificial groups which the poet appears to have devised himself, as an after-thought, to confuse his readers and critics. It is difficult to assign a valid reason for this view, for it does not seem necessary to divide the inspiration of the poems in this arbitrary way in order to give his wife a share, supposing this to be the motive of the upholders of it, generally critics who have received kindnesses from the relatives and descendants of the poet. It is equally difficult to accept the internal grounds on which they could found such a reading of the poems.

In breaking up and re-grouping the poems, and in general embroiling them and confusing them with successive additions in later years, Arnold was, curiously, following the example consciously or otherwise of his acknowledged master, Senancour. Monglond's researches have established most of the salient facts of Senancour's life, and he has given a very sympathetic account of Senancour's attempt to obscure the true story of his unhappy love-affair—in his case, inspired by his friend's sister, Joséphine Marcotte. Senancour had known her as a girl, on her occasional visits to Paris, but it was not until after his unlucky Swiss marriage, and his return to Paris to find her also a married woman, that he became aware of his feelings. A chance encounter brought him full realisation.

He was never to forget her. She became and remained his Egeria, and, according to Monglond, the main inspiration of *Oberman*, his finest work. Without "Madame D**", or "Madame Del **", as he calls her at times, the book would never have been written. The *Rêveries*, a sort of first "brouillon"—no doubt with memories of Rousseau made more vivid by his post with Madame d'Houdetot— appeared in 1799; *Oberman* in 1804.

He fancied he had exercised complete discretion, as he had every reason to do. But, like Arnold in this, he could not stifle his lyric outpourings, although he was reluctant later to republish *Oberman*. Arnold, for his part, could or would not destroy his love-poems; he knew their worth. For Senancour, too, his autobiography was his chef-d'oeuvre, the most personal thing he had written, and in Oberman's exquisite letters he had disburdened himself of his grief and desolation. Passion and renunciation are the mainsprings of the romance of *Oberman*. Senancour's whole attitude to life was modified by his experience (even to his religious beliefs, although one must take into account here the liberalising influences of the times. The starting-point of Arnold's religious speculations could have been a line of Senancour: "La morale est la religion moins raisonnée".)

Meanwhile, identification with real places and persons had to be scrupulously prevented. Josephine Walckenaer was his friend's sister, and married. Senancour was apparently successful in deluding his readers—friends, and critics alike, even to Sainte-Beuve, who learned the story only in the year of his own death.

During Arnold's life-time, a similar need for discretion was imposed, and he appears to have been concerned to prevent any biography of himself appearing. But there surely no longer exists the same need for reticence; and there is little point in wishing to ascribe the inspiration of any members of the series of love-poems to his wife; except for *Calais Sands*, which was never included in either group, and is obviously a poem apart.

Simply put, where all is not conceded to his wife, nothing is conceded. To hunt for poems that can be doubtfully assigned to Miss Wightman's influence seems nugatory, when the indubitable ones, which stand with 'Marguerite's' name in them, are sufficient proof of the earlier love-affair and its importance to Arnold the poet; not least, of the fact that it so closely preceded his courtship and marriage.

If his wife is to be brought in to play a ròle, it might be —Arnold, no doubt, in his way considered it appropriate— that of Iseult of Brittany, who with her sweet temper is imagined as not conceiving of taking it ill that she has a rival. Her rival is humbled, after all. It was Miss Wightman who retained Arnold's final affection, not 'Marguerite'.

It seems an aspersion on both of them to accept the suggestion that he called her "F.-L.", meaning to designate her as Faded Leaves, the initials of her Christian names. One does not usually call a young bride so, or even a young married woman, as she was in 1855. Would Arnold have been capable of punning on his wife's name: "Fanny", "fâné"? The description, "Faded Leaves", with more propriety, surely recalls an earlier experience, a page now become history for Arnold: it may even hold a clue to this earlier story. A critic who argues as above would, without hesitation and also seemingly without authority, date the poems under this head to fall within the period of the poet's courtship of Miss Wightman. But this was almost a whirlwind affair; it went slowly perhaps, in the second half of 1850, but Arnold's diary for 1851 shows him mainly occupied in getting a suitable post and securing thereby the consent of her father to the marriage; certainly too agitated by practical necessities to write the melancholy love-poems in a vein similar to those indisputably written for 'Marguerite'.

Some portions of the many letters which he wrote in this time of stress, and which are mentioned in the diary, are confirmed by their dating in the Russell collection; and from these samples it is clear that Arnold did not send purely amatory notes, but newsy letters, on matters topical and especially political, likely to affect his appointment to the post he was seeking. The ups and downs of politics were very important to him personally just then. "Very anxious about ministers", he writes in his diary of February 2nd.

Miss Wightman's numerous letters to Arnold one can guess were about in the same strain; a query in one of them, which Arnold answers, relates to a possible change in the Ministry. Both were very much concerned in February 1851 about the survival of the Cabinet, in which Lord Lansdowne was President of the Council, and on which Arnold's hopes of a permanent post rested. There is no diary for 1850, but there is a letter of December of that year which shows Matthew and Miss Wightman already discussing possibilities and Arnold offering to show her a letter to Ralph, afterwards Lord, Lingen, Education Secretary at the time and his former tutor, in which he asks Lingen to use his influence on his behalf. Earlier, in September 1850, he had been on a walking-tour with Wyndham Slade in the Lake Country. Slade, who was younger than Arnold, rather than Clough—older, and perhaps jealous —was perhaps a more sympathetic confidant and possibly was more au courant. If Arnold found time, with so much to distract him, to write *Calais Sands* in the summer, this was probably all he managed in the way of love-poetry;

and this seems to have been wrung from him rather by the judge's veto than by Fanny Lucy's coldness. Throughout his courtship of her he seems in fact weighed down with practical considerations. Even the wedding-tour of September 1851, if it may be so called, could have been planned for business as well as for pleasure, with a view to promotion or some addition to his income (see Note B, on the *Grande Chartreuse*). By 1851 he was probably already beginning to think along the lines, suggested in a letter to his sister, of not taking a journey for mere sight-seeing, but in order to visit cities and places where great events had occurred. "I am not sure," he says, in 1858, "but I have begun to feel with papa about the time lost of mere mountain and lake-hunting . . . and to desire to bestow my travelling solely on eventful countries and cities." Dr Arnold's earlier journey certainly was one of the deciding factors that sent Arnold in his tracks to the Grande Chartreuse, Piedmont-Sardinia, and North Italy in 1851. But other motives must have inspired the particular route chosen— the need to avoid covering the ground of earlier journeys and their associations, and to acquire some first-hand knowledge of the troubled situation in Europe. The Italian Question was already a burning one, and he may have been hopeful, as early as 1851, of turning this trip to account. The route taken and all the inconveniences it entailed were not exactly apt to a perfect wedding-tour. How different must his whole attitude have been from that of 1849! There seems little resemblance between the courtship of Miss Wightman, which had a happy ending, and the earlier affair; and only by sheer contrivance can the poems be divided between the two experiences.

It is not, for instance, credible that Judge Wightman could be described as the "iron knot" (he was given to a pleasant humour, and Arnold became much attached to him later) which tied his daughter up from Arnold; and there appears no other obstacle to the marriage. There is nothing to indicate Miss Wightman's unresponsiveness to Arnold's wooing. On the contrary, one would conclude she favoured his suit from the outset, but would not wish to alienate her father—another practical consideration. The judge was to make them a handsome allowance later. From the diary one sees that she answered Arnold's notes with nearly the same frequency and regularity as he wrote them; nor was it her fault that Arnold missed seeing her, on the night he rushed to meet her (at an early stage in the "flirtation"), with a palpitating heart, at Park Crescent, Judge Coleridge's London home! She was not, apparently, a capricious girl; one rather imagines her as temperamentally incapable of inflicting pain. She was fond of pets, but timid and nervous about cows and spiders, as one may judge from some of Arnold's laconic references. She was hardly the type to torment him with the pain and longing which are expressed in the love-poems. There is absolutely no evidence to show that she ever repulsed Arnold. They were two young people, awaiting with natural anxiety her father's consent to their marriage, and Fanny Lucy probably treated Arnold with much affection during a period trying to both.

Nor could Arnold have ever felt it his duty to forget her. "Vain is the effort to forget", was said of 'Marguerite'. Arnold has left eloquent testimony of his many struggles to remember, and to forget her. At one moment he voices the desire to remember; at the next he is imploring forgetfulness. *Separation* is a repetition of the theme of *A Memory-Picture* in reverse. (Possibly Arnold, in the latter poem—as in his enigmatic scribble, preserved in the manuscript papers, about visualising a lost experience—was vaguely recalling Tennyson's similar thought about the dead Hallam. In his undergraduate days Arnold had greatly admired *In Memoriam*.)

But the fair stranger of *Separation* with the "grey eyes" who reminds him of his beloved turns out to be the beloved herself. This poem is, again, a variation on *Absence*; but here "the eyes of grey" which remind him of 'Marguerite' are indeed those of a stranger, perhaps Miss Wightman's, whereas in *Separation* it is 'Marguerite's' own grey eyes, un-recognised, that cause the intolerable pang of remembrance.

In conclusion, the 'evidence' is very unconvincing for the theory of a dual inspiration for Arnold's love-poems. The argument becomes trivial when it attempts to separate the poems on the basis of the faintly different hair- and eye-colouring (see the article, 'Marguerite', referred to above). It seems that Fanny Lucy's eyes reminded Arnold of 'Marguerite's', which were "too expressive to be blue, too lovely to be grey". Was Swinburne inspired by these lines when he wrote the less pleasing:

"Those eyes the greenest of things blue,
    The bluest of things grey"?

To whomever this description applies, it is clear that Arnold himself was not certain about the colour. There were probably glints in Miss Wightman's hair too, which resembled 'Marguerite's'—a confusion from which the advocates of the dual inspiration theory would like to profit. Surely Arnold was attracted to Miss Wightman by these very resemblances—with the added asset of her not repulsing him. She also was intelligent, certainly charming—"exquisite", Arnold says of her on the night of the engagement party; youthful, petite and graceful. She had "very pleasing" eyes, according to Clough, biassed against her. Her appearance altogether could not have been very dissimilar to his memory of 'Marguerite'. Ash-blonde, applied to the latter's hair, has a shaded brightness which could appear brown in certain lights—in dull England perhaps; in the "radiant climes" of 'Marguerite's' Swiss décor, it was "ash-coloured"; (and this fitted the metre better too). But it could have been light brown, or fair (also meaning lovely?). If Arnold hesitated between the different epithets, it does not prove there were different heroines.

No one sensitive to the lyric beauty of these poems and their indescribable poignancy and pain can fail to feel that they are a picture consistent throughout of frustrated love for one woman. A man does not care for two women quite in the same way. As Musset, whom Arnold, following Sainte-Beuve, was not very fond of, says, "N'est-ce pas une vieille maxime que toutes les femmes se ressemblent? Pourquoi donc y a-t-il si peu d'amours qui se ressemblent?" Certainly a man does not write about one woman, his chosen, as though she were the pale reflection, the faded image, of his first love.

There remain the critics who disbelieve altogether in 'Marguerite's' existence. They rely on the famous denial which the poet is supposed to have made to his daughters, when taxed by them. But, as Professor Whitridge has himself pointed out to me, what else could they say, when taxed directly themselves by the importunate questioner?

Apart from the evidence of the letters which Arnold wrote from Thun, and about Thun, there is Clough's laughing reference, before the tragedy had reached its height, in a letter of 1849, where he parodies some lines from A Farewell (see page 124, note 1). The figure of 'Marguerite' herself is too vivid for doubt of its actuality. The very words which Arnold puts into her mouth are simple translations from the French: "C'est toi"; "mon ami, pourquoi souffres-tu?" (later changed from "my friend" to "my love", which is the equivalent anglicism, but certainly not what 'Marguerite' said. "Mon amour" would rather be used of a pet animal or a light-of-love, not very often of the object of a deep passion. The phrase occurs in Longing, one of the poems quite invraisemblablement ascribed to Miss Wightman by the supporters of the dual inspiration theory.) Again, when 'Marguerite' is entering "heedless", Arnold is obviously translating "étourdie", which has quite another meaning from "un-heeding". Arnold might have rendered this better as "feckless" or "light-

hearted"; "giddy" or "full of banter" could be suggested
by the French word. This characteristic may have been a
contributory cause of the tragedy. She was not serious
enough, she had had a flirtation or two, but was probably
already affianced, in the French way, by arrangement, and
enjoying a short spell of freedom before marriage. This
seems a likely cause of her apparent encouragement and
then rejection of him and Arnold's acceptance of the rejection.

Not that, as is well known, Arnold was not fond of fun
and banter too; and he perhaps at first accepted her values,
until he got out of his depth. One fancies he may have
chaffed her by calling her "Margrit" in the Swiss-German
way at times. "My Marguerite smiles upon the strand",
and "Marguerite I shall see no more," only scan correctly
on this assumption. But this conjecture assumes 'Marguerite' was her real name, and of this there is no proof.

There were also eye-witnesses to confirm the reality of
Arnold's affair with her; there were the "friends" of *A
Memory-Picture* (probably of 1848), and the 'Martin' and
'Olivia' of *A Dream*, which might belong to either of Arnold's visits to Thun, of 1848 or 1849, but more probably
to the latter. He may have wished to avoid giving the real
names of the spectators or participants of his adventure;
but it is possible that Martin and Olivia were actually so
called. This might account for the withdrawal of the
poem until 1881, with its reference to perhaps living protagonists. If they are fictitious names, Wyndham Slade—
if he had not left Arnold after the start of their journey
abroad in 1849—might conceivably be 'Martin'. On July
24, 1849, Shairp wrote to Clough: "The said Hero Matt
goes in the autumn to the Tyrol with Slade—he was working at an Empedocles". (Arnold's journey may have been
also suggested by a wish to see the scene of George Sand's
Jacques; in his *Essay* on her he quotes with admiration the
passage referring to the glaciers of the Tyrol.)

The tour was an unforgettable experience. In 1883, less

than five years before his death, he wrote to Slade, "How many years is it since we travelled in the Tyrol together!" From Ischl they returned by Salzburg, which Arnold recalls in a letter of September 12th, 1865 (see Note H), as "the scene of our delightful journey together", and probably by Innsbruck, Landeck and Sargans (the route through Schuls–Tarasp would be less direct) to Zürich, and then went on to Thun, probably by Lucerne. If Slade were with Arnold in Switzerland, and the two stayed at the Bellevue, he might be "Martin". At least his Christian name has the two syllables requisite for the line, and the substitution of a pseudonym presents no difficulty.

But this consideration would also serve for "Henry": the Reverend Henry Wall was English chaplain at Thun in 1845 (see Note H), and might have returned for the seasons of 1848 and 1849; if so, he would certainly have been in Arnold's group, as there is a reference to him in March of this year and Arnold was evidently keeping up relations with him. He was an old Rugbeian, and had also been at Warminster, Dr Arnold's first school before he entered Winchester. Henry Wall was a fellow and tutor of Balliol in 1839, and was to succeed Lake as Rector of Huntspill when the latter became Dean of Durham. Coleridge mentions his having preached at least five times in the English Church at Thun in the summer of 1845. If he were 'Martin', his sister, who usually accompanied him, might have "stood in" for 'Olivia'. (The Reverend Henry Wall died in 1873.)

The most obvious and acceptable suggestion is 'Arthur'; and Clough certainly returned from his visit to Rome and Naples in 1849 via Interlaken and Thun (see *The Letters of Thomas Arnold the Younger*). He writes of this journey, retrospectively, to Tom Arnold on October 29th, 1849. He came back to England, he says, direct from Rome and Naples by Genoa and Turin, and thence to Geneva, which he presumably reached in August (see *The Letters of Arnold to Clough*, page 108). On the other hand, Arnold writing to Clough from Thun on September 23rd [1849], says, "You cannot answer this letter for I know not how I come home." Perhaps, however, Clough did get in touch, and was not too late to join him at Thun. Arnold was back in Oxford towards the end of October, as Clough writes again on November 6th to say, "Matt has been back here [Oxford] for ten days"; and this does not sound as if they arrived together. He had, in fact, been home to Fox How, before returning to Oxford.

The events of this time would be probably clearer if the missing letter which Arnold apparently wrote the year before to Clough from Leukerbad had come to light. "I wrote to you from this place last year" (*The Letters to Clough*, page 109).

There was certainly a group of young people at Thun both years, and no doubt there were parties and excursions, the latter perhaps taken with the responsible guide of whom Arnold speaks in his letter to Clough from Leukerbad, and whom he was to re-engage on his later tour of 1871 with the family—a tour covering much of the same ground (see Note H).

Matthew Arnold almost certainly signed the Fremdenbuch, the Visitors' Book, at the Hotel de Bellevue. His signature is in other hotel registers, but is not to be found at Thun. The pages for these years are missing. The relevant register runs from July 1834 to September 1838, with entries indicating the sort of visitors who stayed and their generally appreciative comments. Our Ambassador at Paris, Lord Granville, made a sojourn at the Bellevue in 1838 with his family, as did the Duke and Duchess of Roxburghe in 1837. (Arnold dined at Lord Granville's at a ministerial function in 1858, according to a letter to Madame du Quaire in Paris, the sister of his old friend John Blackett, M.P. for Newcastle, 1852–1856.) Earlier, in 1836, the French Ambassador at Berne, the Duc de Montebello, who was a son of one of Napoleon's marshals (see Note B) stayed with his family. (He was to replace Count Molé as Foreign Secretary in 1839.) The Duke might well have continued his visits to Thun at the time Arnold was there —in 1848 he had temporarily withdrawn from public life after the February Revolution—and, if accompanied by his family as usual, one finds two charming daughters, the elder, Jeanne, aged sixteen then, who might not have disdained the society of the young Englishmen from Oxford. Actually, the Duke's wife was English and Scottish, an Argyle, and connected with Lord Liverpool's family. The Duke, as Monsieur de Montebello, had been attaché at Rome in 1829 at the time Chateaubriand was Ambassador there. One gathers from these details the sort of international atmosphere of the place, where anything could and did happen; and certainly conventions would not be too strict.

After 1838, however, the record of visitors to the Hotel de Bellevue ceases; two pages at the end are torn off, suggesting that they were deliberately removed. It is not far-fetched to imagine the possibility that Arnold himself asked for them; he had later opportunities of visiting Thun —he was there on two occasions in 1871, and probably before this date. If Arnold, or an interested friend, did take them away, the act appears to indicate that 'Marguerite's' name was entered on them as a visitor. This, with the disappearance of the private diaries for 1848, 1849 and 1850, seems heavy with implications. It appears to have been important to Arnold to obliterate the records of these years. Was this just his way of confirming a decision to turn his back on a period of his life, which had threatened to break with tradition, and away from his whole education and background?

His brother realised that he had married on the rebound, as it were, although Tom could not have known all the details from his station in the Antipodes. Arnold desired marriage, and for this he was more than willing, as he told Clough, to make sacrifices; he had indeed to accept what George Russell called "a life of unremunera-

tive drudgery". His early letters, those to his favourite
sister especially, are not free from self-recrimination. He reiterates his longing for Switzerland, for a job less hum-
drum, and for an escape from what he once describes to
his wife as "hell".

The memory of the past became bearable only as he
entered on his later and worldlier phase. As he himself
significantly said, the "buried self", buried deliberately
because it vexed him to let it live, was only kept quiet
by ceaseless work, by his family ties and official responsi-
bilities; by his writings and the social enjoyments after
which his second self had always hankered. "Rien ne sauve
dans cette vie-ci que l'occupation et le travail." The quotation from Bonstetten keeps cropping up in his diaries.

The period of courtship culminating in marriage could
not have included the experience which inspired the love-
poems. They stand apart from the rest of his output. Their
sad sincerity perhaps springs from a deeper cause even
than regret for lost love; it was his lost youth he mourned.
It must be remembered that Matthew Arnold was twenty-
eight when he married.

J. NOTE TO PAGE 132: *THE RIVER*,
AND TO ILLUSTRATION ON PAGE 100.

A critic who prefers to divide the inspiration of the love-
poems between 'Marguerite' and Arnold's wife has adduced an extended version of this poem, in a manuscript
now in the possession of Mrs Margaret Barnett. In K. Allott's edition of the *Poems*, there are many assertions—
for example, about a crisis in Arnold's relations with his
future wife, which seem without foundation (see Note I)
and which are framed to persuade readers that he is report-
ing facts. But of the truth of his theory, this hitherto unknown manuscript he regards as firm evidence. *The River,*

he states, was inspired by Miss Wightman, and the scene is the Thames at Hampton.

He reproduces the poem in photogravure, the autograph version facing page 230 (*The Poems of Matthew Arnold*, London, 1965) and the imprint given on pages 230–231. These are represented as the original poem.

This extended version contains indeed the five stanzas entitled *The River* in all the editions printed in Arnold's lifetime; but prefixed to these are six new stanzas, for the restoration of which Mr Allott argues in an article in the *Times Literary Supplement* of March 28th, 1958.

A dispassionate study of these stanzas does not confirm Mr Allott's contention. In the first place, they are written in a very different, and very inferior style from that of the consecrated text—their general inferiority is such as to lead immediately to the surmise that they are later additions. The internal evidence points to the conviction, rather than surmise, that this extended version was a deliberately revised one, composed perhaps for family consumption, or even to allay genuine regret on Arnold's part that he had not paid more tribute to his wife in his poetry.

There is some confusion, in fact, about the version in Mr Allott's own mind. Although he gives a photographic reproduction of the manuscript, he does not transcribe it correctly in his printed text; apparently wishing to emend the poem in a scholarly way, he sometimes indicates where he has altered it, but he does not always do so. There result several departures from the text which he fails to mention or explain. The reader is therefore actually confronted with three texts: the generally accepted printed text of five stanzas, the photograph of a manuscript of eleven stanzas, and an incorrectly printed version of the latter. Where emendments are made, they are taken from the familiar 1852 poem, which thus appears to receive Mr Allott's sanction, when he thinks corrections are needed.

Further examination reveals that this manuscript was hurriedly written, obviously with a scratchy pen, so that it is almost illegible in places and would be undecipherable at times without reference to the poem of 1852. So much so, that in one place Mr Allott himself fails to decipher it. Thus, what is surely meant to be "the" voyage, with the pen just missing the paper, he prints as "our" voyage.

(Apropos of untrustworthy deciphering of manuscripts, Allott's edition of the *Poems* has another mistaken reading of the manuscript of *Horation Echo*, on page 59. In the last line, Arnold's alternative version is given as: "My friend, on that just day", which I read in the manuscript: "My friend, on that last day". Another variant, which is erased in Arnold's manuscript, is arbitrarily omitted in this apparently complete edition: "My friend, when comes that final day".)

In general, he omits to point out his changed spellings. Among these, "wrapt" in the manuscript is printed "wrapped"; "controul" becomes "control", and so on. "O'er-used" in the manuscript is changed to "o'er-laboured" in the imprint. This emendation is taken over from the repudiated shorter poem. ("O'er-used" is obviously not so good as "o'er-laboured", as it involves accenting an unaccented syllable. There is some temptation to imagine Arnold here taking up an earlier uncorrected version to dash off the new one, and forgetting his own emendments.)

Changes in punctuation are frequent, but perhaps these are not regarded by Allott as material. He also passes over Arnold's two alternatives for stanza three: "but" and "while". In short, this is not an altogether scholarly handling of the manuscript.

The final impression made by the autograph poem is of a somewhat hastily put together affair. If one compares merely the handwriting with the autograph poem *Longing*, which Arnold Whitridge reproduces in the *Unpublished Letters*—an authentic poem of the period—this is only too obvious. In the latter the word "and" is always written in full. Double 's' is correctly formed with the tail clearly turned back as in 'g', and not as in 'f', or blurred in a single stroke. The writing is altogether neater and more precise.

A later and hastier habit of composing as well as of writing is indicated by the less satisfactory rhymes in the added verses, as when "small" is made to rhyme with "shawl", "balms" with "arms", "Thames" with "flames".

A feature of greater importance, and difficult to explain except on the assumption that this is a re-written form of the poem, is the curious way in which the additional first six stanzas appear like a very lame repeat of the last five. In places, they read almost like a parody, as in the stanza beginning:

> But, ah, the head keeps turned away,
> I only see those fingers small.

This is pure jingle, and seems a spun-out paraphrase of the line:

> None speaks, none heeds; ah, turn thy head.

Another, dare one say clumsy, stanza shows Arnold almost revelling in the sight of the harmless strip of throat between the heroine's fringed shawl and her hair (the last word surely put in for the rhyme, as it makes some nonsense of the line—unless his companion wore her hair knotted under her chin).

"Gaily smile" seems falsely suggestive of the 'Marguerite' manner and her gay smiles; but it has here a bookish aroma as coming pat from Horace—"Amabo Lalagen dolce ridentem"—so perhaps this phrase could serve again. But how could Arnold transfer the epithets "arch" and "mocking", so frankly used of 'Marguerite' in A Memory Picture, to Miss Wightman, who had a firm, decided chin, according to Clough. One would not think it well described as "the archest mockery ever ambush'd in".

> Give me thy hand, and hush awhile,
> And turn those limpid eyes on mine,

Arnold entreats his companion in *The Buried life*, who is almost certainly 'Marguerite'. In *The River*, he says:

> Ah, let them rest, those eyes, on mine,
> On mine let rest that lovely hand,

in almost the same words.

The final lines of *The River* cannot credibly be understood as referring to Miss Wightman. Arnold had known her for only a matter of months at most by August 1850, the date postulated by Allott for the composition of the poem (the summer of no other year will fit his hypothesis), and his sufferings on her account would be quite recent. Mrs Arnold, writing to Tom some time after Wordsworth's death on April 23rd, 1850 (she refers, in a letter lent me by the late Miss Ward, to the change at Rydal "by Wordsworth's being no longer its presiding genius"), speaks merely of her suspicion that more than "Matt's fancy" is engaged with regard to Miss Wightman: this would leave a bare two or three months for Matthew to develop his heart's "deep habitual smart". And indeed why should he be in a state of despair, and "dead to hopes of future joy", whilst being allowed to go out on the river with his beloved, under the very eye of her parents at Hampton? Surely there would be a vestige of hope in this situation!

Arnold uses joy and bliss as substantives to personify Marguerite—"Again I see my bliss at hand"—so often as almost to suggest that one of her names was Félicité.

Falsely suggestive, truly, is the arrangement of stanzas in this manuscript version. Stanza one is given a page to itself. Why? The reason is clear—so that the stanza which begins the poem that we are accustomed to regard as the original can be relegated to the bottom of a page: this run-on effect does seem deliberate.

From a study of this new manuscript it is a relief to return to the text of 1852, surely the authoritative one, and to let Hampton and the Thames fade from the picture, and even Miss Wightman. It does not indeed seem particularly flattering to her to bring her in to share with 'Marguerite' the inspiration of the love-poems. If, out of compunctious regret, Arnold had fancied he could serve up the present mixture, it may have been for the benefit of his children, or friends—hardly to please his wife. He loved his wife in a different way, which satisfied her. In after years she had great sorrow in the loss of their three sons, and Arnold was a compassionate and devoted husband.

Owing to his literary habit of banter, which he expected others, brought up in the same school, to understand without taking offence, Arnold did on occasion offend by what amounted to indelicacy, as in his rough treatment of Francis Newman, and his contemptuous neologism, to "newmanise". C. H. C. Wright said that irony was to Senancour the mark of the superior mind (Wright was no admirer of Senancour!), and he quotes Merlant: "Le mépris du philistin . . . Obermann en a pu être pour sa bonne part responsable". In Arnold's case, one cannot but wonder at what seems more a failure of understanding than an indelicacy in his handling of the love-poetry. He had been irresistibly (more or less) carried away in his youth by love for a strange French girl. No blame attached to this episode, but, once happily married, he hoped to forget it. In the first place, he could not forget; and further he could not bring himself to sacrifice the poems which he was aware were among his best, which were written as he knew he would rarely write again. Far from suppressing them, as his muse dried up, he brought them up anew, or refurbished. But with malaise or complaisance—one hardly knows which—he tried to represent the experience on which they were based as more confused than it was. One fancies he persuaded himself at times that these poems were in fact more literary than real, or perhaps he hoped that this would be their effect on the reader. Feeling the need for some dissimulation, he may have proposed to himself the discipline of re-writing *The River* in a different vein and associating it with his wife. But surely only for the outside world was there any need for camouflage. The facts surrounding the composition of the love-poems must have been known to, and accepted by, his wife, without strained effort on his part to reconcile them with the present.

Why cannot they now, after this lapse of time, be accepted by his critics?

K. NOTE TO PAGE 127: *REQUIESCAT*.

Some critics who demur to the conjectured identification of the subject of this poem with 'Marguerite' prefer a vague parallel with Wordsworth's 'Lucy', although 'Lucy' is not without some basis in fact either.

But *Requiescat* has features that link it with the 'Marguerite' group of poems. There is the very similar imagery to that used in *Parting*; there is the same hope for the future in both poems—for the restless souls of the poet and 'Marguerite', and for the poet and the subject of *Requiescat*. The poet of *Farewell* longs to share this quiet with 'Marguerite', and in *Requiescat* he desires to share it too.

The poem may be a pure generalisation, but there are few of Arnold's lyrics which are not founded on some personal experience.

L. NOTE TO PAGES 178 AND 179, AND TO PAGE 246: "IMENSTRÒM".

It was beside the gorge of Imenstròm, the "Eternal River", that Oberman wished to retire (Monglond, *op. cit.*, p. 272 et seq.).

The image of life as a current or stream might be regarded as a commonplace and not an idea specially characterising Arnold or Senancour. But Matthew Arnold does greatly emphasise his love of running water and small clear lakes; and it is natural that Louis Bonnerot should wish to elaborate on my suggestion (on page 79 of his *Matthew Arnold, The Poet*). He also acquiesces in my view that Arnold's experience of Switzerland and of first love were intermingled.

M. NOTE TO PAGE 216: "A WRITER IN THE *CHRISTIAN REMEMBRANCER*".

The writer was John Duke Coleridge. Arnold refers light-heartedly to his review, in a letter to Wyndham Slade (*Works*, vol. XIV; *Letters*, vol. I, p. 46), airily dismissing it as likely to be read by only a limited public. Another letter, from Arnold to Sainte-Beuve, making a personal acknowledgment of his use of the latter's article, is printed by L. Bonnerot (*op. cit.*, p. 548). This purely private expression of obligation, and the later note added on the second appearance of *Sohrab* in 1854, are characteristic of Arnold's methods, as is also the suppression of the note in later editions, when doubtless he saw no further need to stand before the public in a white sheet.

Henry Coleridge, John Duke's cousin and biographer, states he had reason to believe that John Duke had in fact made his discovery of Arnold's piece of plunder independently, and so felt justified in pointing it out. Arthur Stanley, however, in a letter of October 6th, 1854, apparently protested to Coleridge that he had used information supplied to him by Arnold himself. A letter from Arnold to Coleridge, of November 22nd, 1853, written before the publication of Coleridge's review, does not make any such revelation: it only gives the source of the Greek motto prefixed to the poem. But other information about sources, about Sainte-Beuve, and M. Mohl, might have been given verbally, or in letters not preserved. Stanley, at all events, certainly believed Arnold guiltless of an unacknowledged plagiarism.

A captious critic has objected to my statement that Coleridge should have known Arnold better than to make this reproach. But there is no reason to suppose that Coleridge knew Arnold better than his own family did, who had earlier expressed astonishment at "Matt's" writing poetry in a serious vein at all. Arnold and Coleridge were friends of long standing, and the sons of friends of long standing, but they were not very close in temperament or endowment. After Coleridge's accession to the office of Lord Chief Justice, Arnold in a letter of congratulation asked a little flippantly if he might still presume to sign himself "Yours affectionately". And even if there had not been the slightest reserve between the two in youth, it is doubtful if Coleridge would have succeeded better than Matthew's own family in fathoming his often enigmatic character, or in understanding his literary practices. When Stanley died and Arnold paid him tribute in *Westminster Abbey*, Coleridge praised the poem, but with qualifications; and after Arnold's own death, he expressed doubts as to the soundness of his theological writings. Nevertheless he was always a loyal friend; and it remains somewhat difficult to understand the conscientious motive that prompted his disobliging criticism of *Sohrab and Rustum*.

N. NOTE TO PAGE 242: "THE GREAT ST. BERNARD".

This adventure is recounted by Senancour in the *Fragment* added to the later edition of *Oberman*, published by George Sand in 1840. It does not appear in the original edition of 1804 (which Arnold presumably never read).

A letter which Arnold wrote to his sister on October 10th, 1854, indicates that he knew the *Fragment* and some of the details about Senancour's wanderings onto the Italian side of the Alps. This knowledge may have suggested in part the return route from Aosta of the journey which he took in 1858 with Theodore Walrond in August and September of that year. His diary for 1858 shows he was carefully re-reading the "Méditations d'un Solitaire" (that is, the *Libres Méditations d'un Solitaire Inconnu*) in July, and that Senancour was still an ever-present influence.

For Senancour, the journey had probably been suggested by his reading of Besson. He, however, never went as far as Aosta. Monglond has established that he went only to Etroubles after passing St Rémy (*op. cit.* p. 85), and that he returned on his steps after crossing the pass and frontier. This fact would not have been known to Arnold; however, Oberman's journey and adventure in the *Fragment* almost certainly furnished a motive for his own desire to cross the pass.

He may also have wished to see Aosta again, and revisit the valley down which he had rushed on his honey-moon trip of 1851. English interest in alpinism was very much centered in the region at this time and could have been a further incentive for Arnold's journey (see Note B, on *Stanzas from the Grande Chartreuse*). His meeting with two noted alpinists at Zermatt, T. Hinchliffe and the Reverend Llewellyn Davies, would give him a pleasurable sense of being in the centre of events in the mountaineering world. The Reverend Davies was in fact to make the first ascent of the Dom, the highest of the Mischabelhörner, a few days only after Arnold and Walrond had left.

But Arnold, like Senancour, became with the passing years less interested in the high peaks; his climbing days were curtailed by the companionship of his wife and children, and also by the heart-trouble from which he was beginning to suffer. In Senancour's case, it was the injury which he had sustained in his reckless descent of the gorge of the Drance which gradually crippled him and turned him from further climbing. This infirmity led him to prefer the lower Alps, and in particular the country about his beloved Imenström, near Vevey (see Note H).

O. NOTE TO PAGE 249, AND TO PAGE 249, NOTE 2: "IN 1854 ARNOLD, NOW IN TOUCH WITH THE CRITIC [SAINTE-BEUVE], SENT HIM HIS LATEST VOLUME . . ."

That is, the volume of 1853; this was the first book sent, as Arnold wished to have Sainte-Beuve's opinion of his *Preface*. I hasarded the suggestion that he perhaps added the volume containing *Empedocles*.

Since this guess of mine, the publication of the Chantilly collection of Arnold's letters to Sainte-Beuve by M. Louis Bonnerot, summarised by Professor R. H. Super ("Documents in the Matthew Arnold-Sainte-Beuve Relationship", *Modern Philology*, LX, 1967), has thrown positive light on the correspondence. My conjecture is substantiated—that Arnold first sent the volume of 1853, approaching Sainte-Beuve as a critic of standing, for a pronouncement on his own first essay; and that the volume of 1852, which contained the poem whose rejection was the occasion of the Preface, was sent *en second lieu; in* fact, it was sent as a result of a request from Sainte-Beuve.

Sainte-Beuve asked also for the volume of 1854, which was introduced by a short preface answering Arnold's critics of his 1853 Preface.

It should be pointed out here that the letter from Matthew Arnold, dated September 29th, 1854, which is assumed to follow a letter of Sainte-Beuve to Arnold, dated September 6th, 1854, should in fact precede it. This letter of September 6th is misdated, and the date should be read November 6th. It is the letter which is printed by Arnold

Whitridge in the Appendix to his volume of *Upublished Letters*; and which Professor Whitridge states is the one from Sainte-Beuve referred to in Arnold's letter from Fox How to his sister "K", of October 10th, 1854. This discrepancy was immediately apparent to me on reading through the Chantilly letters. For it was obvious from the context that the letter printed in Professor Whitridge's Appendix is not the letter which gave Arnold the pleasure of which he speaks in his letter to "K". It makes scant reference to his poetry; it even demurs to an observation of Arnold; and it does not mention the proposal to review him, to which Arnold refers in his letter to his sister.

Sainte-Beuve's letter, dated by Whitridge and L. Bonnerot September 6th, 1854, is demonstrably the reply to Arnold's letter of September 29th. (This would have been immediately obvious, if Arnold's earlier letter, with Sainte-Beuve's annotations, had been available.) In it Sainte-Beuve thanks Arnold for sending the volume of poems containing *Empedocles* and mentions that it has been slow in coming. He goes on to say that he has not yet received the 1854 volume with Arnold's further prefatory notes. He makes also a direct comment on a passage in Arnold's letter of September 29th, in which the latter discusses the choice of subjects for epic poetry and in so doing refers to "Virgile ou Apollone de Rhodes". Sainte-Beuve takes him up directly on this point in the (so-dated) letter of September 6th. His annotations, scribbled on Arnold's letter of September 29th, should have been sufficient indication of the correct sequence. Clearly, Sainte-Beuve's letter of September 6th (sic) is subsequent to September 29th, and was written after an interval, since the volume of *Empedocles*, whose receipt he is acknowledging, arrived well after Arnold's letter of September 29th, announcing his intention of sending it.

From this it follows too that Arnold, in his letter to his sister of October 10th, was not speaking of the letter in Whitridge's Appendix, but of an earlier letter.

We can assume that this earlier letter, so far not discovered, was written between the appearance of "Arthur Dudley's" article on Arnold in the *Revue des Deux Mondes* which provoked it (judging by the opening sentence of Arnold's September 29th letter), and Arnold's acknowledgment of its receipt on September 29th—that is, between September 15th and September 27th, or 26th.

This lost letter of Sainte-Beuve's—his first to Matthew Arnold, no doubt—would make interesting reading. It must certainly have expressed his thanks for Arnold's 1853 volume of poems and have contained some comments on its Preface. This is the book referred to in Arnold's letter of January 6th, 1854, which may well have been the start of the correspondence. It begins: "J'ai osé vous envoyer un recueil de mes poèmes". He then asks Sainte-Beuve for his opinion of the Preface; and he also makes a disarming acknowledgment of his use of Sainte-Beuve's article for *Sohrab and Rustum*.

Sainte-Beuve must have praised, or expressed some pleasing criticism of, the volume in question, as Arnold appears to have been delighted with his comments. Sainte-Beuve continued to say many complimentary things to and about Arnold throughout the friendship which followed, although he did not go so far as to say of him, as he did of Hamilton: "On a vu d'autres étrangers, Horace Walpole, l'abbé Galiani . . . posséder ou jouer l'esprit français à merveille, mais pour Hamilton, il est cet esprit même." Did Matthew Arnold not over-rate a little the extent to which he was appreciated in France, and rely too much on Sainte-Beuve as a populariser of his poetry abroad? He may not have been as pleased as he indicates, in his somewhat fatuous words of praise, by Lacaussade's translation of the Obermann *Stanzas*; he might have felt that Madame de Solms, with her acid comment to Sainte-Beuve (of August 26th, 1860) was taking him more literally than he intended: "Je crois bien", she says, "qu'il aimait mieux se lire dans votre traduction."

In fact, at one point in the translation, the substitution of "muette" for "blanche" spoils the sense of the line. Besides removing a favourite epithet of Arnold's, there is a displeasing ambiguity about "muette" in this context. Much later, a printing error in the catalogue of Sainte-Beuve's library refers to the translation by Lacaussade of Arnold's later poem as "Oberon Once More". This would certainly have saddened him.

To sum up, Arnold's letter of September 29th, 1854, is an answer to a letter of Sainte-Beuve's written between September 15th and about September 27th, of which there appears to be no trace; this lost letter followed Arnold's of January 6th, 1854, asking Sainte-Beuve for an opinion on his first essay in criticism; and perhaps also inspired by a wish to forestall adverse comment on his plagiarism for *Sohrab and Rustum*. It is not the answer to the so-dated letter of September 6th. The faulty chronology in Louis Bonnerot's Appendix has unfortunately been repeated in the late Jean Bonnerot's massive edition of the Sainte-Beuve correspondence, where he gives the letter *in extenso*, as in Whitridge's printed text. To those familiar with Sainte-Beuve's practice of using both the ordinary form of dating letters and the form which has regard to the numerical name of the month, following the Roman practice of beginning the year in March (in all but one letter of those written during September 1854 he uses the latter form), and with access to Arnold's letter of reply, it should have been immediately obvious, having regard to the context, that November, not September, is the correct dating. (A sight of the manuscript in Professor Whitridge's collection confirmed my conclusion that Sainte-Beuve wrote at the head of the letter "6—IXbre, 54"; which is, as stated, to be interpreted as "6 Novembre," not "6 Septembre".)

What seems to be a further error in the chronology of the Arnold–Sainte-Beuve friendship has escaped notice.

According to the usual account of Arnold's first meeting with Sainte-Beuve, it is stated that this took place on

August 19th, 1859, when Arnold dined with him at Pinson's.

But it appears from his diary that Arnold first called on Sainte-Beuve on March 30th of that year; it would be only natural for Arnold to pay a courtesy call before being asked to dine. It was a Wednesday, shortly before the day on which he had had the news of his brother's illness and death at Gibraltar (on April 13th or 14th; the diary and journal entries give different dates). On April 16th Arnold bought a mourning hat-band, among other purchases; but the news did not apparently interrupt his round of official and unofficial visits.

Louis Bonnerot states: "Entre 1853 et 1859 aucune correspondance ne semble avoir été échangée entre Arnold et Sainte-Beuve" [he apparently means 1855, not 1853] "Par une lettre fort détaillée du 19 août 1859 [and also one of the 21st], nous savons qu'Arnold a dîné avec Sainte-Beuve à cette même date . . ." There is indeed in this letter to his wife the abrupt announcement: "I dine with Sainte-Beuve tonight." However, the diary entry mentions a call on Sainte-Beuve at 4 o'clock on March 30th, 1859, and this is confirmed in the Guthrie transcription of the (Arthur Houghton) *Journal*.

Arnold's journal at this point appears to have been written up subsequently to the occurrences described, and does not always correspond with the diary entries. When a discrepancy occurs, it may be assumed that Arnold did not recall the exact order of events when writing up the fuller account; or that the diary entry refers to an engagement not necessarily carried out.

The latter was the case for his entry on May 9th, 1859, regarding a call on George Sand. He had delayed making this call, not by a few days, as he says in his *Essay* on her, but after returning from an official journey of inspection into Brittany involving several weeks. By that time George Sand had returned to Nohant. Having so missed her, he appears to have been ever afterwards unwilling to disturb his first impression of her. Even when he found himself again in the neighbourhood, and furnished this time with a formal letter of introduction from Michelet, he hesitated and finally failed to call again. The letter itself he seems to have valued, as he kept it. A singularity of this letter of Michelet's is the spelling Georges Sand. [There is a strange reference to "le communiste Arnold", and to a note of introduction given by this Arnold in 1852 to another pilgrim to Nohant, in W. Karénine's *George Sand: sa vie et ses oeuvres*, vol. IV (Paris, 1926), pp. 221–22. But this "M. Arnold" appears to have been the name adopted by Pierre Leroux during his exile in London and Jersey (1851–1869). In a letter from Leroux to George Sand, dated September 24th, 1854, he says: "Voici mon adresse par voie de Londres. M. Arnold, Hight (sic) Knoll-cottage, Claremont-hill, St Hélier, (Ile de Jersey)."] There is a sketch in Arnold's diary for 1846, on the posterior fly-leaf, which fancy would willingly see inspired by the famous early visit. One figure is almost certainly that of Arnold, in the dress of the time, with tails and topper; the other has a headdress not unlike the squarish article which George Sand is usually depicted as wearing in the country. This gracious (?) figure appears to be holding something in an outstretched hand—a flower?

Apparently it was fore-ordained that Matthew Arnold should follow in the footsteps of Sainte-Beuve. When Sainte-Beuve visited his friends and old schoolfellows the Neates at Tubney Hall (he calls it Tubney lodge, in a letter to V. Hugo, see J. Bonnerot, *Correspondance Générale*), not far from Oxford, on the north side of the road from Abingdon to Faringdon, he surely saw the very spot described in *Thyrsis*, where in May the maidens dance round the Fyfield tree, otherwise the Tubney elm, as it is called locally. It is an old wych-elm, 36 feet in circumference. In his letter he describes his visits to the Bodleian and some of the colleges, including Christ Church. He must have seen, too, in company with the Reverend Neate's sons, much of the countryside—"un joli pays", he says—which later became the haunts of Arnold and Clough. "The wood that hides the daffodil" is almost certainly Tubney Wood. There are 384 acres of it. Tubney Park alone has 45 acres. When Matthew Arnold was at Oxford, Tubney people attended Fyfield church, and Tubney village was simply a tiny outlier of Fyfield (see *The Victorian History of Berkshire*, vol. IV).

Harold Nicolson in his biography of Sainte-Beuve called Squire Neate's home Pudney Hall, and so failed to see the connection.

Sir Francis Wylie in his discussion of the Scholar-Gipsy country seemed also unaware of Sainte-Beuve's earlier presence there. Sainte-Beuve had known Arthur and Charles Neate when they were all at the Pension Landry, rue de la Cerisaie, no. 12 (he went there in 1818, the very year that Senancour took up residence at no. 33); his English visit to the country of the Scholar-Gipsy and Thyrsis took place in August, 1828.

That Emerson in 1853 should call Clough "Lycidas", and perhaps thereby give Arnold the hint of an idea for his elegy of Clough—as we are in a world of coincidences—may be just another one.

P. NOTE TO PAGE 268: "ROSE STEWART".

As "Arthur Dudley", she reviewed Arnold's poetry for the *Revue des Deux Mondes* on October 15th, 1854. (See A. Whitridge, *Unpublished Letters of Matthew Arnold*, p. 25; *Works*, XV, p. 35; L. Bonnerot, *op. cit.*, pp. 520, 521–2).

Q. NOTE TO APPENDIX A, PAGE 258.

"As though", line 13. Apparently this should read, "Although". The manuscript of this early poem was not entrusted to me by Mrs O'Brien, who sent only a copy.

BIBLIOGRAPHY

A. WORKS OF MATTHEW ARNOLD

The Works of Matthew Arnold. In 15 vols., London, Macmillan and Co., 1903.
Unpublished Letters of Matthew Arnold. Ed. Arnold Whitridge, New York, 1923.
The Letters of Matthew Arnold to Arthur Hugh Clough. Ed. H. F. Lowry, Oxford, 1932.
Obermann. In the *Academy*, October 1869, vol. I, pp. 1–3.

SPECIAL EDITIONS CONSULTED

The Strayed Reveller and Other Poems. By A., London, 1849.
Empedocles on Etna and Other Poems. By A., London, 1852.
Poems. By Matthew Arnold. A New Edition, London, 1853. (*Known as the* First Series.)
Poems. By Matthew Arnold. Second Edition, London, 1854.
Poems. By Matthew Arnold. Third Edition, London, 1857.
Poems. By Matthew Arnold. Second Series, London, 1855.
New Poems by Matthew Arnold. London, 1867.
Poems by Matthew Arnold. The First Volume, Narrative and Elegiac Poems. London, 1869.
Poems by Matthew Arnold. The Second Volume, Dramatic and Lyric Poems, London, 1869. (*Known as the* First Collected Edition.)
Poems. New and Complete edition (in two volumes), London, 1877.
Poems. New edition (in two volumes), London, 1881.
Rome-Sickness. In *A Wreath of Stray Leaves*, Rome, 1875.
The Poems of Matthew Arnold: with an introduction by Sir A. T. Quiller-Couch, Oxford [1906], ed. 1930.

B. SOURCES AND CRITICAL WORKS

ADDISON, J. *Remarks on Italy.* 1705.
ARNOLD, THOMAS. *Passages in a Wandering Life.* London, 1900.
BABBITT, I. *The Masters of Modern French Criticism.* Boston and New York [1912], ed. 1923.
BONNEROT, L. 'La Jeunesse de Matthew Arnold.' In the *Revue Anglo-Américaine*, août, 1930.
BONNEY, T. G. 'The Alps from 1856 to 1865.' In the *Alpine Journal*, vol. XXXI, no. 214, February, 1917.
BOUYER, A. *Obermann précurseur et musicien.* Paris, 1907.
BRONTË, CHARLOTTE. *Villette.*
BROOKS, VAN WYCK. *The Malady of the Ideal.* London, 1913.

CARCASSONNE, E. 'Leconte de Lisle et la philosophie indienne.' In the *Revue de Littérature Comparée*, oct.–déc., 1931.

CARO, E. *George Sand.* Paris, 1887.

CESTRE, CH. 'The Church of Brou de M. Arnold.' In the *Revue Germanique*, 1908.

CLOUGH, A. H. Notices of poems. In the *North American Review*, vol. LXXVII, July, 1853.

COOK, SIR E. *Literary Recreations.* London, 1918.

DAWSON, W. H. *Matthew Arnold and his relation to the thought of our time.* London, 1904.

DECAHORS, E. *Maurice de Guérin.* Paris, 1932.

DOUMIC, R. *George Sand.* Paris, 1922.

DUPIN, MADAME A. *Marguerite.* Paris, 1836.

ELTON, OLIVER. *A Survey of English Literature*, 1830–1880, vol. I. London, 1920.

ENGEL, C.-E. *La Littérature alpestre en France et en Angleterre.* Chambéry, 1930.

ESTÈVE, E. *Leconte de Lisle. L'homme et l'œuvre.* Paris, 1922.

FITCH, SIR J. G. *Thomas and Matthew Arnold.* London, 1897.

FOSCOLO, UGO. *Jacques Ortis* [traduit] par Alexandre Dumas, précédé d'un essai sur la vie et les écrits d'Ugo Foscolo. Paris [1839], ed. 1847.

FRANCE, ANATOLE. 'George Sand et l'idéalisme dans l'art.' In *La Vie littéraire*, Première Série, Paris [1888–92], ed. 1926.

—— 'Le Journal de Benjamin Constant.' *Ibid.*

FURRER, P. *Der Einfluss Sainte-Beuve's auf die Kritik Matthew Arnold's.* Zürich, 1920.

HAAS, H. *Die Entwicklung der Stadt Thun.* Thun, 1926.

HARRIS, ALAN. 'Matthew Arnold: the Unknown Years.' In the *Nineteenth Century*, vol. CXIII, no. 674, April, 1933.

KELSO, A. P. *Matthew Arnold on Continental Life and Literature.* Oxford, 1914.

KINGSMILL, H. *Matthew Arnold.* London, 1928.

LAMARTINE, A. DE. *Les Méditations poétiques: Le Lac.* Paris, 1820.

LA VILLEMARQUÉ, THÉODORE DE. 'Les Poèmes gallois et les Romans de la Table Ronde.' In the *Revue de Paris*, Third Series, vol. XXXIV, 1841.

—— 'Visite au Tombeau de Merlin.' *Ibid.* Second Series, vol. XLI, 1837.

LECONTE DE LISLE. *Poèmes Barbares.* Paris, 1862.

LEVALLOIS, J. *Un Précurseur—Senancour.* Paris, 1897.

LOUANDRE, CH. 'L'Enchanteur Merlin.' In the *Revue de Paris*, Third Series, vol. XVI, 1840.

MALORY, SIR THOMAS. *Le Morte d'Arthur.*

MÉNARD, L. *Poèmes: Empédocle.* Paris, 1855.

—— *Les Rêveries d'un païen mystique.* Paris, 1876.

MERLANT, J. *Le Roman personnel de Rousseau à Fromentin.* Paris, 1905.

—— *Sénancour.* Paris, 1907.

MICHAUT, G. *Senancour. Ses amis et ses ennemis.* Paris, 1909.

MICHEL, E. *La Forêt de Fontainebleau.* Paris, 1909.

MONGLOND, A. 'Senancour et un Voyageur au Brésil. Lettres inédites à Ferdinand Denis.' In the *Revue de Littérature Comparée,* vol. XIV, janv.–mars, 1931.

MORAUD, M. *Le Romantisme français en Angleterre de 1814 à 1848.* Paris, 1933.

MOTT, LEWIS F. 'Renan and Matthew Arnold.' In *Modern Language Notes,* vol. XXXIII, no. 2, February, 1918.

MOYRIA, G. DE. *L'Église de Brou,* précédé d'une introduction par M. Edgar Quinet, suivi de stances sur le même sujet, par MM. L. Bruys et X. Marmier. Bourg, 1835.

MURRAY, J. *A Handbook for Travellers in Switzerland, Savoy and Piedmont.* Third Edition, London, 1846.

OLLIVIER, D. (ed.). *Correspondance de Liszt et de Madame d Agoult.* Paris, 1933.

PAUL, HERBERT. *Matthew Arnold.* London, 1902.

PEYRE, H. *Louis Ménard.* Newhaven, 1932.

PHILLIPS, M. 'English Friendships of Sainte-Beuve.' In the *Bulletin of the Modern Humanities Research Association,* vol. I, no. I, April, 1927.

POWELL, A. FRYER. 'Sainte-Beuve and Matthew Arnold.' In the *French Quarterly,* vol. III, September, 1921.

QUINET, EDGAR. *Œuvres Complètes,* Paris, 1881. Vol. VIII, *Des Arts de la Renaissance. L'Eglise de Brou* [1834], in *Premiers Travaux;* vol. I, *Le Génie des Religions.* Paris [1842]. (See also G. de Moyria.)

RÉMUSAT, CH. DE. *Passé et Présent, mélanges.* Paris, 1847.

RENAN, ERNEST. *Essais de Morale et de Critique.* Paris [1859], ed. 1929.

ROBERTSON, J. M. *Modern Humanists.* London, 1891.

ROMER, MRS CARROL (V. L. JACQUIER). 'Matthew Arnold and some French Poets.' In the *Nineteenth Century,* vol. XCIX, no. 592, June, 1926.

SAINTE-BEUVE, C.-A. 'M. de Sénancour.' In *Portraits Contemporains,* vol. I, Paris, 1832.

—— 'M. de Sénancour, *Oberman.*' In *Portraits Contemporains,* vol. I, 1833 (and see also Senancour).

—— 'Pensées.' In *Portraits Littéraires,* vol. III, 1839.

—— 'Le Livre des Rois, par le poëte persan, Firdousi, publié et traduit par M. Jules Mohl.' In *Causeries du Lundi,* vol. I, 1850.

—— *Chateaubriand et son groupe littéraire,* Quatorzième Leçon. Paris, 1860.

—— *Correspondance.* Paris, 1877–8.

—— *Nouvelle Correspondance.* Paris, 1880.

SAINTSBURY, GEORGE. *Matthew Arnold.* London, 1899.

—— *A History of English Prosody.* London, 1923.

SAND, AURORE. *Le Berry de George Sand.* Paris, 1927.

SAND, GEORGE, *Valentine.* Paris, 1832.

SAND, GEORGE, *Lélia*. Paris, 1833.

—— '*Obermann*.' In the *Revue des Deux Mondes*, 15 juin, 1833 (and see also Senancour).

—— *Jacques*. Paris, 1834.

—— *Lettres d'un Voyageur*. Paris, 1837.

—— 'George de Guérin.' In the *Revue des Deux Mondes*, 15 mai, 1840. And in *Œuvres Complètes*, vol. XIV. Paris, 1843–4.

—— *Jeanne*. Paris, 1844.

—— *La Mare au Diable*. Paris, 1846.

SÉCHÉ, LÉON. *Delphine Gay*. Paris, 1910.

SENANCOUR, ÉTIENNE PIVERT DE. *Rêveries sur la nature primitive de l'homme*. [1799–1833.] Ed. J. Merlant, Paris, 1910.

—— *Oberman*. Paris, 1804.

—— *Obermann*, avec une Préface de Sainte-Beuve. Paris, 1833.

—— *Obermann*. Nouvelle Edition revue et corrigée avec une Préface par George Sand. Paris, 1840.

—— *Obermann*. Ed. J. Michaut. Paris, 1931.

—— *Obermann*. Translated and edited by A. E. Waite. London, 1903.

—— *Libres Méditations d'un Solitaire inconnu*. Paris, 1819.

STANLEY, A. P. *The Life and Correspondence of Thomas Arnold, D.D.* London [1845], 1858.

VIANEY, J. *Les Sources de Leconte de Lisle*. Paris, 1908.

VIGNY, A. DE. *Poésies Complètes: Le Mont des Oliviers* [1843]. Paris, ed. 1925.

—— *Journal d un Poète* [1867]. Ed. F. Baldensperger. London, The Scholartis Press, 1928.

VOLTAIRE. *Candide*. Geneva, 1759.

WALBROOK, H. M. 'The Novel in Matthew Arnold's poems.' In the *Bookman*, vol. LXXVIII, May, 1930.

WARD, MRS H. *A Writer's Recollections*. London, 1918.

WHITRIDGE, A. *Dr Arnold of Rugby*. London, 1928.

ZYROMSKI, E. *Maurice de Guérin*. Paris, 1921.

ADDITIONAL BIBLIOGRAPHY

A. WORKS OF MATTHEW ARNOLD

I. *Manuscripts*
   (i) Diaries for 1845, 1846 and 1847, and Diaries for 1852 to 1888, (unpublished: in the Beinecke Rare Books Library, Yale University).
   (ii) Diary for 1851 (unpublished: in the possession of Professor Arnold Whitridge).
   (iii) Manuscript Fragments (Beinecke Library).
   (iv) Manuscript Letters (Beinecke Library).
   (v) Manuscript Poems (Beinecke Library).
II. *The Poetical Works of Matthew Arnold.* Edited by C. B. Tinker and H. F. Lowry. London, Oxford Univ. Press, 1950. Reprinted 1961.

The Note-books of Matthew Arnold. Edited by H. F. Lowry, K. Young and W. H. Dunn. London, 1952.

Matthew Arnold's Diaries: 1852–1888. The unpublished items: a transcription and a commentary by William Bell Guthrie. University Microfilms, Ann Arbor, 1957.

Matthew Arnold: Poetry and Prose. Edited by John Bryson. Harvard Univ. Press, 1963.

The Poems of Matthew Arnold. Edited by Kenneth Allott. London and New York, 1965.

B. CRITICAL AND BIOGRAPHICAL WORKS

ANON. "Charles-Victor de Bonstetten". In *Edinburgh Review*, April, 1864.

BAUM, P. F. *Ten Studies in the Poetry of Matthew Arnold.* Durham, N.C., Duke Univ. Press, 1958.

BEER, GAVIN DE. *Alps and Elephants.* London, 1955.

BERTRAM, JAMES. *The New Zealand Letters of Thomas Arnold the Younger.* Oxford University Press, 1966.

BONNEROT, LOUIS. *Matthew Arnold, Poète: Essai de Biographie psychologique.* Paris, Didier, 1947.

—— *Empédocle sur l'Etna: Etude critique et traduction.* Paris, 1947.

373

BUCKLER, W. E. *Matthew Arnold's Books: Towards a Publishing Diary.* Geneva and Paris, 1958.

CHASLES, PHILARÈTE. *The Legacy of Philarète Chasles.* Edited by A. Levin. vol. I. *Selected Essays on XIXth-Century French Literature.* Chapel Hill, N.C., 1957.

CLIMENSON, E. A. *History of Shiplake.* 1894.

CLOUGH, A. H. *The Correspondence of A. H. Clough.* Edited by F. L. Mulhauser. 2 vols., Oxford Univ. Press, 1957.

COLERIDGE, E. H. *The Life and Correspondence of John Duke Coleridge, Lord Chief Justice.* 2 vols. London, 1904.

EDEL, LEON. *Henry James: The Conquest of London.* New York, 1962.

ENGEL, C.-E. *A History of Mountaineering in the Alps.* London, Allen & Unwin, 1950.

EVELYN, JOHN. *Diary.* Edited by E. S. de Beer. Oxford, 1955.

FERRERO, FELICE. *The Valley of Aosta.* New York, 1910.

FLEMWELL, G. *Chamonix.* Blackie, London, 1913.

FOSTER, J. *Alumni Oxonienses (1714–1886).* Oxford, 1888.

GIRDLESTONE, C. M. *Louis-François Ramond.* Paris, 1968.

HAMMOND, J. L. AND B. *James Stansfeld.* London, 1932.

HARDING, F. J. W. *Matthew Arnold the Critic and France.* Geneva, Droz, 1964.

HAZARD, PAUL. *La Révolution française et les Lettres italiennes . . . de 1789 à 1815.* Paris, 1910.

JONES, ETHEL. *Les voyageurs français en Angleterre de 1815 à 1830.* Boccard, 1930.

JAMES, D. G. *Matthew Arnold and the Decline of English Romanticism.* Oxford, 1961.

KEMBLE, FANNY. *Records of a Girlhood.* New York, 1879.

KING, H. SEYMOUR. *The Italian Valleys of the Pennine Alps.* London, 1858.

KINNARD, NINA. *Rachel Felix.* Boston, 1886.

LANNES, COUNT CHARLES. *Le Maréchal Lannes.* Tours, 1907.

LE GALL, BEATRICE DIDIER. *L'Imaginaire chez Senancour.* Paris, José Corti, 1967.

LYONNET, HENRY. *Dictionnaire des Comédiens français.* 2 vols., Geneva, n.d.

MAILHOL, D. DE. *La Noblesse française.* t. II, Paris, 1910.

MARIO, JESSIE WHITE. *Vita di Giuseppe Garibaldi.* In *due volumi,* Milan, 1904.

MARRIOTT, J. A. R. *The Makers of Modern Italy.* Oxford Univ. Press, 1931.

METZDORF, R. F. *Mr Tinker and his Books.* Yale Univ. Library, 1960.

MILLER, BETTY. *Robert Browning*. New York, 1952–53.

MONGLOND, ANDRÉ. *Le Journal intime de Senancour; Oberman: Lettres publiées par M . . . Senancour*. 3 vols., Grenoble et Paris, Arthaud, 1947.

MONOD, M. O. *Daniel Stern, comtesse d'Agoult . . .* Paris, 1937.

MORYSON, FYNES. *Itinerary*. Ed. Glasgow, 1907.

MURRAY. *Handbook to Berkshire*. 1860.

NICOLSON, HAROLD. *Sainte-Beuve*. New York, 1957.
[In this study, the author refers to Sainte-Beuve's stay with the Neates at "Pudney", a mistake for "Tubney".]

NORMANBY, LORD. *Journal of a Year of Revolution, 1848*. 2 vols., London, 1857.

Nouvelle Biographie Générale. Paris, 1865, 1866.

PAGE, WILLIAM, and the Reverend P. H. DITCHFIELD. *The Victorian History of Berkshire*. vol. IV, London, 1924.

PHILLIPS, E. M. *Philarète Chasles, critique et historien de la littérature anglaise*. Paris, Droz, 1933.

—— "English Friendships of Sainte-Beuve", M.H.R.A., vol. I, no. 1, April 1927.

POPE, W. MACQUEEN. *St James's: Theatre of Distinction*. London, 1958.

POUSSERAN, L. M. *Histoire du Maréchal Lannes*. Paris, 1910.

PROMÈS, CARLO. *Le Antichità di Aosta*. Turin, 1864.

RAYMOND, MARCEL. *Senancour: Sensations et Révélations*. Paris, 1965.

RUSKIN, JOHN. *Modern Painters*. Ed. Everyman.

SAINTE-BEUVE, CHARLES AUGUSTIN. *Correspondance Générale*. Ed. Jean Bonnerot, 15 vols. 1935—1966 (three more volumes to appear).

—— *Causeries du Lundi*. Vol. I, Paris, Garnier.

—— *Portraits Contemporains*. Vol. III, Paris, Garnier.

SAINTS-MARC GIRARDIN. *Cours de Littérature dramatique*. 1849.

—— *Essais de Littérature et de Morale*. 1849.

SAUSSURE, H. B. DE. *Voyages dans les Alpes*. 1779–1786.

SHERSON, ERROL. *London's Lost Theatres*. London, 1925.

SMITH, M. E. *Une Anglaise intellectuelle en France sous la Restauration: Miss Mary Clarke*. Paris, 1927.

STILLMAN, W. J. *The Union of Italy: 1815–1895*. Cambridge Univ. Press, 1899.

TILLOTSON, GEOFFREY AND KATHERINE. *Mid-Victorian Studies*. London, Athlone Press, 1965.

TIMES, THE. July 18th to 23rd, 1846.

—— March 17th, 1873.

WYMER, NORMAN. *Dr Arnold of Rugby*. London, Hale, 1954.

INDEX

Aar, the, 92–3, 95, 99, 100, 106, 135, 239
Addison, Joseph, 81 note 1, 244, 252
Adolphe, see Constant, Benjamin
d'Agoult, Comtesse [Daniel Stern], 9, 33–6, 94, 102
Amiel, Henri-Frédéric, xiii
Amour, De l', see Senancour
Andromaque, 8
Aosta, 40, 242, 245
Aristippus, 43 and note 1, 50–1, 232
Arnold, Edward, 7
Arnold, Jane, 7, 106 note 4
Arnold, Mary, 106 and note 4, 107
Arnold, Matthew: home and school days, xii, 1, 6; an early poem, 257–8; journey to the Pyrenees in 1841, 7 note 2, 9–10, Fontainebleau, 9–10, 17; visits to the Théâtre-Français, 7 note 2, 8; appreciation of French tragedy, 7–9, 221; residence at Balliol, 11; first interest in George Sand, 11–16; reading of *Lélia*, 18, 19, 25; early idealism, 11–12, 14–15; translates a passage from *Valentine*, 15–16; pilgrimage to Nohant, 1846, 11, 16, 27, 28–37; meeting with George Sand, an admirer of Obermann, xiii, 31–7; visits Switzerland 1846[?], 32–3, 37, 245–6; first reading of *Obermann*, 58; epicureanism and sensibility, xiii, 7 note 1, 48, 50, 60–4, 127, 137–8, 140, 163, 165 note 1, 170, 177, 201, 232–3; stoicism, 65–71, 80, 88–9, 151–9, 166–70, 178–9, 222, 234, 236–7; orientalism, 66–8, 76–9, 83, 85–6, 88–91, 188; Alfred de Vigny and, 80–5, 171; Leconte de Lisle and, 85–91, 196; more literary pilgrimages, Thun 1848, 92–106, 245; Thun 1849, 112–26; 'Marguerite' and, 99–102, 105–7, 108–38, 141, 145–8, 173–7, 207, 227, 231, 241 note 3;

philosophy of 'Empedocles' and Obermann compared, 149–65; asceticism in Arnold and Senancour, 47, 51–2, 65–6, 68–71, 168–70, 186–7, 193, 222–3; Nature in Arnold and Senancour, 52–3, 71–9, 163–4, 166–75, 183, 187–95, 199, 201, 225–30, 253–4; pantheism, 72, 91 note 1, 183, 235–6, 254; Arnold and religious problems (and see also Senancour, Sainte-Beuve, Quinet, Ménard and Renan), 66, 195–8, 200, 223–4, 237–8, 240, 247, 248–9; fatalism, 76, 83–4, 116, 125, 136–7, 153, 156, 171, 173, 210–11, 215–16, 218; a debt to Quinet, xiii, 202–7; Sainte-Beuve and, xiii, 149, 208–19, 224–5, 249–51, 255–6; Renan and, xiii, 36, 66, 197 note 3, 220–1, 255; mystery and beauty of imagery in Senancour and, 201–2, 225–8, 230; intellectual loneliness in England, 228–30; a comparison with Wordsworth, 228–30, 253–4; more journeys abroad, 239–42, 244–9; Arnold and Senancour as poetic interpreters of the Alps, 32, 253–4; conclusion: Senancour his acknowledged master, xiv, 58, 238, 255; article on *Obermann* in the *Academy*, 259–67; correspondence with Madame Blaze de Bury, 268–71

Poems: *Absence*, 127, 132 note 1, 133, 134; *Anti-Desperation*, see *The Better Part*; *Bacchanalia*, 235–6; *Better Part, The*, 223; *Buried Life, The*, 83–4, 173–8, 182; *Calais Sands*, 132 note 1; *Church of Brou, The*, 142, 202–7; *Consolation*, 182–3; *Courage*, 68, 166–8; *Despondency*, 135, 137; *Destiny*, 135–6, 166; *Dover Beach*, 223–6, 228, 247; *Dream,*